By Alexis Lichine

WINES OF FRANCE
ALEXIS LICHINE'S ENCYCLOPEDIA
OF WINES & SPIRITS

These are Borzoi Books
published in New York by Alfred A. Knopf

WINES OF FRANCE

Wines of France

by Alexis Lichine

in collaboration with William E. Massee

FIFTH EDITION, REVISED

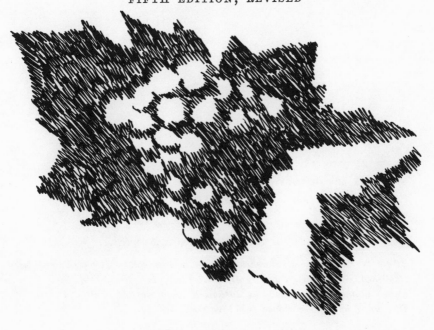

ALFRED · A · KNOPF *New York 1973*

CONTENTS

ILLUSTRATIONS

WINES OF FRANCE

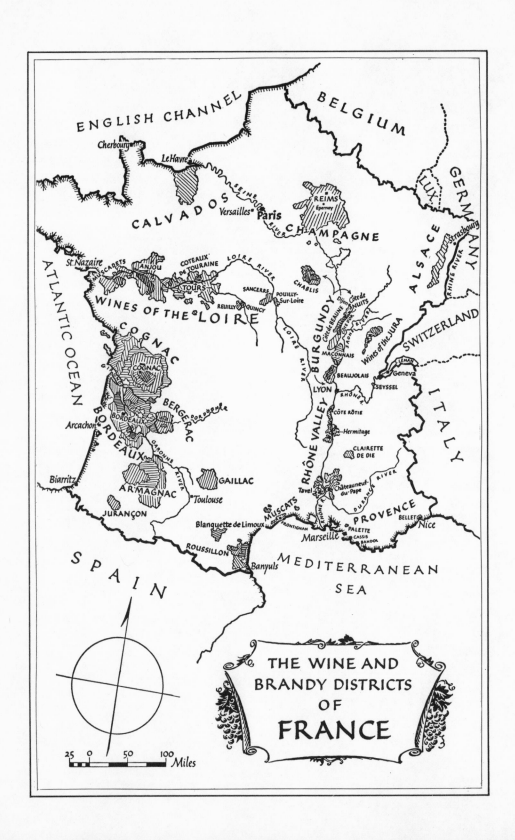

ENGLISH CHANNEL

BELGIUM

Cherbourg

Le Havre

SEINE

Versailles Paris

RIVER

REIMS
Épernay

CALVADOS

CHAMPAGNE

GERMANY

LUX.

Strasbourg

ALSACE

RHINE RIVER

St. Nazaire

MUSCADETS

ANJOU

COTEAUX
de TOURAINE

LOIRE RIVER

TOURS

SANCERRE

POUILLY-
Sur-Loire

CHABLIS

Dijon Côte de
Côte de BEAUNE NUITS
CÔTE D'OR

SWITZERLAND

ATLANTIC OCEAN

WINES OF THE LOIRE

REUILLY QUINCY

COGNAC

LOIRE

RIVER

SAÔNE RIVER

Wines of the JURA

MÂCONNAIS

BEAUJOLAIS

LÉMAN

Geneva

COGNAC

BORDEAUX

BERGERAC

BORDEAUX

Arcachon

DORDOGNE

SEYSSEL

LYON

RHÔNE

ITALY

CÔTE RÔTIE

Hermitage

GARONNE

RIVER

Biarritz

ARMAGNAC

GAILLAC

Toulouse

CLAIRETTE
DE DIE

RHÔNE VALLEY

DURANCE RIVER

JURANÇON

MUSCATS

Châteauneuf-
du-Pape

PROVENCE

Tavel

BELLET

Nice

Blanquette de Limoux

FRONTIGNAN

PALETTE

Marseille

CASSIS
BANDOL

SPAIN

ROUSSILLON

Banyuls

MEDITERRANEAN
SEA

25 0   50   100
                    Miles

THE WINE AND
BRANDY DISTRICTS
OF
FRANCE

THE WINES OF FRANCE

The greatest wines on earth come from France. The wines of this century are the greatest in the history of man. We are now living in a Golden Age of wine, thanks to the one Frenchman in every seven who earns his living making wine, and to his father, and to his father's father, as far back in time as there have been men tending vineyards on the sunny soil of France.

France not only makes the best wine, and more of it, than any other place on earth, but also drinks more per man, because a Frenchman knows a good thing when he tastes it. The 1,600,000 French winegrowers drink more wine than any other group, and it is a wonder that they let the rest of the world have any of it. The economics that forces them to do so will also, according to some, force them to stop tending some of the great vineyards in a decade or so—a reason for taking advantage of what there is while it still exists.

The most elementary details about wine history and wine-drinking form a basis for understanding the wonders that wine possesses. In the excitement of drinking wine these simplest elementals are often forgotten. It may prove useful to know how wines became part of France and to understand the basic things a Frenchman considers when he drinks wine or thinks of it—things so simple and habitual that he may be almost unaware of them.

Nobody knows when or how wines were first tended in ancient Gaul, though it is supposed that they were brought in from the Near East by Phocæan traders some centuries before Christ. There is a feeling among winegrowers that everyone stopped whatever he was doing and took to planting vineyards. In those bad old days when the Romans invaded Gaul, there were vineyards in many parts of France.

With the growing power of the monks during the early centuries of this millennium, more vineyards were planted. From Cluny, in the wine country of Burgundy, bands went out to establish monasteries and vineyards, forever linking the history of the Church with the history of wine. Many of the great vineyards were planted by ecclesiastics, and nearly all of them belonged to the Church at one time or another. There is probably not a hill, slope, or plain in France where vines can grow that has not been planted at one time or another, and it is through the trial and error of the past twenty centuries that today's vineyards have gained their greatness.

French winegrowers would have you believe that the main purpose of the crusades was to bring back new varieties of vine. Perhaps among them were the Pinot, from which all great Burgundies are produced, and the Gamay, which produces an enormous quantity of wine, but only one of any quality, the Burgundy known as Beaujolais. They also state that wine has always been the major produce of France and still is. In 1350 the equivalent of one million cases was exported from the port of Bordeaux. In 1790 six million were shipped, while in 1966 the equivalent of five and one half million cases was exported.

With the French Revolution, vineyards began to pass out of the hands of the Church and the aristocracy and into the hands of the French people, who were more or less pleased with this state of things until the last half of the nineteenth century, when some zealous winegrower imported American vines to see how they would do on French soil. They did well, completely destroying nearly every vineyard in France. On the American roots was a burrowing louse called the phylloxera, which was fatal to French vines. Today almost all French vines are grafted to American roots, which are resistant to the phylloxera.

The wines of France are as varied as they are good. Nowhere else is there such a variety of countryside or such a variety of wine—a special wine to go with every change of scenery. East of Paris is the Champagne country; the vineyards of Burgundy lie just south of it and extend all the way down to Lyon. Along the Rhône Valley are other great vineyards, flanked on the southeast by those of Provence, and on the southwest by a range of lesser wine districts extending to the Pyrenees. Southwest of Paris are the wines of the Loire Valley, and the great vineyards of Bordeaux below that; far over on the eastern borders are the Alsace wines, and below them those of the Jurals. To the north and southeast of Bordeaux are the wines that are distilled into the fabulous brandies Cognac and Armagnac.

All these districts produce wines that are distinctive, but not all are great. By far the largest quantity of wine comes from the vineyards of the Midi, that vast stretch of land in southern France just west of the mouth of the Rhône. Here the wines are rated by the degree of alcohol they contain, and they are shipped all over France in tank trucks that look exactly like the gasoline trucks on American highways. To this quantity is added the immense amount of wine produced in North Africa. These wines and those from the Midi are the ones most commonly drunk in France, where the average consumption per capita is forty-two gallons a year.

A Frenchman drinks wine because he does not drink water. This is partly a holdover from the days when much of the water in France was dangerous to drink. And from those days also comes the much-scoffed-at story that water contains little frogs that get into your stomach and grow there, eventually causing you to die a horrible death while making croaking noises. Now everyone, including the Frenchman who tells you about the frogs, will deny the truth of the story; but the fact remains that hardly anyone drinks water in France.

Bottled water, of course, is something else, and vast quantities of Perrier, Vichy, Badoit, Évian, Vittel, and dozens of other spring waters gush down French throats daily. But these waters are drunk for health and are free of frogs; some of them are said to be full of all sorts of good things to ward off *foie* trouble. At least, they don't harm you, and you can never tell about tap water.

In France, *foie* trouble is the favorite disease, as popular a conversational topic as ulcers in the United States. One of the standard Franco-American conversations is that of a Frenchman explaining to an American what liver trouble is, and that all Frenchmen don't have it, and the American explaining what ulcers are, and that all Americans don't have them.

Foie trouble comes from eating and drinking too much, and every Frenchman can give you a long list of foods that are very bad for the *foie*: eggs, fats, butter, spinach, shellfish, sauces. This explains why the French never eat eggs for breakfast, although they are perfectly all right for lunch and dinner—perhaps the classic example of Gallic logic. But a Frenchman will add that one thing never bad for the *foie*—not in a million years—is wine. Sauces, yes, even though sauces are the basis of French cooking. But wine, never. The fact is, of course, that drinking wine makes it possible to eat rich food, because wine cuts grease, and a sip will leave your mouth perfectly clean and ready for another bite of whatever happens to be bad for the *foie*. Wine is not bad for the *foie,* but wine makes it possible to eat enough to get *foie* trouble.

Wine and food go together, with or without interesting effects on the liver, and it is impossible for the French to think of one without the other. Most Frenchmen drink wine at mealtime every day. It is rarely great, and usually quite ordinary, but it is almost always drunk with food. And there are practically no hard and fast rules as to which wine goes with what, though one rule seems to be that the great wines are not drunk with everyday food, or the other way round. And even the French, who drink wine from habit, also drink it for fun. One thing that makes wine more fun to drink is a series of laws that have made it possible to get what you ask for.

Some thirty years ago few of the vineyards outside of the Bordeaux region were properly rated, nor was nomenclature controlled, and a famous name was often attached to an inferior wine. Probably more wine was fraudulent than genuine. But in the middle 1930's a series of laws began to be passed called the *Appellations d'Origine,* carefully defining which vineyards had the titles to which names, and what variety of grapes were to be used. Also, Burgundy vintners began following a Bordeaux system whereby the grower of the grape made and bottled his own wine, putting his name on the label and personally vouching for its genuineness.

As a result, it is now possible to buy honest wines from every well-known wine district in France. With this guarantee of authenticity, one can gain accurate knowledge about wine from drinking it, something that was hard to do before because you never could be sure of what you were getting.

People have been led to feel that the simple enjoyment of a bottle of wine is out of the question, and that wine-drinking must be surrounded by ritual and pretense. Any advice, suggestions, or rules about wine are not necessarily wine salesmen's hokum, and the best of them should add to your pleasure, giving you greater value for what you spend in effort, time, and money.

There is one pretension about wine that might not be thought of as a pretension at all. It is the matter of descriptive adjectives, the jargon of wine. Through the years these words have become almost meaningless through constant use and abuse, and yet they are used throughout the world to describe wine. You can think of them as clichés, or you can think of them as shorthand terms for a variety of subtle but definable taste sensations. Everyone is born with a tongue in his head, and the tongue can recognize what the terms stand for even if it is hard to put into words exactly what the tongue recognizes. One man's tongue may recognize wider degrees of distinction between the terms, but anyone can get to tell the terms, and the wines, apart.

It is not difficult to tell two wines apart. The wine from one vineyard is not the same as the wine from another, and your tongue can distinguish the difference, but you need to taste the two wines against each other. The greater the wine, the sharper the distinctions. It is easier to make distinctions when the wines are from different districts, and it is not too difficult to distinguish between the wines from the same vineyard and the same vintage, but from different barrels. This is no particular credit to one's discernment, but merely an indication of how widely wine can vary. Wines are living things. Each has its own distinctive character, and most of them are good to drink. The enjoyment is there for everyone, sparkling in the glass. The difficulty comes in trying to talk about it.

The more you know about wine, the more pleasure you can get from it, for knowledge of wine helps you to buy good bottles. Real wine knowledge comes from drinking. The more wines you taste, the more you will enjoy them. It is disappointing, for example, to drink a great red Burgundy or red Bordeaux when the wine is too young, just as it is disappointing to keep an old wine until it is far past its prime. White wines, except sweet ones (which can live for a generation), should be drunk when young, rarely older than ten years, preferably when only three or four; and yet many such wines are kept until they are musty, flat, brown, and unpleasant—a characteristic called maderization, after Madeira wine, whose color they take. On the other hand, some people turn their noses up when a great red wine is only slightly past its prime, ignoring all the good things it contains, merely because its freshness and strength have waned.

Five factors establish the quality in wine: soil, the variety of the grape, yeasts, the vintage year, and, last but not least, the ability of the wine-maker. The greatest distinguishing factor between exceptional wines is soil. The earth is what gives a wine its character, and each winegrower thinks his land is best, perhaps because he knows it best. No group is more chauvinistic than winegrowers, a man from Bordeaux scorning Burgundies as perfumed sun-cooked wine, the Burgundian scorning the wine of the Bordelais because of its full tannic qualities. These prejudices spread, for almost everyone in France is friendly with or related to a vintner and acquires his loyalties.

Wine is a work of art, for it is not only the soil but also the man who makes the wine. Wine-making is a matter of judgment, not only as to the time when the grapes should be harvested, but also as to how long the wine should ferment, how long it should stay in the barrel, how it should be treated if it gets sick, when it should be bottled. It's a vintner's saying that when it comes to wine, as much depends on toil as on rain.

Wine has a great appeal to the eye, both for its color and for its clarity. Many a painter has become excited over light gleaming on wine or the shimmering reflection of wine on a tablecloth. Each wine has its own hue—the yellow-green of a Chablis, the straw of a Meursault or Montrachet, the gold of a Sauternes—and its hue is a characteristic as distinguishable as any other.

But the art of wine can be detected best through the most elusive of our senses, smell and taste. It is one's nose that gives an understanding of what a great wine can be. What you smell is the evaporation of esters and ethers, those elusive chemical components that the wine contains, a collection called "bouquet" because there are so many different ones in each wine. Some people speak of bouquet as the first full smell of the wine. The later odor is called the aroma, and is more lingering. When a wine is too cold or when a bottle is first opened, and before the air has had a chance to evaporate some of the wine, its bouquet is hard to identify. One of the outstanding qualities of young wines from some varieties of grape is "fruitiness," an odor that may remind you of freshly picked raspberries, or violets, or truffles.

Because evaporation increases with the quantity of alcohol, many wines with high alcoholic content have the taste of these fruit and flower odors. Fruitiness is also a taste characteristic of young wines. Equally, many wines have a lingering taste in the mouth, the aftertaste. It is quite distinct from the "original taste," just as the bouquet is distinct from the aroma. Some wines have a tendency to fill the mouth, a characteristic usually defined as "body" imparted to them by alcohol and tannin. Wines heavy in body are pleasantest to sip; of those light in body it is more pleasing to take several swallows at once. Some wines are so full in body that you have the feeling that you could take bites of them and chew on them, a quality called *mordant*.

In great wines a balance of qualities is needed, body being poised against acidity, to give the wine freshness. If a wine is too acid, it tastes sharp; if it is not acid enough, it tastes flat and flabby. What holds the qualities of a wine, so that it will live long enough to develop all its characteristics to the full, is tannin. A wine too strong in tannin will taste heavy and bitter. When all these qualities are integrated, the wine is in balance, which is often called the quality of smoothness. A well-balanced wine is always a good one and can often be a great one.

Edward VII has been quoted as saying: "Not only does one drink wine, but one inhales it, one looks at it, one tastes it, one swallows it . . . and one talks about it." Sometimes wine can be confusing because it contains so many different things, all bidding for attention. But of one thing you can be sure: good wine is good to drink.

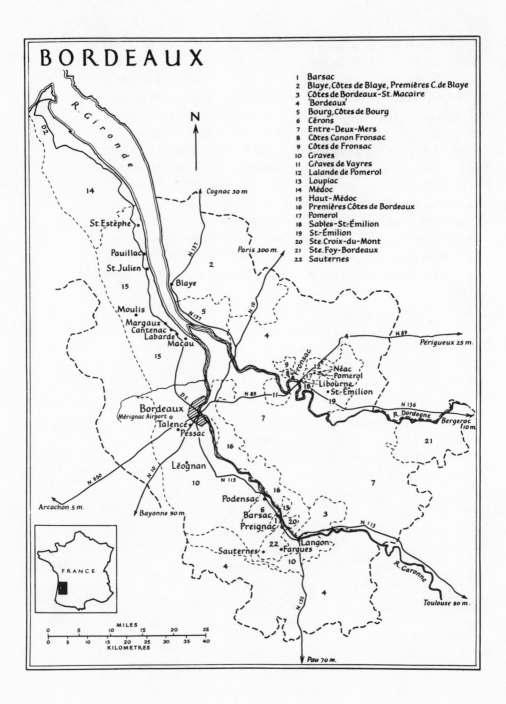

BORDEAUX

1   Barsac
2   Blaye, Côtes de Blaye, Premières C. de Blaye
3   Côtes de Bordeaux-St. Macaire
4   'Bordeaux'
5   Bourg, Côtes de Bourg
6   Cérons
7   Entre-Deux-Mers
8   Côtes Canon Fronsac
9   Côtes de Fronsac
10 Graves
11 Graves de Vayres
12 Lalande de Pomerol
13 Loupiac
14 Médoc
15 Haut-Médoc
16 Premières Côtes de Bordeaux
17 Pomerol
18 Sables-St.-Émilion
19 St.-Émilion
20 Ste. Croix-du-Mont
21 Ste. Foy-Bordeaux
22 Sauternes

BORDEAUX:
The Greatest Wine District

Bordeaux is a seaport sixty miles from the sea, a fan-shaped city on a curve of the Garonne, capital of the province anciently known as Gascony or Guyenne, and its fame was made by the great wines of the vineyards surrounding it. These produce and export more good wine than any others in France. An English possession for three hundred years, the city returned to the French Crown in the middle of the fifteenth century. The stamp of the English remains in *claret*, their name for the red wines of Bordeaux, a corruption of the French *clairet*, which used to mean a light blend of red and white wines.

Bordeaux is the fifth largest city in France. Its 560,000 people talk about wines the way Americans talk about baseball, and wine remains its most valuable export, as it has been for a thousand years. The city, reached by a steel bridge spanning the Garonne, sprawls out from a great riverside square dominated on the quay side by two ugly columns whose principal ornaments are the behinds of four fishes, up near the top under the crowning sculpture. The square is often filled with traveling carnivals and circuses; each spring there is a flea market that lasts for a week, and a gaudy trade fair was held in the month of June. Downstream from the square begins the Quai des Chartrons, a shabby row of waterfront buildings, owning space in which is a mark of distinction, for they contain the cellars and offices of the greatest merchants in the Bordeaux wine trade. In summer the offices are all closed, for the merchants go to Arcachon, over on the Atlantic side of the estuary, and visiting buyers must go to the beaches to do business with the merchants baking in the sun.

On the square is the Hôtel Splendide, which has a honky-tonk nightclub in its basement. The hotel is the Bordeaux headquarters for the visiting wine buyers, and boasts of a wine card that lists over two hundred wines of Bordeaux. A couple of blocks away, near the downtown market, which is an open, circular dome of iron girders and glass whose side walls are hanging awnings vertically striped in red and white, was one of the strangest restaurants in the world, the Chapon-Fin. Built in the nineties, it was made to look like a grotto. It had a rock garden and pool in the back, glass-covered, trellised terraces along the side. The whole was encased under a glass dome, and it was here that the owner of Château Haut-Brion came if he wanted to taste any of the fabulous old vintages that his vineyard produced. Now famous among visiting buyers is the Restaurant Dubern, which you enter by passing through a fabulous delicatessen, and there one can get such Bordeaux specialties as *cèpes à la Bordelaise,* huge mushrooms cooked in olive oil. One of the favorite restaurants of the *bordelais* is the Château Trompette, an excellent restaurant, and one of the specialties is mussels and baby crabs, the former having partially devoured the latter and having been caught before digestion was complete.

Wine is a big business in Bordeaux, complete with brokers, exchange quotations, and speculation on the various vintages and growths. The brokers are called "courtiers," and in the old days when strangers needed protection from marauders, they used to accompany visiting buyers to the vineyards. They still do. At one time things were so bad that the banks of the river were walled to keep out river pirates. All the wine of Bordeaux is sold through brokers, who act as go-betweens for grower and buyer, certifying that the wine bought is genuine and in good condition.

The broker is much more than a necessary evil, for most of the wine is bought directly after the harvest, kept in the château during its two years or so in barrel, and delivered to the buyer after the bottling. Many of the wine châteaux sell the wine in barrel after fermentation is complete, but the broker is still necessary to ensure that the wine lives up to its expectations. Most of the brokers specialize in wine in barrels, but some are concerned with the wine only after it is bottled. There are about one hundred brokers, some of them of English families who have been in the business since the eighteenth century, when a man had to get letters patent from the King before he could set up shop. As one of them says, Bordeaux is smothered with brokers.

The shippers buy from the brokers and send the wines of Bordeaux all over the world. The great bulk of their business is in regional wines, those that carry the names of the district or commune, but not those of particular vineyards, for they are a blend. The five greatest districts are the Médoc, to the northwest of Bordeaux; Saint-Émilion and Pomerol, twenty miles east, which produce red wines; Graves, to the south of the city, which produces both red and white wines; and Sauternes and Barsac, which produce the greatest sweet white wines in the world. The shippers also sell regional wines from the lesser districts and wines from various communes, such as Saint-Julien, Saint-Estèphe, and Margaux, in the Médoc, now called the "Haut-Médoc."

Bordeaux wines are also sold under other labels, usually misleading. One is "Graves de Vayres," a tiny district between Bordeaux and Libourne, having nothing in common with the famous district of Graves to the south of the city. Also, "Graves Supérieur" is a name frequently tacked on wines that are merely regionals and are sold at prices higher than ordinary Graves, being often more expensive than château-bottled Graves. Such wines give the buyer no cachet of authenticity and are often poor values.

The same type of label was one saying "Haut-Sauternes," which was popularly supposed to denote a superior Sauternes—that is, a sweeter one—and these wines often commanded prices higher than the château-bottled wines. The Committee of Place-Names has done much to dispel many myths that had no foundation. Among these was the relation of Haut-Sauternes to Sauternes. Pierre Bréjoux, chief of the technical section of the committee, states: "There is no appellation Haut-Sauternes. The word Haut is theoretically forbidden. It is tolerated, however, as long as shippers supply Sauternes in the event that their customers request 'Haut-Sauternes' labels. The wine, however, must be from the district of Sauternes." There is a myth about Sauternes, particularly on the part of the trade: a belief that there is such a thing as a good dry Sauternes. All good Sauternes is sweet, and a dry Sauternes is a poor one. In an average year a good château-bottled Sauternes is a sweet wine with a dry finish, less full-bodied and not so sweet as the same wine in a good year, when it is characterized by a rich, luscious taste, a much-desired quality that makes for high prices. The better the vintage, the sweeter the wine.

Many poor vintages of Sauternes are dry, and to insist on a dry regional Sauternes is to demand a poor wine. The château-bottled Sauternes can be pleasant in off years, but they are never dry, tasting pleasantly soft and on the sweetish side. Sauternes is not synonymous with white wine, but denotes a small and precisely defined district that specializes in sweet wines.

The heads of the powerful winehouses—such as Cordier; Cruse et Fils, Frères; Calvet; Barton et Guestier; Eschenauer; Kressmann; Alexis Lichine; de Luze; Ginestet; Delor; and Sichel et Fils, Frères—have regular hours when they will see the brokers, usually between ten and twelve and between two and four. The brokers appear with their samples, which look like medicine bottles, each with a sticker on which is printed in ink the name of the wine, its vintage, its alcoholic content, and its price. If the shippers like the wine, they will buy it, and when the wine is ready it will be delivered to their cellars, which usually are behind the buildings that house the offices and the packaging plants.

The regional wines are aged in barrels or stored in glass-lined concrete vats. The wines are cleared, filtered, bottled, corked, capped, labeled, wrapped, and crated in the various rooms above the cellar, and oftentimes there is a carpentry shop where the cases are made, a cooperage where the barrels are made, and a blacksmith shop where the hoops are made.

The workers' lunches are heated in a fireplace in the blacksmith shop and are eaten on barrel tops as often as not. One of the favorite dishes is *chabrot,* a soup bowl containing a thick soup with bread, into which a glass of wine is poured. Each worker gets a ration of one ordinary bottle of wine daily and an additional two or three bottles of a better wine every month, a custom still common throughout France—the theory being that it makes him less likely to tipple the wines he's handling.

Most shippers also buy château-bottled wines, those bottled by the grower himself. The prices of some of these wines increase with demand, but contrary to stocks that go up and down on the New York Stock Exchange, the better Bordeaux château-bottled wines are often a wiser investment, in that they do not go down but constantly increase in value with age and a diminishing supply. Some of the châteaux of Bordeaux from which the wines come are castles in name only; their architecture is not to be confused with that of the noble edifices in the château country of the Loire. The title *château* was adopted over a century ago to lend distinction to that system whereby the owner guarantees the authenticity of the wine from his vineyard. All the great wines of Bordeaux are château-bottled, and all are classified according to greatness.

A great wine is usually defined as one that is true to type, excellent year after year, and long-lived. Such qualities as being distinctive, consistent, and long-lived may seem at first to be arbitrary, but they are not. A great wine should be expected to reflect the outstanding qualities of the soil from which it comes, and to do so

whenever the weather gives it a chance, year in and year out. A wine
has characteristics that take years to develop (balance, bouquet, and
finesse are three), and if a wine cannot live long enough to reach its
prime, it is not considered great. That is why those who make their
living from wine think of wines as individuals and constantly per-
sonalize them. This sometimes sounds ridiculous to people not concerned with wine, but a grower is quick to point out that all wines
are filled with microorganisms that give each wine a life of its own.
The great wines of Bordeaux often live for half a century. Many take
twenty years to develop, and some are still drinkable after fifty years
and more.

The wines of Bordeaux were not thought of as great until the
middle of the eighteenth century. During and after the English
occupation much of the wine was shipped to northern Europe, but it
was then simply known as the wine of Graves. It was so poor that in
the sixteenth century the French passed a law that no other wine
could be exported from the port of Bordeaux until all the local wine
had been sold. At that time, when all wines were drunk young, those
from outlying districts were preferred, and the law made it so
difficult to get them that the English stopped buying claret and
switched to Port, Sherry, and Madeira.

It was not until the days of Louis XIV that Bordeaux came to
be appreciated in France at all, and the Sun King himself thought it
terrible. It was the custom to send momentarily obnoxious nobles
away from the court, and many were banished to Bordeaux. Among
these was the Duc de Richelieu, who loved Burgundy and learned to
like Bordeaux only after his friends foisted on him a bottle with a
fake label. It became his favorite, and this was the beginning of its
popularity.

By the beginning of the nineteenth century certain districts and
vineyards stood out as superior, and by mid-century six growths
were considered supreme: the châteaux of Yquem in Sauternes;
Haut-Brion in Graves; and Margaux, Latour, Lafite, and Mouton in
the Médoc. And there was much argument over which vineyards
deserved second place.

In 1855 Parisians decided to hold an exhibition, and they sent
down to Bordeaux for samples of its best wines. This was as much
excuse as the town fathers needed to set up an official classification of
the wines. The growers from Médoc and those from Sauternes seem
to have run the show, for these were the only two districts classified.
But even amid the storms of jealousy and politics it was felt neces-

sary to mention Haut-Brion, one of the greatest vineyards, but unfortunately in Graves. Actually, the listing followed closely the commercial evaluations of the wines and it has been compared by Henri Binaud, former president of the shippers' association of Bordeaux, to a stud book. He said in a lecture at Vintner's Hall in London that "the competition of quality between them can be compared to a very open race. As on a racecourse, though the horses with the most regular form and the noblest pedigree have a greater chance to win, and in fact often do win, it also happens sometimes that there reach the post before them, in some races, competitors whose form is, on that occasion at any rate, superior to their own." As it has turned out, some of the horses have stumbled badly and others are showing far greater strength than their classification over a hundred years ago even dreamed of. The form sheet has served a useful purpose, but it is time for a change.

Today's prices are not always an accurate valuation of the wines, for promotion and speculation may make an expensive wine out of one that is merely good, not great. Shippers have been known to overpraise wines they hold in large quantities. The wine world has been embarrassed by a succession of amazing years and seems to be somewhat afraid that the drinking public will get to expect surpassing greatness even when vintages cannot supply it. Hence it sometimes plays down a pleasant and enjoyable vintage, such as '58, '60, and '65.

No one possesses greater technical knowledge about the wines of Bordeaux than M. Ribereau-Gayon, a remarkable scientist who with his associate, Professeur Peynaud, runs the Oenological Station of Bordeaux. They give advice to winegrowers and lecture on oenology to capacity wine classes. They superseded a Catholic priest, the Abbé Dubaquié, who was with the Wine Station of Bordeaux for over twenty-five years and was its honorary director. The Wine Station acts as adviser and testing laboratory for the growers of Bordeaux, and the scientists save many vintages from failure and others from mediocrity. The Abbé believed that a man who drinks beer or water exclusively does not give great wines enough credit; that the palates of some people are made of wood or maybe cement; that wine should be part of a meal; and that you cannot taste wines unless you have already learned to taste food. Wine characteristics come out only when the food is discreet, he used to say; too rich foods destroy the taste of the wine, and chances are that all Bordeaux people will not

go to paradise, because they eat and drink too much and concentrate on wine. At times, he used to say, the Bordelais have been known to stop a meal to have another go at the bottle.

The Abbé insisted that drinking wine is a sensation that fires the imagination, one of the greatest things in creation. Knowing wine depends on having drunk enough small ones, in contrast to the great ones, he said, and many French do not know wines because they drink *vin ordinaire* all the time, great bottles very rarely.

To know wines, the Abbé suggested, you should start off with a small but typical wine of the Médoc and drink enough to know it. Then you should try one of the lesser wines from Saint-Émilion, followed by a lesser Burgundy, the two having some resemblance. Or drink only red wines for a while and then begin tasting dry white wines. Tasting is a matter of learning, said the Abbé, for you must compare wines, classifying them by your own standards, which no one else can do for you. After that it is time enough to begin drinking the great wines, especially when a great bottle is preceded by a lesser one of the same type. Learning about wine is one of the pleasantest educational pursuits known to man.

The Abbé thought that no specific classifications of wine can be made, for wine is not arithmetic. There are no sharp standards of measurement, just as there are none for paintings or the perfumes of flowers, and he pointed out that the rose has one smell, the lilac another. The only standard is your own taste.

Many of the good wines of France are lost in the blending vats of the shippers, according to the Abbé. Many Bordeaux wines that could be distinguished are lost in the vats of commerce, in the "big sauce." Ordinary wines and poor vintages should be left to the "big sauce," he stated, for there is a chance to make something mediocre out of what would be merely bad.

The wine trade lives on *coupage*, blending being its only contribution to wine production. The disinterested wine experts, particularly those in the Church, have been fighting the custom of blending ever since the 1600's. Blending may improve the quality of bad wines, but it also destroys the great wines. The system of chopping off the peaks and filling in the valleys is particularly common in Burgundy, where sugar is often added during fermentation to increase the alcoholic content, thus often destroying the individuality of the wine.

In Bordeaux more than in any other wine district of France,

vintages may be relied upon as being authentic, especially in château-bottled wines. In great years one may assume that all of the wines of such a large district are good. In intermediate or poor years, however, one may often find great wines only through careful selection, for they may depend on when a particular château harvested. Generally speaking, the consensus in the Bordeaux trade concerning the vintages of the last thirty-nine years is as follows:

1934 *A very abundant yield, producing excellent wines, which matured much more rapidly than the '28's.*

1935 *A very mediocre vintage.*

1936 *A small yield, irregular in quality, of very little interest today.*

1937 *The red wines had a great amount of tannin and were slow in maturing. Too hard and lacking in roundness and fatness, this vintage was overrated; the wines were not pleasant.*

1938 *Average, on the whole. Poor today.*

1939 *Small wines, of no interest today.*

1940 *A fair year. This was the first vintage to be offered on the American market immediately after the war, and therefore received a great acclaim that is not justified. The wines rested too long in barrel, as there was a wartime shortage of bottles. Many are "seché," or tartly overdry.*

1941 *A very poor year.*

1942 *The white wines were better than the red. Pleasant when young, they are poor now.*

1943 *Many fair wines were produced. However, age has not improved these wines, which were unbalanced.*

1944 *An abundant yield. The wines were very light.*

1945 *A very small yield. These very slowly maturing wines are magnificent. Some of the white wines of the district suffered from hail, and in Coutet and Climens no wine was made. The exceptional quality of the great growths may take thirty years to declare itself.*

1946 *A small year, mediocre in quality in both red and white.*

1947 *A very great year in red wines. These wines have matured faster than the '45's and many are past their prime. Remarkable body and bouquet. When not past their peaks, they can be superb. The whites were still greater than the '45's but most of them have oxidized.*

1948 *Good red wines. This was decidedly an intermediate year. Because it came between the great '47's and the '49's, its prestige was handicapped. In this vintage the wines of Saint-Émilion were better than those from the Médoc. In white wines this vintage was not as good as in red.*

1949   *A very good year. The big red wines matured slowly. Many held their own remarkably well and were most enjoyable through the sixties.*

1950   *A very large yield. Wines matured rapidly; typical of a dependable year without extraordinary greatness.*

1951   *Pleasant wines, at best; poor in general.*

1952   *Red—A great year. The best of these wines are slightly on the hard side and have matured more slowly than the 1953's. Luckily, the '52's came before the '53's, so that they close the gap between these two years. In Saint-Émilion and Pomerol the '52's were greater than the '53's, but the same is not true in the Médoc. White—The Graves soon oxidized. The sweet Barsacs and Sauternes, whose quantity was cut by hail, were superb. The sweetness in the Barsacs and especially in the Sauternes makes for longevity. These wines were great until the late '60's.*

1953   *Red—A very great year. The '53's have great softness, roundness, and perfect balance. They may not last as long as the '52's, but they are certainly sheer perfection now. They will fade from here on in, however. On the whole, don't push your luck beyond the seventies. White—The sweet Barsacs and Sauternes are even more memorable than the '52's.*

1954   *Red—Bordeaux merchants bought heavily in 1952, borrowed to buy the '53's, were delighted by bad prospects during the summer of 1954, and took a strong position against the '54's. Late-September sun notwithstanding, the vintage chartists rated the wines "poor." Many of these represented good value. Although on the thin side, and very light, they were pleasant drinking for fifteen years. White —Of no interest.*

1955   *Red—This very great year was definitely better than 1952. In some cases it was greater than 1953; in others, the contrary is true. Magnificently balanced, although maturing early, the '55's were* vins de garde, *or "put-away wines," a characteristic that the '53's did not have. In 1962 these wines began to show their truly great qualities. White— The perfect year for those who find Sauternes overly sweet.*

1956   *Red—Fair, with a tendency to hardness. A sufficiency of the softening Merlot was lacking because of the February freeze and pre-harvest overmaturing. Here, again, is a year where you could pick and choose some values. White —Rather small wines. The best vineyards proved to be disappointing.*

1957   *Red—Very good. Vineyards that harvested late benefited from a uniquely warm October. A tendency to hardness makes these wines relatively slow-maturing. The best will require several years in the bottle before they can be enjoyed at their peak. White—Tiny in quantity, some wines are very fine.*

1958   *Red—A small yield. The vineyards still suffered from the 1956 freeze. Very light, fast-maturing, lacking the character to warrant keeping for any length of time. Good values could be found. White—The dry Graves were clean and pleasant. The sweet wines lacked the sunshine to make them sweet, full, and rich.*

1959   *Red—Had been over optimistically heralded as the year of the century. Whereas the '29's were unnoticed at birth, owing to world depression and Prohibition, the '59's made banner headlines throughout the civilized world. The wines are big, full, harmonious, and rich in natural glycerine. Because some of these wines were outstanding, they needed time to develop and show their breed. They were bottled between December 1961 and March 1962, but some ten years of aging in the bottle will be necessary to allow them to show their peaks of perfection. White— Although not as great as the red wines, the whites were well rounded and rich in alcohol. The Sauternes are luscious and great.*

1960   *Red—A magnificent early summer followed by a rainy September combined to make light, elegant wines— fast-maturing, pleasant, better than the '54's, '56's, and '58's. Coming after the great '59's, the '60's were prematurely decried. As they matured the wise wine-drinker happily discovered well-selected bottles to be truly excellent values. White—Light, good wines were made in this year. Very good values; they are better than their initial reputation would indicate.*

1961   *Red—As far as quality is concerned, this is the vintage that should have received the clamorous publicity enjoyed by the 1959 vintage. A cold, rainy second half of May, during the flowering, or blossoming, period, however, made for poor pollination and insemination, and curtailed quantity by at least fifty per cent. The hot summer months matured the grapes for an early, mid-September harvest. This very great*

*classical wine produced is superbly well balanced. But the small
quantity, coupled with the great quality and the rising world
demand for fine wines, has brought about the greatest price
increase in the modern history of fine wines. White—
Perfectly balanced, the '61's should help to re-establish a
dying custom, the serving of Sauternes with desserts. The
quantity was sixty per cent less than normal.*

1962   *A dry hot summer produced a very good vintage year for all
red wines; soft, fast maturing, plentiful. The '62's matured
quickly; the '61's have matured now. Although one can find
some good bottles in Saint-Émilion and Pomerol, success there
was not as great as in the Médoc. White—The dry white
Bordeaux were fair to good. The sweet whites are not in the
class of the reds.*

1963   *Some light and drinkable wines in the Médoc, a disaster in
Saint-Émilion and Pomerol. After a rainy summer, the
harvest took place during bad conditions—with a few
exceptions, depending upon the time of harvest.*

1964   *A very plentiful year for red wines. A magnificent summer
was followed by an excellent September, and the grapes
achieved maturity during good conditions. Certain châteaux
in the Médoc waited to harvest late, but unfortunately it
rained incessantly from October 8 onward and this year,
which started so well, proved disappointing for a few wines
harvested in mid-October. However, '64 was generally an
excellent vintage in the Médoc. Very successful in Saint-
Émilion and Pomerol, where the harvest finished before
the rain started. White—A good year for the dry white
wines that were harvested at the end of September or in the
first few days of October, at the latest. For the Sauternes
growers who waited until the end of October it was a
disaster.*

1965   *The summer was rainy. A few vineyards harvested late under
fair conditions. If well selected, there were some good-
quality wines that did not last long, but to those who appreciated
the wines of 1960, some of the '65's proved even
better.*

1966   *Uniformly very great, the best since the great 1961's. Perfect
balance has made these wines outstanding and fast-maturing.
In Barsac and Sauternes only one third was good, the remainder
disappointing.*

1967   *Good vintage—a bit lighter than the '66's. The summer was
ideal, so was the weather during the harvest. The pre-harvest
weather at the beginning of September brought the*

quality somewhat down. In Saint-Émilion the quality was superior to that of 1966. The sweet white wines are turning out to be the best since 1961.

1968 *The lack of sunshine in August followed by a cool rainy September produced a light vintage in the Médoc. These fast maturing wines lack color and character. In other districts, the quality was only fair.*

1969 *A fair vintage in the Médoc, disappointing in Saint-Émilion and Pomerol. These wines should be drunk fast, as they have a tendency to lose their fruitiness and thin out, resulting in a certain degree of tartness. However, the vintage has developed most satisfactorily; they will last a long time. The dry whites are good. Passable sweet wines were made in Barsac and Sauternes.*

1970 *A great year. The abundant quantity, unfortunately, did not lower the prices, as the demand throughout the world for the better red Bordeaux has increased considerably. This vintage was a grower's delight, as there was the rare combination of a very fine quality with a large quantity. The white Bordeaux are excellent. The sweet wines are the best since 1961. The dry Graves are very good.*

1971 *Cold weather during the flowering reduced the quantity considerably. The quality was good. Prices continued to rise to the verge of being unrealistic. Very good sweet white wines.*

1972 *Good vintage year. After a rainy and cool summer the quality was saved by warm weather in late September and during the harvest. Better quality in the red than in the white. Due to high fixed acidity, the red wines will be rather slow in maturing but will be long-lived.*

THE MÉDOC

The Médoc begins just
north of Bordeaux. It is a narrow strip of land, rarely more than a
dozen miles wide, stretching along the left bank of the Gironde.
While the district extends for sixty miles, right down to the spit of
land where the river joins the sea, the best wines of the plain are
grown in the communes of Cantenac, Margaux, Saint-Julien, Pauillac, and Saint-Estèphe, all in that section nearest Bordeaux which is
called Haut-Médoc, or Upper Médoc. Ancient French vintners
taught the Romans the use of wine barrels instead of amphoræ. From
the men of Flanders they learned how to reclaim the land from the
encroaching sea. These reclaimed lands were made into vineyards
that look like nothing more than gravel beds on the well-drained,
slightly sloping soil overlooking the wide, placid Gironde.

Yet the centuries-old saying that fine wines are grown only on
the slight knolls, or *"croupes,"* from which the Gironde River is
visible has repeatedly been proven true. This is where drainage is
best and spring frosts spare the vines that revel on the barely
perceptible gravelly mounds. These vines of the plain grow on both
sides of the vineyard road connecting the insignificant crossroads
towns with Bordeaux, between the pine copses encroaching from the
Landes. The vines share this narrow strip of soil with the wide
meadows, the orchards, the farms, and the vineyards of lesser fame.
On a drive north from Bordeaux over the rolling countryside, the
first place of fame is Macau, which is renowned not only for its wines
but also for its artichokes. Like the wines, the artichokes are classified in growths, but they are not the only produce of France that has
crus, as classifications by quality are called.

Across the river and far to the north is the Cognac country, and
along the inlets are the famous oyster beds where the flat *marennes*
come from. These have *crus.* Over to the east, in Périgord, the truffles
have *crus,* and so do the sardines, the cans of which have to be turned

over every few months like champagne bottles aging in the cellars. The cider of Normandy, cheeses, and practically everything else grown in France are classified. The chicken from Bresse is famous, not merely for its flavor but also for being the only animal to have an *appellation contrôlée,* which is sure to make the *poulardes* both happy and proud. The French love for classification is not limited to wine. However, since 1958 only Médoc wines can be termed *cru classé.*

No wines have been classified so much or so often as those of the Médoc, the business starting back in the fifteenth century and continuing to this very day. The most famous classification is the outmoded one of 1855, in which some sixty Médoc vineyards were included. Later, seven more were rated "exceptional" and placed right after the five original *crus,* and now hundreds of others have been classified into "bourgeois," "artisan," and "peasant" growths. And the "bourgeois" growths have been divided into two parts.

All this categorizing of wine is an attempt to standardize something that varies endlessly. The most important factor influencing the wine is the ground on which the vines are grown, one parcel being obviously better than another. This century-old classification was well made; the soil, the price, and the prestige of the wine—all these factors helped the experts to rate something that was constantly changing. Yet all the wines of Bordeaux have a certain recognizable taste, one that is firm with a distinct bouquet, flowery, light in comparison with the fuller tastes of the hill wines of the Rhône and of some Burgundies.

One of the choicest Médoc soils is in the vineyards of Château Margaux, only fifteen miles from Bordeaux, which perhaps gained its distinguished status because its gravelly sand is so well drained. The estate of Château Margaux consists of nearly 600 acres, of which less than 200 are vineyard. Of those usually planted in vines, some 10 acres are now resting, while another small portion is given over to the making of a white wine, called *Pavillon Blanc,* that is one of the better known dry white Bordeaux.

The great Empire-style château sits in its vast park at the end of a cobbled drive guarded by a great wrought-iron gate. It is a great rectangle of a building, the center of its front façade boasting four columns making a roofed porch modeled after the Parthenon, of all things. The interior is also strictly Empire, however, and here lives the owner, M. Ginestet, who began buying Château Margaux back in 1934 and completed the purchase just in time for Christmas

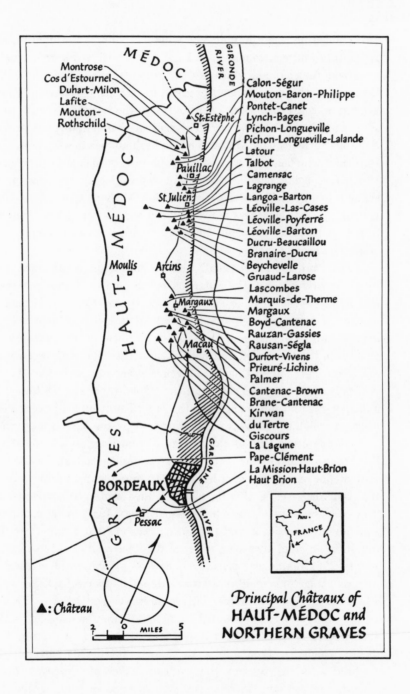

MÉDOC

GIRONDE RIVER

Montrose
Cos d'Estournel
Duhart-Milon
Lafite
Mouton-
Rothschild

Calon-Ségur
Mouton-Baron-Philippe
Pontet-Canet
Lynch-Bages
Pichon-Longueville
Pichon-Longueville-Lalande
Latour
Talbot
Camensac
Lagrange
Langoa-Barton
Léoville-Las-Cases
Léoville-Poyferré
Léoville-Barton
Ducru-Beaucaillou
Branaire-Ducru
Beychevelle
Gruaud-Larose
Lascombes
Marquis-de-Therme
Margaux
Boyd-Cantenac
Rauzan-Gassies
Rausan-Ségla
Durfort-Vivens
Prieuré-Lichine
Palmer
Cantenac-Brown
Brane-Cantenac
Kirwan
du Tertre
Giscours
La Lagune
Pape-Clément
La Mission-Haut-Brion
Haut Brion

St-Estèphe

Pauillac

St Julien

HAUT-MÉDOC

Moulis

Arcins

Margaux

Macau

GRAVES

GARONNE RIVER

BORDEAUX

Pessac

FRANCE
Paris

▲: *Château*

MILES
2   0   5

Principal Châteaux of
**HAUT-MÉDOC and
NORTHERN GRAVES**

1949. When he began buying, the wine had slumped in quality, but replanting and continuous care have re-established its greatness.

Near the château, which is pictured on the label, are the buildings where the wine is made—great low sheds called *chais,* built around a courtyard that opens out on the vineyards and their short-staked, thigh-high vines. The central *chai* contains the presses and the enormous vats, almost ten feet high and six across, typical of Bordeaux wine-making, where the grape juice ferments for a week or two before being barreled, the time depending on the amount of sugar it contains. When the fermentation is complete, the new wine is drawn out of the oak vats into new oak barrels, which are trundled into the adjoining *chai* and lined up in long rows on their sides, resting on heavy timbers.

This *chai,* about the size of a small auditorium, is presided over by the *maître de chai,* the cellar-master in charge of the wine-making. After the *régisseur,* or manager, he is the most important man at a wine château, and helps make the final decision as to when the grapes shall be picked, how long the grape juice remains in the vats, when it is to be barreled and bottled, how the wine is to be treated, and so on. This *chai* of Château Margaux is one of the biggest. Its tile roof is held up by great columns; the whole interior is whitewashed and spotless, and big enough for the great banquets held every year or so, at which as many as fifteen hundred people have been served.

On the other side of the village of Margaux and encircling a knoll that overlooks a sweep of vineyards stands Château Lascombes. Few Médoc vineyards have been owned by as many proprietors in the past forty years. Having now regained and even surpassed its previous greatness, Lascombes, owned since 1952 by a group of wine-loving Americans and the author, has created a minor revolution in an area not always as aware of the times as it ought to be.

In 1961 the author organized the first exhibition of contemporary paintings to be held in a vineyard, on the theme *La Vigne et le Vin,* or The Vine and Wine. This exhibit was restricted to French artists. In 1962 it was extended to include Italian artists, and since 1963 artists from all over the world have been interpreting this theme, which has been a favorite subject for artists through the civilized ages. At present the château makes an average of 250 *tonneaux* of red wine in a normal year, a *tonneau* being a term for four barrels of twenty-four cases each, hence the equivalent of ninety-six cases. The vineyard, by selective exchanges and purchases, has been greatly consolidated and improved. Many experts agree that the 1966 vintage shares with the "first growths" the honors of that particular great year in the Médoc.

Along the vineyard road behind the Church of Cantenac, a couple of miles before the village of Margaux, one sees the walls of Chateau Prieuré-Lichine, an old Benedictine priory, where the author, through some forty purchases and exchanges, reassembled the vineyard to encompass the highest knoll of Cantenac, now included in the place-name of Margaux. Inside the courtyard, the new *chai* at Lascombes, lighted by chandeliers made of vine stalk, is classically modern and, what is more, perfectly clean, a condition unfortunately not completely traditional, but being copied now. The new, well-polished barrels sit with glass stoppers in their bungs, and a curving glass tube called a *pipette* is lowered into the barrel, allowed to fill with wine, and then removed and drained into your glass.

Adjoining is the darker, smaller *chai* where the older wine is kept, the barrels tightly closed with cane-wrapped bungs turned down. It is the Bordeaux custom to tap these barrels for tasting through a small hole drilled in the barrel end and stopped with a wooden peg. The peg is pulled with a vintner's tool that is a combination pliers and hammer, but the wine does not spurt out, because of the vacuum in the tightly sealed barrel. The claw of the tool is jammed under the crossboard braced over the barrel end, and leverage on the hammer handle exerts pressure on the barrel end, squirting wine through the hole and into your glass.

All the châteaux of the Médoc have two *chais* as at Prieuré-Lichine, and it is customary to taste each vintage, starting with the most recent.

The best wines of the *commune,* or parish, of Margaux come from a cluster of vineyards that produce the most exquisitely delicate wines of the Médoc, hence of Bordeaux. Finesse or breed is their main characteristic, yet each château has its own individuality—Margaux, the most famous of all; Lascombes, one of the most popular owing to its year-to-year improvement in quality; Brane-Cantenac, recently the largest; Palmer, whose quality refutes its classification as a third growth, proving the obsolescence of the 1855 classification; Rausan-Ségla, now in wine-loving British hands; d'Issan, the oldest architecturally; Malescot, producing the fullest of all Margaux wines; Prieuré-Lichine, producing early maturing soft wine. Château Giscours is now coming up considerably in quality as its newly replanted vines are becoming older. Some other vineyards exist that produce good wines—Rauzan-Gassies, Boyd-Cantenac,

Pouget, Marquis-de-Terme, Kirwan and Dauzac among the classified châteaux, and Siran and La Tour-de-Mons among the *crus bourgeois* often producing better wines than some of those just mentioned.

A dozen miles up the road is the cluster of buildings called Saint-Julien, which has tacked Beychevelle, once its most famous vineyard, to its name. Now coming up again in reputation are the three vineyards of Léoville: Las-Cases, Poyferré, and Barton. Saint-Julien has given its name to the best-known of regional bottlings, red wines drunk more often than those of its greater château-bottlings because they are more plentiful and cheaper.

Beychevelle is said to get its name from the call of those ancient mariners who used to sail up the Gironde in ships loaded with timber to swap for wine, and who shouted in Gascon: *"Baisses les voiles"* as they struck their sails because of the changing wind and current off the vineyards. The corruption of words was no trouble at all to succeeding generations of Bordelais, and you cannot mention the vineyard in Bordeaux without being told the story, often with gestures.

Adjoining Beychevelle is Ducru-Beaucaillou, a vineyard that had gone down in quality after the war and which in 1961 hit a peak never before reached since its comeback started in 1953. Entering Saint-Julien, one sees, to the left, the simple Empire-style outline of the château of Branaire-Ducru, one that has made some splendid wines. Close by is Château Gloria, owned by Henri Martin, who, as president of all the local wine associations, is Bordeaux's most important wine citizen. He acquired good surrounding vineyards to increase the acreage of his Gloria—some from classified growths such as Saint-Pierre. Unfair as it may seem, the wines lost all their rating because his excellent Chateau Gloria is a *cru bourgeois,* another example of the obsolescence of the 1855 classification.

Just above the town is the big, rambling château of Léoville, shared by Las-Cases, whose *chais* and vineyards are on the right of the road, and Poyferré, whose *chais* and vineyards are opposite. The half of the château belonging to the owner of Las-Cases has a new roof, perhaps to make it easy to tell the two apart. In the twenties Poyferré used to be rated the better of the two. Its '29, for instance, is considered one of the greatest bottles made in the Bordeaux region that year. However, since then it seems to be the consensus that Poyferré has slipped. The wine of Las-Cases has been better than that of its twin, reaching a pinnacle in 1959 and 1961. Its vineyard is entered through an ugly stone arch, which appears on its label. The stone of the arch has been eaten away on its river side by the hard winds and rains blowing down the river. In 1966, M. Delon, contaminated by the renovating fever started by André Malraux, France's minister of culture, and which swept all of France, did away with the quaintness of his gateway by plastering new cement all over it. The arch looks new, but the old label still remains. Nearly 150 acres are in production, producing 300 *tonneaux* in 1967. The quantity increased through the fifties due to new planting. The quality up to 1959 was most disappointing because of the many new vines.

While the Léovilles and Ducru-Beaucaillou are classified as second *cru,* Beychevelle is officially fourth, although the Bordeaux merchants state that it should be a third and often sell it for higher prices than those of second *crus*—a slight confusion often met with in the world of wines. In a fine year, when the alcoholic content is over twelve per cent, Beychevelle has great finesse, but when the percentage is lower, its wines are too light. A good year for Bordeaux means a great year for Beychevelle, the '70's and '66's being magnificent, the '66's very good. 1955 broke the rule, however, being not up to its standard. 1959 re-established it by being very great, while 1961 is big and round, and this year of small quantity is now showing considerable finesse. (*Finesse* is an untranslatable French term that means something like "supreme delicacy," or "fine breeding," or "exceptional elegance.")

The vineyards of the great Château Latour border on those of Léoville Las-Cases, although it is in the neighboring commune of Pauillac, a regional name that rarely appears on a bottle of regional wine. In June 1950 a new promotional order of owners and shippers was created for boosting the sale of Médoc wines. Château Haut-Brion, from Graves, was the only wine from outside the Médoc that was included as a member. At their headquarters in Pauillac one of their chief activities is the holding of dinners at which the members wear long medieval robes and call themselves Commanderie du Bontemps, "good-time companions." *Bontemps* are small wooden pails for the egg whites used in fining, symbolized by the members' white-topped hats. Shouting their slogan: *"Par le Bontemps, pour le Bontemps, toujours Médoc!"* the Commanderie held Bordeaux's first large wine auction in 1951. In 1959 the Commanderie of the Médoc joined up with the wine society of Graves and Sauternes, and it is hoped that the Jurâde will soon be included to form a united Bordeaux Society.

The Château of Latour was burned down at the end of the Plantagenet reign when Talbot, the last English commander of th

British occupation, was defeated there. All that remains of the old château is a domed water tower hulking above the famous vines, a caretaker's small, ugly house covered with ivy, in a grove of trees, and an old stone crenelated gateway that guards the entrance to the *chais* and appears on the label.

A fabulous treasure is supposed to be buried somewhere around the place, and the cellar-master, who is as fond of garlic as he is of the wine, will let you look for it, providing that you don't hurt the vines. The *chais* are among the handsomest in the Médoc, being built around a court planted with rows of vigorously pruned plane trees. The new wine is kept in a long, low *chai* with small windows looking across the vineyards to the river. Production at Latour is small: less than 120 acres, all planted in vines, none resting. Dead roots are torn up and replaced each year. In 1970, 200 *tonneaux* of wine were made, about the average, but in 1971 there were only 130 *tonneaux,* a very small yield.

Constant care is one of the secrets of great wine according to most cellar-masters, says Latour's *régisseur*. One aspect is meticulous cleanliness, particularly the scrubbing of the new barrels before the new wine is poured into them. While aging in the barrels, some of the wine will evaporate, necessitating refilling the barrels frequently to keep the wine sound. Otherwise volatile acidity, the enemy of all wine-makers, will develop. This refilling is called *ouillage,* and it is done so often at Latour that the outsides of the barrels between the two center hoops are stained red with the wine. One visitor insisted that each barrel was painted with a red stripe, and perhaps the symmetry is helped somewhat by wiping the barrels with a cloth after each refilling. In Bordeaux the new wines rest in barrels laid with the bungholes up, stoprered with glass bungs, causing another Latour visitor to allow as how they must look right pretty when they were all lit up.

The wines of Château Latour have an extremely long life. The '64's are only now ready to drink, while the '66's will not be ready until the 1970's. The '70's are big and deep in color. The '60's, decried prematurely by forecasters, are the best in that vintage from the Médoc, and '61 was slow in maturing, a hard, or *corsé,* wine that has developed splendidly and has become a great bottle. Latour makes very great wines year after year, using a combination of stainless-steel vats, representing new techniques, and traditional meticulous care. The new owner, Lord Cowdray, can be deservedly proud of the management of Henri Martin, who is consistently making one of the greatest classical red wines of the world.

Across the small vineyard road from Latour is Château Pichon-Longueville Comtesse de Lalande, usually referred to as Comtesse to differentiate it from the other Pichon across the main Médoc artery, which is known as Baron. The two Pichons are second *crus,* and the Baron, perhaps the more popular of the two, is a big sturdy wine typical of the wines of Pauillac and has naturally a character which resembles those of Latour.

Another fifth growth that is making marvelous wines is Grand-Puy-Lacoste. M. Dupin, its owner, is certainly the Médoc's finest gourmet. He owns one of the best flocks of the sheep that made Pauillac famous and at dinner usually presents old bottles of his beloved "Grand-Puy."

On the road to Pauillac, to the left behind a cross in the vineyard, is Lynch-Bages, a popular fifth *cru.* The name, like so many others in Bordeaux, is an indication of the number of Irishmen who in the eighteenth century settled in the southwest of France to cultivate and exploit its marvelous riches.

Above Pauillac is the other great first *cru* of the Médoc, Château Lafite. One of its neighbors is the first vineyard of the second *cru* Château Mouton-Rothschild, which has never recovered from the shock of being classified a second. The two are owned by rival branches of the Rothschild family.

The name of Château Lafite has lost an *f* and a *t* through the years, though one of the early owners had two of both. It is maintained that the name refers to the old Médoc word *lahite,* which was a corruption of *la hauteur,* meaning "knoll" or "height." In any case, the château is on a rise. It is a jumble of architectural styles, with various towers rising above a great balustraded terrace near the dramatic cellars. Down below, in the great cellars, one discovers one of the world's greatest wine *bibliothèques,* with eighty thousand bottles, containing vintages going back to 1797. As the vineyard was set aside for Goering during the war, the library is still preserved. From its vineyards the great light wines, famed for their finesse, are produced in nearly every good year, the recent classical vintages being '61, '66, and '70. In 1953 Lafite was supreme in this vintage and the '62's and '66's are considered exceptionally good. Château Lafite, as in the case of so many other top vineyards, proves that soil is often more important than vintage years. A wine from a great vineyard of a small year is often better than a small wine from indifferent soil in a great year.

The Château Mouton-Rothschild, near by, has been in the Rothschild family since 1868, and the family has spared no pains to keep the superlative quality of this wine on a par with the four first growths, with which it deserves to be classified. The château is a series of low, Spanish-looking buildings, with the most decorated *chais* in all of Bordeaux. The new wine is kept in a long, low *chai* with indirect lighting and a mammoth cut-out of the vineyard shield, bearing rams. Underneath are cellars lit with hanging wrought-iron hoops holding clusters of tiny electric candles, birthday-cake size. Philippe de Rothschild deserves credit for having been the first promoter of the Médoc. This is too often forgotten. In 1962 he opened a wine museum, which will help make visits to the Médoc that much more interesting. The wines of Mouton claim some of the highest prices paid by the Bordeaux merchants, and are noted for the fact that they develop considerably with age, therefore being hard to fathom when young.

For some reason, the fifth *crus* around Pauillac are particularly well known, Lynch-Bages, Mouton-Baron-Philippe (previously known as Mouton d'Armailhacq), and Pontet-Canet being better known than many of the second, third, and fourth *crus*.

Château Pontet-Canet, which belongs to the shipping house of Cruse, is the best-known château wine that is not château-bottled. Château Kirwan is also a classified growth that is not château-bottled, as is Château Langoa-Barton and Château Batailley. These are the only four wines of the Médoc that were never château-bottled.

Cantenac, where Château Kirwan is located, was granted the right in August 1954 to sell its wines under the much better known place-name of Margaux. In 1952 the author acquired Château Cantenac-Prieuré, built by the Benedictine monks, who were to the Médoc what the Cistercians were to the Clos Vougeot in Burgundy, and the vineyard now replanted and increased in size is known as Château Prieuré-Lichine.

Along with Château Calon-Ségur, one of the best vineyards of Saint-Estèphe, the last town in Haut-Médoc, is the famous Château Cos-d'Estournel, the vineyards of which can be seen from those of Château Lafite. The vineyard boasts a surrounding wall littered with Chinese pagodas. During the war the Germans mounted antiaircraft batteries in each pagoda; they were damaged but have since been rebuilt. The vineyard produces about 210 *tonneaux* a year, with about 180 acres in vines and another 80 resting.

Château Montrose and Château Calon-Ségur round out the list of the Saint-Estèphes. In general, these wines are harder, more *corsé*, or full-bodied, than those of the townships of Margaux, Saint-Julien, and Pauillac. Both these vineyards are living proof that the 1855 classification is but a mere indicator of nuances, or slight shades of quality. The ''firsts,'' owing to their position, have been able to command such high prices because of increasing world demand and limited supply. So often the unwary wine-drinker, wanting to be ''safe'' in his selection, has overlooked many of the great wines that are in a lower classification. Today, thanks to up-to-date knowledge of wine-making, the so-called ''seconds'' are the true great values of the Médoc. In that part of the Médoc north of Saint-Estèphe and running on down to the mouth of the Gironde, most of the wines are lesser *crus*. Many of the wines are excellent, some comparing favorably with the classified growths and surpassing many of the lesser vineyards in that section of the Médoc nearest Bordeaux.

The expensive ''firsts'' have their very rightful place and are good selections for very special occasions. They prove their claim to supremacy as they acquire age, but not to the exclusion of so many others.

Wine-making methods in the Médoc have improved greatly. Painstaking care, cleanliness, modern equipment, laboratory controls, formerly unknown in most vineyards, are now an integral part of the wine-maker's routine. All the wines are, therefore, better made. Also, careless owners are being eliminated. Vineyards that were but a sentimental family relic have suddenly acquired value. Now it pays to make better wines, whereas only a short time ago, after the war, a vineyard was as much a luxury as a racehorse.

If Médoc is complicated from the standpoint of endless classification and the great number of its wines, its world fame is justified by the wide range of wines it produces, extending from small to great. The efforts needed to discover them make for pleasant adventures.

In the early 1970's, increased world demand pushed the prices of all Bordeaux, and especially those of the classified growths, to ridiculous highs. It remains to be seen whether the public will pay the fantastic prices quoted by the wine trade.

SAINT-ÉMILION
AND POMEROL

The red wines of Saint-Émilion are grown in an area not much more than a mile square, on the high plateau and slopes above the valley of the Dordogne. The old town, some twenty miles east of Bordeaux, is reached by driving across that wedge of vineyard formed by the branching of the Gironde and called Entre-Deux-Mers. Much of the lesser wines of the Bordeaux region is shipped from the small port town of Libourne, just downstream from Saint-Émilion, whose shippers are looked down upon by their colleagues of Bordeaux, as are the wines from the minor districts of the *côtes* of Blaye, Bourg, Fronsac, Graves de Vayres, Canon-Fronsac, and Lalande-de-Pomerol to the north of Entre-Deux-Mers. Of these, Fronsac is the most important.

Saint-Émilion stands at the head of a cleft in the plateau, the road turning away from the river and running up the valley floor between two steep, vine-covered slopes to the heights, dominated by a lone steeple. The church is down below, a series of great caverns carved out of the rock, and what would be its roof is the plateau itself, now the flagged terrace of the local restaurant, where you can sit at small tables covered with checked tablecloths, under a canopy of vines, and look out over the valley while you eat your lunch. One of the specialties of the house is lamprey, caught in the rivers below and cooked with the red wines of Saint-Émilion; and the wine card has a long list of the local wines to choose from, to be drunk with a specialty of the town, a kind of macaroon that is not sweet.

Saint-Émilion is one of the loveliest wine towns in the world. It was a stop-over for Breton pilgrims on the way to the shrines of Spain, and a nunnery and hospital were built there to care for the sick trying to reach the sacred places to be cured. Bits of the Romanesque buildings remain: a great moat, the side wall of an ancient church, and part of the hospital. In the forecourt of one of the cloisters a local shipper of sparkling wine has set up shop, using the crypts beneath to store his barrels.

In the lower town, near the entrance to the old church dug out of the rock, is the cavern where St. Émilion, the hermit, lived underneath the crumbling remains of a small chapel. Beside the carved niche where he slept is a block of stone, and if you sit on it, lean far back, and make a wish, it will come true. Also beside the niche is a shallow well full of hairpins; if a girl throws in two and they land on the bottom in the form of a cross, she will be married within the year. The guide will reassure her by insisting that bobby pins count too.

The town and most of the surrounding farmhouses are built of stone quarried out of the soft rock of the plateau. Some of the old quarries were used as burying-places, but those near the vineyards are used as wine cellars in which the local wine matures slowly and superbly in the cool dark.

Coming up the valley cleft to the town are the vineyards of Château Ausone on the left, the château itself being on the edge of the plateau. Contrary to Bordeaux custom, the wines are today allowed to mature in the great fermentation vats during the first winter after the wine harvest. Another break with custom is that during the following spring wines are put into old barrels instead of new ones. Local vintners feel that both practices hurt the wine, and Château Ausone is now thought to be inferior to Château Cheval-Blanc, the other *grand cru* of Saint-Émilion.

The owners of Château Ausone's less than eighteen acres, which are rotation-planted and yield an average of twenty-five *tonneaux,* are also proprietors of the thirty-two acres of Château Belair, which is the adjoining vineyard and a producer of lesser wine. The barrels of wine from both vineyards are kept in the same cellar, also contrary to custom, where they remain three years before the bottling, according to the cellar-master. Château Ausone's '64's seem to be characterized by hardness and bitterness, which are likely to disappear with time. The '66 was very hard, and will not be ready for drinking until 1975; the somewhat softer '62's have become drinkable, while the '61's are not likely to be ready until the 1970's. Both vineyards are extremely old. Ausone was planted by the Roman poet and local governor Ausonius, who gave the wine its name. Belair is even older; the original vineyard was made by gouging trenches in the rock, which were then filled with earth and planted.

Farther down the steep slope are the vineyards of Château La Gaffelière, while across the road and reaching all the way up to the top of the terraced plateau are the plantings belonging to Château Pavie. The qualities of these wines place them among the first half-dozen of the principal Saint-Émilion growths. Just behind Château Ausone, farther back on the plateau, are Clos Fourtet and Château Canon, whose superlative wines are rated right after the two *grands crus*. All these growths vie with each other for first place. In 1961, for instance, which was a Saint-Émilion vintage par excellence, Château La Gaffelière vied for first place with many of the lesser growths, such as Canon, La Dominique, l'Angélus, and Troplong-Mondot.

Such classifications are likely to get you an argument from one or another of the proprietors or the Bordeaux shippers, but they are all agreed that Saint-Émilion wines are the heaviest of the Bordeaux. They are often called the Burgundies of the region, perhaps because many of them are slope wines, which seems to give them a Burgundy character. The bouquet of these wines is generally small in comparison with that of the Médoc wines, which experts feel is a further distinction. Also, it is rare to find a Saint-Émilion with the finesse or breed of a good Médoc. The Institut National des Appellations Con-

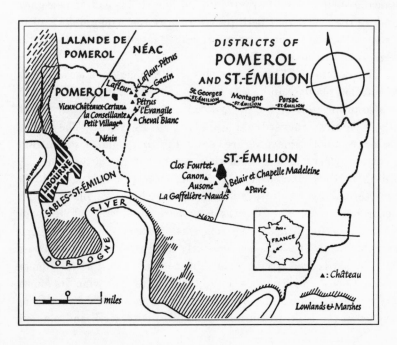

trôlées, or National Institute of Place-Names, has made an official classification of the Saint-Émilion wines. Endless controversy has ensued, for the use of "Crus Classé" or "Premier Cru" has led to confusing these wines with the wines of the Médoc having a similar classification. But none is equal in finesse and quality to the "firsts" of the Médoc.

Château Canon was owned by a man who boasted of never having smoked a cigarette in his life, was a broker of Saint-Émilion wines for forty years, and was a figure in the local promotion organization, La Jurâde, which is mainly concerned with giving, as often as possible, banquets at which only Saint-Émilion wines are served. Part of the *chais* is in an old quarry directly under the local neighborhood cemetery. The nearly fifty acres of vines produce almost an equal number of *tonneaux*. The wine is allowed to ferment for about ten days in the vats and then rests in the barrel for two years. Like the others, the wine was hard, but shorter vatting has rendered these wines much more *souple,* or supple.

Scarcely a mile from Château Canon is the great Château Cheval-Blanc, right on the border where Pomerol begins. It produced one of the greatest Bordeaux of '61 and a memorable one in 1966. Driving down a long avenue of pines, one comes to the court of the low, handsome château, *chais* on both sides, the vineyards all around. The wine is so famous that a local proprietor began calling his vineyard Cheval-Noir, but all he got for his trouble was a lawsuit.

The château owns about a hundred acres, only about seventy-five of which are planted, and makes some ninety *tonneaux* a year. The cellar-master has a short, silver pipette which he uses to draw the wine from the casks for your glass, and he delights in telling you about the trouble they had in 1949, when the vines blossomed three times. This happens every once in a while in all vineyards, a warm spell starting the blossoms, a cold snap stopping the flower, sometimes even killing those that have budded, and the whole growing order beginning all over again when the weather warms up. It is good for the wine if the vines blossom and fall within ten days, for a slow budding cuts down the yield and size of grapes. This phenomenon is called *coulure*. 1961 produced magnificent wines but was the smallest year on record, owing to the great loss caused by poor flowering. 1971 for the same reason was small in quantity.

In spite of all the trouble, '59 is a great wine characterized by fatness, softness, and a comparatively big bouquet, which the vintage has throughout Saint-Émilion. ("Fatness" means a big soft wine, with glycerine, without much body, in contrast to a full wine, which has much body, owing to tannin.) The '70 will be a very great bottle, yet all of Saint-Émilion and Pomerol fared better in 1961. 1961 tends to be *the* vintage for Saint-Émilion and adjoining Pomerol. In 1945 half the vintage was pasteurized, that drastic practice often tried by vintners in order to save the wine from spoiling when the wines are too light and have an excessive amount of volatile acidity, the vintner's greatest enemy. 1947 was one of Cheval-Blanc's greatest years, when, according to some, the wine made was the greatest of all the wines of Bordeaux from all districts.

The wines of Pomerol come from the neighboring commune, and are noted for their distinctive bouquet. One of the best vineyards, La Conseillante, is right across the road from Château Cheval-Blanc. In sight is Château Vieux-Château-Certan, not to be confused with the three or four others with Certan in their names, and Château l'Évangile, which is ranked right after it. However, nearly everybody agrees that the best vineyard of Pomerol is Château Pétrus, deserving greater recognition, whose vineyards are beside those of Vieux-Château-Certan. The Pomerol wines are usually distinguished by greater breed or finesse. They are closer to the Médocs except for their characteristic fatness.

In recent years the winegrowers have tried to recover from the loss caused by the 1956 freeze, which destroyed more vineyards here than in most other parts of France. The crippling blow of the poor blossoming in June 1961, followed by the heat that dried up the grapes in August, has made the better wines from this large wine-producing area temporarily scarce. Since then, with considerably increased production, Pomerol has gained in popularity.

The wines of Saint-Émilion and Pomerol, grown from a cross between the Merlot and the Cabernet Franc called Bouchet, were among the first wines of France to be known, and it is claimed that they were drunk in the times of the Druids, although some argue that the vine was brought to the high plateau by those same early traders who are supposed to have planted it all along the Mediterranean. However and whenever winegrowing got started, the local vintners like to paint the picture of young and tempting Eleanor of Aquitaine gliding over the waters of the Dordogne in her gilded boat, surrounded by musicians and poets, and drinking the heady wine from the high plateau. It is a pretty picture, even without the macaroons.

GRAVES

The vineyards of Graves
run for some thirty-five miles along the western bank of the Garonne,
in a strip rarely more than five miles wide, which starts just above
Bordeaux and continues to just below Langon. The vineyards encir-
cle both cities, as well as the sweet-wine districts of Sauternes and
Barsac, and also that of Cérons just to the north, the wine of which is
considered an intermediary between the often dry white wines of
Graves and the always sweet wines of Sauternes.

Running along the eastern bank of the Garonne are the vineyards called the *Premières Côtes* of Bordeaux, producing fair red
wines in the upper half, fair sweet wines in the lower. Opposite
Sauternes are the sweet-wine districts of Loupiac and Sainte-Croix-
du-Mont, while across the river from Langon is the district of
Saint-Macaire. All these districts produce good secondary Bordeaux
wines.

The wines of Graves are both red and white, and its greatest
vineyard is Château Haut-Brion, in Pessac, a suburb of Bordeaux.
The highway, with its clanking trolley-car line, divides the vineyard.
The red wines come from a plantation of 105 acres, most of which is
on your right as you drive south. It is a large vineyard fenced with
iron grillwork and dominated by a concrete water tank shaped like a
mushroom. Along the back of the plantation is an old concrete shed
that is a shooting range for the French Army, and at its foot are the
château and its park, the *chais* adjoining. Across from the towered
château is a second section, where some red wines and all the white
wines are produced.

Until the turn of the century Haut-Brion produced no white
wine of any importance, but one day its former proprietor was
having lunch with the owner of Château d'Yquem. He complained
about the fact that he owned a tremendous vineyard but produced no
sweet white dessert wines and had to buy them from other growers.

The owner of Yquem agreed that it was a shocking situation, and had some of his vines sent to Haut-Brion the next day. When the plants began bearing, nobody was more surprised than Haut-Brion's proprietor to discover that the wine made from the Yquem vines was very dry. He was still forced to buy dessert wines from other people, but as consolation he became the owner of a dry white wine that has been called the greatest in Bordeaux. Also, he now had something to serve with the fish.

The white wine of Château Haut-Brion is mostly unknown because only some ten thousand bottles are produced each year, less than ten acres on the left side of the road being given over to the white grapes, half Sémillon, half Sauvignon. In an attempt to improve quality and yield, a section on the right side of the road was torn up in 1932 and planted in white grapes. The yield increased, but quality fell, so the old plantation was allowed to rest for six years. When it was replanted, the wine had a different and finer quality,

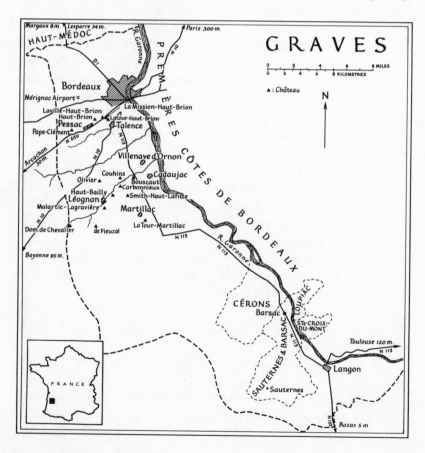

producing an unbelievable white wine in 1945. According to the *régisseur*, who had been at Haut-Brion more than a quarter-century, this is decisive proof that the soil is what makes the wine. Further experiment produced fabulous wines in 1948. The method of making the wine has not changed, except that today it is bottled earlier than formerly. In 1928 and 1929 bottling took place after three years in the cask; today it is done after eighteen months, and the '68's were bottled when barely a year old. Another couple of acres of white vines were planted in 1950, increasing the yield to a present twelve hundred cases.

Château Haut-Brion was producing Bordeaux's greatest red wine in the Middle Ages, when the English began calling it claret. In those days, and for several centuries after, the wines of Graves were the only ones known, and up to the beginning of the eighteenth century Médocs were known as Graves. "Graves" means gravel in French, and the great vineyards of the Médoc, like those of Graves, look like gravel pits. The perfect drainage is a factor in the quality of their wines. At Château Haut-Brion the gravel is as much as sixty feet deep, and the wines from many of the better vineyards in the Médoc have their distinctive taste because of their gravel and pebbly sandstone undersoils. To the north of Margaux, however, the Médoc soil contains more sand, one of the reasons why it was originally named a separate district, for such slight differences in soil make a difference easily detectable to the taste. The abundance of gravel at Haut-Brion is often given as the reason why its wines are good even in off years, the light surface reflecting any excess heat, the porous pebbles draining the vineyard quickly. This good drainage is all-important to the vineyards of the Médoc and Graves, as excessive rainfall is absorbed by the porous soil. With highly skilled methods and modern equipment the wine standards are constantly improving, especially in the lesser years. It is difficult to add quality to the peak years, but what would have been a poor year several years ago can now be a good year, and the wine will sell at a reasonable price.

Talleyrand was once owner of Château Haut-Brion, and the success of his diplomacy at the Congress of Vienna after Napoleon's defeat is often attributed to his chef, Carême. At fabulous dinners Talleyrand pitted his victorious guests against one another, and in the warmth of fine food and the glow of glorious wine they made expansive concessions to that wily representative of a defeated nation. Talleyrand's chief opponent at the Congress was another vineyard-owner, Metternich, one of whose proudest possessions was Germany's greatest vineyard, Schloss Johannisberg, in the famous Rheingau.

The wines of Graves are particularly long-lived, Château Haut-Brion of '59 and '61 being just now about ready to drink. Many of the still older wines taste sturdy and vigorous today.

Proper making of the wine has much to do with its quality, of course, and growers must know precisely when to order the harvest begun. A few days too late may make the grapes rotten or, if rains come during the harvest, allow the character of the wine to be destroyed. A day too early may mean that the grapes will not have reached their peak in ripeness. The acidity in grapes harvested before they are fully ripe would throw the wine out of balance. By waiting, the grower risks losing his harvest in a sudden hail, and by picking too soon, he may make an inferior vintage when others are making a great one. The Abbé Dubaquié used to say that growers possess an extra sense, purely animal, which tells them when to harvest, when to barrel, and when to bottle.

According to the cellar-master at Haut-Brion, the problem each year is not only when to catch the harvest but also what to do with it once you have it. He is in favor of fast vinification, particularly in hot years. The grapes are hustled into the vat room, passed through an *égrappilloir* (a grape hopper that tears off the stems), and emptied into the vats by means of an endless chain of buckets. Some of the stems, the skins, and the pulp remain with the juice; this residue is called the must. The alcohol in the juice dissolves the color from the skins; the longer the must and juice remain in contact, the heavier and darker the wine. Red grapes are never pressed before fermentation. In 1953, when the grapes seemed to begin fermenting while still in the pickers' baskets, the juice and must were left in contact for only seven days. It was only nine days in 1959 and 1961, when the great amount of fermenting grape sugar changing to alcohol caused the wine to color quickly. In 1965, when the alcohol was low, the contact lasted two weeks, and the wine was still too light. White wine, which should pick up no color from the grape skins, is pressed at once and then dumped into the vats, or *cuves*, to ferment.

When the wine has taken its color, and the sugar has been fermented into alcohol, the must is pressed, the juice going back into the vats for further fermentation. The pulpy must can be pressed a second time, although this second press is not mixed with the first, being made into a separate wine of poorer quality. When fermentation is complete, the wine is barreled. Before being bottled, it must be fined. Fining is the process of removing particles from the wine, a fine liquid being put in the wine to collect the particles and drag them to the bottom. Egg whites are most commonly used.

Vintages for Château Haut-Brion follow the normal pattern, except that the wine is supposed to be better than most in poor years, greater than most in good years. The 1960 is ready for drinking, pleasant and full of charm, round and well-balanced. The 1965 vintage was one of the best of all Bordeaux in that poor year. 1945 is the vintage of the century, perhaps the best of all the first growths. Like the 1961, harder than the 1955, it can be drunk now, and will last for another thirty years. The 1946 was so bad that it was not bottled under the château label, and the same thing happened in 1936, when the wine was sold to the shippers to be bottled merely as "Graves." 1970 is another great year, the wine being called less hard, or less full and rich, than 1961. It is less *nerveux*, which means strong and nervy, not nervous, but has great finesse, or delicacy. The soft yet big 1966 is a full wine, which will take long to develop, needing at least ten years, like most of the Haut-Brions. Because the 1959 and 1955 are so great, 1958 is classed as only a good year, for it lacks fat. The three decades are so outstanding in Bordeaux that you can afford to be persnickety, according to the people in the business.

Across the road from Château Haut-Brion is the excellent Château La Mission-Haut-Brion, no relation except in name, its wine being sometimes more like a Médoc than a Graves. All in all, there are some dozen vineyards in Bordeaux that have tacked Haut-Brion to their name. The name is legitimate for those vineyards around Château Haut-Brion, however, as they were all part of the same domain at one time.

La Mission-Haut-Brion claims that it is responsible for getting St. Vincent into trouble. It seems that St. Vincent, the patron saint of vintners, had not been in heaven very long before he was attacked by a terrific thirst and a yearning to taste again the great wines of France, the Burgundies, the wines from the Rhône Valley and the Loire, beady Champagne, and delightful Bordeaux. He applied to the powers that be for a leave of absence, presenting such a pathetic mien that his request was granted provided that he come back on time. There is little doubt that he intended to, but when time was up, St. Vincent was still down on earth, busily tasting wine. They found him in the cellars of La Mission-Haut-Brion, drinking lustily, not just drunk but hopelessly plastered and in no condition to make a journey anywhere, least of all where there might be danger of shocking cherubs and setting a bad example. St. Vincent was turned to stone on the spot, and you can see him there today, mitered cap awry, eyes bleary, and still clutching a rather dilapidated bunch of grapes.

The wine that caused all the trouble comes from a vineyard planted two thirds in Cabernet Franc and Sauvignon, one third in Merlot. No white wine is made. and the red vintages follow those of Château Haut-Brion which they sometimes surpass in quality.

Behind La Mission-Haut-Brion, and belonging to the same owner, is Château Laville Haut-Brion, a vineyard producing white wines exclusively. Across the railroad tracks, which parallel the road, is Château La Tour Haut-Brion, and next to it is Château Fanning-La-Fontaine, whose vineyards adjoin those of Château Haut-Brion in the direction away from Bordeaux. Below Château Haut-Brion is Château Pape-Clément, planted by the pope who moved the papacy to Avignon, near which the vineyards of Châteauneuf-du-Pape are located. These vineyards produce only red wines, similar to, but not so good as, the great Haut-Brion.

Some ten miles south is a cluster of vineyards around the little town of Léognan, the best of which is Château Haut-Bailly, classed as an exceptional growth, a red wine equal to that of Château La Mission-Haut-Brion. Almost on a par with it, and right down the road, is Château Carbonnieux, which produces both white and red wine. Carbonnieux was once owned by monks who, to evade the Mohammedan edict against wine, shipped the wine to Turkey as "mineral water" of Carbonnieux. It was particularly hit by the frosts in 1945, which destroyed much of the vineyard. For the whites, fifty thousand new plants, called "feet" by vintners, were set in 1949. Over 90 *tonneaux* of white wine, and half that amount of red, are made each year, although forty-five *tonneaux* of white were made in 1947. In 1956 the freeze again curtailed production.

Château Couhins, a producer of top white wines, is near Léognan.

To the west is the Domaine de Chevalier, which lost a third of its red-wine plantation—thirty-five thousand vines—in the 1945 freeze. Most of this has been replanted in Cabernet and Merlot. It produces nine *tonneaux* of white wine made from the customary Sémillon and Sauvignon grapes. This very good wine, greatly appreciated in England, is unfortunately not sufficiently well known in this country. Its white wines are considered second to Haut-Brion. To the north of

Léognan is Château Olivier, owned by the firm of Louis Eschenauer, also a producer of red and white. The wine, which is not bottled at the château but in Eschenauer's cellars in Bordeaux, is one of the better-known white Graves. Vintages of both vineyards follow the usual run. Farther south is the handsome moated Château de la Brède, the birthplace of Montesquieu, with a magnificent library, classed as a national monument, but the wines produced from its vineyards are small.

In the listings of the various Graves vineyards, some attempt at a descending order of quality has been made, although any slavish following of the list will get you arguments, for weather changes or bad judgment on the part of the cellar-masters can completely upset the order. Wines and vineyards are hopelessly overclassified, and some of those classed as principal growths will often surpass the two that are classified as exceptional. Few of them, however, are likely ever to come even close to red Château Haut-Brion, and the white is supreme as a dry white Graves in much the way that Château d'Yquem, the greatest of all sweet wines, is supreme in Sauternes.

The first important estate on the Graves-Sauternes road leading to Toulouse is Château Bouscaut. The house is a handsome mixture of medieval and modern, with its tapestries, swimming pool, and huge walled park. The *chais* divide in two for the making of red wines—which are fermented in huge oak vats—and white wines, which are crushed in electric presses, contained in a reservoir the first day but then tapped off directly into barrels in the *chai,* where they both ferment and age. Once in barrel, red and white wines age side by side.

Few large vineyards could start today the expensive process of having to wait over a number of years, without income, before selling bottle-aged wines; but behind the barrel-stores at Bouscaut are a dozen room-sized lockers containing thousands of bottles of wine. This is a usual sight at a shipper's cellar—rare at a château. In 1953, Château Bouscaut was classed among the five top Graves making white wine and the eleven top Graves vineyards making red wine. In October of 1968 a small group of American wine lovers acquired this vineyard, which badly needed new good management. Now it joins the proud ranks of Haut-Brion, Prieuré-Lichine, and Fourcas-Hostein as well-tended American properties.

SAUTERNES AND BARSAC

The place where the sweet wines come from is south of Bordeaux, twenty miles up the Garonne River, and, like Bordeaux itself, surrounded by Graves. The nearest sizable town is Langon, where you will find the good restaurant Oliver in a hotel on the shady side of the public square. A small river, the Ciron, divides the district, Barsac on the north and Sauternes on the south, together forming an area not much larger than half a dozen square miles.

The town of Sauternes is the capital of the district, a few plastered buildings with gray shutters and an ornamental palm tree here and there straggling along its single S-shaped street. Its wines are heavier, sweeter, and more luscious than those from Barsac. The town hall is at one end, the public washing-place at the other, and an odd-looking church is at the center bend. Tucked in a hollow and surrounded by vineyards, it claims a population of six hundred, and even when you tack on the populations of its two flanking villages, Bommes and Fargues, the total is less than two thousand.

Less than a mile north of town is Château d'Yquem, its vines producing the greatest sweet wine in the world. A dirt road passes between two blocks of outbuildings and up to the gates of the fortress-like château. Its crenelated walls have lookout towers at the corners, the great ports swinging wide to open on a graveled court-yard. From the walls, you can look east down the gentle vineyard slope to the river, and all around you, and less than a mile or two away, are most of the great first growths of Sauternes. On the north, Suduiraut; to the east, Rieussec; to the south, Guiraud and then Filhot, the first of the second growths. Sometimes next in quality comes La Tour-Blanche, the vineyard often classified right after Yquem, while also to the west are Clos Haut-Peyraguey, Lafaurie-Peyraguey, Rayne-Vigneau, and the two sections of Rabaud. Particularly in Sauternes is it obvious that the soil has a great deal to do with making a great wine.

The cellar-master at Yquem, who sports a large girth and a small beret, reminds you of a tourists' guide as he leads you from his office. Hung on the walls are various pipes, nozzles, and shiny glass tubes used in wine-making, brass and enamel now, though formerly silver-plated, for no metal except brass or silver must ever be allowed to come into contact with the wine. The shiny red wine-filtering machines, the bottling and corking machines trimmed in brass, the intricate bottle drier and washer, along with the racks of hoses, give the place the look of a spotless equipment room in a firehouse. Round, iron-rimmed tables painted gray are used for the labeling operation, which takes place in a whitewashed room between two *chais,* one for the latest vintage, the other for the older wines, which mature for three years in the wood. The *chais* are dug down into the ground, the vineyards starting at window level. It is a not unusual practice in Bordeaux to dig down into the ground two or three feet for the *chais* floor. This makes for a more even temperature.

The some 220 acres of Château d'Yquem produce an average of 90 *tonneaux* of wine a year. Until 1921 the very best of the wine used to be bottled as a *crème de tête,* a sort of super Yquem, but now the practice is simply to eliminate all the wines that are not exceptional and sell them for bottling as Sauternes. Because the wines are strong and full of unfermented sugar, Sauternes are usually fourteen per cent alcohol, and often more. They can live for decades.

Sauternes are what they are largely because of the way the grapes are picked. Harvest is not begun until the grapes have shriveled on the vine, the grape water dried out by the late autumn sun. At this stage the bacteria on the skin of the grape go to work, and the grapes rot. In Sauternes this is called *pourriture noble,* or noble rot, caused by the mold *Botrytis cinerea,* which gives the wine its sweetness and its high alcoholic content. A vineyard is not harvested all at once, and often the pickers go over the vines a dozen times to find the properly rotted grapes. They are not picked bunch by bunch, but grape by grape, and the harvest sometimes lasts a couple of months. One year at Château Filhot the harvest wasn't finished until Christmas.

At one time the second-best Sauternes came from Château La Tour-Blanche, over near the hamlet of Bommes. This château's rating and reputation are not valid today. A former owner gave the vineyards to the state, and now there is a state-operated school there for boys who want to be cellar-masters someday. The school has nothing to do with the vineyard, however, merely using some of the buildings as classrooms twice a week. The vineyard is rented from the state, the tenant paying an annual rent of five *tonneaux* out of an average yield of fifty. La Tour-Blanche has a tower all right, but it is brown, with a red tile roof, and has no present function, even as a symbol.

In spite of this, the sixty-odd acres of vineyards go on producing good wine; the average age of the vines is thirty-three years, about two acres being replanted each year. The barrels are kept in a long *chai* opposite the school buildings. They rest on beams set on the fine, carefully raked sand floor.

The school, which was started some years ago by the Abbé Dubaquié, is not concerned solely with the wine of Sauternes; it also deals with vineyards and wines generally. Today the professor is an engineer from the Agricultural Service of the Gironde, and one of his main concerns is sulphur.

Sulphur is the vintner's best friend, used for spraying the vines, and sulphur dioxide candles are burned in the barrels to kill unwanted bacteria. Its use was discovered long ago when vineyard proprietors took to spraying the vines along the roadsides with copper sulphate. A mild poison, the spray kept people from picking the grapes and eating them. One particularly bad year it was noticed that the spray also kept the bugs from spoiling them, and the vint-

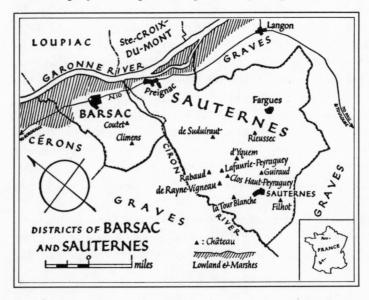

DISTRICTS OF BARSAC AND SAUTERNES

ners have been using it ever since. August 1 is by law the last day
the vines can be so sprayed. In the constant fight against harmful
bacteria, sulphur is used in only the smallest quantities when the
grapes are on the vine and in the barrels being prepared for the
wine.

Sulphur dioxide is also used in exceedingly small quantities as
an antiseptic in the wine, destroying harmful germs, acting as a
binding agent, and preventing wines from refermenting. French law,
however, is very severe on the excessive use of sulphur. The unpleasant odor sometimes given off by cheap Graves once the cork is pulled
indilates that the vintner resorted to sulphur dioxide. Today, improved wine-making methods have taught the vintner the proper
use of sulphur dioxide. As it is volatile, it can easily be evaporated
in the glass if it is perceptible.

Sulphur dioxide is particularly important in Sauternes, according to the professor, because it prevents the yeast in the wine from
growing and thus keeps the sugar in the wine from refermenting, a
special problem in sweet wines. He also has an idea that the sulphur
helps prevent that curse of white wines, maderization. This is caused
by oxidation in the wine, a sort of rusting, which turns the wine
brown. The resulting color is like that of the wine from the Portu-
guese island of Madeira; hence the name. It gives the wine a disa-
greeable, musty, flat taste. Small proprietors seem to have a tendency
to sulphur too heavily, and occasionally sulphur can be tasted in the
wine. This is a case in which shippers are useful, for by blending
different wines and by treating them properly they can make the
sulphur taste disappear from the regional Graves and Sauternes. This
vice of oversulphuring is particularly prevalent in Graves, says the
professor, as the vintners attempt to make the much drier wines taste
more like Sauternes by arresting the fermentation to allow some
unfermented or residual sugar to remain in the wine.

The standard planting in Sauternes is forty per cent Sauvignon,
fifty-five per cent Sémillon, and five per cent Muscadelle, these
grapes blending their properties to make a great wine. Sémillon does
not produce much juice, but its quality is excellent, though some
vintners have tried to stretch their harvest by planting seventy-five
per cent Sauvignon, according to the owner of Château Filhot, the
first of the second *crus*, whose wines are the driest of the great
Sauternes. They deserve to be a first *cru*. Its fine wines are underclassified, in much the way as are those of Mouton-Rothschild in the
Médoc.

In the commune of Barsac, honors go to Château Climens, rightly considered by many to be the greatest sweet white Bordeaux after Château d'Yquem. There are some eighty-five acres of vines, producing somewhat over fifty *tonneaux* in an average year. The vines are tied close to the ground and heavily pruned, which reduces the yield but heightens the quality. Here all of the vines are Sémillon. After the harvest the wine is allowed to ferment for a couple of months, or until it stops itself, although other vintners often stop the fermentation after three weeks.

Vintages at Château Climens are much the same as those in Sauternes. Some twelve hundred cases produced in 1961 may prove that to be the great year of the century. Rich, the epitome of finesse and lusciousness, it may turn out to be as great as in 1929 and 1949, when Climens surpassed Yquem, if not greater. Where the Yquem of 1959 is full and rich, Climens has lightness and finesse. Climens is truly one of the very great sweet white wines of the world.

Right down the road is Château Coutet, like Climens blessed with a rocky undersoil that drains excess water from the vineyards. Its planting is two thirds Sémillon, one third Sauvignon and Muscadelle, its wine somewhat lighter, drier, and more popular than Château Climens. Its wine is classed by many alongside that of Château Climens, but it is on the drier side.

When it comes to Sauternes, there is often an argument about the runners-up, which in some years may be even better than some of the first growths; but for well over a century Château d'Yquem has been consistently the greatest of all Sauternes, and no one will dispute its fame. Average and some poor years produce pleasant wines in Sauternes because they are not oversweet. But a dry Sauternes is a bad wine, since it is characteristically a sweet one. Sauternes is the world's greatest dessert wine. The Marquis de Lur Saluces, owner of Château d'Yquem, and formerly ambassador of the wines of France as president of France's Wine Propaganda Bureau, claimed that Sauternes is also excellent with fish. Many wine-lovers disagree with him.

BURGUNDY:
The Wine Democracy of France

The old domain of the hearty dukes of Burgundy begins near Sens, an old cathedral town past Fontainebleau, seventy miles south of Paris on the national highway running down to the Côte d'Azur. The highway skirts the ancient realm until it crosses a rolling range of hills called the Monts du Morvan, past a bulging promontory from which juts the moated Château de Rochepot, brandishing its turrets above the peaceful valley. It then swings through the town of Chagny, at the foot of the Côte d'Or, then on down through the lesser vineyards of Burgundy, Châlonnais, Mâconnais, and Beaujolais to Lyon. All in all, it is a distance of some 225 miles.

On the way you pass through Auxerre, a medieval town that looks like a movie set for Mark Twain's *Connecticut Yankee,* ancient buildings with modern store fronts with neon signs. Here are the mossy black slate roofs typical of Burgundy, and the jumble of a fourteenth-century cathedral. A net is cast across its central portal, either to protect you from falling bits of the crumbling statues or to keep the pigeons from nesting there. The road to Chablis starts at Auxerre, going across the river and up east into the hills.

Below Auxerre is Avallon, and farther down are Saulieu and the Hôtel de la Côte d'Or, where Alexandre Dumaine served some of the finest food in France and the new owner offers a wine list that is a model of good selections.

Burgundy is surrounded by great kitchens, and while the center of gastronomy has moved south to Lyon, the contribution of Burgundy chefs to great French cooking will never disappear. Although *bœuf bourguignon* may be the most famous dish, *potée bourguignonne* is probably the most traditional, a stew made of salt pork, pig's feet, and vegetables. *Meurette* is famous, a stew of eel made with either red wine or white. *Coq au vin* is a Burgundian dish, and one of its variations is *coq au Pommard,* and there is also *poulet au*

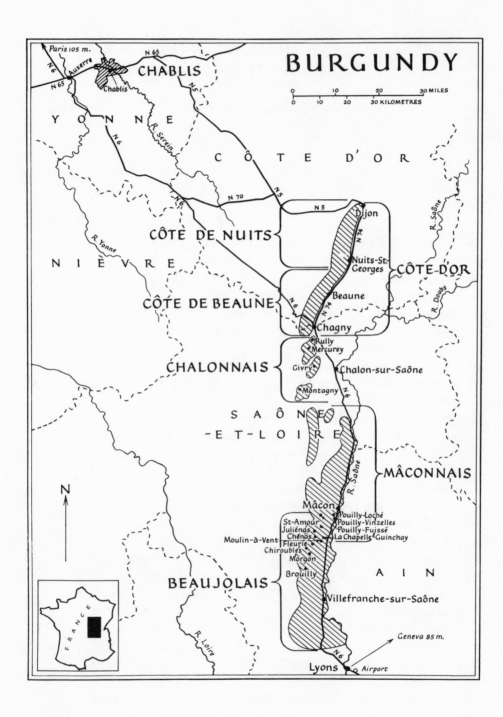

Chambertin. Pauchouse is a soup of eels, pike, trout, and any other
fresh fish available, a sort of Burgundian bouillabaisse made with
white wine. A like dish made with red wine is called *matelotte.* And
there is *quenelles de brochet,* ground poached pike served with a
cream sauce, one of the world's great delicacies when well made.
From the town of Cîteaux, out in the plains, comes a bland cheese
made by Trappist monks, the perfect accompaniment to the wines.
And the people of Burgundy spend their lives making great wines to
go with these great dishes.

Wine-making began in Burgundy some twenty-five hundred
years ago, though no one is quite sure how the vineyards got started
in ancient Gaul. Pliny says that Helvetius, the ancient Swiss, introduced the vine. Livy maintains that it was a Tuscan by the name of
Aaron, while Justin insists that some "Phocæans" landed in a gulf
at the mouth of the Rhône near Marseille and planted vines almost
the instant they waded ashore. At any rate, when the "Phocæans"
founded Marseille, about 600 B.C., a cup of wine was presented to
their chief.

No matter who introduced the vine, the Burgundians took to it
wholeheartedly, and by A.D. 600 the Roman conquest had so spurred
them on that vines were being planted everywhere. The Burgundians
were so successful at glorifying the grape that the last of the twelve
Cæsars, Domitian, in A.D. 89, furious at their supremacy in a delicate
art, ordered all the vines ripped up. They interfered with the growing of wheat, he said. The Burgundians rioted, and the edict was
never enforced, although it remained on the books until the Emperor
Probus re-established the liberty of planting vines in 281. But it took
hundreds of years to get the vineyards going full tilt again, and with
the break-up of the Roman Empire the Church began to take over.
This created a tremendous moral problem.

Wine was wealth, almost as precious as gold, perhaps inspiring
the concept of liquid assets so popular in modern economics. Along
with oil, spices, fabrics, and works of art, it made up the riches of the
ancient world. And when the Church began gathering wealth, wine
was one of the things it was on the lookout for. But being intoxicat-
ing, and exceedingly pleasant to drink, wine was in opposition to the
austerity and privation, the penance and poverty, the mortification
of the flesh, and the strict abstinence that marked the beliefs of many
of the religious orders. Wine's delights weighed heavily on the
consciences of medieval monks.

St. Bernard, the same who made life miserable for Abélard, and thus indirectly for Héloïse, believed in the wealth that wine could bring and in its restorative powers, but he did not believe wine should be drunk for pleasure. Cluny, in the heart of Burgundy, and for some centuries the greatest church in France, came in for some harsh criticism from St. Bernard, largely because the monks drank so much and obviously enjoyed it.

Life was so luxurious at Cluny, in fact, that many of the Benedictines moved out to set up sterner monasteries. One group picked the swampy area near Beaune, calling themselves Cistercians after the *cisteaux,* or bulrushes, all around them, and a group of St. Bernard's nuns also established themselves near by.

One of the ideals of the Cistercians, established in 1098 under the motto "Cross and Plow," was successful agriculture. The sparseness of the hills of the Slope of Gold was a challenge, and the monks soon discovered that the only thing they could raise successfully was vines. They planted the Clos de Vougeot, and the nuns planted Clos de Tart, following the lead of the peasants and of other orders in the vicinity.

The local peasants were descendants of the Burgundii, an invading Germanic tribe who in the fifth century had established a kingdom that extended from the Rhine to Lyon and included Geneva. In the fourteenth century the land was denominated a duchy, to be ruled by Philip the Bold. He married Marguerite of Flanders, thus extending his duchy to include all the land north of Paris, as well as Luxembourg and Flanders. The Burgundian dukes owned the major part of France, felt that they should be kings, and joined the English against the Crown during the Hundred Years' War. At the same time England held Bordeaux. The French King was forced to give up Paris, and it was Joan of Arc who turned the tide in the Battle of Orléans. Subsequently, shrewd and impious Louis XI broke the power of the Burgundian dukes, adding their lands to his realm. Local scholars today claim that Louis was successful because he was desperate at the loss of the two great wine countries, Burgundy and Bordeaux.

All the religious orders added to their holdings throughout the Middle Ages, the rulers of Burgundy giving the Church their most prized possessions, their vineyards, perhaps out of fear of seizure and to ensure a safe hereafter for themselves and their households. In 587 King Gontrand gave the Abbot of Bengine in Dijon all the vineyards surrounding the city. In 1162 Duke Eudes II renounced all rights to the Cistercian vineyards. And so it went. When the

Republic seized the vineyards after the Revolution, most of them either were in the possession of the Church or had been at one time.

The coming of the Cistercians and their schools of agriculture was as tremendous an encouragement to wine-making as the Roman conquest had been over a thousand years before—so much so, in fact, that regulation was needed. The first such rule came from Charlemagne, who owned the vineyards of Corton, and the big news of 809 was that workmen could no longer tread the grapes with their bare feet: it was unsanitary.

But the main trouble came from the Gamay grape, perhaps brought back by a crusader from the Near East. The Gamay grape yields a vast amount of juice, but its quality is low, in no way comparable with that variety known as Pinot, from which all the great wines of the Côte d'Or are made. Today the Gamay is planted all over the world—in Algeria, Chile, California, South Africa, and Australia—and since the Middle Ages it has also been planted in Burgundy. It has been frequently outlawed, one of the most vehement maledictions coming in 1395 from the last Duke of Burgundy, Philip the Bold. He ordered the destruction of all vineyards planted with Gamay, the "disloyal plant makes a wine in great abundance but horrible in harshness." Anyone who disobeyed was to be put in the pillory. At the same time Philip prohibited the storing of wines not grown in the district.

The two greatest evils in wine-making are illustrated by the ancient interdictions. The first is the substitution of an inferior vine for a noble plant. In Burgundy the Pinot Noir and Pinot Chardonnay are considered the noble plants, yields from which are small. Only supreme soils are planted in these aristocratic vines, all others being planted in the heavy-yielding Gamay. To increase the yield of great wines from the choice vineyards, they are often mixed with Gamay pressings, the result being called *passe-tous-grains*. These are often fobbed off as truly great wines.

The second great evil of wine-making is mixing great wines with lesser wines from another district. This blending, or *coupage,* is popularly referred to as the *grande cuisine* in Burgundy. Cheap, heavy Algerian, Midi, or Rhône wines are often mixed with the great wines to stretch them. This, too, is sometimes passed off as real Burgundy.

When a great Burgundy is blended, its greatness is destroyed, for the wine is the result of the soil from which it comes, and a reflection of it. Once the Prince de Condé decided that he would like to establish a vineyard on his lands north of Paris, near Chantilly. He bought vines from one of Burgundy's greatest vineyards. They were fabulously expensive, and when they failed to produce a good wine, he stormed down to Burgundy and complained to the man who had sold him the cuttings. The answer was: "But sir, first it was necessary for you to take the soil."

Not only princes have thought they could make Burgundy wherever they wished. There is more "Burgundy" produced outside of Burgundy than is produced within the province. Vintners in California, Australia, South Africa, Chile, and Spain all sell wines they call Burgundy. The soil is different, the climate is different, the grapes are often different, the way they are grown is different, and the vinification is different. But they still call it Burgundy, as if all wines from Burgundy tasted alike, looked alike, and smelled alike. They do not, for Burgundies do not constitute a type, and it is even hard to distinguish a characteristic family taste. They vary in every way in which wine can vary. In France, at least, Burgundy is merely the name applied to a large and varied region where grapes are grown. The region produces a wide variety of wines, red, white, and *rosé*. Some are magnificent and others are poor. The soil, the grape, the climate, and the men make them distinctive.

Destroying great wines by blending, or by planting poor plants in great soil so that a lesser wine is made, is inimical to the perfection for which vintners strive. The wines are reduced to the lowest common denominator. When such wines are fraudulently offered for sale as great wines at double or treble their worth, the buyer can notice nothing in them to get excited about and dismisses them as a howling pretension. Such wines are.

All this fraud got started in a big way shortly after the Revolution, in 1790, when the vineyards passed into the hands of individuals. Always handicapped by lack of an outlet to the sea, men began to make a business of the dangerous overland hauling. With more stable times, these wine-shippers began to make Burgundy known, and when Napoleon praised the wines, shippers could no longer meet the demand.

Burgundy has never been plentiful, the great wines coming from an area of scarcely twelve thousand acres, and the shippers felt the need of blending in order to make the greatness go further. This was profitable, for Burgundy had become a fabled name. It was so rare that few people had ever tasted the real thing, and frauds were accepted as genuine. To a dangerous degree the same condition persists today.

Fraud by shippers was helped by the confusion in wine names that exists in Burgundy, by the great demand for a small supply, by the complete lack of legal controls, and by ignorance. The practice of blending was even defended by some because by blending good years with bad, and great wines with mediocre ones, a certain year-to-year uniformity was achieved. It was not until 1936 that the first effective controlling laws were passed, known as *Appellations Contrôlées*.

Prior to that date the wines of Burgundy were almost entirely controlled by the shippers. A few growers tried to set up the system followed by Bordeaux vintners, whereby the man who owns the vineyard bottles his own wine, putting the name of the vineyard and his own name on the bottle as a guarantee of an honest wine. The vintners called the system *domaine-* or estate-bottling. It was encouraged by wine-buyers outside the district because it enabled them to get great wines without going to the shippers, and it proved profitable in good years. But in bad years the vintners had no buyers for their wines, and the shippers boycotted them.

The vintners were desperate by the time the depression of the early 1930's rolled around, and they were further crippled by over-production in the cheap wine districts of France and North Africa. To protect their wines and to fight fraud they organized committees to draw up laws that would govern the making and selling of wine.

The passing of these laws and similar ones for all the great wine districts of France has worked a revolution in wine. The laws are one of the great modern achievements in the realm of jurisprudence, forged not by legal experts, but largely by the growers themselves. Not only was science important in drafting the laws, but tradition was involved, for wine is a work of both art and nature, and it is not possible to measure all the characteristics of a great wine with precision.

One of the men largely responsible for setting up these laws in Burgundy, along with the Marquis d'Angerville, of Volnay, was Henri Gouges, a man who had spent most of his life fighting for the wines he loved. "The first thing we had to do was rate the vineyards," he said. "No owner wanted his vineyard classed below his neighbor's, so it was difficult. We examined over a million vineyard deeds in all of France, and allowed only 9,800 of them to be registered. In 1934, some 420,000,000 gallons of wine came from the vineyards being considered for classification, but in 1936, only some

150,000,000 gallons were produced from the vineyards finally approved for classification.''

In addition, the committee on which Gouges served also had to define wine districts, deciding which vineyards should be entitled to which famous names. The kind of vines used had to be agreed upon, as well as the maximum production, how the vines should be tied and pruned, when they could last be sprayed, and the time when the grapes could be harvested. If new vines were planted, it was decided that four years must pass before the wine yielded could be declared.

''The wine is checked periodically by our experts,'' Gouges explained. ''Each commune must produce a wine with a minimum alcoholic content, and the amount of acidity must be checked, for the wine will deteriorate if acidity is slight. Also, there is a legal minimum for tannin content, an element that permits a wine to age well. The production from each vineyard must be registered, but not just to see that the owner does not sell more wine than he makes, by buying cheap wines outside his vineyards. If a man produces more than the average for the permitted grape-variety during a particular vintage, he may have a few vines from lesser varieties, which he may be claiming as top wines. That is not allowed. Geographic boundaries were set up, as the most important factor is the soil. That was defined, and also the undersoil. If the soil did not meet the standard, the wine was given a lower rating. In Meursault, when the slope changes to flatland, the vineyard classification changes. The exposure to the sun also affects the ratings.''

In addition to this, it was necessary to define the bouquet of a wine, that medley of smells which comes from evaporation of elements in the wine. Under the law, bouquet is divided into two parts, the bouquet that the wine has when new and the bouquet wine gains with aging.

Original bouquet is characterized by the smell of the grape, which probably comes from its acids and oils, imparting to wine the fruity taste of fresh grapes. Muscat grapes make wine most outstanding in original bouquet, as do the Sauvignon of Sauternes and Sancerre, the Chenin of Anjou and Touraine, the Blanc Fumé of the upper Loire, and the Traminer of Alsace. When young, these wines are noted for floweriness.

Original bouquet is also believed to come from the action of the grape yeasts in the musts, an important thing to Champagne-makers. This bouquet comes out in the smell from the foam of Champagne when it is poured.

Acquired bouquet begins, and develops, with the aging of the wine, and nobody is yet sure just what reactions form it. It is a characteristic exclusive with wines of great origin, and here is where tasting is necessary. The men making the laws must be not only organizers, lawyers, and salesmen, with an advanced knowledge of soil and geography, but also wine-tasters, for wines with acquired bouquet can never be drunk young. Some of the great Médoc growths do not have a great perfume when young; as one writer puts it, they reserve "the splendid impressions for tasters who know how to wait." When acquired bouquet, which develops after bottling, is sufficiently pronounced to be noticed by the nose, a taster can tell what is going to happen to a wine.

Acquired bouquet is the product of reactions that often lead to maderization of a white wine. It is the taste called *rancio,* which adds to the greatness of Madeiras, Marsalas, and the French Château Chalon, in the Jura district, but spoils other white wines. It is a flaw in dry white wines with insufficient fixed acidity, which then have a tendency to maderize. It is particularly unpleasant in the Montrachets and Meursaults of the Côte de Beaune. Maderization is more unpleasant in Graves than in Sauternes, for instance, because sweetness hides the unpleasant, flat, musty, brownish taste of maderization. Acidity, which imparts freshness and character to a wine, prevents maderization, and the drier the wine, the more unpleasant is the brownish taste.

The two kinds of bouquets combine to produce a distinctive quality, quite noticeable in Sauternes, for instance. Wines possessing them show great nobility, having a combination of fruitiness and bouquet that comes out only with age.

All this has a great deal to do with classifying vineyards and establishing the limits of a wine region. Still another consideration must be taken into account in parts of Burgundy where it is sometimes felt necessary to add sugar to the fermenting must in order to build up the resulting alcoholic content. This process is called *chaptalization,* after Comte de Chaptal, a chemist and a minister of Napoleon, who carried out experiments in it, and it is often referred to as the *Soleil en sacs,* or the "Sun in sacs." Thus, inspectors must taste the fermenting wine and know how much sugar to allow the vintner to add.

All these distinctions are reflected in the classifications of the wines from any particular region. The local committees set the standards for the various wines produced, first defining the area of the region and then the minimum requirements for the vineyards and the wines; and the national legislature formulates the decision into the laws called *Appellation d'Origine* and *Appellation Contrôlée.*

The annual declarations of amount of production filed by each vintner are checked by the local tax authorities, and periodic checks are made to see that a vintner does not sell more wines than he produces. The local governing board watches for fraud. All such boards work under the control of a national board, the Institut National des Appellations d'Origine, or I.N.A.O., and the wines produced under its control bear on the label the phrase: *"Appellation Contrôlée."*

Wines from a region come under regulations whose stringency depends on the *"Appellation Contrôlée"* claimed by them. In this way a set of rules defines regional wines. There is an *Appellation Contrôlée* of "Burgundy." Stricter rules define district wines. There is an *Appellation Contrôlée* of "Côte de Nuits." Still more precise are rules for commune wines. There is an *Appellation Contrôlée* of "Gevrey-Chambertin." Still more exacting regulations define specific vineyards, such as the *Appellation Contrôlée* of "Chambertin." The many varied wines from each of France's great wine regions are thus carefully defined by law. As a result, a Chambertin is one wine, a Gevrey-Chambertin another. The wines are similar; their qualities are not.

Vineyard names are particularly important, although the vineyard itself is not often an *Appellation Contrôlée.* As an example, the wines entitled to the *Appellation Contrôlée* of "Pommard" must contain at least 178 grams of natural sugar per liter, a minimum alcoholic content after fermentation of 10.5 per cent. Pommard wines that include the name of the vineyard on the label, however, such as "Rugiens" or "Epenots," must contain 198 grams of natural sugar per liter, and a resulting minimum alcoholic content of 11 per cent. When the vineyard name is added to the label, it indicates a superior wine.

The laws are detailed and complex, but they make it a simple matter for the buyer to select genuine bottles, for the primary indication of all this attention is summed up in a single phrase on a label: *"Appellation Contrôlée."* By controlling the use of place-names, and by setting up a series of minimum standards instead of merely one, French experts have preserved the distinction of their greatest wines.

A still further guarantee of excellence in Burgundy is the system of estate-bottling, by which the wine is produced by the grower, the bottle bearing his name and that of the vineyard in addition to the township. Because estate-bottled wines are produced in small quantities, by growers whose holdings are usually small, frauds may be checked easily. Where a large shipper may be able to afford fines, a small grower cannot. What is more, the grower feels that his signature is that of an artist. Proud of his name and proud of his wines, he has little desire or incentive to risk discrediting either one.

The Bordeaux label is relatively simple, for a château-bottled wine invariably carries the words *"Mis en bouteilles au Château."* The Burgundy equivalents, however, rarely carry the wording: *"Mis en bouteilles par le propriétaire,"* or *"Mis au Domaine,"* or *"Mise du Domaine,"* or something similar.

French law specifies that an estate-bottled wine, or *"Vin de la Propriété,"* is one of which the bottler is the proprietor of the vineyard. He holds a license to bottle only his own wines and no others.

A *"négociant,"* or shipper, may buy many wines, bring them to his cellars, blend them as he wishes, and bottle them under his label. There are many good and honest shippers, and the quality of the wine will depend entirely on their integrity. A *négociant* must give his status on the label. Many are the shippers who own a vineyard or even several vineyards. Recent French law insists that a shipper may claim being a proprietor or *"propriétaire,"* in addition to being a *"négociant,"* only if the wine shipped is from the township where he owns a vineyard. The label may then state *"Propriétaire"* or *"Négociant et Propriétaire."* But if the wine shipped is from Pommard and the shipper's vineyards are in another commune or another district, he must then label the wines shipped from Pommard as Pommard, and his name can be followed only by the word *"Négociant"* preceding the address of his place of business. If a shipper owns a pocket-handkerchief-size vineyard in Nuits-Saint-Georges, he may buy wines, good or bad, from any part of this township and still state *"Propriétaire et Négociant à Nuits-Saint-Georges"* on the labels of these wines.

The *Appellation d'Origine* laws by no means eliminate frauds, but they do help to reduce them. Many small wines go to market with meaningless phrases that closely approximate the significant ones. A list of phrases appearing on labels, both accurate and fake, appears below. The wise wine-buyer knows that the wording of a wine label is not a pretension, but simple common sense, often making the difference between enjoyment and disappointment.

BURGUNDY LABELS

GOOD HONEST LABELS OF ESTATE-BOTTLING

Mis en bouteilles par le propriétaire—Bottled by the owner or grower

Mise de la propriété—Bottled at the estate or vineyard—same as above

Mise à la propriété—Bottled at the estate

Mis au Domaine—Bottled at the *domaine* or estate

Mise du Domaine—Not necessarily actually bottled on the estate, even though part of the vineyard's production

Mis en bouteilles au Domaine—The same as above

Name (XYZ) followed by the word *Propriétaire*—Owner or grower

Name (XYZ) followed by the word *Propriétaire-Récoltant*—Owner or grower

Name (XYZ) followed by the word *Viticulteur*—Wine-maker or vintner

Name (XYZ) followed by the word *Vigneron*—Vintner

The last word applies often where an absentee owner has a crop-sharing agreement with a wine-maker, the latter getting one half or one third of the production in payment for his work in tending the vines and making the wines. French law provides that the wines sold by the *vigneron* under his name are just as much "estate-bottled" as those sold under the name of the vineyard-owner. Sometimes the same wine may thus be sold legally under two different names.

MISLEADING STATEMENTS

Mis or *Mise en bouteilles dans mes caves* (bottled in my cellars)—If the bottler is not the owner of the vineyard, this statement is meaningless, as all wines are bottled in cellars, and if the bottler is not the vineyard-owner, chances are that by making such a statement he is trying to parade as such.

Mis en bouteilles au Château XYZ—This, again, is meaningless in Burgundy if the so-called château bears no proprietary relationship to the vineyard producing the wine. This is sometimes done by shippers who maintain offices in some château and bottle in its cellars wine purchased on the outside. The wine may be good, but this statement carries no guarantee of authenticity except that of the shipper's reputation.

Although the whole of France follows the same general pattern when it comes to vintages, each district has its own deviations and characteristics. Because grapes are a harvested crop, local weather conditions affect them and the resulting wine. When a great vintage comes along, the wines are quickly bought up when too young for drinking. Some great wines may not be fit for drinking for five or ten years, or longer. Each vintage must be considered in relation to specific wines, those which are good in some vineyards being poor vintages in others.

Such considerations are concerns of those who buy the wines from the vintner. In Bordeaux, when you buy a château-bottled wine, you can be sure you are getting the vintage marked on the bottle. In Burgundy, wines may bear false labels of old vintages. It is best to buy estate-bottlings of a reputable grower or wines of a reliable shipper. Good wines are never cheap. Good old wines cannot be.

When buying wines, it is necessary to decide whether you are going to lay away the wine or drink it up. A great '69 from the Côte de Nuits may not be fit for drinking until 1975, whereas a Beaujolais is at its peak one year after the vintage. To taste the greatness of an old wine, it is wise to buy an old Corton, or an old Côte de Nuits, rather than spend money for an old Beaujolais, which is probably past its prime. A great wine is glorious when old. A good wine can be a disappointment. Equally, it is more of a pleasure to drink young, honest wines than old, fraudulent ones.

RED BURGUNDIES

1949   *The wines have lasted well. Many consider the red '49's the best year of the generation.*

1950   *An enormous quantity of fast-maturing light wine was made among the reds. Now faded.*

1951   *Poor wines.*

1952   *Very great wines were made in both red and white. In some instances '52's were hard, hence had the attributes of longevity.*

1953   *Not as good as the '52's. These wines are not holding. They had the earmark of greatness when young.*

1954   *Despite terrible weather, a few good wines could be found in the Côte de Nuits. Not many red '54's were shipped to the United States.*

1955   *This is another very great vintage similar to 1952 in quality. However, hailstorms partly destroyed many of the top Beaujolais vineyards. In the Côte d'Or over fifty per cent of Beaune and Pommard were destroyed by hail.*

1956   *Very poor wines, including Beaujolais.*

1957   *Very great in Beaujolais, where only a third of normal was harvested. They are far beyond their prime. A normal quantity was produced in the Côte d'Or. The wines were big, strong, and hardy. The prices for authentic estate-bottlings were very high, owing to a general shortage of great wines throughout France in this particular year.*

1958   *As a whole, the red wines of the Côte d'Or were very disappointing, lacking in taste and character.*

1959   *Very abundant. Quantities were so large that the maximum production permitted by law was increased by more than twenty-five per cent. The red wines had depth and enough sustaining backbone to make them into* vins de garde, *wines that recompense patience by the glorious maturity they achieve. Yet the natural glycerine, suppleness, and elegance gave them the roundness that has made Burgundy renowned. And this without the abusive addition of sugar during fermentation. This was undoubtedly the best year since 1949. In Burgundy, as in other districts, faulty fermentation and poor production methods will warrant selectivity.*

1960   *Poor—light and lacking in character.*

1961   *This vintage produced the smallest yield since the war. The red wines were big and supple, and matured relatively early, holding their peak of excellence for many years. In over-all quality, many are comparable to the '59's, although greater selectivity was required in buying.*

1962   *Very fine, light, and well-balanced red Burgundies with a
tendency toward early maturity. Matured before the 1961's.
A good year for red Beaujolais until 1965.*

1963   *Disastrous.*

1964   *In some instances the red Burgundies were better than the red
Bordeaux. These well-rounded wines could be drunk fairly
early, as was the case with the 1962's. They have
plenty of bouquet. Was a very great year for Beaujolais,
now faded.*

1965   *The floods that spoiled many vineyards and the lack of
maturity together made the red wines a disaster.*

1966   *The red Beaujolais resembled the 1962's. The wines from
the village of Brouilly were exceptional. The Burgundies
from the Côte d'Or had many of the 1964 characteristics,
being full, round, and fast maturing.*

1967   *The Côte de Beaune, the southern part of Burgundy proper,
produced wines that lack color. Hail and spring frost
decreased the total quantity all over Burgundy. Hence,
the wines are light with a slight acidity. The reds of the Côte
de Nuits were definitely better than those from the Côte de
Beaune. Beaujolais as a whole produced good, pleasant, and
drinkable wines.*

1968   *Disastrous, excepting some rather pleasant Beaujolais.*

1969   *Great vintage in the Côte d'Or, with a deep color, round,
full, and with a lasting character. The quantity, due to
poor flowering in June, was one third less than normal.
The red Beaujolais are not in the same league, lacking in
color—although fruity and pleasant, they are short on
taste.*

1970   *The red wines of Côte d'Or were fair to good but not exceptional
due to the excessively large quantity produced. Should be
consumed rapidly. Although the '69 Burgundies were far
superior to Bordeaux, the contrary was true in 1970, when
Bordeaux produced a great vintage. Beaujolais produced wines
which were naturally pleasant when young.*

1971   *The average quality was good both in character and in lasting
ability. Part of the vintage was spoiled due to hail, which
caused many wines from leading vineyards to have a slight
taste of rot. These wines lack color.*

1972   *As in all other regions of France, this vintage was lacking
in sun and warmth. Many of the grapes picked were insufficiently
ripe, yet the prices continue to increase to unreasonable levels.
During the course of 1973, it is expected that the wines
will improve, losing some of their greenness and their excessive
acidity, and will round out to a good vintage.*

WHITE BURGUNDIES

1950   *The white wines were better than the reds. The yield was far above average in quantity. Too old.*

1951   *Small yield; fair in quality; much acidity; not worth retaining. The frosts of April 29, 1951, destroyed eighty-five per cent of the vines in Chablis and well over one third of the vines in the section producing white wines in the Côte de Beaune.*

1952   *Excellent wines, beautifully balanced. A very great year.*

1953   *If anything, the great white '53's were better than their red counterparts. Undoubtedly a great vintage. Spring frosts again destroyed approximately eighty-five per cent of all the Chablis. The little that was made was very good but none of it came from the top of the slopes. Too old.*

1954   *Less than average in the great wines; a few fair wines were produced. The Chablis were very good.*

1955   *This vintage was great. Again a spring freeze destroyed a part of the fine Chablis vineyards.*

1956   *Unlike the red wines, the white wines were good in many of the fine white Burgundy districts. The wines had fruitiness and good balance. In Chablis, some '56's were superior to the excellent '55's. Here generalization is impossible, for 1956 was the year for many white Burgundies.*

1957   *Burgundy whites were good. Quantity was half of normal. In Chablis, a frost in May destroyed ninety per cent of the potential harvest; the remaining ten per cent proved to be undrinkable, hard and high in acid.*

1958   *The white wines of both the Côte d'Or and southern Burgundy—namely, those of Beaujolais Blanc, Mâcon, and Pouilly-Fuissé—were very good, or, oftentimes, excellent.*

1959   *In the white wines, the high peaks of perfection were as great as in the reds, but, as usual, the great vineyards proved the supremacy of their soil. The fact that 1959 was a great vintage will not in itself be a guarantee of quality covering all bottles bearing this famous date. Vineyards and growers must be properly selected, and such selections should eliminate the mistakes of fallible man. The white wines matured quickly and did not last much over six years.*

1960   *The white wines were much better than average, many excellent. Too old.*

1961   *Better than the '59's, in that they are better balanced, without excessive alcohol, and have been longer-lived. A high degree of alcohol counterbalanced by acidity gave white*

> *Burgundies an excellent, well-deserved reputation. Now
> too old.*

1962 *The white Burgundies were excellent, lighter in alcoholic
content than the '61's. This factor made the '62's well-balanced,
and when not older than six years, '62 was one of the best
vintages for white Burgundy since World War II.*

1963 *A few drinkable wines were made at best, but no more.*

1964 *Good. Some white Burgundies have a tendency to lack
acidity. They have matured quickly and will not last
beyond 1970. 1964 was a very good year for Pouilly-
Fuissé. Too old.*

1965 *The floods which spoiled many vineyards and the lack of
maturity together made this into a disastrous vintage.
Some light wines were produced which were pleasant
drinking in France.*

1966 *Exceptional, with much of that perfect balance that was
found in the 1962's.*

1967 *Small production, thirty per cent under normal in Burgundy.
Due to hail and a spring freeze there are highs and lows in
the great vineyards where selectivity is essential. The quality
of the Mâcon wines and those of Pouilly-Fuissé was
good. Unfortunately only fifty per cent of a normal crop
was harvested.*

1968 *Light acid wines. Poor vintage.*

1969 *Very good, well-balanced wines with a fruity, heavy, and
vigorous character.*

1970 *Good, better than the reds, without reaching exceptional highs.
Not as full as the '69's. This is a good vintage despite the
large quantity produced.*

1971 *Wines of very good character and with great elegance. Despite
the high prices, the wines are a good value.*

1972 *A good vintage with remarkable lasting abilities for white
wines. The high degree of acidity ensures longevity, although
the wines are marked by a certain amount of hardness.*

White Burgundies should be consumed young. If a generality
must be drawn, one could state that these wines will be pleasantly
fresh after a year and a half or two years, and should be fully
matured within five years. After this time some white Burgundies
may still prove to be great, but there is always the risk of oxidation
diminishing their value. To be on the safe side, shun white Burgundies older than six years with the exception of a few Montrachets
and Corton Charlemagne which may be one of the longest-lived of all
white Burgundies. Lesser wines should be drunk when two years old.

CHABLIS:
Oysters and Vintners

Chablis squats in a valley ten miles up in the hills behind Auxerre. A two-lane country road winds east past barren slopes topped with clumps of young birch and pine. The oiled macadam is a sandy pink because of the red-brown, foot-thick skin of topsoil and the whitish dust from the porous yellow undersoil. On flat stretches the roadside is planted with cropped sycamores, and the dirt roads leading off to farms and settlements are marked with double rows of slim, tall poplars, with dark-green balls of the killing mistletoe in their higher branches. Damp and cold in winter, bursting with color in summer, it is like any back country in Westchester, or Wisconsin, or Washington, until you round the flank of the last hill and drive across the slanting valley floor to a huddle of stone houses where sixteen hundred people live for the wine of Chablis.

A thin slate steeple rises above the sandy walls of split limestone and the black, mossy roofs. It faces east to the curving slope, shaped like an oyster shell, and here are the seven outstanding vineyards of Chablis: Bougros, Les Preuses, Vaudésir, Grenouille, Valmur, Les Clos, and Blanchots.

The vineyards classed "outstanding" occupy 90 acres. The next most important "first growths"—Vaillon, Les Forêts, Montmain, Mont de Milieu, Montée de Tonnerre, Fourchaume, and Séchet—comprise fewer than 520 acres. Today only one third of this land is being worked, while the remaining two thirds are resting. And an outstanding Chablis vineyard must rest for twenty years.

The road from Auxerre leads straight into the square in the center of town and continues on out to the foot of the slope. It crosses over a shallow stream, never more than ten yards across, overhung with willows. Reeds line its banks, and ducks dip in the pools or skim through the shadows cast by the old stone walls. The stream is called Le Serein, meaning either "serene" or "evening dew"—no one in Chablis is quite sure which. But Le Serein, which north of Auxerre empties into the Yonne, which then empties into the Seine, gives the name to serene Chablis, a happy, quiet country town.

The town square in Chablis was much more spacious than it is now. One night in June 1940, when the vineyards were in bloom, a fleet of Italian bombers blasted the place. Chablis vintners are still trying to figure out the reason for the raid, for the town is so far off the beaten track that it had no strategic importance. They will tell you about the centuries-old houses that were knocked down, adding happily that no bombs fell on the vineyards of either the great or the first growths. The square is now rebuilt, cluttered up with big houses and narrow streets.

On the left side of the square is the Hôtel de l'Étoile, completely repaired now. The owner, M. Bergerand, a towel tied bandana-fashion around his neck, tall chef's cap atilt on his big head, big white apron clinched around his bulk, urges you to try the specialties of the house: a terrine of rabbit to be eaten with a glass of Chablis, *écrevisses*, which are crayfish swimming in Chablis, Burgundy ham in a reddish sauce laced with Chablis, slices of veal cooked in Chablis, chicken poached in Chablis, or a soufflé served in scooped-out oranges, to be followed by a coarse, leathery marc made from distilled Chablis. He'll be only too glad to tell you that oysters and fish aren't the only things that are good with Chablis, and to give you his recipes, printed on little slips of paper, to prove it.

One of the best of the sixty-seven growers in Chablis is Dauvissat, a short, birdlike little man who thinks his wine the best in the world, and takes you down into his cellars to prove it to you.

If you don't have a *tastevin,* the shallow, dimpled silver saucer about the size of a small ashtray that is used by the wine-taster when he tests the wine, the grower will take out some clear glass goblets. On the way to the caves he will ask you which vintages and growths you want to taste, taking out of his pocket a *tastevin* wrapped in a handkerchief and polishing it.

Most tasters use the *tastevin* in Burgundy, although some prefer glasses, either because they believe they can see the color better or perhaps from habit. The *tastevin* is silver, so no foreign taste will be imparted to the wine; it is dimpled along the sides so that you can better see the color of the wine at different depths. Some *tastevins* have ridges along one side to reflect the shimmer of light through the wine. In the center is a knob almost as high as the lips of the "taste," and in the old days you could stick a candle on it. This must have

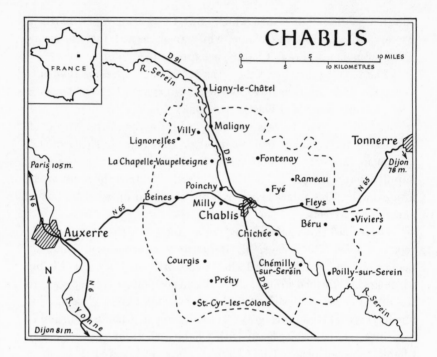

made the utensil hard to drink out of, and wine-tasters of other times could probably be identified by singed forelocks and smoke smudges on their foreheads. The grooves of the "taste" darken quickly because of the wine. The handle is a silver ring, often with a thumb-rest on its top edge, shaped like the rest for a cigarette on the side of an ashtray. Others are in the form of a snake, with a middle loop by which you can hold the "taste."

After unlocking the door to the cave, the grower picks up a sort of crowbar from the top of a barrel and takes the pipette down from a hook near the light-switch. Curiously called "thief" in English, a Burgundy pipette is about a foot long and an inch thick, a glass tube tapered at one end and having a metal ring at each side of the other end so that it can be held by the fingers. On top of the barrel is the bung, a wooden stopper around which a disk of burlap has been pressed. Working it out with a few bangs of the crowbar, the grower gently lowers the pipette into the barrel, tapping on the rounded hole with his thumb. If the pipette does not fill fast enough, the grower sucks the air out of the pipette through the thumb-hole, then covers it with his thumb and pours some of the wine into your "taste."

Dauvissat will wave at some barrels in the corner with his free hand. "That's La Forêt over there, and this is Les Clos." Like any grower, he is happiest when talking about his wines. "In Chablis we often store the wine above ground, but in the rest of Burgundy it's always kept in the *caves,* the cellars. After pressing, the wine is drawn off into the barrels, where it remains until it's ready for bottling, which will be in eighteen months or two years for Chablis. Then it's bottled, and ages for another six months to one year, depending."

Wine has two ages: the life in the cask, and the life in the bottle —childhood and adolescence. Here they usually use a special size of barrel, smaller than in other places. The big ones used in Burgundy, which contain the equivalent of 288 bottles, are called *pièces.* These Chablis half-size barrels are called *feuillettes.* On the average, all the wine from the *Grand Crus* and the *Premiers Crus* amounts to an equivalent of 62,000 cases. In addition, the lesser wines labeled Chablis and Petit-Chablis produce the equivalent of 120,000 and 150,000 cases respectively. Part of these 270,000 cases is sold in barrel for French consumption.

Dauvissat will look around the *cave,* which contains perhaps thirty barrels against the walls, with another double row of twenty down the center. "I would say that less than a quarter of all the Chablis drunk every year is genuine. Maybe less than ten per cent."

When tasting, you hold the "taste" in front of you, about waist-high, so that you can see the wine's color under the bare light-bulb. The silver sparkles under the wine, and a good wine picks up and adds to the sparkle. These Chablis in the casks are young, green wines, but they should be clear, free of floating particles, and not cloudy. The color should be a pale yellow with a faint green tinge. The smell of the wine should be clean and fresh, with no unpleasant odor of wood or sulphur, nor any musty or vinegary smell. These green wines taste sharp and often acid, but you can recognize the traditional taste behind the roughness and the bitiness: a flinty, clean taste that is supposed to come from the Kimeridgian chalk in the vineyards. This particular chalk also comes to the surface in Champagne. Wines change in the cask, one tasting fine one week and bad the next, while another barrel will be the reverse. Because young wine works in the barrel, these differences are easy to distinguish, and vary noticeably from barrel to barrel, vineyard to vineyard, and vintage to vintage.

After looking at the wine, and smelling it, you take a small sip and, holding it in your mouth, purse your lips as if to whistle, sucking in air and making a gurgling sound that tumbles the wine about on the tip of your tongue. Then you spit it out on the earthen floor. Both gurgling and spitting are somewhat scandalizing to a novice, but after a couple of *caves,* the rankest of amateurs is spitting like a master, with a certain nefarious delight. Some of the growers swallow the wine, because it is precious even when green and undrinkable, but a taster cannot, because the green wine in his stomach deadens his taste. Not only that, but green wine acts as a purgative, and a wine-taster samples as many as fifty barrels in a day, which would be disastrous if he swallowed the wine, to say nothing of the fact that he would be roaring drunk every night and would ruin his kidneys in a week.

Another typical grower, not only of Chablis, but of all Burgundy, is Marcel Servin, who grows and bottles his own wine and owns parcels totaling seven acres in Les Preuses, Blanchots, Bougros, and Vaillon. Because he, like Dauvissat, handles the wine himself from vine to bottle, he is called an estate bottler. His name as proprietor and the name of his vineyard where the wine comes from are on the label of the bottle. He is a winegrowing peasant of Burgundy, and he is proud of it. His wine is his life.

Servin's place is down from the town square in Chablis, just beyond the spot where the road crosses the river. Standing at his front gate, which is of sheet iron painted a gray in which there is a little blue—a color typical of Burgundy and on most of the metal and wooden shutters and gates—you can look square at the vineyards of the *Grands Crus.* The slope is a little less than a quarter of a mile away and faces somewhat west of south. Servin, his wife, and his son work in the vineyards or for the vineyards all year round, getting up at dawn and going to bed at dusk.

The gates of Servin's place open on a court about the size of a tennis court. The house is on the right, two stories high, the *chais* and storerooms along the back and on the left, their black roof slates uneven and mottled with thick green moss. The door of the house opens into a low, flagged room with a sink in one corner, a wood stove beside it, and a table in the rear, backed by a sideboard. The indoors activity during the daytime takes place in this combination kitchen, dining room, sitting room, and office. It is typical of the Burgundian peasant, and although other houses will be a little bigger or a little smaller, only the details vary.

Servin is a stocky, mustached man in his sixties, who wears felt slippers in the house and wooden sabots when he goes out of doors, dressed in corduroys the color of ripe olives when new and the color of dried ripe olives when old. Although many vineyard workers now wear rubber boots, Servin clings to the heavy wooden clogs that used to typify the peasant. His son is a polite, cheerful man in his thirties. His wife is a pretty, gray-haired woman. With them lived his father, who at ninety-three, had a hearty wheeze, was bent double from working among the vines all his life, and, with nine decades of knowing it behind him, strained the hard, white wine of Chablis through his yellow mustache. Up to his death, on good days he still did some puttering about the vineyard.

With the coming of winter, the vineyards are plowed and fertilized with manure and phosphates. Servin and his son guide the tractor between the narrow rows, and by January usually have them ready for the pruning. Both roots and the vine tendrils must be pruned so that none of the energy of the soil or vine will be wasted on parts that will not produce good grapes. Pruning begins on January 22, the day of St. Vincent, the winegrower's patron saint. Any sick or dead plants are ripped up and new ones planted. The vine used is the real Pinot, called Pinot Chardonnay in Burgundy, Beaunois in Chablis; it is grafted to American roots, the only roots strong enough to resist the dreaded phylloxera. According to the tradition of Burgundy, all the planting must be done by late April.

Servin is likely to reach behind him at this point in the story of his life and begin setting out glasses. His son, as if on signal, will come in carrying a dirty bottle. Servin will carefully break the wax seal on the bottle, carefully insert the tip of the corkscrew into the center of the cork, and begin to twist its handle, which is made of a shiny grapevine root.

"The best moon for planting is a red moon, or that's what they say," he tells you with a smile. "If the vines are planted too soon, the grapes will fall. It is very important, the planting. A good vine should live between forty and forty-five years, but things happen. And after every storm we must go out with baskets, for the earth washes down the slope to the bottom of the vineyard, and it must all be carried back. After every storm. It is heavy, carrying the mud."

On one occasion Servin held the bottle pressed between his knees, and the cork came out with a pop. Everyone was suddenly quiet, watching as he poured a few drops into the glass before him. It was clear and whitish yellow, faintly green. He began to fill the glasses on the table. "Nowadays everybody wants clear Chablis, with all the sediment strained out—the particles of grape, the lees as a result of fermentation, everything—but when you do that, it takes some of the good out of the wine. But the color is what counts. They used to put white of eggs in red wines, and isinglass in white wines, and even blood, or milk, or gelatin. Now we use pills.''

He tasted the wine, sucking in air, and then nodded his head and grinned. ''After Easter, all through April and until the 20th of May, we have vacation. Nothing much to do, no plowing.''

His wife laughed and, reaching behind her, picked up a willow stick about a foot long and a quarter-inch through. ''I'll show you what we do on vacation.'' She put the end of the willow stick between her teeth, biting it, then tore a strand loose and following it with her finger, stripped it off; then she wrapped the sliver around the stem of the glass, twisting it, turning it back on itself to make it stay. ''This is the way we tie the vines to the wires. We sit up all night making the strands, and spend all day tying.''

Servin nodded at his wife. ''In the fall we pull up the rotted stakes, replace them with new ones, string wires across their tops about three feet from the ground, and tie the vines to them. Then in June the vine flowers into tiny whitish blossoms along the slope, and after that it must be warm. However, with lots of sun the blossoming may be over in ten days' time and then we will have an abundant harvest; if it is cold or rainy the blossoming may take up to a month, and this is when we lose quantity. The pollen should inseminate the other blossoms, being carried by wind or insects. Before and after the flowering we spray every other week with copper sulphate until Bastille Day, July 14, but after that we spray only after it rains. In June we begin the tilling, then in August we plow again. And once in June, once in July, and again in August we trim the vines. With this.''

Out of his belt Servin pulled a short, hooked blade, perhaps four inches long, with a smooth wooden handle. His son reached into his belt and pulled out an identical knife. Mme Servin waved her hand at the knives. ''Everybody in Burgundy carries the *serpette* in his belt. It's like the carpenter's hammer or the mason's trowel. But it's the women who do most of the trimming. You must be deft and fast. It's a woman's work.''

Servin nodded at his wife. ''Then in September, vacation again, hunting and fishing. Perhaps a trip to Paris to sell some wine to old friends. And in September we put the wines in bottle if we haven't done it during the spring vacation, and we cooper the barrels, and clean them, and let sulphur candles burn in them to kill the molds. And then there's the wheat-planting. We have wheat for bread and feed. In October comes the harvest, and we must keep the cellar warm for three weeks while the wine ferments, and then in November we make new stays and clean the vineyards. There are no Sundays in Burgundy. Every day is work.''

This is the life of the men who make the wines of Burgundy, gamblers all, working for a good year. Proud of their great wines, the growers resent the fact that so many poor wines are sent to world markets as great Chablis.

In the town is the shipping firm of J. Moreau et Fils, unique because it specializes solely in the wines of Chablis. The firm is now run by two brothers, the younger of whom was in charge of wines at the French Pavilion of the New York World's Fair of 1939. The firm owns two acres of Valmur, two acres of Les Clos in the *Grands Crus,* and twelve acres of Vaillon in the *Premiers Crus.*

As for vintages, great ones occurred in 1966 and 1967, wines difficult to find anywhere today; many of them are now too old. Because of the extreme heat in the summer of 1947, the wine was one of the greatest vintages Chablis has ever had. The wines were extraordinarily high in alcohol, many of them containing more than 14 per cent. A criticism has been that the full richness of these wines is not characteristic of the dry steeliness usually associated with Chablis. The same was true of certain '69's. But, like true Burgundians, the vintners of Chablis are uncomfortable when you mention a bad year like 1945 or 1957. These were good vintages in most Burgundy vineyards, but not in Chablis, where every vine was frozen and practically no grapes were harvested. In spite of this, many casks have been sold bearing the tag ''Chablis '45'' or '' '57,'' and many a bottle of '' '57'' was imported into the United States.

The frosts on the night of April 29, 1951, froze eighty-five per cent of all the great vineyards. Hence in 1951 only a few barrels of Chablis were produced. The freeze of 1953 took up to five sixths of the normal crop, Marcel Servin, for instance, harvesting 20 instead of 120 *feuillettes.*

The vineyards were partly frozen in 1960, and some of the *Grand Crus* in 1961 did not need harvesting. The great wine-to-be did not exist because of the freeze in early May.

CHABLIS VINEYARDS

Grand Crus, or Outstanding Growths

Blanchots	Les Preuses
Bougros	Valmur
Les Clos	Vaudésir
Grenouilles	

Premiers Crus, or First Growths	Township
Beauroy	*Poinchy*
Beugnon	*Chablis*
Butteaux	*Chablis*
Châpelot	*Fyé*
Châtain	*Chablis*
Côte de Fontenay	*Fontenay*
Côte de Léchet	*Milly*
Fourchaume	*La Chapelle-Vaupelteigne*
Les Forêts or La Forest	*Chablis*
Les Lys	*Chablis*
Mélinots	*Chablis*
Mont de Milieu	*Fyé and Fleys*
Montée de Tonnerre	*Fyé*
Montmain	*Chablis*
Pied d'Aloup	*Fyé*
Séchet	*Chablis*
Trœsme	*Beines*
Vaillon and Côte de Vaillon	*Chablis*
Vaucoupin	*Chichée*
Vaulorent	*Poinchy*
Vaupulent	*Fontenay (part), La Chapelle-Vaupelteigne (part)*
Vosgros or Vogiras	*Chichée*

THE CÔTE D'OR:
The Heart of Burgundy

Burgundy's greatest wines come from the Côte d'Or. Geographically the Slope of Gold begins at Dijon, one of the main stops for the Paris-Riviera Express. The railroad and National Highway 74 parallel the strip of vineyards, which run on down to Santenay, forty miles south.

The Golden Slope is a low and rolling range of hills, topped by brush and scrub, along the western edge of the great Burgundian plain, which spreads eastward to the Jurals and Switzerland. The greatest vineyards are a tenderloin of Pinot grapevines planted just above the point where the hill slopes meet the flatland, a strip rarely more than a mile wide and more often barely a couple of hundred yards across. Below these, and on across the railroad tracks into the plain, are vineyards which produce rather poor wines. All the vineyards look the same, but the wine is not.

The Côte d'Or's favorite proverb says: "If our slopes were not the richest in Burgundy, they'd be the poorest." It is pure accident that this poor reddish earth provides the precise combinations of soil and sun to make the great wines.

Driving south along the Golden Slope, a stranger does not pass through all the famous vineyards. The first vineyard he is able to identify is probably Clos de Vougeot, where there is a stone arch every few feet. Some of these arches are quite ornate, opening onto a slightly tilted field of grapevines. He would pass through Nuits-Saint-Georges, Beaune, and near Pommard, but he would have to take a small dirt road to see the great Montrachet vineyard. He might be surprised to find in a stretch of carefully marked plantations one that was singled out to have a wall around it, with small square arches opening into the vineyard, some carefully marked with neat metal plaques bearing the owners' names. Such walled vineyards are called *clos*. One parcel of greenery looks much like another, and there is little way of telling which are great.

Yet the stories about the great vineyards would do credit to Babe, the big blue ox. There was the general who made his troops present arms when passing Clos de Vougeot, a custom that persists; and Pope Gregory made a cardinal of the man who was clever enough to send him thirty barrels of the famous wine. One historian says the reason Burgundian cardinals never visited Rome was that they didn't want to be away from their vineyards so long. Erasmus said that the only good reason he could think of for going to France was to drink Burgundy on the home grounds. Rabelais says: ''How good is God to give us of this juice!'' And Dumas is said to have declared that Montrachet ought to be drunk kneeling, with head bared. Almost everybody has something commendatory to say about great Burgundies, and usually the same thing, several times.

Today the Côte d'Or is divided into two sections. The Côte de Nuits, to the north, produces three quarters of all the great red wines; the southern Côte de Beaune makes the rest of the reds and all the great white wines. The red wines get steadily lighter in every way as you go south, and most of the whites are in the vineyards of Meursault and below. Some Burgundians insist that the Golden Slope should today be divided into three parts, the third being called the Côte de Meursault, in order to distinguish more clearly the white wines of the Beaune Slope from the reds. As usual, there's an old local saying about it, in rhyme:

> *La Bourgogne a trois côtes ou je ne suis qu'un sot,*
> *Côtes de Nuits, de Beaune, et Côte de Meursault.*

In the old days there actually was a third slope, the Côte de Dijon. Once most of Burgundy's wines came from the vineyards surrounding Dijon, and at the little town of Chenôve is the world's largest winepress to prove it. Officially it is called ''the Duke's winepress,'' but long ago it picked up the name of ''Big Maggie,'' after Marguerite, that lusty Duchess of Burgundy.

She was the mother of Philip the Bold, a gay old girl mentioned tantalizingly and often in all Burgundian chronicles, but so discreetly that you would never suspect her tremendous prowess. Marguerite presided over the harvest festivals, which have been described as bacchanalia; she has been called ''amiable''; it is said that she bestowed her favors on the fastest harvesters and best vintners; and after her was named the biggest winepress in the world.

The winepress and its memories are all that remain of the Dijon Slope's fame, and the suburbs have engulfed many of its vineyards.

Dijon used to be famous for its food, but today it is known principally as the world's mustard center, and mustard is a condiment that
spoils the taste of great wine. Also made there is an alcoholic currant
syrup called cassis. A teaspoonful in a third of a glass of French
vermouth, which is then filled with seltzer and ice, makes the famous
vermouth cassis. More popular in Burgundy is the drink made by
adding a teaspoonful of cassis to a glass of chilled white wine. It is
called *rince cochon* ("pig rinse"), and is the Burgundian Alka-Selt-
zer. Lately this drink has become popular in the wine-drinking world
as *Kir* (pronounced keer), named after the promotion-minded priest
who became the mayor of Dijon. Kir died in his nineties in 1968.

Dijon's wines became famous in those days because, due to poor
transportation, only local wines could be drunk. But when the Cistercian monks began producing their wonders, no amount of civic pride
could make the people of Dijon keep on drinking their own lesser
wines. The vineyards declined steadily, and when the phylloxera
destroyed the plantings in the 1870's, the vineyards were replanted
in Gamay grapes. But even forgoing quality for quantity was a
failure, for Midi and North African wines more than took care of the
cheap-wine market.

Recently most of the old vineyards have again been planted in
Pinot, particularly around the little town of Marsannay. Burgundy
produces no famous *rosé* wines, and it was believed that these vineyards might produce an excellent pink wine. The result was a *rosé*
that is light and fresh, less high in alcohol than other *rosés,* sold
mostly by restaurants in carafe. Although it can be shipped, it rarely
is, for it is little known. The best *rosé* is made by the cooperative of
Marsannay, and most of the wine sold by shippers as a Burgundy
rosé is made in that town.

To counteract this lack of fame, a fête was held in Marsannay in
1949 in honor of St. Vincent. The *Chevaliers du Tastevin* climbed
into their robes and presented a colorful pageant to publicize the
rosé. It is thus that shippers perform a service for the lesser-known
areas of the Côte d'Or. With their methods of promotion and distri-
bution, they encourage people to try the lesser wines, where differences are not great, and fairly large quantities can boast of an
average goodness.

The great vineyards of the Côte d'Or, however, are some half-
dozen miles south of Dijon, where the Côte de Nuits begins. And a
confusion at once arises, because the various towns of the Golden
Slope have long since added to their names that of the nearest

famous vineyard. Gevrey, for instance, has become Gevrey-Chambertin, Chambolle has become Chambolle-Musigny. And the town name applies not only to the village, but also to the commune, or parish, surrounding it.

To get around such difficulties, Burgundians will give you a phrase: *"Respectez les crus."* This means: learn the name of the best growths, or vineyards, and pay little attention to any other names.

In Bordeaux little attention is paid to the names of towns or communes or to the geographical listing of vineyards. The vineyards are listed in order of merit, as a group, for an entire district. There has never been such a list of Burgundy vineyards, and while the wines of each commune have been rated, the wines of the whole Côte d'Or have never been given in one master list.

It may be helpful for the outstanding wines of the Côte d'Or to follow the Bordeaux system of listing. In this tentative list, local prestige, world reputation, the soil, the year-to-year consistency of the wine, the grower, and the value of the wine in relation to its price have been taken into consideration. The list in order of over-all quality is a consensus of many experts' opinions, and because wine is a product of nature and of man's skill, any wine in the following list could jump up or down half a dozen places for any particular vintage. Many an argument can be started among wine-lovers by bringing up this list, but it has a value to the novice of wines, it is of interest to the amateur, and it can be a basis of soul-searching for the expert. If nothing else, it shows that many of the most famous Burgundies are not the best, that many Outstanding Growths rank below many First Growths. Any complete agreement with this list is entirely coincidental.

RED

Vineyard or Climat	Township or Commune	Principal Owners
Romanée-Conti	*Vosne-Romanée*	Domaine de la Romanée-Conti; de Vilaine et Chambon (sole owner)
Chambertin-Clos de Bèze and Chambertin	*Gevrey-Chambertin*	Pierre Damoy; Domaine Marion; L. Latour; Remy; L. Camus; Domaine Rebourseau; Domaine L. Trapet;

RED   *(continued)*

Vineyard or Climat	Township or Commune	Principal Owners
		Drouhin-Laroze; Jaboulet-Vercherre; J. Drouhin; Peirazeau-Groffier; Mme Thomas; Livera; Jantot; Elvina Dupont, J. Prieur; de Marcilly; J. & H. Dufouleur; Consortium Vinicole; Gelin; Groffier; Tortochot; Clair-Daü; etc.
La Tâche	*Vosne-Romanée*	Domaine de la Romanée-Conti, de Vilaine et Chambon (sole owner)
Richebourg	*Vosne-Romanée*	Domaine de la Romanée-Conti; Gros Frère et Sœur; Jean Gros; Charles Noëllat; J. Méo; etc.
Musigny	*Chambolle-Musigny*	Domaine Mugnier; Comte de Voguë, Domaine J. Prieur; Conrad; M. Drouhin; Roumier; Hudelot; etc.
Clos de Vougeot	*Vougeot*	See list of owners on page 106.
La Grande Rue	*Vosne-Romanée*	Lamarche (sole owner)
Bonnes-Mares	*Chambolle-Musigny*	Clair-Daü; Mugnier; Drouhin-Laroze; Comte de Voguë; P. Ponnelle; Groffier; F. Grivelet; Hudelot; Roumier; Alexis Lichine–R. Newman
Grands-Échezeaux	*Flagey-Échezeaux*	R. Engel; Domaine de la Romanée-Conti; Mlle C.

RED   *(continued)*

Vineyard or Climat	Township or Commune	Principal Owners
		Gros; Veuve Mongeard-Mugneret; L. Gouroux; Grivelet; Georges Noëllat; Bissey & Collet; H. Lamarche; E. Lenternier
Romanée-Saint-Vivant	*Vosne-Romanée*	Charles Noëllat; Pierre Poisot; Domaine de la Romanée-Conti now producing the wines for the heirs of G. Marey-Monge; A. Galtic; L. Latour
Clos de Tart	*Morey-Saint-Denis*	J. Mommessin (sole owner)
Cuvée Nicolas Rollin	*Beaune*	Hospices de Beaune
Saint-Georges	*Nuits-Saint-Georges*	Domaine H. Gouges; Morizot-Pelletier; Misserey; Hospices de Nuits; E. Michelot; Liger-Belair; Union Des Vins de Bourgogne; M. Guilleminot; V. Delatraute; Consortium Vinicole de Bourgogne; L. Bruck; Bocquillon Liger-Belair; L. Audidier; L. André; etc.
Latricières-Chambertin	*Gevrey-Chambertin*	Drouhin-Laroze; J. H. Remy; Alexis Lichine; L. Trapet; L. Camus; Consortium Viticole et Vinicole R. Launay
Corton-Clos du Roi, Les Bressandes	*Aloxe-Corton Beaune*	Prince de Mérode; L. Latour; P. Gauthrot;

RED *(continued)*

Vineyard or Climat	Township or Commune	Principal Owners
		Thevenot; Senard; Jaboulet-Vercherre; Arbelet; Comtesse Chandon de Briailles; Dubreuil-Fontaine; M. Quenot; Poisot; Debraye; Martin; etc.
Clos des Lambrays	*Morey*	Mme Cosson (sole owner)
Renardes	*Aloxe-Corton*	P. Petitjean; Delaroche; J. Collin; Gounoux; Maldant; Gille; etc.
Cuvée Dr. Peste	*Aloxe-Corton*	Hospices de Beaune
Clos des Porrets-St.-Georges	*Nuits-Saint-Georges*	Domaine H. Gouges (sole owner)
Les Porrets	*Nuits-Saint-Georges*	J. Jarot; E. Michelot; Hospices de Nuits; Consortium Viticole de Bourgogne; Union Commerciale des Grands Vins; R. Dubois, Société Civile du Clos de Thorey; Domaine H. Gouges; etc.
Mazys-Chambertin	*Gevrey-Chambertin*	Camus; A. Rousseau; P. Gelin; Tortochot; Alexis Lichine; Rebourseau; Thomas; Marchand-Simeon; Girod-Aliex; Jaquesin; Seguin; Chouiller; Thomas-Collignon; Geoffrey; Consortium Viticole et Vinicole de Bourgogne;

RED (*continued*)

Vineyard or Climat	Township or Commune	Principal Owners
		Dr. Bizot; Maume, Tisserandot; Magnien; Ciroty; Drouhin-Laroze
Les Pruliers, Les Cailles	*Nuits-Saint-Georges*	Domaine H. Gouges; Marcel Gessaume; Misserey-Rollet; J. Jarot; Chicotot; M. & R. Chevillon; Pidault Père et Fils; G. Jeanniard; E. Grivat; Union Commerciale des Grands Vins; C. Bezancenot; etc.
Les Caillerets	*Volnay*	H. Boillot; H. Bitouzet; Bouchard Père et Fils; Bouley-Duchemin; Marquis d'Angerville; Clerget; Delagrange; Veuve Fabregoule; Mme Boillerault de Chauvigné; Soc. de la Pousse d'Or; etc.
Clos de la Perrière	*Fixin*	Jehan-Joliet; Bellote; etc.
Échezeaux	*Flagey-Échezeaux*	R. Engel; Domaine de la Romanée-Conti; L. Gros; Groffier; Mongeard-Mugneret; L. Gouroux; J. Bossu; R. Bossu; Confuron; Jayer; Marius; Mugneret-Gibourg; Gerbet; Noblet; Mugneret-Gouachon
Amoureuses	*Chambolle-Musigny*	Domaine Mugnier; F. Grivelet; L'Héritier-

RED   (*continued*)

Vineyard or Climat	Township or Commune	Principal Owners
		Guyot; Gardey-Jouan; M. Drouhin
Clos Saint-Jacques, Ses Varoilles	*Gevrey-Chambertin*	Esmonin; Clair-Daü; A. Rousseau; Monopole Ste Civ. Domaines des Varoilles à Gevrey-Chambertin
Beaux-Monts (also Beaumonts)	*Vosne-Romanée*	Charles Noëllat; Lamarche; Grivot; etc.
Malconsorts	*Vosne-Romanée*	F. Grivelet; Massart; Clos de Thorey; Pidault Père et Fils; A. Bichot; H. Lamarche; Ch. Noëllat; etc.
Clos de la Roche	*Morey-Saint-Denis*	H. Ponsot; A. Rousseau; H. Remy; A. Jacquot; Groffier; Marchand; Mlle Ory; Veuve Tortochot; G. Lignier; etc.
Les Suchots	*Vosne-Romanée*	Lamarche; Mme Blée; Maitrot; Domaine de la Romanée-Conti; J. Confuron; H. Noëllat; Ch. Noëllat; L. Jayer; R. Roblot; R. Arnaux; H. Noirot (succession); R. Mugneret; M. Noëllat; H. Lamarche
Clos des Réas	*Vosne-Romanée*	Gros (sole owner)
Chapelle-Chambertin Charmes-Chambertin Griotte-Chambertin	*Gevrey-Chambertin*	P. Damoy; J. Camus; Drouhin-Laroze; J. H. Remy; L. Trapet; Veuve Tortochot; J. Coquard; Livera; Biguyot; Gaité; Clair-Daü; S. Thomas;

RED   (*continued*)

Vineyard or Climat	Township or Commune	Principal Owners
		Jousset-Drouhin; F. Pernos; E. Marchand; Roty; etc.
Clos du Chapitre	*Fixin*	P. Gelin
Rugiens	*Pommard*	J. Guillemard; Pothier; Comte Armand; Clerget; Jaboulet-Vercherre; B. Gonnet
Épenots	*Pommard*	Domaine Lejeune; Chandron de Courcel; M. Parent; Delagrange; J. Monnier; Loubet; G. Parent; H. Boullot; H. Gonoux; Domaine Lejeune; L. Ricard; Bouchard Père et Fils; L. Chenot; L. Latour; Hospices de Beaune
Didier, Saint-Georges	*Nuits-Prémeaux*	Hospices de Nuits
Fremiets, Champans	*Volnay*	Marquis d'Angerville; F. Buffet; C. Rapet; P. Emonin; M. Voillot; J. Prieur; R. Caillot; Bouchard Père et Fils; de Monthille; Montagny; etc.
Clos des Corvées	*Nuits-Prémeaux*	Gouachon; Hospices de Nuits-Saint-Georges; Noireau; C. Renow; J. Cognieux
Vaucrains	*Nuits-Saint-Georges*	Domaine H. Gouges; Michelot; J. Confuron; Misserey; Chauvenet; Domaine de la Poulette; Mme P. Leger; L. Au-

RED (*continued*)

Vineyard or Climat	Township or Commune	Principal Owners
		didier; A. Chicotot; Union Commerciale des Grands Vins; V. F. Dupasquier; etc.
Santenots	*Meursault*	Marquis d'Angerville; E. Bouley; Clerget; Thévenot; Ste Civ. de la Pousse d'Or; Mme Philippon; Lag; Glantenay; G. Mure; etc.
Fèves, Grèves, Clos des Mouches	*Beaune*	J. Drouhin; L. Voiret; Bouchard Père et Fils; Champy Père et Fils; Chanson Père et Fils; L. Latour; J. Guillemard; H. Darviot; F. Clerget; Martin-Bourgeot; Goud de Beaupuis; Dard; M. Marion. Hospices de Beaune
Clos de la Boudriotte	*Chassagne-Montrachet*	Claude Ramonet; L. Jouard; E. Guillon; etc.
Clos de la Maréchale	*Nuits-Prémeaux*	Domaine Mugnier (sole owner)
Clos Saint-Jean, Clos Morgeot	*Chassagne-Montrachet*	Claude Ramonet; L. Jouard; E. Guillon; André Colin; J. N. Gagnard; M. Moreau; etc.
Les Angles	*Volnay*	H. Rossignol; Mme Boillerault de Chavigné; Mlle Douhairet; M. Bouillot

RED *(continued)*

Vineyard or Climat	Township or Commune	Principal Owners
Clos Blanc, Pézerolles	*Pommard*	Jaboulet-Vercherre; Poirier; F. Clerget; Cavin; L. Michelot; Lochardet; Grivot; H. Bardet; Pidault Père et Fils; etc.
Clos Saint-Denis	*Morey-Saint-Denis*	Bertrand; J. Coquard; A. Jacquot; G. Lignier; A. Rameau; E. Seguin; M. Sèze (Domaine Graillet); etc.

OTHER WINES

Note: In buying wines bearing the commune name with no vineyard name, the important factor determining your selection should be the integrity of the shipper.

WHITE

Vineyard or Climat	Township or Commune	Principal Owners
Montrachet	*Chassagne and Puligny-Montrachet*	See list of owners on page 140.
Chevalier-Montrachet	*Puligny-Montrachet*	See list of owners on page 140.
Clos des Perrières	*Meursault*	Mme Bardet-Grivault (sole owner)
Bâtard-Montrachet	*Chassagne and Puligny-Montrachet*	See list of owners on page 139.
Corton-Charlemagne	*Aloxe-Corton*	L. Latour; A. Duc; L. Jadot; Jaffelin-Rollin; Louis Cornu; Rapet; Dubreuil-Fontaine; Laleure-Piot; Chabot; Bonneau-du-Martray; Klein; Hospices de Beaune; Delaroche; M. Moine; Mme Duchet

WHITE *(continued)*

Vineyard or Climat	Township or Commune	Principal Owners
Perrières	*Meursault*	Ampeau; Joseph Matrot; Domaine Lafon; Lochardet; Maurice Ropiteau; Camille Chouet; Grosyeux-Polet; J. Boulard; A. Cauvert; P. Gauffroy; A. Michelot; E. de Moucheron; J. Belecard; H. Prieur; E. Loupon; P. Latour
Musigny-Blanc	*Chambolle-Musigny*	Comte de Voguë; Domaine Mugnier
Ruchottes	*Chassagne-Montrachet*	Claude-Ramonet
Charmes	*Meursault*	P. Boillot; A. Bouzereau; Y. Latour; Latour-Boissard; A. Michelot; Bernard Michelot; Michelot-Truchot; E. Jobard; Jean et René Monnier; E. Morey; Comte de Moucheron; Percebois-Marchal; Perronnet-Chouet; Perronnet-Latour; Veuve J. Vasseur-Boillot; Veuve Vitu-Pouchard; C. Ropiteau; Hospices de Beaune; Domaine J. Matrot; Comtes Lafon; C. Chonet; H. Prieur; R. Cavin; C. Martenot; P. Ampeau; E. Poupon; Patriarche; Loiselet-Matrot; C. Girard; A. Brunet

WHITE *(continued)*

Vineyard or Climat	Township or Commune	Principal Owners
Blagny	*Meursault*	C. Bondeau; J. Bondet; Domaine Matrot; Comtesse de Montlivault; Domaine J. Leflaive; B. de Cherisy
Combettes	*Puligny-Montrachet*	Etienne Sauzet; Domaine Leflaive; etc.

THE CÔTE DE NUITS
and Its Regal Reds

The Côte de Nuits vineyards begin near the village of Fixin and extend southward along the Golden Slope for a good dozen miles, down to a stone quarry just below Nuits-Saint-Georges, its biggest town, from which the Côte de Nuits takes its name. Within its carefully defined limits are some of the greatest vineyards in the world.

Making wine from even the greatest vineyards, however, does not always mean success. Too many things can ruin the wine. There are parasites like the phylloxera and diseases like mildew, which can destroy the vineyard. Insects are now and then so voracious that if it were not for sprays entire crops would be ruined. Back in the fifteenth century all men were ordered to go to confession and give up swearing so that the insects would go away, and in the following century insects were formally excommunicated and banished to the woods. Today copper sulphate is used to save the vine and its grapes.

There are dangers in the natural growing process. The vines pass through three crucial stages each season: vintners watch the grapes closely when the new shoots sprout, when the vine flowers, and when the grapes are ripe, just before harvest. At each step they can assess the possible quantity and quality of the vintage to come.

A late frost in April or May, a beating rain or high wind during the summer, a drumming hail in August, or an early frost in September can undo the year's work. A wet summer may rot the grapes, a dry one keep them small. And yet weather quirks can upset all predictions. On the sixth of September in 1957 there was gloom all along the Golden Slope. Every vintner was convinced that the vintage would be bad, for the summer had been wet and cloudy. The grapes were small on the vines. But on the seventh the sun came out, shining bright and hot for three straight weeks, and the grapes filled. The 1957 vintage was suddenly turned into a good year.

Hail is the greatest danger. The great vineyards are parceled

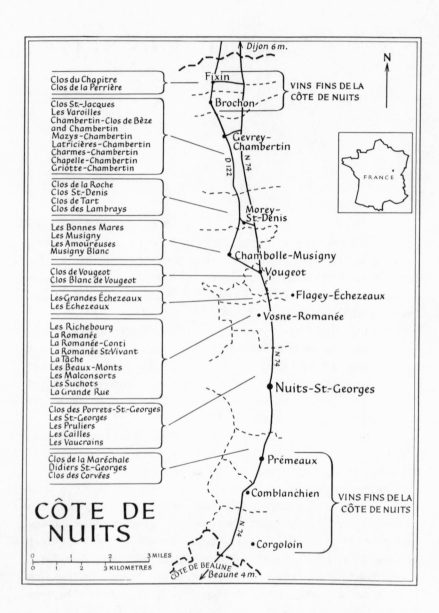

Clos du Chapitre
Clos de la Perrière

Clos St.-Jacques
Les Varoilles
Chambertin-Clos de Bèze
and Chambertin
Mazys-Chambertin
Latricières-Chambertin
Charmes-Chambertin
Chapelle-Chambertin
Griotte-Chambertin

Clos de la Roche
Clos St.-Denis
Clos de Tart
Clos des Lambrays

Les Bonnes Mares
Les Musigny
Les Amoureuses
Musigny Blanc

Clos de Vougeot
Clos Blanc de Vougeot

Les Grandes Échezeaux
Les Échezeaux

Les Richebourg
La Romanée
La Romanée-Conti
La Romanée St.-Vivant
La Tâche
Les Beaux-Monts
Les Malconsorts
Les Suchots
La Grande Rue

Clos des Porrets-St.-Georges
Les St.-Georges
Les Pruliers
Les Cailles
Les Vaucrains

Clos de la Maréchale
Didiers St.-Georges
Clos des Corvées

Dijon 6 m.

N

Fixin

VINS FINS DE LA
CÔTE DE NUITS

Brochon

Gevrey-
Chambertin

D 122

N 74

FRANCE

Morey-
St.-Denis

Chambolle-Musigny

Vougeot

Flagey-Échezeaux

Vosne-Romanée

N 74

Nuits-St.-Georges

Prémeaux

Comblanchien

VINS FINS DE LA
CÔTE DE NUITS

N 74

Corgoloin

CÔTE DE
NUITS

0   1   2   3 MILES
0   1   2   3 KILOMETRES

CÔTE DE BEAUNE
Beaune 4 m.

into small sections, one man owning several in different areas, in the
hope that hail will not destroy them all. Early hail is perhaps the
most dangerous, for the stones break off the young sprouts. The vines
may grow again, but not in time to produce mature grapes.

Quirks of weather and pestilence, though they occur in all
vineyards, and to many other crops besides grapes, are particularly
important on the Côte de Nuits. In the Côte de Nuits are grown
grapes that cannot grow successfully in a more extreme climate. If
they were planted farther north, the character of the wine would
change, becoming thin and acid. And when Pinot varieties are
planted farther south, the wine produced is softer and less robust. In
much warmer climates, too much sun or rain destroys the delicate
grape. You cannot grow the Pinot Noir easily in the Côte de Nuits, or
grow it well anywhere else. It is in this tiny area that the Pinot
produces its greatest wines. And only certain sections have the soil
that can bring the supreme from the vines. This is why the great
vineyards are so small, why the wine from one spot is good and that
from a hundred feet away only average.

On the Côte de Nuits the vineyards are called *climats* (climates)
for this very reason. Each one is slightly different in exposure,
drainage, and soil, composing a different "climate." The name has
spread to all the vineyards of the Golden Slope.

All the great *climats* face southeast on the Côte de Nuits, where
the dawn sun hits the vineyards, drawing moisture up through the
vines. The vineyards are on a slope so that the hottest noon sun
strikes the plants at an angle. Farther south, the vines would wither;
farther north, the sun would not be hot enough. With such extremes
in such a limited district, where a little too much or a shade too little
can ruin a vintage, it is no wonder that the vintners talk about their
vineyards in terms of music or of making love. They are talking
about an art.

Nobody knows for sure why the vineyard of Clos de Bèze should
be better than that of Charmes-Chambertin, right next to it, but you
can taste the difference in the wine. It may be the tilt of the soil, the
way the rain hits it, the composition of the soil itself; but part of it is
the man who makes the wine.

A careful and conscientious vintner will make better wine than
a careless, sloppy one, but the distinction is probably more subtle.
Burgundians like to point to the fact that a race horse will run better
for one trainer than another, that a great orchestra will sound

different in the hands of various conductors. Just as children take on the mannerisms of their parents, a wine seems to pick up some of the character of the man who makes it. When Burgundians are tasting wines together, they sometimes joke about whether the picker during harvest was a virgin, a mother, or an old woman, for it used to be believed that such things made a difference. For generations, women were rarely allowed in the wine cellars, a pregnant woman never.

When all the minor differences in winegrowing and wine-making reach a conclusion in a particular bottle, that wine will have a character all its own, distinct and recognizable. Tasting one wine against another, anyone can tell the difference between a Côte de Nuits and a Côte de Beaune. between a Chambertin and a Musigny.

FIXIN

The northernmost of the eight communes of the Côte de Nuits is Fixin, just above Gevrey-Chambertin. Its wines are similar to those of its famous neighbor, the vineyards having much the same exposure and soil. But out on the highway, at the dirt turn-off that leads back to the town, a large sign boasts, not of the wines, but of a statue of Napoleon. Executed by Rude, the statue, called the *Awakening of Napoleon,* shows the great man just about to open his eyes, a dead eagle at his feet. The statue portrays the legend that Napoleon will come to life again almost any day now. It stands in a glade up in the woods behind the town, near a great avenue of pine trees leading to a museum honoring Napoleon. The building is a replica of the house on St. Helena where Napoleon died, reproduced in two thirds of its actual size.

The center of tourist interest may well be this small museum, but the center of local activity revolves around a circular building containing a circular pool, some fifteen feet across. It is the town *lavoir,* a laundry pool that is short of water these days, where some of the women of the town gather to wash their clothes and exchange gossip, some of the most ribald in the world. Near the *lavoir* is one of the oldest churches in the region, built in the eleventh century, with tombstones askew in the churchyard, and looking as if it had been excavated, not constructed.

The wines from the vineyards near Fixin have a deep red color and a strong bouquet. Because of their high alcoholic content, they develop with age. When well made, they can almost equal the great wines of Gevrey-Chambertin. The wines from the First-Growth Vineyard, Clos de la Perrière, not quite twelve acres in size, are better than the wine from such First-Growth Chambertin vineyards as Charmes or Chapelle.

FIXIN

First Vineyards (*Premières Cuvées*)	Acres
Clos de la Perrière	12.
Clos du Chapitre	11.25
Les Hervelets	9.+
Les Meix-Bas	1.25
Les Arvelets	8.2
Aux Cheussots (Clos Napoleon)	4.5

Note: Names listed in capitals indicate vineyards whose wines are likely to be imported into the United States. The others are not at present imported.

GEVREY AND ITS CHAMBERTIN

The town of Gevrey-Chambertin lies nearly a mile back from the main road, on what is hardly more than a crossroad, with a few short side streets now and then breaking the jagged line made by stone walls and stone house fronts. The building line is the gutter, but over the walls or through the grilled gates there is a glimpse of a large old house now and then. Most of the houses belong to the winegrowers, and each has its wine cellar underneath, low and vaulted.

Many of the growers still sell their wines in barrels to the shippers, but some have taken to tending and bottling their own wine and sell it under their own label. This practice of estate bottling is called *"mise au domaine"* in French, and the phrase *"Mis en Bouteilles par le Propriétaire,"* or a variant, appears on the label. See pages 61–3.

It is at Gevrey, where the *"Route des Grands Crus,"* the road of the great growths, begins, that the vineyard road, which wanders south along the Golden Slope, skirts the greatest vineyards of Burgundy. It is not much of a road, rutted by the vineyard carts, narrow and bumpy, muddy after a rain, dusty in hot weather. It is little more than a wagon track, with an occasional cowpath leading off to a tool shed or farmhouse, and an iron cross at the turn to bring good luck. Down this road to the south is the great vineyard that gives Gevrey its second name, the *Tête de Cuvée* of Chambertin. The phrase can be translated as "Outstanding Vineyard," or "Outstanding Growth."

Not too long ago practically every vineyard within the commune had Chambertin added to its name. To protect their greatest wines, the owners of the best growths formed an association in the 1930's and passed a ruling that limited the use of the name Chambertin to the two greatest vineyards, Le Chambertin and Chambertin Clos de Bèze, and those immediately adjacent to them. Latricières, Mazoyères, Charmes, Mazys, Ruchottes, Griotte, and Chapelle can also legally add Chambertin to their names.

All the confusion began shortly after the year 630, when Almagaire, Duke of Burgundy, gave some land to the local Abbot of Bèze. The abbot increased the size of the vineyard that was already there, and walled it. Some six hundred years later the adjoining field was made into a vineyard and called Champ Bertin, after its peasant owner. The two vineyards were eventually joined together, and were finally bought by a man named Jobert. He followed custom by adding Chambertin to his name, and his efforts made the wine famous. All the furor is caused by the less than 340 barrels produced each year by the two vineyards, now split up between some two dozen proprietors.

Chambertin is one of the greatest red Burgundies, and its vineyards are farther north than those of any of its peers. Along the Golden Slope, Chambertin is called *"Le Grand Seigneur,"* and nobody disputes the title, perhaps out of respect for Napoleon, who called it his favorite wine.

Even without latitude and Napoleon, Chambertin would be a glorious wine. Burgundians talk of its *robe,* or deep, rich, red color, and of its balance and fullness, all its various taste characteristics blending to make a majestic unity. Its tremendous nose—*bouquet* is too delicate a word—makes it a veritable Cyrano. When you have drunk Chambertin, you remember it.

On the way out of town on the Route des Grands Crus, the great vineyards begin just beyond the last house, which belongs to Mme Drouhin-Laroze, a vineyard-owner in Clos de Bèze, Latricières-Chambertin, and some of the lesser vineyards. On the right is Mazys, followed by Clos de Bèze, Chambertin, and Latricières. On the left are Chapelle, Griotte, Charmes, and Mazoyères, the commune boundary separating these vineyards from those of Morey, to the south.

The two Outstanding Vineyards gain their greatness from the soil and its exposure to the sun, their honor and good name protected by the *Appellation Contrôlée*. Nearby vineyards that do not have the same blessings of soil and exposure, and are not allowed to add Chambertin to their names, are Les Varoilles, Clos Saint-Jacques, Fouchère, Étournelles, and Cazetiers. Clos Saint-Jacques and Les Varoilles must be sold with the name of the commune, Gevrey-Chambertin, preceding it. Almost as good as the seven permitted to add Chambertin to their names, and classed with them as *"Premières Cuvées,"* or "First Vineyards," it is regrettable that these two, at least, are not also permitted to add the glorious vineyard name to their own. All have less distinction than the two greatest ones, rarely rising to the level of Chambertin or Chambertin-Clos de Bèze.

Probably the most skillful winemaker producing Chambertin today is Louis Trapet, whose home and cellars are right on the main highway going through the village of Gevrey-Chambertin.

The largest and best producer of Chambertin-Clos de Bèze is Pierre Damoy, whose relatives own the second-largest grocery chain in France. He sells a good part of his wine to shippers, particularly in bad years, but recently he has gone increasingly into estate-bottling.

In the fifties, two of the best producers of Chambertin were Armand Rousseau, one of the first to dare to go into estate-bottling, and Dr. Marion, one of the greatest surgeons in France. He spent much time in his vineyard, and the local growers agreed that his section produced the Chambertin of greatest finesse. A good shipper, J. H. Remy, whose firm is in Morey-Saint-Denis, owns a large section.

An English-teacher at Chalon-sur-Saône, a man named Deschamps, rode the bus that travels along the main highway to be near his vineyards on the weekends and on Thursdays, the French school holidays. He died in 1950, and now his heirs continue to produce about one hundred cases of Chambertin each year.

Many of the lucky owners of the *Têtes de Cuvées* also own parcels of first and second *cuvées*. The Chambertin of Rousseau, for instance, should not be confused with Rousseau Charmes-Chambertin, or with Rousseau Gevrey-Chambertin, the last being the generic term for all the wines of the commune. In this respect, it is interesting to note that some of the lesser vineyards are more famous than the two *Têtes*, largely because lesser wines are much cheaper in price and there are more of them. The two great vineyards produce only about 7,500 cases in a good year like 1969, the splendid wine of 1961 being about half that in quantity. The quality of wine varies tremendously in the various communes along the Golden Slope, the two

Outstanding Growths of Chambertin, for instance, being vastly superior to such generic wines as those sold simply as Gevrey-Chambertin.

Wine quality also depends enormously on the age of the vines, the older the better, although the yield decreases. New vines make small wines. Today the majority of the vines of the great Gevrey

GEVREY-CHAMBERTIN

Outstanding Vineyards (*Têtes de Cuvées*)	Acres
Le CHAMBERTIN	32.5
CHAMBERTIN-CLOS DE BÈZE	37.5

First Vineyards (*Premières Cuvées*)	
LATRICIÈRES	17.5
MAZYS or MAZIS	31.5
MAZOYÈRES	47.5
CHARMES	31.
RUCHOTTES and the CLOS DES RUCHOTTES	8.5
GRIOTTE	13.5
CHAPELLE	13.
CLOS SAINT-JACQUES	17.5
VAROILLES	15.
Fouchère	2.5
Étournelles	5.
Cazetiers	20.

Second Vineyards (*Deuxièmes Cuvées*)	
Gémeaux	5.
Échezeaux	9.
Lavaut	24.
Combe au Moine	5.5
Carougeot	14.

Note: Names listed in capitals indicate vineyards whose wines are likely to be imported into the United States. The others are not at present imported.

vineyards are in their prime, thirty years old, and the introduction of rotation planting will tend to keep their wines on a high level. The official yield for the commune is about 373 U.S. gallons to the acre, a fairly representative figure for much of Burgundy. This means that each acre yields about 100 cases of wine, when evaporation and loss in handling are taken into account. Of the great wines, most of them are drunk in the large cities of the world. In the village of Gevrey itself you can't find a bottle of the *Têtes de Cuvées* in either of the local restaurants, and it is even hard to get one of the few bottles of the *Premières Cuvées*. Many of the growers rarely drink their own wines. They're too valuable.

MOREY-SAINT-DENIS

La Route des Grands Crus runs straight into Morey after passing the great vineyards of Gevrey-Chambertin. Morey is even smaller than its neighbor, with a shady public square, and its few houses huddled around it like frightened children clinging to the skirts of the mother superior. On the right is a sandy stone wall in excellent repair, on which are the names of Clos des Lambrays and Clos de Tart, the great wines of the commune.

In the seventh century a nunnery was founded here, between the two monasteries of Bèze and Vougeot. Like the monks, the nuns started a vineyard, calling it Clos de Tart. Today the steep vineyard is owned by a shipper from Mâcon, J. Mommessin, while the neighboring Clos des Lambrays, which had seventy-four owners in the early part of the nineteenth century, now belongs to one—big, burly, jovial Mme Cosson. This magnificent vineyard is a heritage from the late M. de Bahèzre, who spent the better part of his life reassembling the vineyard.

The wines of this commune are the forgotten wines of the Côte de Nuits, their magnificence almost unknown. There are intermediate years in wine, vintages overshadowed and forgotten because the preceding and following ones were so exceptional. The same thing happens to vineyards. Morey-Saint-Denis vineyards are intermediate because of their famous neighbors north and south, and yet their wines are among the best values in Burgundy, selling at lower prices than the much-bid-for wines of Gevrey or Chambolle.

Until the laws governing *Appellation d'Origine* were passed, Morey wines went to market under the names of their neighbors— one reason why they are almost unknown. Morey long ago added Saint-Denis to its name, a vineyard that is one of the *Têtes de*

MOREY-SAINT-DENIS

Outstanding Vineyards (*Têtes de Cuvées*)	Acres
BONNES-MARES	5.
CLOS DE LA ROCHE	37.9
CLOS SAINT-DENIS	16.2
CLOS DE TART	17.5

First Vineyards (*Premières Cuvées*)	
Les Charnières	6.
Les Chenevery	8.
Aux Cheseaux	6.
CLOS DES LAMBRAYS	14.8
Clos des Ormes	11.
Les Faconnières	4.5
Les Millandes	11.
Monts-Luisants (white wine)	8.
Morey	8.
Clos Sorbet	8.

Note: Names listed in capitals indicate vineyards whose wines are likely to be imported into the United States. The others are not at present imported.

Cuvées. The wine of Clos Saint-Denis is lighter than its peer, Clos de la Roche, a full, rich wine.

The great wines of the commune, Clos de Tart and Lambrays, are strong, heavy, and sturdy. They take from ten to twenty years to mature, depending on the amount of tannin. Another magnificent vineyard is Les Bonnes-Mares, but as only a fifth of it is within the commune, the wine is usually associated with Chambolle.

It is here that the character of the wines of the Côte de Nuits makes a great change. That from the Clos Saint-Denis is a bridge between the sturdiness of the Moreys and the soft, elegant distinction of the Bonnes-Mares, Musignys, and other wines from the adjoining commune of Chambolle.

The vineyards are slightly further south, the exposure to the sun is slightly different because of the steeper slope, the soil is slightly

different in composition and drainage, and these infinitesimal variations make a pronounced change in the wines. It is in Morey-Saint-
Denis that one begins to discover the wonder there is in wine.

CHAMBOLLE-MUSIGNY

Past the vineyard of Bonnes-Mares, the vineyard road swings right
into the town of Chambolle, tucked under the highest mountain of
the Golden Slope. Flanked on the north by a craggy outcrop, the
town has the feeling of a mountain village.

The main street of the town runs straight back to the wall and
park surrounding the Château de Chambolle-Musigny, a large rectangular building in the massive nineteenth-century style, built over
a splendid series of vast cellars and handsome vat rooms. The 1950
and 1951 vintages were managed by the author. The house was used
as a barracks in the last war, first by the Germans, and then successively by the French and Americans. Near it is a modern structure
which is also called Château de Chambolle-Musigny by its owner. The
Mugnier family, who have owned the old château for nearly a
hundred years, maintain that the owner of the modern building has
no right to call his property Château de Chambolle-Musigny, which
creates confusion.

Les Bonnes-Mares, north of the town, yields superb wines, which
are softer than those from Morey, possessing a combination of delicacy and the more robust qualities of those to the north. One of the
finest of Burgundies, still unknown and little appreciated, it over-
shadows all the wines of the other Côte, that of Beaune, with the
exception of Corton, more famous than Bonnes-Mares but equal in
quality.

As you drive east out of Chambolle toward the main road, the
vineyards produce wines noted for supreme delicacy. The dirt road
swings right and heads south, the crossing marked by an old stone
cross, and on your right hand are the Musigny and the Petits-Mu-
signy vineyards, producing wines known simply as Musigny. The
vineyard road is downhill from these great vineyards, separating
them from plantations that are only slightly less magnificent, the
greatest of which is Les Amoureuses, ''Women in Love.'' Burgundians feel that it is one of the loveliest vineyard names of the Golden
Slope. Its wines are reminiscent of the bouquet and delicacy of the
vineyard across the road.

Musigny has a glorious perfume and a lingering bouquet; it is truly one of the great wines of Burgundy, and the least masculine of them all. Rather, its charm is its lightness, its femininity. The largest owner is the Comte de Voguë, related to the Champagne family that owns Moët et Chandon—an example of how families who work in wine have holdings in other districts. Other large owners are the Domaine Mugnier and, to a smaller degree, Berthaut-Hudelot.

The Domaine Mugnier was one of the largest owners of topnotch vineyards in the Côte de Nuits. In addition to its large holdings in Chambolle-Musigny, others include a section of Clos de Vougeot and sections in Prémeaux of Nuits-Saint-Georges. It is one of the few Burgundy domains large enough to employ a *régisseur*. Most of its wines, beginning with the 1950 vintage, were estate-bottled, in the hands of a man trained in the art of wine-making by Henri Gouges, one of Burgundy's great champions. Unfortunately, in the hands of a shipper, the wines have now lost their reliability.

Below Les Amoureuses is a steep bank that drops down to a narrow plateau, then plunges down another hundred feet to the valley floor, dividing the slope into four levels in all. It is here that the Vouge River chooses to burst out of the mountainside, to wander

CHAMBOLLE-MUSIGNY

Outstanding Vineyards (*Têtes de Cuvées*)	Acres
Les MUSIGNY	25.
Les BONNES-MARES (in part)	34.

First Vineyards (*Premières Cuvées*)	
Les AMOUREUSES	13.5
Les Baudes	9.
Les Charmes	14.5
La Combe d'Orveau	12.5
Les Cras	10.5
Les Fuées	15.5
Les Gruenchers	7.5
Les Noirots	7.5
Les Sentiers	12.5

Note: Names listed in capitals indicate vineyards whose wines are likely to be imported into the United States. The others are not at present imported.

down across the valley. Standing on the plateau above its mouth, you can look southeast and see the whole of the Clos de Vougeot spread out below you. The main valley road bounds the walled vineyard on the east; the vineyard road bounds it on the west. Toward the back, the turrets of the château glint yellow in the sunlight, while the great vineyards of Musigny slant up the slope behind you. For many, here lies the heart of Burgundy.

It is in Chambolle-Musigny that you again notice the startling differences in the wines of Burgundy. The tiny plots produce wines of widely different character. It is in the Musignys that you find an outstanding delicacy, a contrast that is unexpected but one which confirms the fact that natural Burgundies are lighter than Bordeaux.

VOUGEOT AND ITS CLOS

The river Vouge flows out of the hill near the vineyards of Vougeot, watering and naming them at once. From the vineyard road on the high land of Le Musigny, you can look across to the main highway, with its avenue of trees, the buildings of the town along its length, ending near the vineyard wall. The town now claims less than two hundred inhabitants, but there were many more working to dry the swampy lands when the monks moved in and began building their monastery in the twelfth century. The Cistercians, around the same time, built another monastery, dedicated to the making of great white Steinbergers at Kloster Eberbach along the Rhine.

At Vougeot the monks set out the vineyard on the slopes above the monastery; its 125 acres then composed the largest in Burgundy. It still is the biggest of the top-notch plantations. Once the monastery was finished, a great wall was laid out around the vineyards, and toward the back of the enclosed area it was decided to build a castle and a press house. The monk who was given the drafting job was so proud of his efforts that he signed the plans before taking them to the abbot, and that worthy resented the act. The plans were turned over to another monk for doctoring and were ruined. The abbot called in the architect, showed him the botched plans, and ordered the castle built as shown, with all the flaws and errors intact, as punishment for his sin of pride in signing the plans. The architect is said to have died on the spot, out of mortification, but the abbot had no trouble finding others to push the building through. The building is all that's left of the ancient monastery.

It was not finished until the fifteenth century, and has been constantly repaired ever since. Since the Second World War millions of francs have been poured into restoring the building, which had been used as a billet by the Germans during the occupation, and later as a prison camp by the Americans. At one point the disgruntled German prisoners tried to burn up the centuries-old presses, claiming they needed the wood for fires. The caretaker hotfooted it to the American commander, who slapped up a barbed-wire barricade around the massive machines. The press levers are enormous chestnut trees squared roughly with the ax, held in place by other squared tree trunks only slightly smaller.

The money for restoration came in through contributions to the *Chevaliers du Tastevin,* Burgundy's promotional organization, made up of growers, shippers, and various dignitaries interested in wine. The order bought the castle for their meetings, and every other month they throw a big dinner for themselves, dressed up in red robes and square black hats, with silver *tastevins* dangling from a red and orange ribbon looped around their necks.

To hear Burgundians tell it, the wall around the Clos was almost as big an effort as China's Great Wall, for it took more than a hundred years to build. Between eight and ten feet high, it is built of split stone. Along the rear section on the inside are espaliered fruit trees; along the short terraced drive to the castle itself is the tombstone of one Léonce Boquet, who united the vineyard into a single domain in the nineteenth century. Today the Clos is split up among more than sixty owners.

Rosebushes are planted along the drive, and as you walk up to the great doors and yank at the vine root at the end of the bell-pull chain, the odor of the roses is in your nostrils. The caretaker's hound barks at the clanging and pelts across the yellow gravel of the court, waiting for the caretaker to open the gates and let you in. The great roofs of the older buildings to the back and on the right come slanting down almost to the ground itself, supported by heavy, timbered posts painted a purplish red, the color of wine.

Across the court is the great room that used to be a storage shed for casks, where as many as five hundred members of the *Chevaliers du Tastevin* can eat and drink, shouting out between songs and mouthfuls the slogan of their order: "Never in vain, always in wine." The pillars of the great hall are giant stone monoliths, tapering up some twenty feet to enormous beams, and hanging on the pillars are the leather back-baskets formerly used for gathering grapes. The baskets are decorated with a painted coat of arms and dates of the most famous vintage years, the oldest being 1108.

From this walled earth comes another great Burgundy, a wine so superlative that it is a tradition for passing regiments of the French Army to salute the vines. When Napoleon once ordered some of the wine, the crusty guardian is said to have replied: "If he wants to taste this glorious wine, let him come here and drink it." It will always be one of the great Burgundies, magnificently full and per-fumed, with a velvety robe and splendid balance.

But the wine varies enormously. Clos de Vougeot is as large as some of the vineyards that produce the great growths of Bordeaux, but there all the wine is blended by the single owner; here the wine is made by over sixty different owners. Also, the wine varies with the soil, and with its makers. Each man decides when his section is to be picked and when the grapes shall be pressed. In his own cellar he supervises the wine-making, decides when it shall be drawn off the lees, when it shall be bottled, and so forth. To see how any single wine can vary, all one need do is taste various bottles made by different men in the same year.

The wine also varies with the soil. Clos de Vougeot used to be divided into three growths, the best on the sloping land up behind the castle, near the back wall. Centuries ago wine from this section was reserved by the abbot for royal gifts to crowned heads and princes of the Church. The farthest corner is called Musigny de Clos de Vougeot, because it is nearest the Chambolle vineyards. This is owned by the sons of Louis Gros.

The top third of the vineyard also includes sections known as Garenne, Plante Chamel, Plante Abbé, Montiottes Hautes, Chioures, Quartier de Marci Haut, and the Grand and Petit Maupertuis. The middle section, whose wine is only slightly less glorious than that from the top, has always commanded high prices. The sections are: Dix Journaux, the *journaux* being an old vineyard measure; Baudes Bas; and Baudes-Saint-Martin. Even the wines from the lowest section, which are excellent in good years, sell for high prices. The sections are: Montiottes Bas, Quatorze Journaux, Baudes Bas, and Baudes-Saint-Martin. The various owners live up and down the whole length of the Côte d'Or, from Gevrey in the north and down even as far as Chalon and Mâcon, for being the owner of a slice of Clos de Vougeot is a sign of true wine nobility. Every Burgundian aspires to that.

Wine from Clos de Vougeot can be one of the greatest wines of Burgundy. It is one of the most famous of the Côte de Nuits, as well known as Chambertin. Its wine has a distinct perfume, full and flowery, and often said to resemble that of violets. Like the other great Burgundies, it has been famous for centuries—eight of them. The toast of kings, the pride of princes, it has outlived them all. As long as wine is made in Burgundy, Clos de Vougeot will be among the great.

Just outside the walls, near the entrance of the castle, is the vineyard of La Vigne-Blanche, known as Clos Blanc de Vougeot. It produces white wine, made from the Chardonnay grape. The vineyard is very small, less than five acres in all, and most of it is owned by L'Héritier-Guyot, who is also a maker of cassis.

Alphabetical List of Principal Owners and Addresses in the Clos de Vougeot

Adrien, Marie-Antoinette	Dijon
Arnoux-Salbreux, Charles	Vosne-Romanée
Bichot, A.	Beaune
Bocquillon-Liger-Belair	Nuits-Saint-Georges
Capitain, R.	Ladoix-Serrigny
Carrelet de Loisy, C.	Nuits-Saint-Georges
Clair-Daü, J.	Marsannay-la-Côte
Clerget-Philibert, F.	Beaune
Confuron, Christian	Prissey
Confuron-Bouchard, J.	Prissey
Confuron-Jayer	Vosne-Romanée
Consortium Viticole et Vinicole de Bour- gogne (Faiveley)	Nuits-Saint-Georges
Coquard, Firmin	Morey-Saint-Denis
Coquard, Louis	Morey-Saint-Denis
Corbet-Jayer, Maurice	Morey-Saint-Denis
Drouhin-Jousset, Maurice	Beaune
Drouhin-Laroze, Alexandre	Gevrey-Chambertin
Dufouleur Bouillot, Joseph	Nuits-Saint-Georges
Engel, René	Vosne-Romanée
Fage, A.	Paris
Gouroux, Louis	Flagey-Échezeaux
Gouroux Gremeaux, Henri	Flagey-Échezeaux
Grivot, Gaston	Vosne-Romanée
Gros, Colette	Vosne-Romanée
Gros, François	Vosne-Romanée
Gros, G.	Vosne-Romanée

Haegelen, Émile Victor	Nuits-Saint-Georges
L'Héritier-Guyot	Dijon
Hudelot-Mongeard, Georges Henri Noel	Vougeot
Hudelot, J.	Chambolle
Indelli, P.	Paris
Jaboulet-Vercherre	Pommard
Jaboulet-Vercherre, Michel	Pommard
Jaffelin Frères	Beaune
Lamarche, Henri Emman	Vosne-Romanée
Lecrivain, L.	Vosne-Romanée
Lejay-Lagoutte	Dijon
Le Roy	Auxey-Duresses
Leymaris-Coste, J.	Clos Mazèyres, Libourne
Machard de Grammont, Maxime	Nuits-Saint-Georges
Méo, J.	Vosne-Romanée
Mérat-Piot, André	Beaune
Misset-Bailly, Paul	Dijon
Mongeard-Mugneret, Eugène	Flagey-Échezeaux
Morin, Jean	Nuits-Saint-Georges
Mugneret, Georges	Vosne-Romanée
Mugnier, Étienne	Dijon
Noblet-Guienot, Alfred	Vosne-Romanée
Noëllat, Charles	Vosne-Romanée
Noëllat-Jayer, Henri	Vosne-Romanée
Nourissat, J.	Dijon
Parfait-Sallot	Chambolle-Musigny
Piat et Cie	Mâcon
Pierre Ponnelle	Beaune
Rameau-Saguin, A.	Morey-Saint-Denis
Domaine H. Rebourseau	Gevrey-Chambertin
Roblot, Raymond	Vosne-Romanée
Ropiteau, J.	Meursault
Roumier-Quanquin	Chambolle-Musigny
Salbreux, Maria	Dijon
Soc. Civ. au Clos de Thorey	Nuits-Saint-Georges
Société Vinicole Beaujolaise	Saint Georges de Rheneins
Tardy-Voyement	Fontaine-Française
Thomas-Chaissac, J.	Nuits-Saint-Georges
Domaine J. Thorin	Romanèche-Thorins
Tortochot, Vve	Gevrey-Chambertin
Tourlière	Beaune

FLAGEY-ÉCHEZEAUX

The vineyard road angles down the hill from the vineyards of
Chambolle and along behind the rear wall of Clos de Vougeot. The
wall bends off to the left, but the road cuts straight, and to the right
is the vineyard of Grands-Échezeaux. The great vineyards are still to
the right of *La Route des Grands Crus*. The town is across the main
highway, down by the railroad tracks, important only because the
vineyards have been included in its commune.

The wine from Grands-Échezeaux is little known, and the English insist it is because the name, which sounds like a drunk's
exclamation, "esh-eh-zo," is so hard to pronounce. This is as foolish a
reason as any, the wines being excellent values, intermediates like
those from Morey. The wines are a bridge between the full and
sturdy Vougeots and the lighter, more delicate wines of Vosne-Roma-

FLAGEY-ÉCHEZEAUX

Outstanding Vineyards (*Têtes de Cuvées*)	Acres
Les GRANDS-ÉCHEZEAUX	23.
Les ÉCHEZEAUX	106.

First Vineyards (*Premières Cuvées*) *	
Les BEAUX-MONTS or BEAUMONTS	14.
Champs-Traversins	9.
Clos Saint-Denis	4.5
Les Cruots or Vignes-Blanches	8.
Les Loachausses	10.
En Orveau	25.
Les Poullaillières	12.5
Les Quartiers de Nuits	6.
Les Rouges-du-Bas	10.
Les Treux	12.5

* These wines may also be sold as Vosne-Romanée. Les
Beaumonts is the only vineyard listed under *"Premières
Cuvées"* that is not included in Échezeaux. The others are,
although at the same time they may call themselves *Premières Cuvées* of Vosne-Romanée.

Note: Names listed in capitals indicate vineyards whose
wines are likely to be imported into the United States. The
others are not at present imported.

née, the commune just to the south. They have great balance and distinction and are outstandingly good for the most part, largely because no one has been tempted to tamper with a wine so little in demand.

The ten first *cuvées* are never sold under the name of the *climat*, or vineyard, but always as Échezeaux, without Grands as a prefix. They combine body and strength as do all the other Côte de Nuits wines, improve considerably with age, and are closer to the Vosne-Romanée wines than to those from Clos de Vougeot.

The Domaine de la Romanée-Conti is one of the owners of Grands-Échezeaux; René Engel also owns a section; and others are the heirs of Louis Gros, and men named Groffier, Jayer, Gouroux, and Mugneret. Engel is a writer on the wines of France, his studies, essays, and columns appearing in various French wine journals, and he is highly respected among the Burgundians who make the wines.

The intermediate wines are particularly popular with those wine-lovers who want outstanding wines at reasonable prices even though they can afford the more famous and more expensive Burgundies. These intermediates of the Côte de Nuits are usually better wines than any of those from the Côte de Beaune, with the exception of the great Cortons. The Pommards and Volnays rarely reach the excellence of these Grands-Échezeaux and Moreys. These are wines for those impressed by what's in the bottle, not by the label on it.

VOSNE-ROMANÉE

The vineyard road crosses the boundary of Vosne-Romanée scarcely a hundred yards from the wall surrounding Clos de Vougeot. This commune produces more great wines than any other, and the fewest small ones, and yet its top-notch vineyards total less than 150 acres. The wines from these are the most expensive on earth, and wine-lovers revel in their greatness. Even their names are a source of delight, and P. Morton Shand, the British wine authority, once said they were "the mingling of velvet and satin in a bottle."

The greatest of the great is Romanée-Conti, scarcely 4½ acres in size, which was bought in 1868 by the ancestors of the present owners for 330,000 gold francs, a sum equal to nearly $100,000 today. It is the most precious vineyard in the world. Mme de Pompadour, the mistress of Louis XV, once tried to buy it, but it went to the Prince of Conti, who had the King's ear, being director of secret diplomacy for Louis XV.

Closely following this magnificent vineyard are La Tâche, a vineyard only fifteen acres in size, and La Romanée, which is only two acres in all. The biggest of the greats is Richebourg, almost twenty acres, the largest owners being the sons of Louis Gros, the Domaine de la Romanée-Conti, and Charles Noëllat. The production of Richebourg is too small for the demand, while bottles are so rare from the smaller vineyards that drinking the wine is always a great event.

The largest owner in Vosne-Romanée is the Domaine de la Romanée-Conti, which takes its name from the vineyard that is its prize. The Domaine also owns all of La Tâche, which is better known as a *climat* than the actual commune of Vosne-Romanée and never carries the parish name on the bottle. The Domaine owns parts of Grands-Échezeaux as well, in addition to its portion of Richebourg. La Romanée is owned by the shipping firm of LeRoy.

The Domaine de la Romanée-Conti is owned by M. de Vilaine, who lives near Vichy, and who was the first in Burgundy to begin bottling his own wines. His introduction of estate-bottling has revolutionized the wine industry of Burgundy. His wines have set the standards for all great Burgundies.

Shortly after the phylloxera struck in the last decades of the nineteenth century, growers began grafting vines on American stocks. The Domaine refused to, and until 1946 the gnarled old roots produced wines from the pre-phylloxera vines. They were preserved through constant care, but the war made this difficult; the yield was becoming smaller each year; and the Domaine was forced to succumb to the modern practice of grafting. Other old-fashioned and proudly successful methods were clung to, such as making a mulch of the old vines. But disease in the cuttings used for mulch ended this practice also, and now the Domaine uses fertilizers and manures like the other growers. The tenacity of the Domaine in holding to old ways has kept the wine great, and the magnificent care lavished on the vineyards continues to produce great wines which, unfortunately, are over-abundantly sugared or chaptalized.

The greatness of the wines would lead you to expect that the cellars of the Domaine would have marble columns and perhaps a choir chanting in one corner, but the buildings in Vosne are as modest as the wines are great. The house stands at the head of a walled court, two long *chais* forming the sides, with the immaculate cellars underneath. M. Noblet lives in the house, acting as the *caviste*. And in the center of the court there is usually a manure pile. Here

VOSNE-ROMANÉE

Outstanding Vineyards (*Têtes de Cuvées*)	Acres
ROMANÉE-CONTI	4.5
La ROMANÉE	2.
La TÂCHE	15.
Les GAUDICHOTS	3.
Les RICHEBOURG	20.

First Vineyards (*Premières Cuvées*)

La ROMANÉE SAINT-VIVANT	24.
Les MALCONSORTS	15.
La GRANDE RUE	3.25
Les BEAUMONTS or BEAUX-MONTS	6.25
Les SUCHOTS	32.25
Aux Brûlées	10.
Aux Petits-Monts	7.
Aux Reignots	4.25

Second Vineyards (*Deuxièmes Cuvées*)

CLOS DES RÉAS	5.
AUX RÉAS	25.
La Colombière	11.
La Combe-Brûlée	4.
La Croix-Rameau	1.5
Cros-Parantoux	2.5
Les Damaudes	6.
Derrière-le-Four	2.5
Hauts-Beaux-Monts	10.
Hautes-Maizières	6.
Les Jacquines	9.
Aux Raviolles	15.

Note: Names listed in capitals indicate vineyards whose wines are likely to be imported into the United States. The others are not at present imported.

the wine and its needs are all-important, and aesthetic considerations are incidental.

Behind the cellar where the new wine is kept are two back cellars, where in the racks are some of the greatest bottles in the world. Here you can see the tradition behind a great label. As the Domaine has always bottled all its wine, a wine-lover opens a Romanée-Conti with the respect and anticipation he has gained through years of tasting. Romanée-Contis, more than any other wine, often reach the ultimate in absolute perfection due to the combinations of bouquet, flavor, body delicacy, and intensity. The connoisseur knows that the wine will be great, and he is in a frame of mind to appreciate the fine old wine, prepared for its magnificence. This is why these two back cellars are thought of with such awe and delight, for the Domaine has all the great bottles that are left of the splendid vintages.

Because of these bottles, other growers have begun estate-bottling of at least part of their production. Formerly much of it was sold in the barrel to restaurant-owners in Belgium or Switzerland, who made annual trips to the vineyards to replenish their cellars. Shippers bought much of it, and most of the bottles went to Belgium, which is the largest buyer of Burgundy in the world, followed closely by Switzerland. The only bottles of the great Romanées that got out to the rest of the world came from the cellars of the Domaine. Today most of the wines from Gros and Noëllat are also being estate-bottled. Just because the Domaine was the first major estate-bottler in Burgundy, wine-lovers are apt to believe that their wines are great to the exclusion of all others. Not only is this wrong but it also shows the inexperience of those making such judgments.

These great wines of Vosne-Romanée are, to many, the supreme examples of great Burgundy. Their balance is magnificent, no one characteristic standing out, but all being superb, and together forming a wine that has a perfection almost unequaled. All are big, sturdy, full-bodied, with a velvety richness and the characteristic of acquiring a splendid nose with age. Les Richebourg is perhaps the fullest, Romanée-Conti, La Romanée, and La Tâche being somewhat more delicate, in descending order. The only Burgundian equals of these are the two Chambertins, Le Musigny, Corton, and the best wines of Clos de Vougeot.

But these are not all the great wines of Vosne-Romanée, for the first *cuvées* are outstanding. They are on a par with the Bonnes-Mares and Grands-Échezeaux, and often superior to many Clos de

Vougeots. The best of these are: Romanée-Saint-Vivant, Les Suchots, Les Beaumonts, Les Malconsorts, and La Grande Rue. Here it is important to note that wines from Les Verroilles, an Outstanding Growth, are never sold under their own name, but always under the name of Richebourg, while the third *cuvées* are sold simply as Vosne-Romanée.

Perhaps the outstanding characteristics of the greatest wines of Vosne are their lingering bouquet and rich, full character, coupled with a certain delicateness. Some connoisseurs claim that the wines are sometimes too highly chaptalized, the sugar added making for an occasional aftertaste that errs in the direction of sweetness. The wines of Vosne are among the most glorious in the world, and a bottle is a symbol of the greatest magnificence in wine.

NUITS-SAINT-GEORGES
AND PRÉMEAUX

Nuits-Saint-Georges is the capital of the Côte de Nuits because it is the biggest town and produces more wine than any other. It lies on both sides of the highway and is the home of many shipping firms, whose contribution to the world has been Sparkling Burgundy and grape juice.

Sparkling Burgundy was created by shippers to help them compete with Champagne sales and fame. It is made of small wines that could not normally demand a good price. These are seldom worth drinking and are poor values in markets where the duty is the same as that for Champagne.

Living in this den of shippers was the late Henri Gouges, a winegrower who spent his life combating fraud in Burgundy. He was one of those responsible for the success of the *Appellations d'Origine* laws, which have meant so much to the winegrowers of the Golden Slope. He led a full life, being vice-president of the French national committee of fine wine-producers, and a most important member of the Committee of Appellations, the group responsible for unearthing cases of wine fraud and seeing that they are prosecuted. Along with all this he and his two sons had time to make some excellent wine.

The wines of Nuits are noted among the local vintners for firmness, meaning that they are full of texture, or tannin, with so much body you can actually take bites out of them. Dark in color, as well as full in body, they mature slowly. Heavy in tannin, with age they acquire a remarkable consistency in body.

NUITS-SAINT-GEORGES

Outstanding Vineyards (*Têtes de Cuvées*)	Acres
Le SAINT-GEORGES	19.
Aux BOUDOTS	16.
Les CAILLES	10.
Les PORRETS or PORETS	17.5
Les PRULIERS	17.5
Les VAUCRAINS	15.
Aux Cras	7.5
Aux Murgers	12.5
Aux Thorey and Clos de Thorey	15.

First Vineyards (*Premières Cuvées*)	
Les Chabœufs	7.5
Les Chaignots	14.
Château Gris	6.
La Perrières	10.
Les Poulettes	6.
Les Procès	5.
La RICHEMONE	6.
La Roncière	5.
Rue-de-Chaux	7.5

Note: Names listed in capitals indicate vineyards whose wines are likely to be imported into the United States. The others are not at present imported.

Just south of Nuits is the town of Prémeaux. Its vineyards have much the same characteristics as those of Nuits-Saint-Georges, the soil, the undersoil, and the sun being almost identical with that of the more famous commune. Because the wines are so similar, unlike those from other neighboring communes along the Golden Slope, the *Appellation* laws specify that Prémeaux wines go to market bearing the name of Nuits-Saint-Georges. The best vineyards are Les Didiers, Les Clos des Forêts-Saint-Georges, Les Corvées, and the Clos de la Maréchale, its twenty-five acres making up the largest single vineyard in Burgundy belonging to one owner, the Domaine Mugnier. It was formerly called Clos des Fourches.

In addition to the above, the best vineyards around Nuits are: Les Saint-Georges, fullest in body; Les Vaucrains, noted for bouquet; Les Pruliers, which has both body and bouquet; and Les Cailles and Les Porrets, lighter and more delicate than the others. The commune name usually precedes that of the vineyard in Nuits-Saint-Georges.

NUITS-SAINT-GEORGES-PRÉMEAUX

First Vineyards (*Premières Cuvées*)	Acres
CLOS DE LA MARÉCHALE	24.
Les DIDIERS	7.
CLOS DES FORÊTS	12.5
CLOS DES CORVÉES	20.
Les Corvées-Pagets	6.
Les Clos Saint-Marc	7.5
Clos des Argillières	12.5
CLOS DES ARLOT	10.
Aux PERDRIX	8.

Note: Names listed in capitals indicate vineyards whose wines are likely to be imported into the United States. The others are not at present imported.

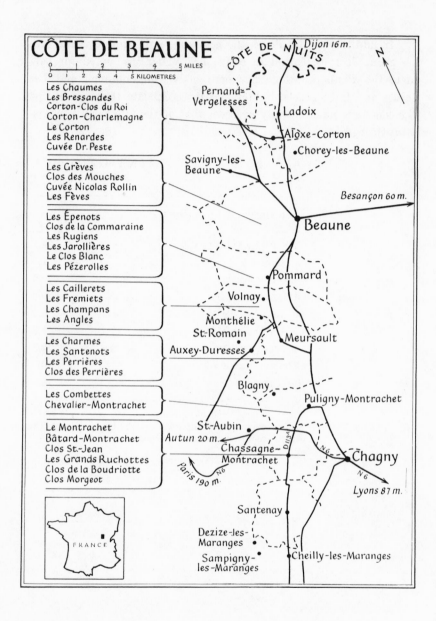

CÔTE DE BEAUNE

0 1 2 3 4 5 MILES
0 1 2 3 4 5 KILOMETRES

Les Chaumes
Les Bressandes
Corton-Clos du Roi
Corton-Charlemagne
Le Corton
Les Renardes
Cuvée Dr. Peste

Les Grèves
Clos des Mouches
Cuvée Nicolas Rollin
Les Fèves

Les Épenots
Clos de la Commaraine
Les Rugiens
Les Jarollières
Le Clos Blanc
Les Pézerolles

Les Caillerets
Les Fremiets
Les Champans
Les Angles

Les Charmes
Les Santenots
Les Perrières
Clos des Perrières

Les Combettes
Chevalier-Montrachet

Le Montrachet
Bâtard-Montrachet
Clos St.-Jean
Les Grands Ruchottes
Clos de la Boudriotte
Clos Morgeot

FRANCE

CÔTE DE NUITS
Dijon 16 m.
N

Pernand-
Vergelesses
Ladoix
Aloxe-Corton
Chorey-les-Beaune

Savigny-les-
Beaune

Besançon 60 m.

Beaune

Pommard

Volnay

Monthélie
St.-Romain
Meursault

Auxey-Duresses

Blagny

Puligny-Montrachet

St.-Aubin
Autun 20 m.
Chassagne-
Montrachet
D 113A
N 6
Chagny

Paris 190 m.

N 6
N 6
Lyons 87 m.

Santenay

Dezize-les-
Maranges
Cheilly-les-Maranges

Sampigny-
les-Maranges

CÔTE DE BEAUNE:
Famous Reds and Montrachet

T he vineyards of the Côte de Beaune begin below the limestone quarry where the Côte de Nuits leaves off and continue on below Santenay, some fifteen miles in all. Most of the wines are red, getting steadily lighter in color, smell, and taste until you reach Meursault. The name Meursault is derived from the Latin for mouse-jump, where red wines and white wines are produced in adjacent vineyards, only the jump of a mouse apart.

Beaune, the barrel city and wine capital of the Côte d'Or, with a population of some ten thousand, gives its name to the slope stretching above and below it. It is an old, walled town, full of shippers and their cellars, and the homes of the proprietors of many of the surrounding vineyards. Burgundians say that when the wine is in the vineyard, you must be a good lover, and when it's in the barrel, you must be a good father. Beaune, especially, is a town full of wine fathers, anxiously watching their barrels.

One of the town fathers was Georges Yard, who owned part of Les Bressandes, a *Tête de Cuvée* of Corton, one of the best red wines of the Beaune Slope. Yard got into the art of wine-making because his father fell in love with Corton, moved down from Paris, and bought one of the vineyards that make it, perhaps to ensure a steady supply for himself. He gave the vineyard to his son, and during the harvest spent most of his time prowling around the vines, watching the grapes suspiciously.

In the old days the local lord set the day when the vineyards could be harvested, seeing to it that his own were finished first, there always being a shortage of pickers at harvest time. The monks, of course, outside the control of civil law, paid no attention to these edicts, and harvest time was one long glorious battle to get workers. It used to be fashionable for Parisians to go down to Burgundy for the harvest. The *vendange* is still a gay affair, the thirsty pickers drinking much new wine, for the sun is hot in the vineyards.

Today a board of vintners sets the dates for the picking of the grapes. Most vintners like to wait as long as possible after the permitted date, so that the grapes will contain as much sugar as possible. This is a risky time. Hail can destroy the whole crop, and even a high wind can knock the ripe grapes off the vines.

"Sometimes we're up all night," said Yard. "At the last possible moment I give the order, and the workers start combing the rows, bringing the bunches to the head of the rows in baskets, where men load them into bigger baskets, then dump them into trucks and haul them to the vats. Mine are right downstairs."

Yard owned a house in the business section of Beaune, looking like any city house anywhere, wall to wall with the houses beside it. A garage door opens into a large room, two stories high, and on one side are the vats, two of them a dozen feet high, flanked by a large screw press, and the *égrapilloir*. Beneath are the cellars.

"A ripe grape has a bloom on the skin," Yard explained. "It looks like dust, and you can wipe it off with your finger. The bloom is made up of ferments, containing yeasts. Nobody knows why they should cling to grapeskins, but they do, and one of them, *Saccharomyces ellipsoideus,* helps change the sugar in the grape to alcohol. The stalk of the grape is full of tannin, and when the grapes don't have enough tannin themselves, some of the stalks are allowed to stay in the crushed grapes during the early fermentation. This usually takes four or five days here in Burgundy. After pressing, the juice is run into vats, where it continues fermenting. This is usually over in a week and the wine is then drawn off into barrels.

"What's left in the press may be distilled, the result being called marc."

Yard spoke of this pressing as a simple process. It is not. The sugar content of the grapes should produce at least 11½ per cent alcohol after ferment, and can produce as high as 14 or 15 per cent. The more alcohol, the better, for this helps determine the keeping quality of the wine. Also, fermentation is a heating process, which varies with the amount of alcohol, and the temperature must be carefully controlled. In the vats the liquid seethes and bubbles, sometimes quite violently.

"It is when the wine is in the *cuves* that we can get an idea of whether it's going to be any good or not. Before then, it's a matter of hopes and guesses.

"Once the wine is in the barrel, its life begins. Quite literally.

The wine is full of organisms, and these cells grow, changing the wine. Once it's in the casks, all we can do is guide it, and try to keep it from getting sick."

In addition to the cells that help the wine to grow are many chemical actions that help to kill it. F. C. Lloyd, in his book *The Art and Technique of Wine,* lists five that have been clearly identified, and there are many others. *Acescence* fills the wine with specks of matter that change the alcohol into vinegar; *tourne* changes the wine to brown or purple, tiny bubbles appear on the surface, and the wine tastes as if it were watered; if the wine is low in alcohol or tannin, *graisse* destroys the unconverted sugar, and the wine tastes flat; *amertume* makes the wine bitter; *casse* makes it cloudy.

Yard used to shake his head at all the dire evils that can affect the wine. "The big thing is the change to alcohol," he said. "During ferment, the grape sugar is transformed to carbon dioxide and alcohol. In 1947 there was so much alcohol that the wines were too difficult to handle. The alcohol can chloroform the ferments, and too much paralyzes them. Chances were you would get one very great barrel of wine, but two others would be terrible. I sold all my '47's to the shippers. There was no way of counting on the wine. You couldn't trust it."

Yard used to worry about his great red wines, and all during the five days or so of ferment they had to be watched closely, checked every hour or so. This was easier for him than for most, because his apartment was on the top floor of the building, above the vats and the equipment.

It is a different matter for Claude and Pierre Ramonet, who live in Chassagne-Montrachet and own sections of the *Premiers Crus,* Ruchottes and Morgeot. Their father came to the Côte de Beaune in the nineteenth century and bought a small parcel of Ruchottes, and the two sons have gradually increased the holding through the years. The Ramonets make red and white wine, and their *cuves* are under various houses in the neighborhood.

"We were up all night as long as the '47's were in the *cuves,*" says Claude Ramonet. "Nobody around here has ever seen anything like it. The alcohol was 15 per cent, and some of it even a little more. We had to hold down the covers of the *cuves,* which were only half full. Usually we fill them to within a foot of the top, but the wine was so active we had to sit on it to keep it down."

It often happens, particularly as in 1947, that the wine contains so much sugar that it cannot all be changed to alcohol, the alcohol itself stopping the fermentation. This ruins the wine. Fermentation can be speeded up by heating, and one of the first processes in making wine is to get the *caves* to the right temperature, for the wine has a second ferment once it is in the barrel. In the making of white wines, which differs from the making of red, the presence of excessive sugar in the wine, coupled with lack of acidity, causes it to turn brown when the air gets at it, and the wine becomes what is called maderized or oxidized.

"In making the white wine, when white grapes are used, they're pressed before fermentation starts; to make white wines from red grapes, as in Champagne, the juice does not remain in contact with the skins. By removing the skins you can make a white wine out of the same grapes you use to make red, although we use Pinot Chardonnay instead of Pinot Noir. To make *vin rosé*, you leave the skins of red grapes in the must for a time, then fish them out. *Rosé* wine is also made by blending red and white wine, but it's not the same thing."

For Ramonet, as well as many of the other vintners up and down both *côtes,* wine-making doesn't end until the wine is in the bottle. The wine changes and develops in the barrel, reaching what is called the point of fermentation three times a year. These coincide with the growth of the vine, occurring when new tendrils sprout, when the flower blossoms, and when the grapes are harvested. The seasons act on the barreled wine in exactly the same ways they act on the grapes. This point of fermentation can be tasted in the wine, and it is at these times that adverse chemical reactions are most likely to take place.

Once bottled, the wine is known as *vin vieux,* "old wine," and it begins a life of its own, some air getting into the wine through the cork and enabling the wine bacteria to continue developing. Once the wine is in the bottle, the vintners can do nothing about it, and while they watch the wine as it ages, hoping for the best, they feel a certain remoteness toward it.

In Burgundy, wine is made neither for profit nor for entirely and purely altruistic purposes. Making wine is something inevitable and irresistible, and it is not merely because of the endless risks that vintners are realistic. The making of wine is absorbing, and the vintners know it.

ALOXE-CORTON AND
PERNAND-VERGELESSES

The finest red wine of the Côte de Beaune, comparable to some from
the Côte de Nuits, comes from the vineyards around the little town of
Aloxe (pronounced "Aloss," for no good reason). It is reached by
driving in from the highway, and from here the vineyard road
meanders down to Beaune. Up the slope behind Aloxe is the little
town of Pernand, whose claim to distinction is that it is the most
primitive of all hamlets along the Côte d'Or. Its neighbors call it
culterreux. On the label the great vineyard name of Corton precedes
the names of the other fine vineyards, such as Corton-Bressandes and
Corton-Charlemagne. The great wines take the name of the greatest
vineyard and not the commune name.

A good vineyard of Aloxe is Le Corton, the principal owners of
which are the excellent shipping firms of Louis Latour, thought by
many to be the best shipper in Burgundy. Thévenot and the Prince
de Mérode also make excellent wines. On a par with this vineyard is
Les Bressandes, Dubreuil-Fontaine and Thévenot being the principal
owners. Sometimes better than these two, and perhaps more famous,
is Clos du Roi, the principal owners of which are Baron Thénard and
Thévenot. The Hospice de Beaune sells the wine from five parcels in
Aloxe, the equivalent of six hundred cases in 1967, under the names
"Charlotte Dumay," who donated the parcels to the hospice, and
"Cuvée Dr. Peste."

Voltaire loved the wines of Corton and attributed his longevity
to them. Swept with enthusiasm, he wrote to the owner of Château
Corton: "Your wine has become a necessity to me. I give a very good
Beaujolais to my guests from Geneva, but, in secret, I drink your
Corton."

The Clos du Roi was planted by the last Duke of Burgundy,
Charles the Fearless, in 1477. Originally a pond, the land was filled
and planted with vines from ducal lands, and eventually became part
of the royal domain of the kings of France, hence the name.

The red Cortons age faster than wines of the Côte de Nuits,
but are the slowest-maturing of all the red wines of the Beaune
Slope. Their outstanding characteristic is a beautiful balance, by far
the best of all the Côte de Beaune reds, wines that have a delicacy
combined with strength, which makes them a true transition wine
between the sturdier wines to the north and the lighter wines to the
south.

Charlemagne was an early owner of those vineyards that bear

his name, which produce white wines. He gave his vineyards to the Abbot of Saulieu, and the subsequent dukes of Burgundy and kings of France followed the custom, bestowing their vineyards on other monasteries. In the 1500's, war, brigandage, and plague forced the local inhabitants to flee, and the Church could no longer tend the vines. A Beaune innkeeper named Charles leased the lands from the Church and for many years served the wines in his inn. By the seventeenth century the great holdings were divided up, and several of them eventually passed into the hands of the Hospices in Beaune.

The white wine from Corton-Charlemagne is one of the great Burgundies. Less known than Chablis and the Côte de Beaune white wines, it can be classed with Montrachet in great years. Harder and perhaps more steely than the softer white Meursaults, it is a rare wine because production is small. The wines of Corton-Charlemagne, which must be made out of Chardonnay grapes, are big and golden in color. Some connoisseurs assert that they can identify the perfume of cinnamon in the wine.

Like Gaul, the vineyard is divided into three parts, nearly half of the best section belonging to Louis Latour, who is proud of his possession and makes excellent wine from its grapes. Another excellent shipper is Louis Jadot. The rest is owned by some half-dozen

ALOXE-CORTON

Outstanding Vineyards (*Têtes de Cuvées*)	Acres
Les BRESSANDES	42.5
Le CORTON	28.
Le CLOS DU ROI	26.
CORTON-CHARLEMAGNE	42.5
Les RENARDES	37.5
Les Chaumes	6.

The great white wine is CORTON-CHARLEMAGNE. Pinot Chardonnay, however, is planted in small parts of the following vineyards:

Le CORTON

Les Pougets

Note: Names listed in capitals indicate vineyards whose wines are likely to be imported into the United States. The others are not at present imported.

superb growers, the largest of whom makes only two hundred cases, while the smallest makes but fourteen, or one *feuillette,* which is half of a Burgundy *pièce.* This famous wine is slowly decreasing in quantity, largely because the vineyard is so difficult to tend. Its slope is as steep as many of those in Chablis, and it must be worked without the aid of teams. After every rain the dirt must be hauled back up the slope on the backs of men. Old growers complain that their sons don't love the wine enough to do the work, and the great wine may soon disappear.

Formerly the lesser sections of Corton-Charlemagne could be planted in the cheaper and coarser Aligoté grapes. This, however, is no longer permitted.

The firm of Louis Latour sells a fine wine from the unclassified vineyard called Corton-Grancey, whose name has become a trademark. The outstanding wine of Pernand is the red wine from the vineyard of Iles des Vergelesses, whose character is similar to that of the red Cortons.

BEAUNE

The vineyard road, which runs down from Aloxe-Corton, leads straight into the town of Beaune, for it was in Beaune that most of the wines from the surrounding slopes were sold. Today much of it still is, by the firms of shippers and through the annual auction at the local charity hospital, the famous Hospice de Beaune.

Beaune is a wine town, proud and wealthy because of the fact. The city is tunneled with wine cellars, and even the old town walls have been turned into storage places for wine. For the tourist, Beaune is a quaint little town full of buildings in a jumble of styles, with a pleasant square where there is a restaurant serving fair food, and several curio shops where you can buy miniature barrels and other souvenirs suggestive of wine. For the wine-buyer, Beaune is crowded with shippers, and it is hard to learn which are good, or even which are real firms, for the phone book lists several company names under one number. A good firm, as often as not, may have its name aped by a bad one, as closely as is legal. Underneath all this, however, is the sincere and honest love for the great wines of Burgundy. In Beaune, one is always aware that wine is not merely a curiosity, or a product for exploitation, but a glorious addition to good living. Burgundians love their wine, and Beaune is its capital.

The Hospices de Beaune, the heart of the city, is quite properly near the center of town, just off the main square. The Hospice, which is crowded into the midst of other old buildings, presents a stern, four-story facade to the street. An archway leads through the building into the main court, and above the entrance is an ornate, ninety-foot steeple, projecting out over the sidewalk and unsupported by a tower. It has been there for several hundred years and shows no signs of crashing, in spite of its lack of underpinning. The building is in medieval Flemish style, translated to Burgundy, and the steeple was the model for the Sainte-Chapelle in Paris.

In the immense and cobbled courtyard, steep, slanting roofs come down over the balconies, their colored slates laid in patterns of yellow and green and black—the traditional Burgundian roof. It is here that the wine auctions are held, usually on the third Sunday in November. The bidding on each lot, or *queue*, lasts until a measured bit of candle has burned down to the mark. On the Saturday before the sale, bidders taste the wines from the barrels, which are kept in the cellars beneath a smaller inner courtyard. The prices paid are a barometer of what the vintage is worth, and of its quality, and buyers come from all over the world to attend the auction.

The tasting for the auction is usually the first chance outsiders have to analyze the vintage. Often the wine is still fermenting, making judgment difficult. There are always more buyers than barrels; hence the bidding is high, and although the Hospice owns vineyards only in the Côte de Beaune, the wines and prices are a basis for judging all those of the Côte d'Or. The prices, which are usually ridiculously high, are justifiable only by the fact that the proceeds go to charity.

Much of the wine goes to European restaurant-owners, for every good restaurateur likes to boast that he has wine of the Hospice, just as American chop houses boast of serving only blue-ribbon steers. Shippers buy many of the barrels for much the same reason, for it is a mark of honor to have your name printed in the list of buyers published shortly after the auction. The wines are taken away by the buyers after the sale, and some suffer from inept handling, particularly after the barrels leave the country, an argument for estate-bottling by the Hospice.

The Hospice was founded fifty years before Columbus discovered America, by the tax collector under Louis XI, Nicolas Rollin, of whom it was said that he could well afford to donate a charitable institution to the poor because he had made so many of them. Its entire income derives from the sale of its wines, which have been auctioned annually for a century. The various vineyards under its control throughout the Côte de Beaune were donated to the Hospice. Its scattered parcels total a little more than 125 acres, about the size of Clos de Vougeot. The wine is always sold under the name of the donor and not under the name of the vineyard. The wines are not uniform, because they come from all over the Côte de Beaune, and while many are overpriced, there is some consolation in the fact that all the money goes to support the sick and the poor.

The vineyards of the commune of Beaune and of its satellite Savigny-les-Beaune are among the largest of the Côte d'Or. There are nearly 2,500 acres of classified vineyards, and more planted in Pinot Noir than in any other commune. The best wines come from several smaller vineyards owned by the Hospice.

Beaune wines are characterized by softness and lightness, pastels after the brilliant primary colors from the Côte de Nuits. The wines have less pronounced characteristics than those from the Nuits Slope. Among the best vineyards are: Les Fèves, which is noted for its finesse and delicate aroma; Les Grèves, which has more body and is therefore more velvety; and Clos des Mouches, also noted for body, and called *"très élégant"* by the local growers. Part of the vineyard of Clos des Mouches, which is near the commune boundary of Pommard, is planted in white grapes. A white wine is made from them by the excellent shipping firm of Joseph Drouhin.

Drouhin, an honest shipper with fine cellars that are old stone quarries built by the Romans, was a liaison officer attached to General MacArthur in the First World War. He was wounded in combat and was awarded the Distinguished Service Cross. He was one of the directors of the Hospices de Beaune, and also controls the sale of that portion of Montrachet owned by the Marquis de Laguiche.

Beaune wines that are not sufficiently good to carry a vineyard name are sold simply as Beaune. For the better wines, the town name precedes the vineyard name, such as Beaune Clos-des-Mouches or Beaune Bressandes. The last is a vineyard different from Bressandes in Aloxe-Corton. Some of the *cuvées* of Beaune-Grèves are sold as Beaune-Grèves de l'Enfant Jésus. The name comes from a favorite Burgundy expression for wines that are easy to drink: "wines that go down as easily as a little Jesus in velvet pants." It is used without any feeling of sacrilege or rancor.

In these wines of the Côte de Beaune, *Têtes de Cuvées* are not so important, there being relatively slight differences between the best growths. Beaune wines should be less expensive than those from the

BEAUNE

Outstanding Vineyards (*Têtes de Cuvées*)	Acres
Les FÈVES	11.
Les GRÈVES	79.5
Les MARCONNETS	25.5
Les BRESSANDES	46.
Le CLOS DES MOUCHES	62.
Aux Cras (or Crais)	12.5
Les Champimonts	41.5
Le Clos de la Mousse	8.5

First Vineyards (*Premières Cuvées*)

A L'ÈCU	8.
Sur-les-GRÈVES	11.5
CLOS DU ROI	35.
En Genêt	12.5
Les Perrières	8.
Les Cent-Vignes	58.
Les Toussaints	16.
Le Bas-des-Teurons	18.
Les Teurons	39.
Aux Coucherias	56.5
Blanche-Fleur	23.
Les Chilènes	42.5
Les Epenottes	34.
Les Boucherottes	22.
Les Vignes-Franches	25.
Les Aigrots	35.7
Pertuisots	14.
Les Sizies	21.
Les Avaux	33.5
Chaume-Gaufriot	48.
Montée-Rouge	41.5
Les Montrevenots	20.

Note: Names listed in capitals indicate vineyards whose wines are likely to be imported into the United States. The others are not at present imported.

Côte de Nuits and from Aloxe-Corton. The exceptions are the wines
sold at auction by the Hospice, especially those from its prize *Cuvée*,
named after the founder, Nicolas Rollin. This wine usually fetches
the highest prices of all Burgundies, with perhaps the exception of
Romanée-Conti.

All Côte de Beaune wines mature early, and few of them are
considered *vins de garde,* wines to be laid away in the cellar. The
wines of the commune of Beaune from the 1959 vintage, for instance,
are now definitely ready to drink.

PRINCIPAL CUVÉES
OF THE HOSPICES DE BEAUNE

The year-to-year variance in the quantity of the wines produced
from the 125 acres of the Hospices de Beaune is demonstrated in the
official figures issued by the committee in charge of the auction sales
at the charity institution.

RED WINES

No. of *Pièces* Produced and Sold			
1966	1967	Appellation	Cuvées
34	28	*Beaune*	Guigone de Salins
41	35	*Beaune*	Clos des Avaux
41	29	*Beaune*	Nicolas Rollin
33	27	*Beaune*	Hugues et Louis Bétault
21	16	*Beaune*	Dames Hospitalières
24	31	*Beaune*	Pierre Virely
27	14	*Beaune*	Estienne
28	16	*Beaune*	Brunet
34	27	*Beaune*	Rousseau-Deslandes
26	22	*Pommard*	Dames de la Charité
36	30	*Pommard*	Billardet
25	16	*Savigny-les-Beaune and Vergelesses*	Fouquerand
30	26	*Savigny-les-Beaune and Vergelesses*	Forneret

RED WINES *(continued)*

No. of *Pièces*
Produced and Sold

1966	1967	Appellation	Cuvées
34	28	*Savigny-les-Beaune*	Arthur Girard
31	32	*Corton*	Charlotte Dumay
32	29	*Corton*	Dr. Peste
13	11	*Volnay (Santenots)*	Jehan de Massol
25	22	*Volnay (Santenots)*	Gauvain
29	22	*Volnay*	Général Muteau
30	27	*Volnay*	Blondeau
9	4	*Auxey-Duresses*	Boillot
16	11	*Monthélie*	Jacques Lebelin
29	25	*Beaune*	Maurice Drouhin
5	4	*Pernand*	Rameau-Lamarosse

WHITE WINES

No. of *Pièces*
Produced and Sold

1966	1967	Appellation	Cuvées
13	13	*Meursault*	Loppin
9	0	*Meursault*	Jehan Humblot
5	9	*Meursault-Genevrières*	Baudot
13	5	*Meursault*	Goureau
9	7	*Meursault-Charmes*	Albert Grivault
8	0	*Meursault-Charmes*	de Bahèzre de Lanlay
3	3	*Corton-Charlemagne*	François de Salins
9	6	*Meursault-Genevrières*	Philippe-le-Bon

Most of the wines are sold under the name of the donor. The holdings of the Hospice are somewhat scattered all over the Côte de Beaune.

The best wines are sold in barrel when less than two months old, and the lesser wines are distilled into eau-de-vie de Marc de Bourgogne. In 1966 the Hospice sold 643 *pièces* [1] of red wine, and 89 *pièces* of white wine, besides 29 hectoliters, or roughly 750 gallons, of eau-de-vie de Marc. In 1967 the Hospice sold 534 *pièces* of red wine, 43 *pièces* of white wine, and in addition 12 hectoliters, amounting to some 310 gallons of eau-de-vie de Marc. This illustrates how widely quantity of sale can vary.

POMMARD

South of Beaune the Golden Slope begins to rise somewhat, crooking to the west, so that the vineyards have a more southerly exposure. The slope of the land is less abrupt here, and the highway branches off to Pommard, running beside the walled vineyards whose wines bear the name of the handsome village.

Through a pass in the hills behind Pommard flow the headwaters of the Dheune River, to be channeled between thick stone walls as the stream flows through the town. Its canal runs along beside the main street. The water gurgles against the stones, sliding swiftly under the squat, arched bridges overhung with tall trees. Pommard is a town full of sunlight, greenery, mossy stone, and the sound of flowing water.

One of the handsomest buildings in Burgundy is the Château de la Commaraine, built in the twelfth century. It is a simple rectangular mass, with two square pyramids of tower at each end, low roofs of outbuildings extending on either side. The vineyard starts at the back door, looking like an immense lawn in summer, deep and green. Its owner is M. Jaboulet-Vercherre, one of Burgundy's most hospitable hosts.

The Pommard vineyards begin less than half a mile from Beaune and, like those of its sister commune, are among the largest in Burgundy. The wines are sturdier than those from Beaune and are apt to keep better. They are lighter in body and texture than those from the Côte de Nuits, unless chaptalized, the addition of sugar giving more body and slightly higher alcoholic content. Some

---

[1] A *pièce* contains approximately 288 bottles, or 24 to 25 cases of 12 bottles each.

Burgundy shippers overchaptalize their Pommards, a regrettable practice that does away with the typical characteristics of the wine. As in Beaune and Nuits-Saint-Georges, the town name always precedes the vineyard name on a wine label.

Pommard is probably the best-known of all Burgundies, not only because its name is easy to remember, but because the big vine-

POMMARD

Outstanding Vineyards (*Têtes de Cuvées*)	Acres
Les ÉPENOTS	26.
Les RUGIENS-BAS	15.
Le Clos Blanc	11.

First Vineyards (*Premières Cuvées*)	
La PLATIÈRE	14.5
Les PÉZEROLLES	16.
Les PETITS-ÉPENOTS	51.
Les RUGIENS-HAUTS	19.
CLOS DE LA COMMARAINE	10.
La Chanière	25.
Les Arvelets	21.
Charmots	8.9
Les Charmots	9.
Les Argillières	9.
Les Saussilles	9.5
Le Clos Micot	7.
Les Combes-Dessus	7.
Les Fremiers	12.5
Les Bertins	9.
Les Poutures	11.
Les Croix-Noires	11.
Les CHAPPONIÈRES	8.
Les JAROLLIÈRES	8.
Les Chanlins-Bas	18.
Village de Pommard	65.

Note: Names listed in capitals indicate vineyards whose wines are likely to be imported into the United States. The others are not at present imported.

yards produce a great deal of wine. The wines from Les Épenots are soft and round, with a good bouquet; those from Les Rugiens are considered the firmest of all Pommards; those from Les Argillières are the lightest.

The wines of Pommard are the most abused as far as frauds go, probably because they are more famous than most. Pommard gained its great fame in the seventeenth century, when it was spread by thousands of French Protestants who left the region to find religious freedom. But its great fame led to fraud, especially in European countries, where wine is exported in barrels, and where a barrel of ordinary wine can become Pommard overnight. In the United States any fraudulent Pommards must come to us in bottles, for importation of barrels is impractical because of duties.

VOLNAY AND MONTHÉLIE

Volnay is less than a mile below Pommard, the vineyard road cutting straight through Les Rugiens-Bas and Jaroillières and into the commune. Higher up on the slope, from Volnay rooftops you can see the vineyards stretching north to Beaune and south to Meursault, an almost unbroken stretch of green. Farther up behind the town, from the terrace belonging to the Marquis d'Angerville, one of the principal owners, you can see across the whole Burgundian valley and sometimes as far as the snow-capped Jurals.

The land is somewhat rolling here, some vineyards being more exposed than others, so that certain sections are now and then endangered by frost, while others are undamaged. Because of the frosts, and also as insurance against hail, which strikes in scattered areas, the vineyards are much parceled. Attempts have been made to use smudge pots and to disperse storm clouds with cannon, but these have been only slightly successful. Volnay takes its name from the ancient goddess of hidden springs, and today's vintners are as likely to appeal to her as to smudge pots.

Volnay wines are extremely pleasant, round and light, yet with a fine bouquet. Their bouquet is the most pronounced of all the wines of the Côte de Beaune, excepting the Cortons. They are lighter in color than the wines of Beaune and Pommard, perhaps the most agreeable wines of the Beaune Slope. Because of their perfume, that first fresh whiff you notice after opening the bottle, and because of their flowery bouquet, the more lasting aroma, they could be called the Musignys of the Côte de Beaune. Volnays mature rapidly, but an

VOLNAY

Outstanding Vineyards (*Têtes de Cuvées*)	Acres
Les CAILLERETS	36.
Les CHAMPANS	28.
Les FREMIETS	16.
SANTENOTS	20.
Les Angles	9.

First Vineyards (*Premières Cuvées*)	
Les CHEVRETS	15.
CLOS DES DUCS	6.
La Gigotte	9.
Grands-Champs	17.5
Les Brouillards	17.
Les Mitans	10.
L'Ormeau	11.
Les Pointes-d'Angles	3.
Pitures-Dessus	9.
Chanlin	10.
Carelles-Dessous	5
En Ronceret	5.
Les Aussy	7.5
Les Lurets	21.
Robardelle	10.5
Carelle-sous-la-Chapelle	9.5
Les Clos des Chênes	41.
Taille-Pieds	18.
En Verseuil	2.
Village-de-Volnay	32.5
La Barre	3.
La Pousse-d'Or	5.

Note: Names listed in capitals indicate vineyards whose wines are likely to be imported into the United States. The others are not at present imported.

old Volnay from a good grower is a wine of fine balance, flavor, and bouquet.

Volnay's best vineyard is Les Caillerets, and there is an old French saying that the vintner who doesn't have vines in Caillerets doesn't have Volnay. Another saying about Volnay comes originally from old Latin: "You can't be gay without drinking Volnay." It sounds better in French: *"On ne peut être gai sans boire du Volnay."*

The vineyards date from the Gallo-Roman period, and relics are often found in them. In the old days, from the thirteenth to the seventeenth century, Volnay and Pommard made a gray-pink wine called *vin de paille,* one of the most famous of the ancient wines. The grapes were laid on straw mats to dry before being pressed. In those days more white Chardonnay was planted than Pinot Noir, giving the wine its color and its name, "partridge's eye," *œil de perdrix.*

Just south of Volnay, off to the right and up a small dirt road, is the tiny village of Monthélie. Its wines can occasionally be found, and because they are much less known than Volnay, they are much cheaper. They are lesser wines, failing to reach the high quality of the fine Volnays.

Still farther south is the village of Auxey-Duresses, whose wines can also be found now and then. Both red and white wines are made, and the red Cuvée Boillot is auctioned off by the Hospices de Beaune. The wines are on a par with those of Monthélie.

MEURSAULT

Below Volnay, *La Route des Grands Crus* begins to pass through the vineyards of Meursault, the hills rising fairly steeply above the sloping land. The town itself is an old one, a strong garrison having been quartered there during the Roman occupation, and some of the vineyards were planted then. Meursault is a wealthy town, and the streets leading out from its central square pass solid stone houses.

In the square is the country hotel and inn called Le Chevreuil, one of the few to be found in the small Burgundy towns, where some of the lesser local wines can be drunk with such specialties as hot *terrine de lapin* and *escargots.* The Château de Meursault is just outside of town in a spacious park, owned by Comte de Moucheron, a proprietor of several vineyards and also a shipper.

The best wines of Meursault are white, and the Hospices de Beaune owns several vineyards of them, auctioned as the following *cuvées:* Bahèzre de Lanlay, Jehan Humblot, Loppin, Goureau, Baudot, and Albert Grivault. Meursault has its own hospice, founded in the twelfth century, its gate on the main highway just below the town.

A great bottle of Meursault is a symbol of great hardship as well as great joy, for the vineyards are hard to tend. A custom still exists, called *La Paulée*, a rest taken by the vineyard workers in the middle of the day, the name perhaps derived from the Greek *paula*, which means "rest." A newer custom was begun in 1922 by Comte Lafon, one of the patriarchs of the town, a great lover of Burgundies, and an extensive vineyard-owner in Meursault as well as in Montrachet and Volnay. He began giving a yearly dinner for some three hundred growers and shippers following the sale of the wines of the Hospices

MEURSAULT
WHITE WINES

Outstanding Vineyards (*Têtes de Cuvées*)	Acres
CLOS DES PERRIÈRES and Les PERRIÈRES	42.5

First Vineyards (*Premières Cuvées*)	
LES GENEVRIÈRES (Dessus & Dessous)	42.5
Les CHARMES	68.
SANTENOTS	Varies *
Sous-BLAGNY	5.5
Les Bouchères	10.5
La GOUTTE D'OR	14.
Le Porusot-Dessus	4.4
La Pièce-sous-le-Bois	28.
Sous le Dos d'Âne	13.3
La Jennelotte	12.

Note: Names listed in capitals indicate vineyards whose wines are likely to be imported into the United States. The others are not at present imported.

* Most of the good red wines are permitted to be sold as Volnay. Some Santenots is planted in white-wine vines, the small area varying in size.

de Beaune. Each person brought his own wines, and the Comte donated a barrel of his best Meursault as a prize for the best book written that year on Burgundy wines. The Comte died during the war, and a token award is still made, but it is no longer a barrel of Meursault.

In Burgundy the three greatest feasts following the sales at the Hospices de Beaune, of which *La Paulée,* a lunch bringing together the winegrowers, is one, are called *Les Trois Glorieuses.* One is held in the cellars of the Hospice, another in the vat rooms of the Clos de Vougeot.

The white wines of Meursault are among the greatest of white Burgundies, somewhat softer, slightly less powerful, and perhaps less distinctive than the Corton-Charlemagnes or Montrachets. The wines are dry, though somewhat less so than steely Chablis, and are delicate and perfumed, with a color that is like straw.

The best vineyard today is Les Perrières, the principal owners of the forty-three acres being the heirs of Mme Grivault, Comtesse Lafon, and two men named Ampeau and Matrot. Its finest section is the Clos des Perrières, owned by the heirs of Mme Grivault.

Matrot is also an outstanding owner in the other top vineyard, Charmes, and in the section known as Blagny.

The red wines are full, with plenty of bouquet, and the best-known vineyards are Les Santenots (sold as Volnays), Les Cras, and Les Petures, part of this last producing some white wines. The red wines are good, but not in a class with the excellent whites.

PULIGNY AND ITS MONTRACHET

Just below Meursault lies the village of Puligny. The vineyard road swings into the town square and then out past some of the greatest vineyards in the world, those which produce what has been called "divine Montrachet."

The great vineyards, up behind the town, are walled in along the road. Square stone arches every dozen yards or so lead into the various parcels. On the right is the great Montrachet, with Chevalier up the slope behind it, and beside this is the vineyard that used to be called Les Demoiselles. Across the road are Bâtard-Montrachet, Bienvenue-Bâtard-Montrachet, and Criots-Bâtard-Montrachet, and there were so many jokes about the Chevalier and the Demoiselles that the latter's name was changed to Cailleret some years ago, a word that means to curdle or clot. The intimation is said to be that the jokes were so bad that the wine was turned to vinegar.

The Montrachets are the greatest of all white Burgundies, and one of the greatest white wines in the world. The greatest is Montrachet itself, whose nineteen acres produce around one thousand cases in a good year—nowhere near enough to meet world demand. As a result, much fraudulent Montrachet is sold, and for no other wine is it more important to know the names of the owners.

It is more difficult to make white wine than red, and some owners hire experts to tend the vineyards. These men receive half the yield as their share for doing the work. This system is called *mie-fruit,* and though the expert's name may not appear on the vineyard deeds, it will appear on the label of the bottle as a stamp of authenticity. For such great wines, only estate-bottlings should be bought.

The largest holdings are as follows: the Marquis de Laguiche, Baron Thénard, Bouchard Père & Fils, Mme Boillereault de Chauvigné, Prieur, Comte de Moucheron, Fleurot-Larose, and Lafon.

PULIGNY-MONTRACHET

Outstanding Vineyards (*Têtes de Cuvées*)	Acres
CHEVALIER-MONTRACHET (in totality)	15.5
BÂTARD-MONTRACHET (in part; see village of Chassagne)	24.
BIENVENUE-BÂTARD-MONTRACHET	6
MONTRACHET (in part; there are an additional nine acres in the village of Chassagne)	10.

First Vineyards (*Premières Cuvées*)	
Les COMBETTES	17.
BLAGNY BLANC	11.
Le CHAMP-CANET (a part is classified as 2ème Cuvée)	11.5
Les PUCELLES	16.5
Les CHALUMEAUX	17.5

Note: Names listed in capitals indicate vineyards whose wines are likely to be imported into the United States. The others are not at present imported.

Bavard is *mie-fruit* with Mme Boillereault de Chauvigné. Milan is the new proud owner. An excellent producer up to 1948 named Roizot owned a portion, which was sold to a shipper at a price higher than that of any white Burgundy vineyard on record.

It is a great honor to own part of the vineyard that produces the prototype of all great white Burgundies. Ownership is a sign of wine nobility.

Baron Thénard, whose cellars are in Givry, down in the Chalonnais, was chairman of the board of St. Gobain, France's greatest glass trust, which makes most of France's wine bottles. He was the owner of Dijon's largest paper, and yet he asserted that he was proudest of his small slice of Montrachet, that it was his most prized possession.

The little town is handicapped by a lack of cellars, for an underground stream prevents digging them. These are necessary for coolness, which helps keep the pale green color of the wine.

The lack of deep cellars makes wine-making difficult, a further reason for selectivity for without the protecting coolness, the wine may have a tendency to maderize.

Chevalier-Montrachet is the best vineyard after Montrachet itself, a third of which is over the line in the commune of Chassagne. Bâtard-Montrachet ranks next. The other vineyards produce superb white wines, and sometimes a better-made wine from a lesser vineyard can be compared with the great Montrachet. This tiny bit of soil, whose stone wall gives it the look of a cemetery, produces what many believe to be the greatest white wine on earth.

CHASSAGNE-MONTRACHET AND SANTENAY

The vineyard road cuts across the main Paris-Riviera highway a few yards from Montrachet and immediately enters the backward little cluster of stone buildings called Chassagne, which has also pegged the famous wine to its name. Although only a third of Montrachet is in the commune, the inhabitants of the town are proud of what they have, and the two local owners of small parcels are looked to with respect.

Most of the vineyards are to the south of town, and are underclassified by the *Appellations d'Origine* laws. The classification is now being reviewed. The best vineyard producing white wines is Les Ruchottes, whose principal owner is Claude Ramonet, an impeccable wine-maker. Fifteen growers own portions of Bâtard-Montrachet, and while that vineyard is considered better than Les Ruchottes, Ramonet's wines often equal and sometimes excel some of those from Bâtard-Montrachet.

The wines of Chassagne have an unmistakable flavor. They are

CHASSAGNE-MONTRACHET
WHITE WINES

Outstanding Vineyards (*Têtes de Cuvées*)	Acres
Bâtard-Montrachet (in part; see village of Puligny)	14.4
Montrachet (in part; see village of Puligny)	9.
Criots-Bâtard-Montrachet	4.

First Vineyards (*Premières Cuvées*)	
Les Grandes ruchottes	7.5
Morgeot	9.75
Les Caillerets	15.

RED WINES

Outstanding Vineyards (*Têtes de Cuvées*)	
Clos Saint-Jean	36.
Clos de la Boudriotte	5.
Les Boudriottes	40.
Le Clos Pitois	14.

First Vineyards (*Premières Cuvées*)	
La Maltroie or La Maltroye	23.
Les Brussanes, Le Grand Clos, Le Petit Clos	45.
Champgain	71.5
Les Chaumées	2.5

Note: Names listed in capitals indicate vineyards whose wines are likely to be imported into the United States. The others are not at present imported.

dry, without hardness, and have a little floweriness, though without any sweet aftertaste. The wines possess a certain expansiveness, with no hard core. Those from Morgeot are similar, and live longer.

The red wines of Chassagne are little known and, because of this, are excellent values. They are soft and well balanced, reaching perfection in about five years, though they can be drunk when younger. They are a transition wine between those of the Côte d'Or and the lighter Burgundies from the Côtes of Chalonnais, Mâconnais, and Beaujolais. The Clos de la Boudriotte has more tannin than any of the others, with a resultingly fuller body, the French saying that the wine is more *corsé*. Clos Saint-Jean is somewhat lighter than Clos de la Boudriotte.

Below Chassagne is the last wine town of the Côte d'Or, Santenay. Santenay produces no great wines, all of them being red and light. Again, it is possible to recognize in the wine the transition from the Côte d'Or Burgundies to those of the Côte Chalonnaise. They are rarely sold under their vineyard names.

PROPRIETORS OF THE MONTRACHET VINEYARD

In the fall of 1967 a local vintner, in order to illustrate the unbelievably small quantity of genuine Montrachet, volunteered the following estimates of the amount of *pièces* or barrels produced. Taking into account the age of the vines, very young or very old vines having a small yield, his total estimate for the 1966 vintage did not exceed 1,200 cases. At least 10 per cent of this total is kept by the growers for their own personal consumption. An additional 200 to 300 cases are sold to friends. Hence the maximum of authentic Montrachet available for sale throughout the world barely exceeds 750 cases.

At the present time the local production of Chevalier-Montrachet is less than a thousand cases of authentic wines.

The Bâtard-Montrachet vineyard is partly in the township of Puligny and partly in the adjoining township of Chassagne.

The principal owners on the Puligny side are: Messrs Leflaive, Poirier, Bavard, Sauzet, Petitjean, Maurice Jacquin, and A. Monnot.

The principal owners in the Chassagne part of the vineyard are: Messrs Coffinet and Gagnard, Julien Monnot, Morey, Jouard, Déleger-Lagrange, Ramonet, and Brenot.

Proprietors of the Montrachet Vineyard	*Ouvrées*	*Pièces* *
Marquis de Laguiche	42½	5
Baron Thénard	42	12
Bouchard Père et Fils	21½	11
Mme Boillereault de Chauvigné	19	5
Le Roy	11	6
Domaine Jacques Prieur	9	4
Les Comtes Lafon	7½	3
Fleurot-Larose, shipper at Santenay	7½	4½
Dr. J. Blanchet	6½	2½
Milan Mathey	6½	3
Thevenin	3½	3
Pierre Amiot	1½	½
Mme Vve Petitjean	1½	½
Mme Girard-Eichman	1	½
Mme Vve J. Colin	1	½
Mlle Marguerite Girard	1	½

* A *pièce* contains approximately 24 cases of 12 bottles each.
The *ouvrée* is an old Burgundian measure still widely used in the Côte d'Or. There are 23 *ouvrées* to a hectare, and a hectare is 2.4 acres, which means that there are about 10 *ouvrées* in an acre.

Principal Owners of the Chevalier-Montrachet	*Ouvrées*	*Pièces*
Bouchard Père et Fils	31½	16
Héritiers Leflaive at Puligny	28	12½
Jean Chartron, grower at Puligny	16	9
Jadot, shipper at Beaune	12	4
Latour, shipper at Aloxe-Corton	11½	4
Déleger-Lagrange, grower at Chassagne	8	4
Charles Poupon, grower at Meursault	3½	2
Jacques Prieur, grower at Meursault	3	1½
Henri Clerc, grower at Puligny	2½	1
Joseph Bavard, grower at Puligny	2	1
Charles Danser, grower at Chassagne	2	1
Hochardet, grower at Chassagne	2	1

THE WINES OF
SOUTHERN BURGUNDY:
Chalonnais, Mâconnais,
and Beaujolais

The Côte d'Or ends at Chagny, where the main Paris-Riviera Route No. 6 swings down from the hills to meet the Golden Slope highway coming from Dijon. From Chagny to Lyon is ninety miles, and from the scattered vineyards off to the right of the road come most of the Burgundies seen on French wine lists. Divided into three *côtes,* the vineyards also make up most of the Burgundy exports to Switzerland, the second largest importer of Burgundies. Swiss imports are large because Chagny is only some six hours from Geneva by car. The two restaurants in the little town are well known to the wine-loving Swiss, who like their good food and their carafe Burgundies.

After leaving Chagny, you barely have time to catch your breath before you skirt the Côte Chalonnaise, which takes its name from the small city perched glumly on the banks of the Saône, a dozen miles to the southeast. The land is flat, the vineyards sparse and small, and over to the west is what is left of Cluny, once the great monastic center where medieval monks tended vines, then migrated all through Burgundy to found new monasteries and vineyards. The ancient vineyard road that runs straight south from Chagny instead of swinging east to Chalon, passes through the four best-known communes: Rully, Mercurey, Givry, and Montagny. The commune names have become the *Appellations Contrôlées* recognized by the *Appellation d'Origine* laws, for the Chalon Slope.

The change in soil marks a change in the wine, but the Chalon wines still bear a resemblance to those of the Côte de Beaune, perhaps because the Pinot Noir is the grape used in the vineyards. The best wines of the Chalon Slope are the reds of Mercurey, lighter than Beaunes, though sometimes almost as rich, the sort of wine that is often called "unpretentious and good."

The wine of Givry is a little lighter than that of its neighbor Mercurey, fresh, clean, and pleasant, the best vineyards being Clos

Saint-Pierre, Clos Saint-Paul, and Cellier aux Moines. The owner of
the last is Baron Thénard, whose cellars are under the little town.
The town buildings are in the Louis XIV style, the open market is a
domed roof supported by stone columns, and the streets are noisy
with the sound of water splashing from ornate fountains. The great
cellars are much more ancient, however: huge stone rooms with
twenty- and thirty-foot ceilings, with gravel on the floor under the
barrels, and wide stairs and archways that seem a better setting for
sword fights than for fine wines.

The commune of Rully produces a small red wine, some of which
is made into sparkling wine. Montagny produces a white wine, the
most apt description of which is "pleasant."

On down the valley of the Saône is Mâcon, a pleasant town
rising up from the river banks to the high hill. Four miles above the
town is the Château Saint-Jean, now converted into a deluxe hotel, a
large handsome building set in the middle of an immense park. In
Mâcon there is an excellent restaurant in the Hôtel de France et
d'Angleterre, on the quay, whose specialties are *écrevisses à la Nage,
quenelles de brochet, jambon en croûte,* and *poulet à la crème.* The
chef used to be M. Burtin, who cooked for Wilhelm II of Germany
before the First World War.

It is from the Mâcon Slope that one of the best white Burgundies comes, in a rolling valley half a dozen miles west of Mâcon. It is
the first truly southern valley in Burgundy, where people speak more
slowly and move more quietly, and the men wear berets creased into
a peak to shield their eyes from the glaring sun. Five neighboring
communes have the right to call their wines by the famous name
Pouilly-Fuissé.

The best comes from Fuissé, which tacks Pouilly to its name.
The town is reached by turning south off the west-running highway
and going down a back road and across a railroad crossing, which is
called Patte d'Oie. Three or four country lanes come together, looking like a goosefoot, hence the name. The road winds through a fold
in the hills into the boomerang-shaped valley, with Solutré in the
crook, and the neighboring Fuissé in the farther tip. Behind is a
bulging crag that looks like a miniature Gibraltar, and one has the
feeling that the sea is just beyond the cratered valley's rim.

Here the Pinot Chardonnay is allowed to grow much taller than
elsewhere, almost chest-high in places, for the sun is warm enough to
swell the grapes without the aid of heat reflected from the chalky
earth. The harvest is the latest of all Burgundies, often two weeks

after that in the Côte d'Or, the wines being allowed to contain much sugar. Altogether, there are some eleven hundred acres planted in vine in the Mâconnais.

The white wine from Solutré is more feminine than the other Pouillys. The best vineyards are Les Chailloux, Les Boutières, Les Chanrue, Les Prâs, Les Peloux, and Les Rinces. In Fuissé the wine is stronger and more masculine, the best vineyards being Clos de Var-ambond, Clos de la Chapelle, Château Fuissé, Le Clos, Menetrières, Versarmières, Les Vignes-Blanches, Les Châtenets, Les Perrières, and Les Brûlets. Below Fuissé is the commune of Chaintré, where there is a good vineyard, Clos Reissier, and above Solutré is Vergisson, all four of these communes having the right to the name "Pouilly-Fuissé." Occasionally there will be a good wine from the neighboring communes of Pouilly-Loché and Pouilly-Vinzelles.

The vineyard laws permit use of some Aligoté and Merlan vines in the vineyards, but when the wine contains pressings from these grapes, the label on the bottle must say so. The same is true in Burgundy, where Aligoté is sometimes planted. Putting the grape name on the label is rare in France, Sancerre, in the Loire Valley, and Alsace being the only other places where it is necessary or customary.

In France the laws control what grapes may be used in the vineyards, so variety names are unnecessary in most places. This is not so in California, for example, where wines can be made from any grapes, making it necessary to check on the vineyard district, the grower, and the variety of grape before you have much of an idea of what you are getting.

The pale-golden wine of Pouilly-Fuissé, with its slight greenish tinge, can be drunk young. Because of its strength and vigor it can keep quite well, but keeping doesn't pay, for after five years the sturdy wine no longer develops much.

When chilled, it is wonderful with sea food and white meats, and is particularly delightful with what the French call *charcuterie*. That all-embracing term generally means prepared pork meats such as sausages, *pâtés*, and the other spicy meats that can be lumped under the term *delicatessen*. The country is famous for its hot sausages and the variety of its *charcuterie*, as well as game such as hare, venison, and pheasant or woodcock, stuffed with truffles. A strong cheese is made in the region.

In Chalon-sur-Saône begins the famous food and fabulous eating for which Burgundy was always famed. The country inns and little towns serve good food to travelers, something you can't say for many of those in the Côte d'Or. Just to the south is Charolles, from whose deep green pastures comes the famous Charollais beef. From Chaintré you can look east across the Saône to the plains of Bresse, the home of chicken and birthplace of Brillat-Savarin. Mâcon is famous for its fish, the perch and pike from the river, frogs from Bresse ponds, snails from the vineyard hills. And to wash it down is the wonderful Pouilly-Fuissé. The Mâcon Slope also makes a small red wine, but in Mâcon the wines that are drunk are Pouilly-Fuissé and Beaujolais, both red and white.

The district of Beaujolais begins just south of the Pouilly vineyards, and on the maps the vineyards sometimes seem to intermingle. In these northern valleys of the district many have the right to call their wine either Mâconnais or Beaujolais, but in the valleys farther south are the classified growths of Beaujolais. Each successive valley is watered by a stream or two, the slopes facing generally southeast, soaking in the sun from the time of the first tendril to the cutting of the last bunch of grapes.

Beaujolais is made exclusively from the Gamay grape, which reaches heights here because the Burgundian soil becomes granitic, rather than calcareous and chalky. Everywhere else the Gamay is a despised vine, but here it becomes one of the noble plants.

Beaujolais is one of the most widely drunk red wines in the world, one reason being that it is excellent when young. It is the great carafe wine of France, sold in barrels, and drawn off in bottles for drinking. Many Paris cafés specialize in young Beaujolais, which is called *vin bourru,* with a rolling Burgundian *r*—probably indicating the contented sound you make after drinking some.

The northernmost important commune in Beaujolais is Juliénas. Its wines are fresh and fruity, the prize of gastronomic Lyon, where it is the carafe wine supreme, drunk when scarcely a year old. It is a red wine that can be drunk very young, from six months to two years. Its neighboring commune is Saint-Amour, whose wine is very similar in character to Juliénas though somewhat lighter.

The best-known of all Beaujolais wines is that from the *appellation* of Moulin-à-Vent. Chiroubles is now the best-known Beaujolais in France, Moulin-à-Vent is the best Beaujolais exported, somewhat heavier than any other. It is second largest among the districts. The vineyard soil is thin and pinkish, and on a hill above the main valley is the windmill that names the wine. Without vanes now, it is classed as a national monument, a symbol of Beaujolais. The best vineyards

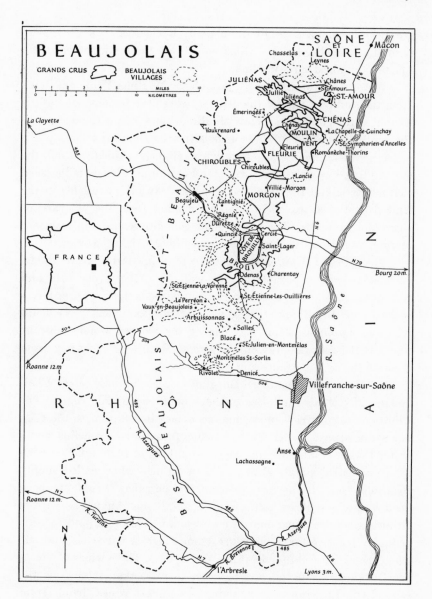

BEAUJOLAIS

GRANDS CRUS   BEAUJOLAIS VILLAGES

MILES

KILOMETRES

FRANCE

SAÔNE ET LOIRE

Mâcon

Chasselas

Leynes

JULIÉNAS

Chânes

St-Amour

ST-AMOUR

Jullié

Juliénas

Émeringès

CHÉNAS

Chénas

MOULIN-A-VENT

La Chapelle-de-Guinchay

St-Symphorien-d'Ancelles

Vauxrenard

FLEURIE

Fleurie

Romanèche-Thorins

CHIROUBLES

Chiroubles

Lancié

Villié-Morgon

Beaujeu

Lantignié

MORGON

Régnié

Durette

Quincié

Cercié

CÔTE DE BROUILLY

Saint-Lager

BROUILLY

Bourg 20 m.

N 79

Odenas

Charentay

St-Étienne-la-Varenne

St-Étienne-Les-Ouillières

Le Perréon

Vaux-en-Beaujolais

Arbuissonnas

Salles

Blacé

St-Julien-en-Montmélas

Montmélas St-Sorlin

Rivolet

Denicé

Villefranche-sur-Saône

Roanne 12 m.

R. Saône

HAUT-BEAUJOLAIS

BAS-BEAUJOLAIS

RHÔNE

R. Azergues

Anse

Lachassagne

La Clayette

Roanne 12 m.

N 7

R. Turdine

N

R. Brevenne

l'Arbresle

R. Azergues

Lyons 3 m.

are Les Carquelins, Le Moulin-à-Vent, Rochegres, Les Chants-de-Cour, La Rochelle, and Les Gimarets. In all, the commune has some fourteen hundred acres in vines.

The district of Chénas is just above Moulin-à-Vent, and wine from the southern part of the district, where the famous windmill is located, often goes to market as Moulin-à-Vent. Below the district of the windmill is Fleurie, whose wine is fruitier than the others, and is a very typical Beaujolais, best when slightly chilled. Of all the outstanding Beaujolais that will stand shipping, Fleurie is the most characteristic and thus the most typical Beaujolais available in the United States, an excellent example coming from the vineyard of Clos de la Roilette. The other good communes of Beaujolais are Morgon and Brouilly. Morgon wines last longer than the others.

The wines of Beaujolais flow to Lyon as inevitably as the Rhône and Saône, and a parable on the wall of almost every café and restaurant throughout southern Burgundy reads thus: "Three rivers bathe Lyon: the Rhône, the Saône, and the Beaujolais." No doubt it's true. Lyonnais claim that one of the modern wonders of the world is the fact that the city lets some Beaujolais get away from them, to the rest of France and even overseas.

All the wines of southern Burgundy from the three *côtes*—Chalonnais, Mâconnais, and Beaujolais—should be drunk young. The wines bearing district and commune names in addition to the *Côte* name are always better buys, a wine from Les Carquelins being better than a Moulin-à-Vent, which would be, in turn, a better wine than one called simply Beaujolais. In France wines called simply Beaujolais may be perfectly wonderful, but they would not be a good value bought in bottle, and certainly not anywhere outside France, where the same import costs would have to be paid for this ordinary wine as for a truly great one. This is not true, however, when the wine is sold for less than two dollars. These wines of southern Burgundy should always be lower in price than those from the Côte d'Or. In France very young Beaujolais wines drunk from carafes taste better when slightly chilled.

Vintages mean less in southern Burgundy than in the Côte d'Or. The good ones in the past decade are 1957, 1966, and especially 1964. None of the wines show much improvement after five years.

These wines of southern Burgundy are different from the great Côte d'Or wines in another way: you swallow them, you don't sip them. The reason is simple. That's the way people seem to like to drink them. It is almost impossible to take swallows of the Chambertins, or Musignys, or even Cortons, and it is difficult to take large swallows of the lighter Beaunes. But when you get to southern Burgundy, all that changes. When drinking, one has a desire to take big draughts of the wine, in much the way one drinks beer or cider. One reason may be that cold drinks can be drunk faster than hot ones. But it is more than that. The wine itself is light and refreshing and makes you want to have a lot in your mouth at once. And this is particularly noticeable when you are eating food. The Côte de Nuits produces sip wines, the *côtes* of southern Burgundy produce swallow wines. By the time you get down to Provence, the wines are guzzle wines. It's not a question of temperament, but of geography.

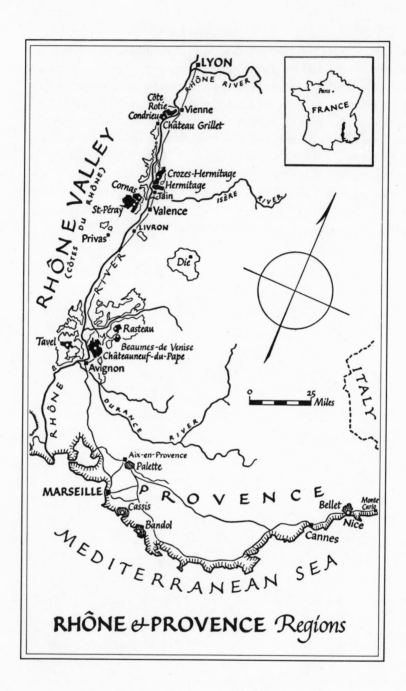

RHÔNE & PROVENCE Regions

Lyon, that sprawling metropolis of central France, surrounded by hills and divided into sections by the two rivers that flow through it, with the greatest tradition of cooking of any city in the world, stands at the head of the Rhône Valley. To the east is the country of Bresse chicken and Brillat-Savarin; to the west is the Massif Central and Périgord, from which come truffles and *foie gras;* from the north come the wines of Burgundy, and from the south come the riches of the Rhône Valley: fruits, fish, and the full-bodied wines. Lyon is the mouth of the horn of plenty.

From the kitchens of its great restaurants, Auberge Paul Bocuse, Troisgros, Mère Brazier, Nandron, and Mère Guy, come *poulet en vessie* (chicken cooked in a pig's bladder to retain all its juices, also referred to as *en demi-deuil,* or half-mourning), *quenelles Nantua,* and its famous *charcuteries.*

The first great vineyards begin across the river from Vienne, an old Roman town thirty miles south of Lyon. Here is the great restaurant of the Widow Point, near an old Roman obelisque called La Pyramide, which gives its name to what is often called the greatest restaurant in France, the Restaurant de La Pyramide. Many of Point's wines come from the vineyards across the river—reds from the Côte Rôtie, whites from Condrieu.

The Roasted Slope is a steep hillside less than two miles long and averaging about a hundred yards from top to bottom. Terraced every few feet with old stone walls that hold the precious earth in tiny pockets, some of the vineyards are no bigger than a living room. The slope faces southeast, and while the seasons here are two weeks ahead of those in Burgundy, the grapes broiling on the vines all through the summer and early fall, the *vendange* or harvest is at the same time.

The principal Côte Rôtie vine is the Syrah. Like the Gamay, it was brought back from the Near East by the crusaders, according to the legends. The grapes are grown from a single length of vine held by a tall stake, the vine arching over to be tied to a second bracing stake. When the vines are bare, the stakes bristle along the steep slope, looking like stacked rifles.

The best slopes are those just below the town of Ampuis and are divided into two sections, the *Blonde* and the *Brune*. The story goes that one of the early lords had two daughters—he left them the vineyards and these took on the personalities of the girls, the Côte Blonde being young and gay at first but petering out with age, the Côte Brune being quiet and reserved in youth but turning into quite a grand old dame. The vintners tell you that's the reason why the reds from the Brunette Slope are more *corsé*, holding their strength longer, having a heavy body and strong character, while those from the Blonde Slope, just to the south, are lighter and softer and much more *tendre,* a word that means much the same thing when used in connection with wine as with women.

Some of the vineyard names of the two slopes are occasionally found on bottles, but the wine is usually sold as Côte Rôtie. The best vineyards are La Brocarde, Les Chavaroches, Les Clos and La Clape-ronne, Fontgent, Grande Plantée and La Garelle, Grosse Roche and La Balaiyat, La Landonne, Le Mollar, Le Moulin, Les Moutonnes, Le Pavillon Rouge, La Pommière, Tharamon de Gron, and La Turque. The best owners of the some 130 acres are Bonnefond, Cachet, Chapoutier, Dervieux, Pouzet, and J. Vidal-Fleury, who owns the most, plus some hundred others who own small parcels.

The red wines of the Côte Rôtie do much of their aging in the cask, some longer than five years. This practice sets the pattern for the reds of the Rhône Valley, for it takes time for the wines to cast off their heavy deposit and a still longer time to clear. The wines gain enormously with age, developing slowly, often taking a dozen years to round out, and then holding for an amazingly long time. If well kept, many last for thirty or forty years, and if some old bottles from the end of the last century happen to turn up now and then, they are usually marvels. Many think that the rich, deep-red wine, full and generous, is the best of the Rhônes. Unlike other wines, the Côte Rôtie reds have a strong taste of truffles, or of raspberries, a taste easily distinguishable and not a mere suggestion, as flavors often are in other wines.

The laws controlling place-names, which went into effect in the fall of 1940, specify that eighty per cent of the vines must be Syrah, and although the laws limit the amount of production per acre, the vineyards never reach the maximum figure because of the terracing. The entire production of Côte Rôtie wine averages less than the equivalent of twelve thousand cases. The production looks greater when you walk through the caves and sheds where the barrels are kept, but you can easily spot the older vintages and their small yield by the thick mold on the old barrels. The few new ones are almost untouched, standing out dark against the mold-white walls and floors, the whiteness looking like snow.

Condrieu is the neighboring district, just downstream on the bend of the river. There the production of wine is much smaller than on the Côte Rôtie. The vines start at the town and run south, some two dozen growers owning the seventeen acres planted in the Viognier grape. The white wine is full of perfume and has a strong distinctive taste imparted by the local soil, a characteristic called *goût de terroir* in French. Most of the wine is drunk in Vienne and Lyon.

The best white wine of the Rhône Valley comes from the vineyard just south of Condrieu, called Château Grillet. Its four acres, owned by a single proprietor, Henri Gachet, produce less than a hundred cases a year. They also are planted in Viognier. The wine is considered the outstanding *vins du pays,* or local wine, of France. Superlatively dry and well-balanced white wines, not so soft as Meursaults, they are as great as those from Pouilly-Fuissé, with a slightly drier and more austere ''finish,'' or aftertaste. Finish is the lasting end-taste of a wine, such as dryness, floweriness, sweetness, or softness.

Americans have little chance to taste these good wines of France for it is the habit to import only the great names. Local pride in some Rhône wines, however, have made their names known, and today many of them are being brought in. Among the most famous are those from the vineyards near Tain, some fifty miles south of Lyon.

Above Tain is the steep slope called L'Hermitage, supposed to be one of the oldest vineyards in France, and taking its name from a legendary hermit. One story goes that he was hiding from some invading Romans on top of the hill. When he got hungry, wolves and foxes brought him food. The food made him thirsty, so God sent down a group of vintners from heaven, which is where all good vintners go. The vintners planted vines, which grew grapes and ripened in a single night, and the hermit drank the glorious wine all his life, praising God with each swallow.

You couldn't pick a pleasanter spot in which to be a hermit, high up above the Rhône on the south-facing hill. The grapes are the Syrah, a planting made compulsory in the third century by the Emperor Probus. Even though it is the southernmost of the great French wine districts the vines may suffer from *coulure,* a malformation of the budding grapes caused by excessive rain or storms during the time of flowering.

In Hermitage and the other vineyards of the Rhône Valley sections are called *quartiers,* perhaps because they are so small. Both red and white wines are produced, and both are rough when young. With age, however, and when exceptional and carefully selected, the reds rank with a great claret or Burgundy. Harsh and bitter when young, after four years in the cask, where they throw a heavy sediment, the red wines can become soft and velvety. When old, the red Hermitages are enormously rich in aroma and aftertaste, with a fine perfume and a marvelous bouquet, only slightly less than the Côte Rôties, and a color all their own. Instead of having the complete red spectrum, the wines have a brownish tinge, which the French call *pelure d'oignon,* or onionskin. They are essentially a big wine, and George Saintsbury has called them the manliest of French wines.

The full white wines are among the longest-lived of all dry whites, and many of them are good after twenty years. The whites will eventually maderize, however, and taste best when somewhere between six and fifteen years old. They have a marked tendency to be hard when young and are one of the few dry white wines that cannot be drunk then, taking three or four years to soften. The wines are excellent with highly seasoned foods such as curries and spicy creamed dishes.

The white wines come from vineyards in the center of the Hermitage Slope, most of which are planted in Marsanne vines, with some five per cent planted in the Roussane variety. Less than thirty thousand cases of white wine are produced each year. One of the most famous is that called Chante-Alouette. This is the name of a vineyard, but the name has also been used as a trade name by the firm of Chapoutier, and the wine is usually a blend of those from the better vineyards. The best vineyards are Beaumes, Maison-Blanche, Chante-Alouette, Les Recoules, and La Chapelle.

Twice as much red as white Hermitage is produced by the sixty-odd vineyard-owners. It is a common practice for an owner to have vines in several different *quartiers* and blend the wines from the various sections. It is also permitted under the laws to plant other varieties than the Syrah in small quantity, and these varieties add special qualities to the wine. The best red-wine vineyards are Les Bessards, Le Méal, Les Murêts, L'Hermite, L'Homme, Gros-des-Vignes, La Chapelle, Varogne, La Croix, Les Diognères, Les Greffieux, Les Signaux, and La Pierelle.

L'Hermitage is just below that group of vineyards that produce wine sold under the name of Crozes-Hermitage, but the wines of Crozes cannot be compared with those which are entitled to the simple name, Hermitage. As in the Côte Rôtie, the vine-growers are publicity-conscious, and the stone walls that divide the terraced vineyards are whitewashed with many of their names: Chapoutier, Paul Jaboulet Aîné, and Jaboulet-Vercherre.

Just south of Tain, on the right bank of the Rhône just opposite Valence, are the two small districts of Cornas and Saint-Péray. The vineyards were given to the monks some time before the beginning of the tenth century, on condition that the tending brothers give an annual luncheon to their colleagues, the main dish to be a big fish caught in the river. Cornas produces a red wine, while Saint-Péray produces white, some of which is made into a sparkling wine. Occasionally, the Saint-Péray vintners wait for the noble rot, carefully picking the grapes one by one and placing them on large plates. The wines are small and rarely distinguished.

For some reason, the fame of Hermitage has been overshadowed in the past decade or two by the red wines from a district far to the south, Châteauneuf-du-Pape. You reach the district by driving south along the Rhône, through Valence, where the great Restaurant Pic serves its glorious food, on down through Montélimar, famous for its chewy nougats, where the restaurant of the Relais de l'Empereur has been taken over by the former chef of London's Savoy Hotel, and almost to Avignon. Avignon, 140 miles down the Rhône from Lyon, is where the French popes had their seat in the Middle Ages. Some ten miles away the popes built a summer residence, deep in the midst of vineyards, and while the vineyards still produce a great red wine, all that is left of Châteauneuf-du-Pape are a few crumbling walls. The town boasts two restaurants, both excellent, La Mère Germaine and La Mule du Pape, and one of the most famous wines of France. The road follows the crenelated remains of the castle and goes through the town, past a small triangle of dirt called the town square, which has a handsome old fountain, moss-covered and shaped something like a chocolate fudge sundae. Nights and weekends the square is full of local vineyard workers talking politics, the favorite activity of southern France, indoors or out.

The winegrowers of Châteauneuf-du-Pape were the first to pass regulations concerning place-names and qualities for labeling and marketing their wines, setting the pattern for the *Appellations d'Origine* laws that today control the production of all France's great wines. The prime mover of these early laws was the late Baron Le Roy de Boiseaumarié, a winegrower and a great hunter, who until recently was president of the International Wine Office, the world-wide special association for wines, as well as president of the National Institute of the Appellations d'Origine and owner of the Château Fortia vineyard.

The vines are planted farther apart at Châteauneuf than in any other of the fine-wine districts of France, often with five or six feet between the rows, the vines spreading out bushily from a single root. You can't see the soil for the flat round stones that cover the vineyard, stones as big as your fist, and the grapes ripen baked in the southern sunshine and the boiling heat reflected from the stones. A dozen varieties of vine go into the making of Châteauneuf, which accounts for such great differences in the wine.

Production varies immensely, because if the sun is not hot enough, the grapes stay small. A million gallons of red wine were made in 1966 and some 4,000 gallons of white; in 1967, 460,000 gallons of red and 2,800 gallons of white. Most of the wine is sold in barrels to French restaurateurs. The white wine is a good small wine, merely a novelty.

The red wines of Châteauneuf must have an alcoholic strength of 12.5 per cent, the highest minimum for any of the wines of France. Because they are a blend of so many varieties of grape, a fact that gives them body and outstanding flavor, the grapes must be sorted by hand; Châteauneuf is the only southern red wine where this is necessary. Lighter than the Côte Rôtie reds, softer and faster-maturing than both Côte Rôtie and Hermitages, the red Châteauneufs can be drunk when scarcely three years old. Strong in alcohol, they are cheaper than the other two famous reds of the Côtes du Rhône. The best-known vineyards are Château Fortia, Château Nalys, Château de la Nerthe, Château Fine-Roche, Domaine de Montredon, Vaudieu, and La Gardine, but there are many other good vineyards. The best growers and shippers are the heirs of Baron Le

Roy, Doctor Dufays Mousset, Brotte-Armenier, Brunel, Chapoutier, Jouffron, Ponson, and Tacussel.

Châteauneuf-du-Pape and the nearby district of Tavel make up the southern wine districts of the Côtes du Rhône. Tavel produces one of the best *rosé* wines of France for export, and it is the most famous, for its high alcoholic content preserves it during travel.

Tavel is walled in by cliffs, small hills of sandy limestone baking in the sun, and, above the vineyards, knolls covered with olive trees and brush. The town square reminds one of Louis XIV architecture; and there is a daily game of bowls in the dust, called *boule* in France, the players crouching over the balls in their wide berets, smoking pipes, and joking in the thick accent of Provence.

Tavel is mainly made from Grenache grapes, and the pink wine has a ruby color as a result, with none of that orange tint so characteristic of many poor *rosés*. One of the largest producers is the local cooperative, and another is Château d'Aqueria. The young mayor of Tavel, Armand Maby, is also, naturally enough, a grower, and one of the best.

Tavel tastes best when drunk chilled, and goes with any food that can be eaten with wine, red or white. Because of its universality and light, refreshing taste, it is a superb luncheon wine.

Vintages along the Côtes du Rhône are not so important as in those districts farther north, being more uniform. The 1955's and 1952's are excellent, particularly the long-lived Hermitage reds, which are well matured and are great wines, but hard to find today. The 1957 is a glorious wine, robust and long-lived, which will last for decades. 1945 reds were full and heavy, rated excellent, classic.

The more recent vintages may be rated as follows:

1959 *The sun-drenched valley of the Rhône got an overabundance
of heat, which scorched the vines. The grapes matured so
rapidly that they rotted before they could be picked and
it rained during the harvest; hence, selectivity should be
shown in buying Châteauneuf-du-Pape. The grapes from the
other Rhône districts enjoyed the same healthy ripeness
as the other districts of France.*

1960 *The best year in very many, 1960 was to the Rhône Valley
what the great 1959 turned out to be for the other districts
of France.*

1961 *Unlike any other region in France the Rhône Valley produced a good vintage, but nothing more.*

1962   *A small vintage that gave flat wines lacking in character.*

1963   *A very small vintage. Wine completely lacking in color. Very clearly inferior to the 1962's.*

1964   *An average vintage. Slightly similar to the 1961's.*

1965   *A good vintage. The Côtes du Rhône region, unlike other parts of France, did not lack sunshine. The harvest weather was ideal.*

1966   *A top vintage.*

1967   *The Rhône, which is blessed with more good vintages than other wine districts in France, has outdone itself in 1967 as in 1966.*

1968   *A few quite pleasant wines were produced.*

1969   *Small in quantity, and short in quality—disappointing color.*

1970   *Excellent vintage year. Magnificent color. Large quantity.*

1971   *Wines of very good quality and character.*

1972   *Lack of heat and abundant rains reduced the quality of this vintage; nevertheless, it has turned out to be better than fair.*

Wines bearing district names and vineyard names are always better than those merely called Côtes du Rhône. The wines from the Rhône Valley have always been somewhat underrated, perhaps because the country is so full of tall tales, most of which revolve about the mistral, that extraordinary wind which begins somewhere in the neighborhood of Lyon and blows all the way down to Marseille, always for an odd number of days. The stories, the history, and the food always seem to go down easier when swallowed with the local wines.

The wine districts are sparse along the Rhône Valley, but in between are other fabulous things from old France. Aix-en-Provence has perhaps the most beautiful main street of any town on earth; the Roman ruins of Arles, Orange, and the other great outposts of the ancient conquerors are here; and everywhere is the scent and savor of southern France, and its warm-blooded people. Nowhere is their spirit reflected more brightly than in the wines they make.

PROVENCE
and the Sunny Wines
of the Riviera

Aix-en-Provence, that ancient capital of the ancient province, is a watering-place, the scene of one of France's most wonderful music festivals, a university town, and the birthplace of Cézanne. It sits astride the Paris-Riviera highway. The southern road leads to Marseille and bouillabaisse, the marvelous and unctuous fish stew simmered best at the Strasbourg and also Campo. Here live Marius and Olive, those two great characters who are the Pat and Mike of France, and whose prototypes can be seen sipping their *pastis* along the Cannebière, the Broadway of France's second-largest city. The road that turns east over the high plateau takes you to Saint-Raphaël, the first town of the Côte d'Azur, that Golden Horn of sand and rocky seacoast called the Riviera.

The towns, the beaches, the perfume of Grasse, and the famous people who holiday along the coast may be better known than the wines, but they are no more wonderful. Vineyards are planted all across the twenty-mile-wide coastal strip in the valleys from Marseille and on over to Monte Carlo and the Italian border. Yet only four districts are recognized by the *Appellations d'Origine* laws: La Palette, Bellet, Bandol, and Cassis.

La Palette is a district some twenty miles east of Aix toward Saint-Raphaël, the only fine-wine district not along the coastal strip. As in the other districts, both red and white wine are made as well as the *rosé*, which is made from a wide variety of grapes, principally the Grenache and the Ugni Blanc, but none of the Burgundy varieties are grown. The best vineyard of La Palette is Château Simone. The climate and soil are similar to those in the winegrowing valleys of northern California.

The wines of La Palette and the others of Provence are rarely drunk outside of France, sixty per cent slaking the thirst of those on the Riviera, another thirty-five per cent being served in other parts of France, and only some five per cent being exported. Half the wine made, by far the best, is *rosé,* a sturdy, heady wine that travels well because of its high content of alcohol. The red wines are rough, much like the Italian wines, and they were famous in the days of Cæsar, who issued them to his legions when they headed home. The white wines are dry and strong—one vintner says they are like tarpaulin with lace around it—but production is so small that they are never shipped, their virtues in no way comparing with those of the other fine white wines of France.

Bellet is the only recognized district on the Riviera itself, a group of vineyards up in the mountains behind Nice. Nearly all of the *rosé* it produces is drunk in the splendid hotels and restaurants between Cannes and the border; at Eden Roc, where celebrities bathe; at La Réserve in Beaulieu, one of the most luxurious seaside hotels in the world, where no better food can be had when you're wearing bathing garb; at the Château de Madrid, high above the Grande Corniche between Nice and Monte Carlo; at the Casino in Monte Carlo, or the fabulous old Hôtel de Paris. Perhaps the finest restaurant on the Riviera is the Bonne Auberge on the road near Antibes, which is one of two great restaurants of France that have a woman chef, and where the pride of the establishment is wine from the owner's own vineyard. The *rosé* comes to the table as accompaniment to that most delicate of all fish, the loup, the pride of the Mediterranean.

The other two wine districts lie along the coast road between Saint-Raphaël and Marseille. Bandol vineyards produce a *rosé* second only to that of Cassis, and its white wine is also of fine quality. Just off the coast from Bandol is the tiny island of Porquerolles, which boasts a single hotel, a magnificent beach, and one of the least-known wines of France, a *rosé* that is rarely obtainable anywhere else, kept on the island to be an accompaniment to the excellent food served in the quiet hotel.

All the wines served along the coast do not come only from the recognized districts. Other wines are placed in a special category called "Superior Quality," and these are produced by domaines such as Château de Selle, Château de Saint-Martin, and Ste. Roseline, three of the best-known. Their pink wines are famous locally, and some of them are exported, but they are made without any legal controls over grape varieties, soil, or vinification.

One of the finest *rosés* of the Riviera, and the one most popular in Marseille as an accompaniment to the rock fish of the Mediterranean and the simmering bouillabaisse, comes from Cassis, the tiny seaport from which Marseille gets most of its fish. Of all the varying shades of *rosé* wines from Provence, those from Cassis are the most beautiful—truly pink and dry, with no orange tint. James Beard, the American cook and author, was one of the first outside France to discover the wonder of this perfect summer wine, one that should be drunk slightly chilled, and with a flavor delicate enough to complement the most delicate of the rock fish, as well as distinct enough to hold its own against the more highly seasoned Mediterranean dishes.

The harbor of Cassis is shaped like a fishhook, with the main buildings of the town along its shank and around the curve. The road in front of them doubles as a quay, the fishing boats tied up along its length, the nets stretched out on the cobblestones to dry. The waterfront buildings, three stories high and painted in pastels—pink, lemon, bone-white, or faded blue—house the antique shops, the fish markets, the stores and restaurants, where the talk is mostly of fish, wine, women, and weather, depending on which is the most trouble at that particular moment.

In summer the tourists arrive in the restaurants, demanding to be served the fresh-caught fish and the white or rosy wines made in the valley. These wines are usually served too cold, which ruins their flavor. The waiters are much more casual about wine than in other vineyard districts of France, perhaps counting on the hot sun to warm it up quickly to a more proper temperature.

Behind the town on the slopes of this beautiful valley are the vineyards and the houses of the growers, looking as if they were about to slip down on the houses near the water—an Alpine village gone Mediterranean. One of the growers was a retired English colonel, former commander of the 14th Bengal Lancers, who came to Cassis in 1921, bought a house for himself and companion, and proceeded to enjoy life industriously. To do this, he started raising chickens.

"Even chickens are happy in Cassis, although it gets terribly cold in winter, in spite of what people say," said the colonel. "But the chickens didn't make me happy. Beastly devils had to be fed on Sunday. We'd planted grapes right away, and when the vineyard next door came up for sale, we got rid of the squawking devils and went in for wine. Get three or four free days a week that way."

The colonel, who first impressed you as an enormous man, perhaps seven feet tall, with a great nose, immense mouth, massive forehead, and enormous ears, but who was actually a man a little under average height and with normal-size features, claimed he knew nothing about winegrowing and even less about the studied technicalities of wine-making, in spite of the fact that all the local people insist he made the best wine in the valley. "When we started out, I bought a book, second-hand. We figured that just about everything else in the world had changed, or would soon, except the making of wine. Book was published in 1803, and I follow its orders like a good subaltern. We're slaves to that damn book. The wine of Cassis is good, sometimes it's wonderful, and we make a natural wine. No need to muck it all up with dosing and doctoring and cutting. Might ruin the wine."

The colonel liked to keep the alcohol content of his wine down. "There's no reason for wine being as strong as whisky. It will last longer and travel further, but I don't want to wait ten years to drink it. And it travels far enough. Fellow wrote me from India to send him a cask. I wrote him a letter telling him I'd send it, but wasn't sure how it would stand that hot trip. Tarred up the ends of the barrel and sent it off, and a few months later the fellow wrote me to send another barrel. Don't like to ship it that way, though. Safer in bottles. We've got some we made before the war, keep it out of curiosity. Tastes fine."

The colonel didn't go out of his way to ship his wine abroad. "I can sell all my wine right here. And it's a damned nuisance making out all those forms, and fussing with the labels and the shipping. Nobody knows about Cassis wines, anyway, and I don't know how anybody can sell it abroad. Then there's all that stinking business of proof that has to go on the bottle. Once I got a book and boned up about it, under-proof and over-proof. A ghastly English system, but I memorized it all pat. But I forgot it the next day."

There is, of course, a story of how the good wines came to Cassis.

Once upon a day, God was up in heaven, taking a vacation after creating the world. Gabriel came over to Him to report that people were complaining, down on earth. "What's the matter down below?" God asked, and Gabriel began polishing the mouthpiece of his trumpet with his thumb. "Well, they're complaining that everything is too flat and smooth down there. Oh, they like it, mind You, they think it's a wonderful world, but they're just a bit bored with it all." God scowled and looked hard at Gabriel's trumpet for a long moment, and then He smiled. "I've put so much time and effort into the world, it seems a shame to end it all. Listen, Gabriel, take a big sack of hills and crags, and boulders and alps, and sprinkle them around. But do it neatly, mind. I don't want the world all messed up, even if the mortals do.''

So Gabriel loaded up a big sack and went down to spread some roughness around. It took him all day, and by quitting-time he was pretty tired, and he still had a lot of mountains left. There was nothing to do but carry the leftovers back up the highway that leads to paradise. Now, as everybody knows, the earthly gate of the Highway that leads to Paradise is at Cassis, and as Gabriel started up, he gave the big sack on his shoulder a hitch. The sack had been in for some pretty rough wear during the day, and that last extra hitch was too much for it. The bottom tore open and all the leftover hills tumbled down on Cassis.

Gabriel went up the Highway that leads to Paradise and reported his day's activity to God. But he didn't tell Him about the torn sack.

The next day God heard the sound of weeping coming up from the earth below, and, listening closely, He could hear the bawling of children, and the dry, hard sobbing of bitter men. He jumped up and went down to find out for Himself.

As He came through the earthly gate of the Highway that leads to Paradise, which, as everybody knows is right at Cassis, a terrible sight met His eyes. A bent and twisted man was hacking at the hard, steep earth with a wooden hoe, sobbing bitterly; and seated on a rock beside the road was a humped and crooked woman, holding a skinny baby to her shriveled breast. They, too, were crying as if their hearts were cracked.

''What's this?'' God bellowed, and the noise made the baby wail even harder. ''Are you the fine creatures I put on this fine earth? What's happened to you? Why are you so crooked and lean, and, man, why are you grubbing at that poor earth while your wife and baby sob?''

The man looked up at God and rubbed the back of a dirty hand across his nose. ''Look at this earth,'' said the man. ''Every day I work it, trying to raise a few poor olive trees and tend these miserable grapevines. But the trees bear no fruit, and all we get from the vines is thin, sour wine.''

God looked at the scrawny vine the man had been hoeing and then at the huddled woman and the bony child. He was deeply touched, and a tear rolled down His cheek and fell on the withered vine.

And suddenly, as God's tear splashed on it, the vine began to grow, strong, green leaves sprouted along its length, and bunches of golden grapes formed under the leaves. And as the vine grew, its strength spread to the other vines, and in an instant the entire slope was covered with a fruitful vineyard. In another moment the entire valley was a mass of emerald vine leaves and ruby grapes. And that is how the glorious wine of Cassis, which, as everyone knows, is at the gate of the Highway that leads to Paradise, came to be.

THE CHARMING WINES
OF THE LOIRE

The source of the Loire, the longest of all French rivers, is in the mountains of the Massif Central, far below Lyon, but its famous vineyards do not begin until the stream winds north past Nevers. The districts of Pouilly-sur-Loire and Sancerre lie on opposite sides of the river north of the town; over west near Bourges are Quincy and Reuilly; and after the great bend in the river begins, along the placid banks and up-lands of the valley of the Loire, stretch the other districts that pro-duce the most charming minor wines of France: Vouvray, Chinon, Bourgueil, Saumur, Layon, Anjou, and Muscadet.

The vale of the Loire is the oldest civilized part of France, the retreat of kings; and the residence of royalty in this garden of France perhaps accounts for the fact that its people speak the purest French of all. The gentle countryside and the famous châteaux have earned for the region the title of the Smile of France, and the wines are as pleasant as the countryside. Bourges, that old cathedral town which dominates the land in the bend of the Loire, was the capital of the Duchy of Berry, and is the fountainhead of the early royal history of France, perhaps because Jacques Cœur came from there, the man who became treasurer for Charles VII and supplied the King with enough money to begin uniting France into one kingdom. The chances are that he also supplied the King with domestic help, for Berry still supplies most of the nursemaids and servants who staff the mansions of France, and Berrichonne is synonymous with servant. The country is full of the old Romanesque churches and their painted frescoes, which attract as many to the Loire Valley as its châteaux and its wines. The Loire peasant is as gentle as the coun-try he tends, easygoing and cheerful, a farmer interested in the won-ders of the land as well as what it produces, and that sets him apart from his Burgundian counterparts, who are concerned with more earthy matters. *"Vieille France"* is what the French call the vale of

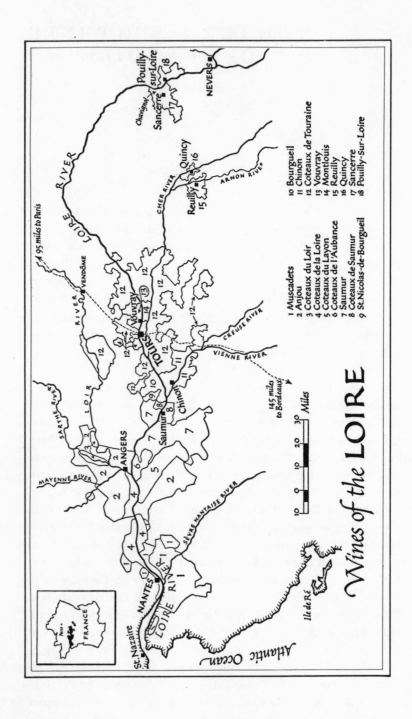

Wines of the LOIRE

1 Muscadets
2 Anjou
3 Coteaux du Loir
4 Coteaux de la Loire
5 Coteaux du Layon
6 Coteaux de l'Aubance
7 Saumur
8 Coteaux de Saumur
9 St.Nicolas-de-Bourgueil

10 Bourgueil
11 Chinon
12 Coteaux de Touraine
13 Vouvray
14 Montlouis
15 Reuilly
16 Quincy
17 Sancerre
18 Pouilly-Sur-Loire

the Loire, and if Paris is the heart of France, the Loire is its soul.

The first wines that reflect the delights of this country come from the district producing Pouilly-Fumé, often confused with the Pouilly-Fuissé wines of the Côte Mâconnaise in Burgundy. The white wines of the two Pouillys are strikingly similar; they are of the same quality, coming from similar soil, the result of the same methods of vine-tending and wine-making. Yet there is a pronounced difference in taste, for the wines of Pouilly-Fumé are made from the Sauvignon vine used for Bordeaux white wines.

The grape is called white smoke in Pouilly-Fumé, for a reason lost in the darker smoke of the Middle Ages. Some say it is because of the look of its white blossoms in flower; others point to the white bloom on the grapes at harvest time for an explanation. At any rate, the wines have a flavor of cheese or truffles, a taste characteristic that is a reflection of the *goût de terroir,* that distinctive tang of the wines reflecting the soil from a certain locality which German growers call *Schmeck.*

It is odd that such a distinctive dry white wine should come from the grape that produces sweet wines in Bordeaux. It is little known in France, even though it was Marie Antoinette's favorite and was admired by Napoleon. Little of it is produced, and it tastes best when young. The best-known wine comes from the vineyards of Château du Nozet, which was built in the nineties as a reproduction of an older Renaissance château by the grandmother of the present owner, the Baron de Ladoucette. Other good vineyards are found in the communes of Saint-Andelain, Les Loges, and Tracy. It is extremely rare to find the name of a specific vineyard on the label. The control laws for the district went into effect in 1937, when a distinction was made between Pouilly-Fumé and the wine called Pouilly-sur-Loire, which is made from a lesser grape variety called Chasselas. The light, fresh wine of Pouilly-Fumé has a unique and fruity flavor of clean delicacy, in which one can almost taste the essence of spring.

Like Pouilly-Fumé, the 2,500-acre Sancerre district across the river produces a fine white wine, clean and dry. Because it is short-lived, this wine should be drunk young. From the Château de Sancerre, on top of the hill behind the town, is one of the most beautiful panoramas in France, a long sweep of its longest river. It is perhaps here that the wine tastes best.

The best-known communes in the Sancerre district are, besides Sancerre itself, Chavignol, Bué, Armigny, and Verdigny. Part of the production is *rosé* wines, made from the Pinot Noir, delightful when one to three years old, but so low in alcoholic content that they do not always travel well.

In the village of Bué, the proprietor of the local café, M. Lucien Picard, acts as "courtier" for the local growers, a representative group of whom may be found gathered in the café almost any night of the week. M. Picard is a grower in his own right, owning choice sections in one of the best vineyards, Clos du Chêne-Marchand.

Thirty miles west of Sancerre is Bourges, near which are the two small districts of Quincy and Reuilly, both producers of white wines. These are also rarely exported because of low alcoholic content. Their characteristics are much like those of their bigger neighbors.

The center of the wines of the Loire is Tours, 150 miles south of Paris in the heart of the château country—not wine châteaux like those in Bordeaux, but beautiful castles that were the homes of kings. The Touraine is reached by driving south through Chartres, the most famous cathedral town in France, dominated by magnificent Gothic spires. Near Tours are the great châteaux, Amboise, Chenonceaux, and Chambord. The first is situated on top of a hill, and beneath its crenelated walls is a delightful open-air restaurant on the river bank, the Hôtel de Choiseul, where such countryside specialties as *terrine de lapin* and blood sausage are featured, along with local wines. Tours is on the south bank, and above and below the city are scores of châteaux. The most famous vineyard district is just upstream, across the river.

The vineyards of Vouvray lie on the high slopes above the river, and eight communes produce the wine, although some of their names rarely appear on the bottle: Rochecorbon, Vouvray, Vernou, Sainte-Radegonde, Chançay, Reugny, Parçay-Meslay, and Noizay. Much of this wine is served in the local restaurant of Pont de Cisse, which also specializes in that local pork *pâté, rillettes,* and whose terrace looks across to the vine-covered slopes.

The casks of wine from these vineyards are stored in deep caves cut into the hill rising above the river. But the caves weren't dug for storing wine. People have lived in them from prehistoric times, and still do; as you drive along the river bank to Vouvray, you can see houses, the back halves of which are caves, and some of them are merely façades, the rooms being dug back into the hillside.

Among the handsomest of the caves turned over to wine are those of Marc Brédif. Brédif's house has four sides, the caves opening at a proper distance behind it. They are high, vaulted caverns; and deep in the back, some three hundred feet beneath the hilltop, is a circular tasting-room, with an old round grindstone set up in the center for a table. In the chalky walls niches have been cut to hold bottles of the various vintages, the oldest dating back to the 1870's.

The white wines of Vouvray are soft and dry, with a slight taste toward sweetness, which may become complete, depending on the vintage and the lateness of the time of picking. The soil also affects the sweetness, some vineyards producing wines much less dry than others. Unlike the Sauternes, most of the Vouvrays produced from the Chenin grapes are short-lived, characterized by a youthful, fruity freshness. The most expensive Vouvrays are old and sweet, but few of these are exported, for most people prefer their Vouvrays young and dry. There are exceptions, however, for occasionally a vintage can live half a century.

One such was that of 1893, when there was an enormous harvest and wild rejoicing in Vouvray. Halfway through the harvest the growers ran out of barrels. Here was a glorious vintage, the greatest in the memory of living men, and no place to put it. The juice was stored in pitchers and crocks; even bottles were filled; and people coming to the press rooms with containers had them filled free. Vases and pots crowded every room, not overflowing with flowers, but filled with the sweet fermenting wine. At the harvest festivals old men jigged, grandmothers flirted with the boys, and joy and love were everywhere.

In the spring of 1895 everybody was still raving about the harvest two years earlier, and at harvest time the growers found that the same thing was happening all over again, but even bigger and

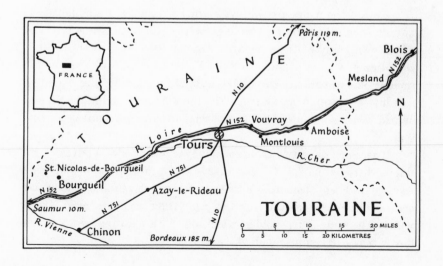

better. It was unbelievable. This time there was an even greater shortage of containers, and people were still so enthralled with the 1893 vintage that the growers had trouble convincing outsiders that the harvest was worth raving about.

Both these wines are in their prime today, more than half a century after the harvest. But of the thousands of bottles made, there are probably less than a hundred left. Such an old wine is unusual among the great wines of Burgundy and Bordeaux, and fond old wine-drinkers spend many happy hours talking about them, but it is incredible when a district that produces good small wines comes up with such a great vintage.

Like all the Loire Valley wines, those from Vouvray are supposed to be short-lived. They are bottled the spring after the harvest, reach their prime after five years, and are thought of as being nice little wines that taste good with a light lunch. For years they were considered too delicate and light in alcohol to be shipped and were passed off by connoisseurs as local wines, *vins du pays*, pleasant enough to drink when passing through the château country. They were good enough to wash down *andouillettes*, the local sausage made of tripe and lights, and tasted fine with *rillettes*, a *pâté* that comes in little pots and is spread on bread. But once or twice a decade the Loire Valley districts produce wines that are more than something to drink with local specialties. When a great year comes along, the most scorned of vineyards may produce a fine wine. As the vintners insist on telling you, it's impossible to make any hard and fast rules about vineyards or vintages. Each district is a family, and the poorest can have great children.

Few of the wines are sold with vineyard names on the labels, so buying should be from reputable growers and shippers, the latter of whom own many of the vineyards. One of the best growers is Mouzay-Mignot, who is president of the Vouvray syndicate of growers; some good shippers are the Château de Montcontour, once classified as a historic monument, destroyed by the Germans during the Second World War, and now rebuilt, Ackerman-Laurence, and Monmousseau.

There are some two thousand vineyard-owners of Vouvray producing between half and three quarters of a million gallons of wine each year. Their alcoholic content is between eleven and fifteen per cent. Vintners often wait for the *pourriture noble* to make sweet wines. The wines turn golden when old, with a full, sweet, flowery flavor that still retains much of its fruitiness.

Vouvray vintages set the pattern for all those of the Loire. Production in 1971 was small, sixty per cent of normal, but the wines were excellent—big, full, and sweet. The vintage of 1970 was fair; 1966 was a great year, definitely on the sweet side.

As in most districts that produce sweet wines, the greater the year, the sweeter the wine. As in most other districts in France, the '71's and '61's vie for first honors.

Across the river from Vouvray is Montlouis, whose white wine was so little known that it once went to market under the name of its bigger brother, Vouvray. Much of it is sold directly to local or Parisian restaurants in either barrel or bottle. As in Vouvray, the vineyards are planted in what is called the Pineau of the Loire or in Chenin, a larger grape of the Gros Pinot variety of Burgundy's great vine.

Wines from both are evenly balanced, ranging from slightly dry to somewhat sweet. This last characteristic the French call *mœlleux*, and Rabelais spoke of the "wine of taffetas" because of its velvety and silky, somewhat foamy texture in the mouth.

Some wines are particularly heavy in sugar. Bottled before all this sugar has been transformed into alcohol, they develop carbonic acid gas, becoming somewhat sparkling without any added doses. The French call this characteristic *pétillant*. Much of the Vouvray is made into a fully sparkling wine called *mousseux*, a dose of dissolved cane sugar being added to the wine when it is bottled, and the second fermentation changing the sugar to carbonic acid gas and making the wine bubbly.

From these vineyards come the sparkling wines given away as prizes on the wheels of chance that are so much a part of every French fair or carnival. The *mousseux* wines, which are rarely distinguished, are a Frenchman's substitute for Champagne, taking the place in France that Sparkling Burgundy holds in the United States. *Mousseux* and *pétillant* wines are rarely imported into the United States, largely because these lesser wines carry the same high duties as fine Champagnes, and the resulting prices make them poor values.

North of Vouvray is a small district that produces pink and white wines called Jasnières, but these are rarely shipped, even to Paris. Its white wine rarely has that creamy quality called *mœlleux*, and often takes a half-dozen years to develop.

Downstream from Tours and Vouvray are the red and pink wine districts of the Touraine slopes. Bourgueil and Saint-Nicolas-de-

Bourgueil are on the northern bank of the Loire. Chinon is opposite, in the wedge of land formed by the Loire and a tributary called the Vienne, reached by driving past Azay-le-Rideau, that loveliest of all Loire châteaux, which was built as a sixteenth-century Versailles by the treasurer of Francis I and was confiscated by the King on its completion.

The high plateau of chalky soil that makes up the vineyards of Bourgueil is planted in what is locally called the Breton vine, actually the Cabernet Franc of Bordeaux, and so Chinon is, too. Both wines are much alike. The smaller the wine, the less distinctive are its characteristics, and even neighboring districts may be remarkably similar.

Rabelais, who drank more wine during his lifetime than some would consider seemly, and whose Pantagruel and Gargantua do the same, was born near Chinon, lived there for years, tended a vineyard, and was a monk, in name if not in spirit. The town is sandwiched in between the river bank and a great bluff on which crumble the ramparts of the enormous castle of Chinon. The castle's massive walls were stormed by Joan of Arc, and its stones were pilfered by Richelieu to build his own castle near by. Parts of the town haven't changed much since the days of Rabelais. It is easy to imagine him reeling homeward up the steep cobbled streets after a heavy all-night bout with the local wine of Chinon, which he praised as lavishly and often as he drank it. His spirit permeates the town, and his ghost is supposed to appear whenever there is some particularly heavy drinking. Even the old hotel overlooking the rooftops to the river is called Gargantua. The local promotion organization, the Chantepleure, has gone so far as to design a special glass for the local wine, with the Rabelaisian phrase: "Always drink, never die," etched on the side.

In the old days, when all French wines were drunk mostly where they were made and the great wines were not as good as they are today, Chinon and Bourgueil lived up to their reputation. Their wines are better now than then, but so are the great wines, and in spite of Rabelais, whose sentiments are echoed by Balzac, who came from Tours, these red wines are rarely shipped.

On down the Loire lies the old town of Saumur, dominated by an ancient and rambling castle that is now a horse museum, the most famous in the world because the great cavalry school and mounted troops of the French Army are located there. Of the six districts of the Anjou Slope, Saumur stands first, not only because its sweet white wines can also be made into a good sparkling wine, but because the riverside bluffs are tunneled with vast, high caves, perfect for aging.

The sparkling wines of the Loire differ from those of Champagne, keeping the taste of the wine, where Champagne actually is transformed into a sparkling something unique. Saumur, particularly, is overpriced if it costs as much as Champagne, and suffers from the fact that it is usually taxed as much as Champagne. Heavier and fuller than the sparkling wine of Vouvray, it is made of two thirds white Chenin and one third Cabernet. The big shipping firms in Saumur that make the sparkling wine had bad luck in 1949, when late rains rotted the grapes, turning the harvest into a small sour wine.

Just down the river from Saumur begin the wine districts of the Anjou. There are over fourteen thousand wine producers in the Anjou. They make both pink and white wines. Many of the pink wines are not true *rosés;* they are pale and tinted faulty wines, with an orange cast instead of a true pink, yet they have a clean, fresh taste, and, like all the wines of the Loire, are ones that can be enjoyably drunk in quantity.

These average only nine to eleven per cent alcohol per volume, and, like all Loire Valley wines, lose their characteristic charm and lightness when the percentage of alcohol is higher, the wine becoming hard and its fresh bouquet disappearing. As wines need at least eleven per cent of alcohol to be shipped safely, that degree protecting them from the rough handling and temperature changes, these pink Anjous are usually better when drunk on the home grounds.

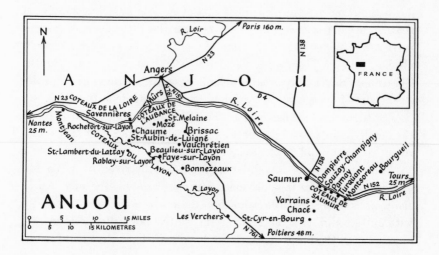

The two best and most famous of the Anjou districts are the Coteaux du Layon, thirty miles of vineyards scattered along the banks of the small Layon River, south of the Loire, and the Coteaux de la Loire, on the north bank of the river. The wines from the slopes of Layon are extremely high in alcohol, and the best vineyards are picked only after *pourriture noble* has set in. The best vineyards of the Layon slopes produce sweeter, more full-bodied wines, which last longer than those from the best vineyards of the slopes of the Loire.

The best wine from the Coteaux du Layon is the sweet white wine from a vineyard called the Quart de Chaume, one of the vineyards near the town of Chaume in the commune of Rochefort. Quart de Chaume wine is the sweetest of the Anjou whites, much like a sweet Vouvray, more flowery than Sauternes. It has a lightness and bouquet that make it unique, in spite of the fact that its alcoholic content is between thirteen and fifteen per cent in most years. Originally all the Chaume vineyards were owned by one man, rented out to workers in return for a quarter share of each vintage. The lord reserved the right to choose which section of the vineyards his quarter should come from, and it came to be called Quart de Chaume, and was, of course, the best in Anjou. Now the vineyard is owned by three proprietors: Lallane, Courtillé-Roynet, and Marcel Breyer, who also owns one of the choicest sections of Quart de Chaume, called Château de Belle-Rive, and the neighboring vineyards of Château de Plaisance and Château de Suronde, of Chaume.

North of the Coteaux du Layon is the Coteaux de l'Aubance, a small district that produces noteworthy *rosés*. It also produces some white wine, much drier than those from the slopes of Layon. Farther down the river are the vineyards of Coteaux de la Loire, mostly on the north bank, where the best surround the little town of Savennières. The wines are drier than those from Layon, very high in alcohol, and very slow in maturing. The best vineyards are the Château de Savennières, La Coulée de Serrant, Château d'Epiré, La Roche-aux-Moines, Clos du Papillon, and Château de la Bizolière.

Still farther downstream is the Coteaux du Loir, a district on the small tributary of the great river, whose wines are white and sweet, red and indifferent, *rosé* and charming.

The vineyards of Muscadet lie far down the river, near the city of Nantes. They are the only classified vineyards in Brittany. All of the wine is white; pleasant and dry, these wines are most appealing with oysters and sea food. Prior to the control laws, they were openly blended with Chablis, to stretch the supply of that scarce and famous wine. Now these wines have achieved great popularity not only in French restaurants but also abroad. The constant price increases of white Burgundies coupled with greatly improved wine-making methods have helped to give Muscadet a justified vogue.

That most of the pleasant Loire wines are not much exported is not so great a loss as it might seem. Nearly every tourist drinks some while sightseeing through the château country, between bouts of listening to the guides tell the fabled tales of the kings and queens who fell in love with the garden of France. And if amour and intrigue become tiring, there is always the legend of Joan of Arc to delight you between swallows, or the lusty stories of Rabelais and Balzac—stories as varied as the wines.

Recent vintages of the Loire may be rated as follows:

1959   *Great, from one end of this river to the other. Starting with
        the very inexpensive Muscadets, through the rich and
        perhaps overly sweet Vouvrays, to Pouilly-Fumé, which will
        show its particularly positive character more than ever,
        the wines were outstanding.*

1960   *Good and fair wines were produced.*

1961   *A good vintage, but a small harvest. The wines had a high
        degree of alcohol but lacked balance because the alcohol,
        fruit, and body were out of proper proportion.*

1962   *A very great success. Better balanced than 1961's, and in
        some cases a better quality. Too old.*

1963   *A small vintage. Ordinary wine.*

1964   *A good vintage. Rather like the 1962's, but a bit lighter and
        more hollow. The wines have oxidized.*

1965   *An ordinary vintage. Too light.*

1966   *A very good quality. A little more sprightly than the 1964's,
        with the exception of Muscadet, much of which was disap-
        pointing.*

1967   *A good vintage.*

1968   *Poor.*

1969   *A good vintage for all the wines of the Loire, stretching from
        Pouilly-Fumé to Muscadet—the latter were excellent.
        Generally fruity, this vintage was blessed with wines having
        a remarkably good color.*

1970   *Good to fair quality.*

1971   *Excellent vintage. The wines are perfectly balanced with
        considerable character.*

1972   *Good, with a tendency to excessive acidity or greenness. Will
        improve with age.*

THE WHITE WINE
OF ALSACE

Alsace, the martyred province of France, and along with Champagne the only one whose wines are not fully controlled by *Appellations d'Origine* laws, stretches its vineyards and orchards along the left bank of the north-flowing Rhine, separated from Lorraine and the rest of France by the Vosges Mountains. Most of its vineyards and towns were battlegrounds during the last war, and the destruction was enormous.

You would never suspect it, going east from Paris across the Île de France and skirting the Champagne country, then through Lorraine and up into the mountains. War damage has almost disappeared, and tourist interest focuses on the wonderful *quiche Lorraine* and preserves served in Bar-le-Duc at the Hôtel Metz, or on the watering-place of Vittel, where much of France's bottled waters come from, or on Münster, to the south, the cheese from which is famous the world over. As you drive up through the peaks and crags of the mountains, the country is peacefully Alpine, and when you break through into the valley where the town of Orbey perches, you are ready for the fabulous *foie gras* and trout, the ham and sausage, the mounds of ice cream and whipped cream that are the specialties of the Hôtel Beausite, the town's famous restaurant. But when you come through the pass into the foothills, you can see some of the price that France has paid for peace.

The best-known wine towns are Ammerschwihr, Kaysersberg, Kientzheim, Mittelwihr, Riquewihr, Ribeauvillé, and Bergheim, all north of Colmar, although the vineyards begin farther south. Mittelwihr was completely destroyed in the drive across the Rhine; only a few walls were left standing. Along one of them, called the Wall of Martyred Flowers, the Alsatians planted red, white, and blue flowers during the occupation, in defiance of the German order that the French national colors should not be displayed. In Bennwihr there used to be 184 houses; four were left standing. The ruins of the Château of Koenigsberg stand on the heights; the ancient stones looked down on a newer havoc.

The towns were rebuilt, workers taking the stones from the piles of rubble to build new houses, but it is a changed Alsace now, with only patches of the old. Once the Germans were routed, the first task was replanting the vineyards, and the first buildings built were large modern cooperative cellars, so that the vintners of each town could again make their wines. It has been a giant's task.

Strasbourg, the capital of Alsace, and famous for its *choucroute*, its brownstone cathedral with the handsome stone ladies above the portals and the immense and ugly clock on the inside, lies 275 miles straight east of Paris, in the middle of the Alsatian plain, on the banks of the Rhine. The plain was once a vast lake, now shrunk to the meandering Rhine, and coming across the towering Vosges, crowned with forests and old castles, you can look down and across the wide plain, rich with orchards and fields of hops and wheat, to the Black Forest of Germany.

Twenty miles south of Strasbourg is Sélestat, and twenty miles still farther up the Rhine is Colmar, whose museum contains the weird and famous Grünewald altarpiece. All three towns have an ancient quarter ribboned with canals and crammed with old half-timbered buildings, surrounded with the ugly rash of modern suburb and factory developments. The towns divide the winegrowing district of Alsace in two, the best being that called the Haut-Rhin, between Colmar and Sélestat; that called Bas-Rhin stretches north along the foothills and slopes between Sélestat and Strasbourg.

The wine villages lie back from the Rhine, on the slopes and rises of the Vosges foothills, surrounded by their vineyards. Some of them survived the most recent war, as well as a thousand years of earlier ravages, and the half-dozen that are left are as magical as ever was. Perhaps the loveliest wine town of France, next to Saint-Émilion in Bordeaux, is Riquewihr. Fifteenth- and sixteenth-century houses and courts lie within the encircling town walls. There is an old inn where the flowery wines are served in green-stemmed glasses, the color of the stem adding to the green gold of the wine. And above the stone arches leading into the old *cours* are long flowerboxes full of blooms, and trained against the sandy walls are vines and fruit trees, leafy green along the old streets. Wrought-iron painted signs hang above the shops, oxcarts rumble over the cobblestones, and the water from the town fountains splashes from the mouths of mythical beasts to burble down the open gutters. Kaysersberg is almost as lovely, with a stream running through the town. Houses are built right over it, the water slipping darkly under the arched stone channels. Here and there on the rooftops is a platform made out of a barrel top, a stork's nest perched on top, to bring good luck.

To taste the wine from the neighboring vineyards, you go down into the cellars under the houses, full of great casks, some of them taller than a man and twice as long. Many of the cellars date from

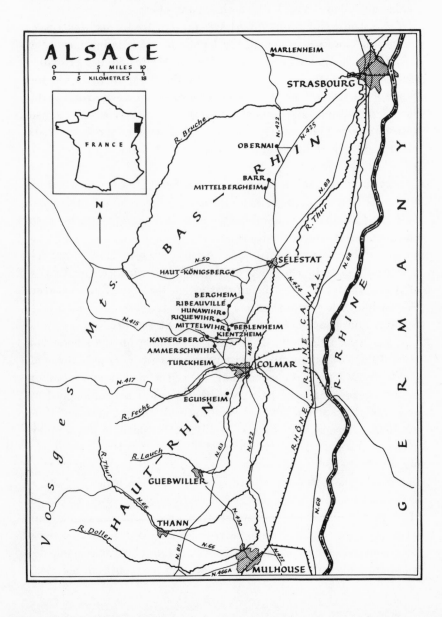

the fourteenth century, and some of the barrels date from the eighteenth. The heavy braces across the ends are carved with harvest scenes or garlands. The new wine is put into old barrels in Alsace, where it rests from October till March before being bottled, being racked once in the first month of the year. Old barrels are especially prized, particularly one in which an exceptional vintage has aged, for the wood soaks up some of the wine, and a great old barrel will lend its greatness to the new wine. To taste a wine, the vintner twists a wooden spigot in the end of the barrel, squirting the wine into a straight-sided glass not much bigger than a three-ounce glass. And in Alsace it's the custom never to spit out the wine being tasted, as you do everywhere else in France.

The Germans ruled Alsace from 1870 until 1918, claiming the province as spoils of the Franco-Prussian War, and when the province returned to France, the winegrowers had a problem. Under German control Alsace vineyards were planted in poor-quality vines that gave a large yield, and in 1918 all the vineyards had to be replanted. Few regions in France have shown the great improvement in quality that is shown by Alsace. To make it clear that poor grapes were no longer being grown, it became the custom to label Alsatian wines with the name of the grape on the bottle, and the custom has continued.

The best vine is the Riesling, that grape which produces all the great German wines; and the next-best is called Gewürz-Traminer, which is not quite so dry, a selection of Traminer vines that boast of a slightly more prominent bouquet than Riesling and make the most highly perfumed white wine of France. The wine is dry, not containing much sugar, but its spicy perfume makes it taste somewhat sweet.

A belief has grown up that the Gewürz is much better than the Traminer, but the difference is slight. Some wine is grown from the Muscat grape, which gives the richest wine, and two Pinot varieties are planted. The better is called Tokay, a Gray Pinot that gets the name Tokay because it is supposed to have been brought in from Hungary. The other variety is the Pinot Blanc, planted in the hope that it would produce wine as great as that grown from the same vines in Burgundy. It hasn't, and the wine of Alsace is a comparatively small wine, though fresh and good; gourmets call it a luncheon wine. The French say it's a wine that lets itself be drunk, meaning one that you take big swallows of, not one you sip.

Far down the list comes Sylvaner, a vine that produces a smaller wine, and that has somehow become one of the best known. The

Sylvaner is planted most extensively in the lesser vineyards of the Lower Rhine. *Edelzwicker* is a blend of wines made from the best grapes; a wine blended from noble and ordinary varieties is called *Zwicker*. *Vin gris*, famous in the world as the Alsatian *rosé*, does not exist in Alsace and comes from neighboring Lorraine. A true *rosé* of Alsace comes from only three or four vineyards and is made from Pinot Noir grapes.

The wines of Alsace are often compared with the great German wines of the Rheingau and the Moselle.

The best of Alsace are certainly better than the run-of-the-mill Liebfraumilchs and other shippers' blends from the Moselle enjoying unwarranted popularity. For one thing, they are usually drier, as they are completely fermented out and leave no unconverted sugar. Hence the average Alsatian wine is higher in alcoholic strength, averaging eleven to twelve per cent, whereas the sterilized bottling methods perfected by Seitz permit many German wines to have an alcoholic content as low as eight to ten per cent and to contain ten to forty grams of unconverted sugar.

Only the domaines, or original *Abfullungs*, made by the producers belonging to the "Natur" wine association, surpass the producers of Alsace in quality. Unquestionably these can be among the greatest white wines of the world.

The Riesling grape produces the best wine of both districts, but the similarity ends there, the soil and climate producing wines with very different characteristics. The Hocks of the Rheingau, which are supposed to take their name from the adjacent town of Hochheimer, are white wines made from grapes picked late, often after the noble rot has begun. There are four classifications of these wines. Those called *Auslese* are wines made from select bunches of grapes. *Beeren Auslese* are wines made from the best grapes selected from these bunches. *Trockenbeeren Auslese* are wines made of selected over-ripe grapes that have been left on the vines until they have lost their excessive moisture. Each successive class is progressively sweeter and more distinctive. *Spätlese* is the word used to indicate late picking with no special selection of grapes.

In Alsace there is late picking, and sometimes you can find a selected wine or an *Auslese*. But although the German vintners use old barrels too and the wine-making is much the same, the wines are entirely different.

The Alsatian vineyards bristle with tall stakes, higher than a man, to each of which a vine is tied, and the tendrils are looped down on each side of the stake, looking like loving-cup handles when in leaf. Each town is surrounded by its great blocks of flowing green, following the contour of the land. There is no official classification of all the vineyards as yet, although many say this will be the tendency as elsewhere in France and within a decade Alsace may fall in line. Until then, you can only buy wines from a particular commune, the name of the vineyard rarely getting on the bottle. As it is, the wine from any one type of grape is blended together with other varieties by the owner, who usually has several different parcels.

Many different *eaux-de-vie* are made in Alsace, and right among the vineyards are great raspberry and strawberry patches and orchards which yield the fruit that is distilled to make the strong colorless spirits. Some thirty pounds of raspberries are needed to make a bottle of *Eau-de-Vie de Framboise*, which makes it fabulously expensive and almost impossible to find. While genuine *Framboise* is dying out on account of its prohibitive cost, *Fraise*, made from strawberries, *Mirabelle*, from yellow plums, and *Kirsch*, from cherries, are still around to take its place. Even these are expensive, and the commercial brands are mixed with alcohol and synthetic flavors as often as not.

Some wine merchants and shippers of Alsace are like those anywhere else in France, or worse, making it almost impossible to buy a genuine Alsatian wine from a good vineyard. Some shippers overblend the wines, selling them so cheaply that the genuine Alsatian bottles seem highly overpriced. The honest shipper or grower who wants to bottle his own wine is faced with the dilemma of meeting the unscrupulous shippers' prices or charging higher prices for his wine. When the vineyards are eventually classified, this difficulty will lessen, and the tall bottles cooling in the high ice buckets will then contain a wine that will take its place with the other fine wines of France.

Vintages, strangely enough, follow the Burgundian, not the German, pattern. Recent years have been very good, and may be rated as follows:

1959   *Very great. Here is a vintage for which the top growers will claim the consideration and respect generally reserved for their German counterparts.*
1960   *Fairly good.*
1961   *Owing to the marvelous weather, the wines of this year were very great, with considerable fruit and flower.*

1962   *A very good vintage. Remarkably well balanced. A wine which will last.*

1963   *A small vintage.*

1964   *A good vintage. Some wines lacked roundness and fruitiness.*

1965   *A very small vintage.*

1966   *Excellent wines. Well balanced.*

1967   *Good wines, well balanced.*

1968   *Poor.*

1969   *Good vintage year with a typically pronounced character.*

1970   *Good quality despite tremendous quantity. Lacking the character that was so prevalent in the '69's.*

1971   *Fair to good quality, well balanced.*

1972   *Average quality with a tendency to excessive acidity.*

Alsatian wines taste best when drunk young, not over five years old, their freshness being one of their main attractions, which they lose with age. Like most dry white wines, those from Alsace also have a tendency to maderize.

THE LESSER WINES
FROM MOUNTAIN
AND PLAIN

Tere are vineyards all over France. Even in Paris the vine grows, and each year an auction is held at which the wines grown in the vineyards of Montmartre are sold. Some people insist that the wine isn't at all bad, and what it lacks in quality it makes up in novelty. It's plain to see that when a Frenchman finds himself in a spot where he can plant a vine, he does.

In the middle of the nineteenth century there were some five million acres under vine, and wine was France's principal source of income. Even today winegrowing in France is big business, although only half as many acres are planted. Last century saw the beginning of scientific research in wine, after many centuries of by-guess-and-by-God study of vines and wine-making. Wine exports were being hurt by the tendency of the wines to go bad during a sea voyage, and Louis Pasteur was requested to find out why. He went to the Arbois, his native province in the Jurals, to experiment, and while his studies made it possible for vintners to discover why wine acted as it did, his findings were more useful to dairymen. Pasteur found that wine could be made to age faster by running oxygen through it, causing it to become soft, losing that greenness of acidity that makes a new wine taste unpleasant. To age wine through oxidation, it is stored in large vats, where it is cooled before being placed back in the barrels. Pasteur also found that heating wine kills the organisms that cause fermentation, thus permitting wine to live longer. But the process made wine lose its liveliness. Even so, wines that are too light in alcohol or that might deteriorate quickly can often be saved by pasteurization.

For sterilizing, the wine is brought up to a temperature of 55 to 65 degrees centigrade, depending on the composition of the wine. For an acid and highly alcoholic wine, 55 degrees centigrade is needed, 60 degrees centigrade for a wine of average acidity and alcoholic content, and 65 degrees centigrade for a wine having little acidity and little alcoholic content. The temperature should never rise above 70 degrees centigrade. Pasteurization is carried out in the complete absence of air.

Pasteur's findings about the cause of fermentation, the effect of oxygen, and the usefulness of heating for preserving poor wines were of help to vintners in making great wines greater because it enabled them to understand the processes wine went through.

Pasteur selected Arbois for his experiments because immense vineyards were planted there and the wines were light. The Côtes du Jura produced wines of every kind—red, white, pink, and yellow—from a strip of vineyards across the Burgundian plain from the Côte d'Or. The phylloxera wiped out more than half of the vineyards, and production is slowly decreasing today. Among the best wines are those of Arbois, white or pink. Many Frenchmen believe that the *rosé* d'Arbois is one of the best in France, on a par with Tavel, although expert opinion ranks it lower. Its white wines are particularly well liked in Bourg and the Bresse country, that marvelous farm area just to the south of the vineyard district. Below Arbois is Château Chalon, famous for its yellow wine, the longest-lived of any in France. After fifty years the wine is deep golden, completely maderized. This is the only wine of France in which maderization is a desired characteristic. Another wine is called *vin de paille,* not merely because it is the color of straw, but because the grapes are laid on straw mats after picking and allowed to dry in the sun for a time to make them richer. Some of these wines are splendid after more than sixty years. Southwest of Château Chalon is the best white wine of Côtes du Jura, from the tiny district of L'Étoile, which also produces *vin jaune, vin de paille,* and sparkling wines.

The Jurals give way to the mountains of the province of Savoy to the south, and from their slopes come white wines from a district, called Crépy, on the French shores of Lake Geneva, and another wine from a district near the headwaters of the Rhône, called Seyssel. From farther to the south comes the light wine called Clairette de Die from the district of the same name. These wines, rarely shipped outside the district where they are made, are typical *vins du pays.*

Inland from the wine districts of Bordeaux, and southeast of the city itself, are the minor districts of Bergerac and Monbazillac. Bergerac is properly more famous for Cyrano, who came from there, than for its heady red and white wines. Between Bergerac and

Saint-Émilion are the districts of Montravel and Sainte-Foy-de-Bor-
deaux,[1] whose wines resemble mediocre Sanit-Émilions. Near by is the
Côte de Duras, whose red and white wines are even smaller than
their reputation or production. The best wines from this area are the
sweet wines of Monbazillac, drunk as dessert wines in many French
homes. The wines have a big body, and while they are often called
"poor man's Sauternes," the quality of some of them is fair and
makes them worth sampling.

The wines of the Pyrenees come from three districts in the
foothills. Jurançon wine was put to the lips of newborn Henri IV
immediately after his birth, in 1553, and this may explain why he
called it his favorite wine. The whites, left four years in barrel, are a
deep golden color when drunk, and would probably be better if
bottled younger. The wine has a perfume all its own, often described
in flowery terms, for it is sweet, spicy, and unique. Farther east and
north is Gaillac, from which come the sweetish white wines frequently made sparkling, and also some dry white wines that are
better to ignore than consider. The best thing in the district is the
Toulouse-Lautrec Museum in Albi. Near by are the small vineyards
of Blanquette de Limoux, where the sparkle is also exploited, many
of the wines being slightly crackling. The wines are small, and are an
argument for insisting on Champagnes.

On the Mediterranean border between France and Spain, and
stretching along the coast, are a series of districts that produce some
acceptable wines with little distinction, rarely exported. Banyuls
produces a sweet wine known as *vin de liqueur* in French, of little
interest in countries where Sherry and Port can be had. Banyuls is a
sweet natural wine, often drunk by those French who like sweet
apéritifs before eating, and as a dessert wine in France. Similar and
also of slight distinction are the wines from the nearby districts of
Maury, Rivesaltes, Côtes d'Agly, Côtes de Roussillon, and the district of Muscat de Frontignan. These wines often taste like Spanish
wines, heavy and slightly sweet, although not fortified, reminiscent
of poor Sherries, while others are close to the Chianti wines of Italy,
and often better.

Some of the coarsest wines of France come from the Midi and
that great plain of Languedoc which stretches from Arles, near the
Rhône, over toward the Spanish border. These are the common wines
of France, sold by alcoholic percentage because they have little else
to recommend them. When old, the dark-red wines look brown on

[1] A district of the Bordeaux region.

the side of your glass, and these wines are often called *pelure d'oignon.*

These plantations were vastly extended at the time of the phylloxera, as were the vineyards in North Africa, particularly those of Algeria, and when the great vineyards of France were rebuilt and began producing, sale of their lesser wines suffered from the competition of the cheap Midi and Algerian growths. This competition is one of the reasons why the great districts worked so hard to clear up fraud, and attempts were made to improve even the smaller wines of the great regions.

At the same time, these cheap wines came to be used as blend wines to stretch out the more famous regionals, a practice that does credit to no one. Tank trucks and tank cars roll north daily to the shipping firms of France, and by the magic of malpractice the cheap wine from Algeria and the Midi are transformed into wines with famous names.

Half the wines of France come from the Languedoc, from the four departments of Gard, Hérault, Aude, and Pyrénées-Orientales. The best are from Corbières, just north of Perpignan, and Minervois, just inland from the coast behind the bulk-wine center of Béziers. Good red wines also come from Saint-Georges; and from near Montpellier, which boasts of the Wine University of France, comes Costières de Gard. All these have their names controlled by law. The only white wines from the area having an *Appellation Contrôlée* are Clairette de Languedoc and Clairette de Bellegarde.

The wines of the beautiful island of Corsica are heady, especially the *rosés* made in the southern part of the island between the Cap Corse and Île-Rousse. Patrimoniaux, once the only superior wine exported to the French mainland, is strong, pink, and high in alcoholic content. Found on many a wine list in small Riviera restaurants, its virile taste complements the pungent bouillabaisse. With the influx of Algerian refugees, the wines have improved, and large quantities are shipped to metropolitan France. But if Corsica has little right to international fame as a wine-producing country, it rests on its laurels as the birthplace of Napoleon Bonaparte and for contributing the word *maquis* to the language, the name for its uncrossable sagebrush and symbol of the French resistance movement. Corsican wines were much more popular at the beginning of the century and found a market in metropolitan France prior to the large plantings of Provence wines.

France imports more wine than any other country, and most of it used to come, before an embargo was placed on its importation, from the North African vineyards around Oran, Algiers, and Constantine. Together these sections make Algeria the largest and most abundant producer of table wines on earth. Wine is also imported from Morocco and from Tunisia.

Former French North Africa is largely Mohammedan, and Islam prohibits drinking. Today's inhabitants might have been happier if the Christianized Berbers, who took over from the Romans during the fifth century, had not been thrown from power, first by invading Arabs and then by the Turks. Descendants of all three groups in the eighteenth century became the Barbary pirates. This scourge of the Mediterranean was laid low by the French, who completed colonizing the area by 1850. Shortly thereafter the French extended the ancient vineyards originally planted by the Phœnicians in the ninth century. When the phylloxera struck the vineyards of France proper, in the second half of the nineteenth century, the vineyards were greatly extended. Recently the large vineyards of Algeria totaled more than 750,000 acres, and were owned by some 5,000 growers. These produced over 400,000,000 gallons (15,000,000 hectoliters) each year, equivalent to a seventh of all that was produced in France.

Algerian winegrowing really became important in the early decades of this century, when modern methods and large-scale production were introduced. Chain-line production brings the wine to vat rooms, where it is stored in glass-lined vats as large as houses. The vineyards are about the size of those in California, Australia, Argentina, and South Africa, planted in the same lesser varieties of grapes. Carignan, Alicante Bouschet, Aramon, Mourestel, and Mourvèdre are the principal red varieties, all heavily planted in California, while Clairette and Ugni Blanc are mostly used for whites. Anybody who has tasted French wines has tasted those from Algeria, for these were used as a base for many of the shippers' wines sold as Burgundy and Bordeaux.

Attempts have been made to standardize the wines, but have failed, for many of the wines are distinct. Plains wines come from the areas of Mitidja and Issers surrounding the city of Algiers, Mostaganem around the port of Philippeville, and Bône in the department of Constantine. The wines are heavy, coarse, and undistinguished and are used primarily for blending. Hillside wines come from areas between Cherchell and Ténès, from near Oran, near Philippeville, and from Sidi-bel-Abbès. Cherchell is where the American submarines landed General Mark Clark's party just before the African invasion, and Sidi was famous as the headquarters of the French Foreign Legion. The wines from the mountain vineyards run from twelve to fifteen per cent in alcoholic content, and often can be a delightful surprise. The districts of Miliana, Médéa, Aïn-Bessem, and Bouira produce small quantities of very creditable white and *rosé* wines. In Oran the vineyards of Tlemcen, near the Moroccan border, and those near the town of Mascara, after which the eye-paint is named, produce some of the better table wines.

Some of these wines can be very good, even though plantations of fine grape varieties are rare, and good wines suffer from the bad reputation of the general run of Algerian wines. Probably the best came from the Domaine de la Trappe de Staoüeli and the Domaine de l'Harrach, near Algiers; but other good ones came from the Domaine de la Lorraine, near Bône, Domaine de Guebar, Domaine du Comte d'Hestel, near Constantine, and the Domaine Saint-Pierre, near Oran.

Algeria has a climate similar to that of southern California, and while Californians claim that every year is a vintage year, the Algerians feel that their vineyards are so far south that vintage years are not important. All the Algerian vineyards produce still table wine, and no fortified wines, such as Sherry, Port, or Muscatel. But in California, over two thirds of the vineyards are devoted to the making of fortified wines, an indication of how small is the amount of natural wine drunk by two hundred million Americans, how much is drunk by fifty million Frenchmen.

Lack of exacting supervision has drastically brought down the quality, and any discussion of Algerian wine today is academic, because of the embargo France has placed on its importation.

CHAMPAGNE:
Most Famous Wine of All

Champagne made its place in the Gay Nineties, when the salesmen from French firms spent thousands every month to convince people that it was impossible to have a good time without a bottle of the sparkling wine. These men were the most elegant salesmen in the world, and one of the best was a gentleman who dwelt in a magnificent house on upper Fifth Avenue and drove around New York in an open carriage with four horses and two liveried footmen. Whenever he entered a restaurant, he ordered free Champagne for everybody in the house.

Although some people feel that Champagne should be reserved for launching ships, most feel a pleasant surge of excitement as the wire muzzle is twisted off the cork and it is slowly pried loose, the expectant pause giving away to happy chatter as the cork pops, the wisp of smoke curls up, and the sparkling wine foams into the tall glasses. Many frown on the practice of allowing the cork to pop, but others believe that the pop is half the fun, and the Champagne-makers are more tolerant about this than the connoisseurs, merely suggesting that the cork should come out into your palm and not go flying off across the room. They are also pleased if the Champagne is properly cold, so that it won't foam all over everything, and if it is served in tulip-shaped glasses, not the shallow sherbet type, which dissipates all the carefully manufactured bubbles and destroys the flavor of the wine.

Anyone who loves Champagne is shocked by the current ridiculous fad for swizzle sticks, those abominations which allow the uncomprehending to twirl all the bubbles out of the sparkling wine. Some even go so far as to have their own special swizzles made out of platinum and gold, always handy for instant use in the fashionable bars and night clubs of Paris and Rome, London and New York. With a few twirls of the swizzle, years of special care and labor can be destroyed in seconds.

The makers of the gay, sparkling wine of Champagne have their capital in Reims, the old cathedral town one hundred miles east and slightly north of Paris. Although Reims is out of the vineyard district, in the middle of a wide and rolling plain, the city is blessed with deep catacombs and old stone quarries, and when the Champagne-makers were in need of a storage place for their bottles, the chalk tunnels of Reims were just the thing. Some of them are a hundred feet underground, and in times of war practically the entire population has gone underground to live. One firm has over fifteen miles of tunnels.

The actual center of the old province of Champagne, and the center of the vineyards that produce the wine, is Épernay, a town of 23,000 people, seventeen miles south of Reims, on the southern bank of the Marne, that calm and winding river which joins the Seine near Paris. Across the river are the vineyards of the Marne Valley, the best of which are on the slopes above the town of Ay (pronounced *AH-ee*), one of the oddest place-names in France. Ay has cellars directly under the vineyards, and it was once said that the grapes did not have to be picked; the workers merely squeezed them, and the juice ran straight down into the *caves*.

Épernay boasts of a stately avenue called Champagne, naturally enough, which begins at a modernistic column erected in honor of the resistance movement, and continues along the slope parallel to the river. Across the flats on the other side you can see the beautiful vineyards, and up the southern slope, behind the rows of impressive buildings that house the Champagne firms, are vent holes of various shapes and sizes, the air shafts leading down into the cellars, which burrow back into the hill.

Over the hill below Épernay, and running south, is a string of towns separated by vineyards, a long, curving ridge that looks like a vast amphitheater. It is the Côte des Blancs, some fifteen miles long. The principal towns are Cramant, Avize, and Mesnil, all looking as if they were about to slip down onto the valley floor. Many of the big firms have press houses in each town throughout the Champagne districts, *vendangeoirs*, to which the vineyard-owners bring their grapes at harvest time and where the baskets of white grapes are inspected by a member of the firm. Each firm accepts grapes at different hours of the day, and when a load is rejected by one, the owner hustles on to another press house in hopes of making his sale there. The single vineyard road is jammed with carts in harvest time.

All the vineyards of the Côte des Blancs are appropriately planted in the white Pinot and the Chardonnay. Some hundred years ago all the vineyards were classified on the basis of one hundred, all those between Cramant and Mesnil being rated over ninety per cent. These are the *Têtes de Cuvées* of the White Slope. Before harvest a representative committee of the growers meets and sets a price. At the same time a committee of the Champagne firms decides on a price they are willing to pay, always lower. The two groups meet, warily, and talk about the price. If they can't agree, as is not unusual, the prefect in Reims is called in to arbitrate, and if his figure is not agreeable to both groups, as happens rarely, that year's grapes are not sold. Since the late 1930's, vineyards have not produced enough to meet the demand, and firms buy under a quota system, which is a constant cause for complaint. Many of the firms own vineyards, each identified by a stone marker that looks like a headstone, to ensure themselves of a portion of each harvest, at least. When the price is

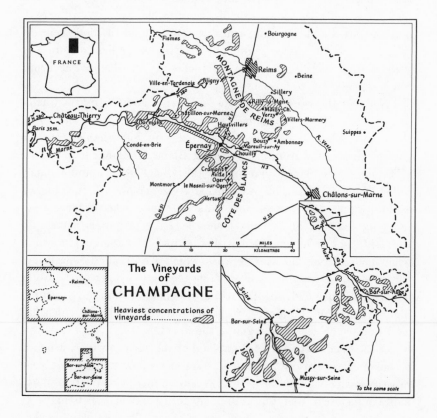

The Vineyards
of
CHAMPAGNE

Heaviest concentrations of
vineyards

fixed there is no haggling. Each owner sells his grapes at a figure reached by multiplying the agreed price by the percentage rating of his vineyard.

Such forehandedness is necessary in Champagne, for the grapes must be gathered and pressed quickly. Except for some of the vineyards of the Moselle, those in Champagne are the farthest north, so the harvest is set as late as possible to increase the sugar content; but this is dangerous, because the frosts come early in Champagne. The vineyards are full of smudge pots, and by each stands a jerry can full of kerosene, leftovers from the war, some painted the olive drab of American field equipment, others the dull blue of the German. In 1960, however, the harvest was begun in mid-September because of an early attack of rot.

Once the prefect sets the date for the beginning of the harvest, pickers stream into the vineyards, carefully rejecting grapes and bunches that are under-ripe, and their loads are hustled into the press houses and quickly squeezed. The presses are large, some dozen feet across, and so made that the heavy press block can be swung over a second press pan, the juice running into vats on the floor beneath the presses, so that, once begun, the pressing never has to stop. The juice is then rushed off to the vat rooms of the Champagne firms, where it is allowed to ferment.

Some of the wine of the Côte des Blancs is made into a Champagne called Blanc de Blancs, white Champagne from the white Pinot only, whose light color makes it easy distinguishable from the golden wines made from black grapes. Blanc de Blancs is not often sold under firm names, but under the village or commune name, called Blanc de Blancs of Cramant, or Avize, or Mesnil. It is known as *Champagne de Cru*, and is most liked by those who prefer exceedingly light wines. Some wine from the white grapes is made into Crémant (not to be confused with the town of Cramant), a white wine, made of red and white grapes, which is only partly sparkling. But most of the white wine made from the white grapes of the Côtes des Blancs is blended with the white wine made from the red grapes planted north of the Marne, to make those Champagnes which are most familiar to celebrants around the world.

Each firm has its own secret blend of the various wines, which it is constantly modifying because of differences in the wine from year to year, changes in the taste of different countries, and attempts to improve its blend. Blending is difficult, for each firm tries to make its Champagne taste the same from year to year. The new wine is raw, hiding its potential qualities, and the tasters must know what it is going to taste like once it matures. What makes this harder is that the sugar content varies from year to year, so before fermentation cane sugar dissolved in wine is added, in order that when the fermentation changes it into alcohol, all the wine will have the same alcoholic content, usually twelve per cent by volume.

All the white grapes come from south of Épernay, out of the vineyards of the White Slope, but all the black grapes come from the vineyards to the north of the Marne, those along the river and those from the slopes of the mountain that rises out of the plain beween Épernay and Reims, which is called the Montagne de Reims. These vineyards stretch in the shape of a question mark around the wooded mountain. Those of Mailly and Verzenay face north across the plain to Reims, five miles away, where the cathedral rises out of the distance. These are *hors classe* vineyards, rated at one hundred per cent. Next to them on the curving slope, facing northeast, are the first-category vineyards of the commune of Verzy. Facing southeast are the one hundred per cent vineyards of Ambonnay and Bouzy, also in the district called Montagne de Reims. Facing south along the Marne Valley, to make the shank of the question mark, are the one hundred per cent vineyards of Ay, flanked by those of the first category in the communes of Mareuil and Dizy.

All these vineyards are planted in Pinot Noir, or a variety, the same that is used to make the great red wines of Burgundy. But in Champagne the wine is small and acid because of the soil, an outcropping of the same Kimeridgian chalk you find in Chablis. There the warmer sun matures the grapes better, but in Champagne sugar must often be added. Here bare chalk outcroppings break up the stretches of vineyard, and even the plantations look white when plowed, the soil often being only a couple of inches deep. The vines are trained high, with double or triple rows of wire stretched along the root tops, and three or four long vine tendrils stretched along the wire, looking like a woman's hair pulled back from her head.

When the black grapes are pressed, they are run through as quickly as possible to avoid prolonged contact with the skins, which might impart their color to the juice. For pink champagne, the juice is left with the skins a little longer.

Some firms make special blends of wines coming from only the one hundred per cent vineyards, but most of the Champagnes are blends of several different grades. In Mailly a cooperative was formed during the depression, when the firms refused to buy the harvest, which began making a Champagne from the black grapes of the member growers. They've had tough going, starting with no capital, and building their own *vendangeoir* during the off season. After regular working hours the members dug the caves in the soft chalk underneath, progressing during the winter at the rate of a yard a day. Today the cooperative has nearly sixty members, and produces a vintage Champagne, both pink and white, the favorite wine at the George V and Plaza Athénée hotels in Paris. Such a sparkling wine from only one commune is rare in the black Pinot districts.

Most houses produce vintage Champagne, all the wine the product of one particular harvest, but most also produce cheaper nonvintage Champagne, a blend of two or more years. This is perfectly logical for a manufactured wine, the addition of wine from good years improving the quality of those from bad vintages.

Although Champagne is what it is because of the soil and climate that produce the wine, the manufacturing process is important too. Everyone denies that it was Dom Pérignon who devised the process, but because nobody knows who it actually was, the blind old monk still gets the credit, from tradition. All over Champagne you can see his statue, reproductions of the original, which is in the court of Moët & Chandon in Épernay, standing in his monk's robe, holding up a goblet, with a couple of bottles at his feet, and a beatific expression on his Roman face. He was the first to think of putting a hunk of cork bark in the neck of a bottle instead of a wad of cloth, and as he was a cellar-master, he probably noticed that wine had a second fermentation the spring following the vintage, even if he didn't think of adding some sugar to increase it.

In any event, a dose of sugar is what makes all the bubbles, called a bead by Champagne-makers, who will tell you that the smaller the bead, the better the Champagne. After the wine has been hauled to the vat rooms, it is poured into glass-lined tanks the size of a small room, where the wine is allowed to ferment for three or four weeks.

The different wines ferment separately, each in its own vat, until sometime in December or January, when all the doors and windows of the vat room are thrown open; the cold air stops any last vestiges of fermentation. The wine is then drawn off its lees. This operation, called racking, is usually performed three times. Each time the wine is cleared, or fined, with fishtails or the whites of eggs, which helps rid the wine of suspended impurities. After the first racking the new wines are blended, and after the third any wines from other vintages that are considered needed to make the proper blend are added. By March the wine is bottled, with a dose of cane sugar dissolved in wine added to each bottle. Then the bottles are sealed with a temporary cork held down by a steel-wire clamp and are stored in the cellars, neck nestling into neck, piled like so much cordwood.

With spring, the miracle of Champagne begins. The sealed bottles of wine are dozens of feet underground, stored at a low constant temperature, one that never varies. But when the sap begins to rise in the trees, somehow the bacteria begin to work in the wine. A second fermentation begins. The sugar is turned into alcohol, the process forming carbon dioxide gas, building up a pressure in the bottle that is often more than a hundred pounds to the square inch. In the old days, before the cellar-masters knew how much sugar to add, and before bottles were uniform, one would sometimes explode, often starting another bottle, until the echoing pops sounded like firecrackers; but this rarely happens today.

The bottles rest flat for four years, during which time the fermentation forms a deposit in the wine. When fermentation has finally ceased, the side of the bottle opposite the deposit is painted with a blob of whitewash, and a line of whitewash is smeared on the punt, that thumb-deep depression in the base of each bottle. The bottles are carefully placed in slanting racks, neck down. These racks, called *pupitres,* are tables with oval holes in them big enough for the bottle necks and shoulders. For four months a worker labors to get the sediment down in the neck of the bottle, wiggling it one day, turning it a bit the next, and gradually tipping the bottle more upright. Gradually the deposit moves down, and when its tail is against the cork, the bottles are stacked, standing on their heads, the cork of one resting in the punt of the bottle beneath it.

They stay that way until the firm gets an order for shipment. Then they are placed neck-down in a heavy, partitioned wicker basket holding six, and lugged to that part of the cellar where the disgorging, or sediment removal, takes place. A worker holds the bottle upside down against a gauntlet on his left arm, with corked mouth in his hand. Standing in front of a barrel with a hole cut in its side, he works the cork loose with a pair of pliers. It flies into the barrel with a bang, the man twists the bottle upright, runs his left thumb around the neck, smells it, tastes his thumb, and before the wine begins to foam, slaps the bottle in a circular rack, the mouth against a rubber nipple, the punt against a breast-shaped pad.

The trick is to have the sediment shoot out with the cork, and the bottle is held upside down so that the air space in the bottle pops up through the Champagne, blowing out the sediment before it has a chance to fall down into the sparkling wine. Some firms freeze the necks of the bottles, so there is no risk of losing any of the wine. Other firms do not, because they think freezing hurts the wine.

Next to the disgorger is another worker, who takes the bottle from the circular rack and sets it in a similar one in front of him. This machine has a superstructure of silver-plated knobs and tubes, and a couple of bottles hanging on it, upside down. One contains a bottle of the same Champagne that is being handled, from which to fill up any bottles that have lost too much in the disgorging. The other bottle contains cane sugar dissolved in wine. A dose of this is added to the wine, depending on which type of Champagne is wanted: *Brut, Extra Dry,* or *Sec.*

In the old days before the turn of the century, people liked sweeter Champagne than they do today. Champagne was then a dessert wine more than anything else, but it has become less sweet through the years because people's taste has tended toward dryness. Occasionally Champagnes are made without the addition of sugar, but not many people care for them. The favorite of the Champagne firms is *Brut,* to which up to 1½ per cent of sugar by volume is added. Up to 3 per cent is added to make Extra Dry, up to 4 per cent for Dry, which amounts to about a teaspoonful of syrup per bottle. *Demi-sec* Champagne contains up to 8 per cent, and sweet or *Doux* up to 10. The amount of sugar added varies with different firms, some making a *Brut* containing only the minimum ¾ per cent, and they change their formulas from time to time.

Brut costs more than the others, because the smaller dose of sugar does not disguise the taste of the wine under a smothering sweetness. Good Champagnes have little sugar added, their natural sugar content being enough to form the bubbles. But sugar is often added to the cheaper Champagnes to hide the shortcomings of the wine.

The dosing is gauged automatically. The bottle is then handed on to the corker, whose machine squeezes the thick cork, which is made in sections. By means of a rope attached to a weighted metal plunger, the cork is forced down into the mouth of the bottle. This is another ticklish operation, for the bottle then goes on to the fourth man of the disgorging team, whose machine puts the metal cap on the cork and tightens the wire muzzle around the top of the cork and the bottle lip. The banging on of the metal cap forces the cork in farther, and if the cork goes in too far, the wire muzzle won't hold properly, the cork will work loose, all the bubbles will fizz away, and the wine will go flat.

The bottle then goes to the packing-room, where it is labeled and wrapped. All in all, a bottle of Champagne goes through eighty-four hands from cellar to shipping crate, and the workers must be highly skilled. In addition to his wages, a worker gets a bottle of ordinary wine a day so he won't be tempted to tipple the Champagne, and as further encouragement to abstinence he also gets two or three bottles of Champagne a month, which he often sells.

Champagne costs so much not only because it has to be handled so often, but also because it has to be kept in bottles so long. In addition, press houses in the vineyard districts are needed to process the grapes. Some firms have as many as a dozen such *vendangeoirs*, and each one costs something like $30,000 a year to run. But the main reason Champagne costs so much is the heavy taxes leveled against it, extra taxes because it is sparkling. There is nearly a dollar a bottle duty and tax on Champagne imported to the United States, ten times more than those on still wines.

The vineyards of Champagne are probably the most subdivided in the world, as insurance against hail, the theory being that a storm will hit one section and miss another, and if the grower has sections in different areas, the chances are he won't lose all his grapes. The result, of course, is that expensive farm equipment is impractical, for a grower would spend too much time moving it from parcel to parcel and would not have enough time for working. And as labor costs rise, so will the price of Champagne.

In 1964, Champagne firms sold approximately 90,000,000 bottles of the sparkling wine, close to 76,000,000 in France, in France's former colonies, and in England. The United States imported less than 3,000,000 bottles.

Champagne vintages are less important than vintages in other wine districts, for Champagne is a blended and manufactured wine, but there are a few that are outstanding: 1948, 1949, 1952, 1953, 1955, and 1959. Recent vintages may be rated as follows:

1959   *The very great 1893 alone can claim to be a peer of 1959.*
       Fortunately, the excellent weather toward the end of May
       and the beginning of June permitted bountiful flowering
       of the vine; hence, the quantity—approximately 65,000,-
       000 bottles—is more than three times that produced in
       1957, and ten per cent more than that of 1955.

1960   *Not a vintage year.*

1961   *In contrast with the yield of most of the other districts of*
       France, the quantity was satisfactory. Quality was excellent.

1962   *Some firms produced a vintage, others did not.*

1963   *A lack of sunshine produced wines on the acid side, which*
       are useful in the blending of nonvintage wines.

1964   *A very good vintage, plentiful in quantity. The wines are*
       round and full. Ninety-three million bottles were pro-
       duced.

1965   *A nonvintage year.*

1966   *Magnificent wines. Excellent bouquet with great finesse. Well*
       balanced. Some eighty million bottles were produced.

1967   *What could have been an exceptional vintage was diminished*
       by pouring rains between the fifth and twenty-first of Sep-
       tember, just prior to the harvest, which started one week
       later. Rot developed in grapes that lacked maturity. 420,-
       000 barrels were produced and the high price of a thousand
       dollars was paid by the champagne firms to the growers for
       each ton of grapes brought to their local fermenting cellars.

1968   *A nonvintage year.*

1969   *A good vintage, well-balanced and full-bodied. A small*
       quantity produced.

1970   *Abundant quantity, breaking all previous records. Fair to*
       good in quality with excellent balance. Part of this vintage
       was sold in France as still Champagne.

1971   *Good vintage, fruity. Very small quantity.*

1972   *Strangely enough, this northernmost region of France was*
       the most favored of all in this year. Both quality and
       quantity were good.

Like all white wines, sparkling or not, Champagne should be drunk fairly young, say within ten to fifteen years after the harvest. This, in spite of the fact that some connoisseurs like to talk about bottles decades-old. Like all white wines, Champagne has a tendency to maderize with age, turning brown and musty. Because of the gas pressure in the bottles, Champagne is also more likely to become corky.

THE BRANDIES OF FRANCE:
Cognac and Armagnac

Brandies are perhaps the most wonderful spirits ever devised by the genius of man. The wonder of their excellence is known around the world. A fine old brandy has become a symbol of the richness of civilized living, and its powers of resuscitation have been lauded for centuries. The drinking of a glass of fine brandy is one of life's great luxuries. Time makes brandy, man can only help.

Tasters buy brandy by smell, and more than half the pleasure of a great brandy comes from its heady aroma. The most sensible glass is one of good size, with a small amount of brandy in the bottom. While many people insist on large balloon glasses, others prefer the long and comparatively slender tulip shapes. Both are excellent, for they permit of swirling the brandy in the glass, which brings the liquid into contact with the air, while their shapes form an enclosing chimney so none of the fine bouquet is lost. Such glasses are pretentious, however, when the brandy is young and mediocre, and many people who serve fine wines follow them with insignificant brandies. A great wine deserves to be followed by an old brandy.

Brandy is an *eau-de-vie,* the water of life, the French term for all distilled spirits, which in northern Europe are called *aqua vite.* By European nomenclature, even whiskies and bourbons are classed as *eaux-de-vie,* or spirits.

In France, the term *brandy* is usually limited to distillations of wine, mainly Armagnac and Cognac, although undistinguished brandies come from other districts, and to distillations of the residue of stems and pulp remaining in the vats after the pressing, which is called *marc.* Marcs are made in most of the wine districts of France, but the best come from Champagne, Burgundy, and the Rhône Valley. The finest bear the names of the vineyards from which they come, are produced in very small quantities, and rarely reach the market. When well aged, they have a distinctive, grapy, earthy, leathery taste. A fine Marc de Champagne is light, with much finesse. Burgundy marcs are fuller and heavier. Most of them are sold simply as Marc de Bourgogne, although better ones carry the name of vineyard or domain, such as Marc de la Romanée-Conti, Marc de Musigny, Marc de Chambertin, Marc de Nuits-Saint-Georges, and Marc du Marquis d'Angerville. The most expensive is the Marc des Hospices de Beaune, sold at the annual auction sale. The most notable of those from the Rhône Valley is the Marc de l'Hermitage.

Many brandies are called *alcools blancs* because of their white color. Quetsch is distilled from purple plums, Mirabelle from tiny yellow plums, Framboise from raspberries, Fraise from strawberries, and Kirsch from the tiny pits of small cherries. They are often drunk in Europe, but have not as yet become popular in the United States. They are colorless because they are not aged in wood, but in crockery, and are slow in maturing. All are exceedingly dry, and some of the best ones can be found by searching out the small producers and peasant growers who make them—a practice followed by good French restaurateurs.

In Normandy, cider is distilled to make *Calvados*, the finest apple brandy in the world. The name is taken from the department of Calvados, and the best comes from the Vallée d'Auge, its greatest cider-making district. When old, Calvados can be a magnificent brandy, but fine ones can rarely be found outside the cellars of Normandy. A good number of New York importers bring in some excellent Calvados. A distillation is made from the residue of apple pressings when making cider, and this is usually called Apple-jack, in France *eau-de-vie de marc de cidre*.

In Normandy, dinners are so enormous that something called the *trou normand* has become a custom. This is a pause between courses, when the diners take a short rest, fortifying themselves for following courses by downing a shot of Calvados.

All of these brandies bear only a family resemblance to liqueurs, which are distilled from various concoctions of herbs and berries, sometimes with a brandy base. There are hundreds of liqueurs, and in the nineteenth century new ones were created whenever some great event was worthy of being commemorated. Among the best are Chartreuse Verte, which contains more than one hundred separate ingredients, Chartreuse Jaune, which is made of fewer ingredients and is less powerful, and the world-famous Benedictine. Others are Crème de Menthe; the Cherry liqueurs, of which the best come from

Denmark; and the triple secs, such as Cointreau and Orange Curaçao, these being the most commonly drunk liqueurs in France. Many are still made by monks, who began the making of liqueurs in the first place. But liqueurs are not brandy.

The distilling of wine began centuries ago, because the resulting product could be transported easily and made bad water safe and palatable. It was the only hard drink then known to man, and up to the last century brandies had complete control of the spirits market. As a result of the inroads made by whiskies, brandy-makers have tried to reduce brandy to the level of whiskies by recommending it for highballs and mixed drinks, thus sacrificing its position as the greatest of all distillates in the effort to regain economic supremacy. Brandy still remains unique, however.

The name probably comes from the Germanic word *brannt,* *Branntwein* meaning burned wine, a name forever preserved in the annals of American history by Brandywine, the scene of the Revolutionary battle. And, as one would expect, the greatest brandy comes from France.

Ships from the north used to stop off along that part of the French coast just above the Gironde estuary, mostly at the port of La Rochelle, to pick up cargoes from the salt deposits. It wasn't long before the local inhabitants figured out that they might also sell the traders wine as well. What was good business for Bordeaux, down to the south, would be good business for the townspeople who lived along the Charente River.

Unlike many good ideas, it worked too well, and by the seventeenth century too much wine was being produced. Although Villeneuve talked of the water of life as early as the fourteenth century, it was a knight named Croix-Maron who is supposed to have popularized the idea of distilling the wine, the product being easier to ship, taking up only one tenth of the hold space wine would occupy, and being harmed not at all by the sea journey. He was also pleased to discover that it tasted magnificent, which prompted him to announce without a trace of modesty: "In cooking my wines, I have discovered their soul."

He was right, for by the time Napoleon arrived on the scene, nearly two hundred years later, almost every brandy made anywhere in the world had come to be called Cognac, after the town of that name on the Charente River. Spanish brandies came to be called *coñac* in imitation, and the name persists today, although the only resemblance is that both are distilled from wine. The same name is also still applied to brandies from South America. Until the 1930's, when reciprocal treaties forbade the practice, brandy made in the United States was also called Cognac, with no attempt to convert the spelling.

Cognac was properly incensed at this imitation, for it was the wine from which the brandy was distilled that set Cognac apart, making it uniquely great. The small white wines of the vineyards along the Charente were hard and acid, but all the unpleasantness disappeared in the cooking. What's more, the casks were made from specially seasoned oak from the nearby province of Limousin. The best oak comes from the edge of a forest, it is said, and certain sections are supposed to be better than others, being classed in separate growths, or *crus*. The tannin picked up from the wood during aging gives another special distinction to the brandy, to say nothing of the precious secrets of the distilling itself, or the fine art of blending the brandy from different vineyards.

Napoleon re-established the supremacy of real Cognac over its spurious competitors by drinking Cognac brandy exclusively and carting it all over Europe on his campaigns. During the nineties the only fashionable brandy was the one called Napoleon's "Return-from-Russia" Cognac, and one of the favorite gambits of wine wags is to state that the main task of Napoleon's armies was to lug Cognac around so that it could bear his name.

Many firms still call their best Cognacs Napoleon Brandy. They

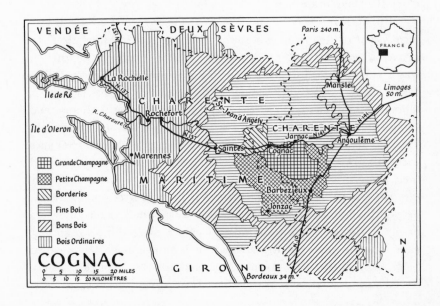

claim that it has become a tradition in the industry, but it is more accurate to say that a firm calls one of its grades Napoleon Brandy in the hope that unknowing buyers will really believe the Cognac is from the same stock from which the Little Corporal was supplied. There is no real Napoleon Brandy on sale anywhere today, and even if there were, it would not be so good as an old Cognac bottled yesterday. The name is false and purposely misleading. Cognac does not age in bottle, and for that matter, neither does any other *eau-de-vie* or liqueur, though a few believe they can detect a slight mellowing in a long-bottled *alcool blanc*. The high alcoholic content preserves it in exactly the same state as at the moment it was bottled.

The brandy of Cognac comes from a district now limited by law. No other brandy in France is entitled to be called Cognac, the name of the main town in the center of the vineyards. Many of the big firms are located there, while most of the others have their offices and plants in Jarnac, a small town ten miles farther up the Charente toward Angoulême. Before World War II the Charente was used to transport the Cognac to the port of La Rochelle for shipment, and the rows of horse-drawn barges was one of the sights of the region. Today most hauling is done by truck.

During the winter after the harvest, the vineyard-owners get a permit to distill their wines, and they sell the raw colorless brandy to the shipping firms, which store it, barrel piled on barrel, in warehouses; and there it rests, waiting while time turns it into great Cognac. All the buildings near Cognac firms are stained black, as if the buildings had once been afire and the sooty smoke had leaked out through the cracks. The stain is made by evaporating alcohol fumes, which, according to local intelligence, cause the growth of a microscopic fungus when the fumes hit the air.

The vineyards of the Cognac district are divided into six classes: those called Grande Champagne, to the south of the town of Cognac; Petite Champagne, south of that, with the town of Jarnac in its center; the Borderies, to the west of Jarnac; and all three surrounded by those vineyards called Fins Bois. These, in turn, are surrounded by Bons Bois, while over on the coast and on the two islands just off shore are vineyards classed as Bois Ordinaires. Originally the word *Champagne* meant chalky soil, the districts being at that time land surrounded by woods. The bois were later cleared and planted with vineyards. Brandies from the districts are aged separately, then blended by the shippers.

This is not a wicked practice, as it would be if wines were

blended, however, for the brandy from each district lacks certain qualities, according to brandy experts. The brandy from Grande Champagne, for instance, ages very slowly, and is heavier, more pungent, and finer than that from Petite Champagne, which ages quite rapidly. Most firms sell a Cognac called Fine Champagne, a blend of the two, but it is expensive, not only because it has to be aged so long, but also because it takes some ten bottles of wine to make one of brandy. To put brandy within the reach of everyone, the "Champagnes" are blended with Borderies, a soft, fat, supple, full-bodied, quickly aging brandy, and with Fins Bois, which lacks finesse, and Bons Bois, which has a taste imparted by the earth, this *goût de terroir* destroying what finesse it has. Each of these brandies ages successively faster, and ordinary brandies are made of a large proportion of the distillate from Bois Ordinaires vineyards.

All these vineyards used to be planted in Folle Blanche, which is being replaced, about two thirds of the plantations now being in Saint-Émilion vine, a variety of Ugni Blanc. This vine produces more, and flowers later, and is therefore not so likely to be frozen by spring frosts. The name of the vine has nothing to do with the Bordeaux district of the same name.

The vineyards were almost completely wiped out when the phylloxera struck in the late 1870's. That misery was added to by the fact that the grafted American stocks were subject to another disease characteristic of the extremely chalky soil of Cognac, called green sickness. As a result, the number of acres in vines dropped from nearly three quarters of a million to less than one fifth, which is what is in vine today.

The wine is distilled twice. It is first brought to a boil and yields a spirit of some 25 per cent alcohol, or about 50 proof. Then it is distilled again, the first and last of the steam, the head, and tail being discarded; only the middle distillate, called the heart, is kept. The heart ends up at between 60 and 70 per cent of alcohol, 120 to 140 proof, and raw enough to corrode the hide off a mule.

Some say that the secret of a great Cognac is the temperature at which distillation takes place, which may account for the present-day use of old-fashioned pot stills. New-fangled stills and distillation methods are constantly being introduced in the district, but few are successful, the centuries-old methods and equipment still proving best.

The new Cognac is next poured into barrels of the Limousin oak, where it remains anywhere from six to fifty years. The brandy loses about two per cent of its alcohol each year through evaporation, more at the beginning and less toward the end of the aging period. After half a century the proof is down to eighty or ninety, which has proved to be the best strength at which to drink it, for then the brandy is at a peak of perfect balance, and longer aging would only weaken it still more, with no increase in flavor or body or aroma.

At one time it was thought that the alcoholic content steadily declined, and then after thirty years or so suddenly increased again. Where the increase came from remained in the realm of mystery, and while this change is physically impossible, a few of the old brandy-makers still believe in the miracle. In any event, once bottled, a brandy ceases to improve with age, kept from change by its high alcoholic content. A fifty-year-old brandy bottled yesterday is on a par with a fifty-year-old brandy bottled a century ago, and is probably better if the brandies were of the same quality to begin with.

Most Cognacs are a blend of different years, as well as of different districts, the label indicating the age of the oldest brandy, not that of the most in quantity, unless more specifically identified. For this reason United States laws do not permit the labeling of brandies as to age. Some firms now and then bottle vintage Cognac, all of it coming from a particular year, but this is rare.

Although all other *eaux-de-vie* come to market clear and color-less, it has become the habit to prefer a brandy that is brown. In really old brandies this color comes from the tannin in the barrel wood, but in the less expensive grades burned sugar is added, the caramel coloring the Cognac to the desired shade. To improve the smooth flavor of their cheap Cognacs, some unscrupulous firms add vanilla flavoring, which is relatively hard to detect. A good brandy should taste dry and smooth, with little or no aftertaste, and because vanilla flavoring lingers in the mouth, it can be detected in this way, even if you can't smell it. This doctoring might not be thought so wicked if it was mentioned on the bottle, or if cheap brandies weren't thus disguised to sell as fine Cognacs. Fortunately, there are enough honest firms to make it possible to get good brandy at fair prices.

There are all sorts of letters and galaxies of stars on Cognac bottles, each firm having its own system. The use of the star was introduced after the phylloxera, when it was decided that good vintages ought to have a star to represent a comet. The comet became a symbol of excellence in 1811, the year of Halley's comet, when the vintage was of an astounding excellence; the wines are still spoken of with awe. The second good year after the phylloxera was to have two stars, and so on. But the star markings soon became cumbersome.

Three Star usually means the cheapest brandy of a firm's line, at least three years old, and often six, diluted with distilled water to bring it down to about forty-two per cent or eighty-four proof. Nearly all brandies are diluted to this strength, and while you can find brandies that have reached this witching point merely through age and evaporation, such half-century-old brandies are extremely expensive. Brandies between seven and twelve years old are usually called VO or VE, "very old" or "very extra"; VSO, VSOP, and VVSOP are older than ten years, the last meaning "very very superior old pale." There are some remarkable VSOP's, which are scarce and hard to find. They may be from thirty to sixty years old. It is strange that old brandies should be called "pale" when darkness has become a criterion of distinction.

These signs and their meaning change, with whim and regulations. The best way to buy brandy is by price, but *only* if it is a bottle put out by a good firm, when price expresses its value, and provided it is sold by a reliable merchant.

The young brandies, which start at about seven dollars a bottle, taste fine when mixed with soda or made into cocktails or toddies, but such mixing is sacrilege to older brandies. It takes years to get the smooth, wonderful flavor into an old brandy, and mixing or diluting destroys it. Young brandies are a let-down after a fine meal, and older ones can be bought for only slightly more. In the 1930's an old brandy cost at least twice as much as the young ones, but in the fifties they cost less than a quarter more, and are today one of the best values in things to drink. You don't save money by buying good brandy, but you get more for it.

Brandy evaporates rapidly because of its alcohol and ethers, and as it is drunk rarely and in small amounts, small bottles are good value—just the opposite of wine. It is still the fashion to use large display bottles, but the last half never tastes as good as the first.

Gravity is an important element in the making of Cognac. That is why most of the big firms are built on hillsides. The barrels are trundled into an upper floor of the blending plant after being brought from the *chais* where they have been aging, and then dumped into great vats, which are the size of a hall bedroom and hold over six thousand gallons. Pipe lines lead from these vats to others, in which the blending takes place, the Cognac passing through thick wool filters, which look like the top of a bass drum. Wooden paddles whisk the various Cognacs together to make for thorough mixing, and here and there are wooden manhole covers so that the blenders can watch the flowing. The blended brandies are run into man-high vats on the floor below, and these are tapped when needed, pipes carrying the blends down another floor to the bottling-room, where machines rinse the bottles with brandy, and men place them on an endless chain, where other machines fill, cap, and label them. This bottling-room is monitored by a man in a glass-enclosed booth that looks like the control room of a battleship, where with a system of spigots he can control which vats are being tapped. Small firms do all this by hand.

Blending is an art, for each part of the world seems to have special preferences in color and flavor. The English climate, for instance, imparts a musty taste to brandies, and the blender must see that bottles slated for England have that particular mustiness the English associate with good brandy. Because each barrel tastes slightly different, it is difficult to make a brandy type that will taste the same all the time, and it is the blender's job to make the taste as consistent as possible. From time to time, firms change their formulas, always trying to make new blends more popular, which is why bottles of any particular brand may taste different from shipment to shipment.

If it were not for its brandy, the great flat stretch of sunbroiled land with Cognac in its center would be known only as the birthplace of Francis I and because good melons are grown there. Cognac is a quiet, stolid town, its streets and buildings bleached gray by the scorching sun, and even its large park still and dusty in the hot summers. But the heat is what makes the wine from which Cognac is made, and everybody agrees it is worth the discomfort. And as is usual, there's the classic Cognac story, probably apocryphal, a little worn by now, but still told to everyone who comes to the hot little city on the winding Charente. It seems that a party of bishops was having dinner in Rome, and one of the party was asked where he came from. "I am the Bishop of Angoulême," he informed the company. The announcement was greeted with silence and blank stares. "I am also the Bishop of Cognac," he stated, and at once there was a chorus of gasps, and the other bishops exclaimed in chorus: "Ah, the splendid See of Cognac!"

It is good to know that Cognac tastes better than any of the stories about it.

ARMAGNAC

Armagnac comes from the land of d'Artagnan, a fabled region once rich and famous, where witches can still be found to bring you luck or curse your enemies, where husking bees and barn dances are the favorite winter sport, and where mourners sit down and eat a dish of beans together after a funeral. The cold wind howls down from the Pyrenees in winter, and the rolling land broils brown under the searing southern sun in summer. This is the land of the Gascons.

The city of Auch is on the eastern edge of the Armagnac district, a hilltop town of some sixteen thousand people, crowned by a cathedral that was started in the fourteenth century and finally completed by Louis XIV. It boasts an almost unknown marvel of France, a magnificent choir seat decorated with hundreds of tiny carved wooden figures, each a minor masterpiece. The artist was a pupil of Michelangelo's, and the wood he worked had been left to harden and blacken in water for a hundred years.

Many of the townspeople and those from the countryside have Spanish names and faces; they are descendants of Goths and Visigoths, returned from raids into Spain, who liked the wide spaces of Gascony so much they settled there. Because Gascony was the birthplace of Protestant King Henri IV, many of the local people are Protestant and many of their farms are marked by identifying cypress trees so there will be no doubt of their faith. But even the Protestants have kept to the old custom of church seating: women in front, men behind. It's a strange land.

The brandy of Armagnac is as distinctive as the people who make it and the land from which it comes. Strong and heady, a fine Armagnac boasts a full-bodied pungency when well matured and properly cared for, which gives it a powerful character of its own. Most of it goes to market in a bottle as distinctive as its taste, round and flat, with a long neck, and called a *basquaise*, after the neighboring region where it originated. But the way Armagnac is made bears only a family resemblance to the process of making Cognac, for all the Armagnac firms are small, and there are no great blending plants.

Following the harvest, portable stills travel about the countryside to the different growers. The apparatus looks like a small old-fashioned locomotive, and growers insist that one still can be better than another. Distillation is a single continuous process, carried on very slowly, the new wine becoming raw brandy that comes out at

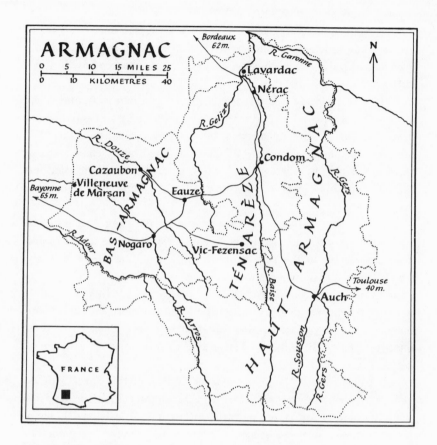

about 52 per cent or 104 proof. The brandy is then poured into barrels made from local oak, the oak of Armagnac imparting more tannin to the aging brandy than other oaks. Local growers feel that a good third of the Armagnac character comes from the oak in which it ages.

The best vineyards of the district are in a region named Bas-Armagnac, called Lower Armagnac because the country is less hilly than the rest. The very center of this district is called Grand Bas, the special vineyards being somewhat sandier and for that reason producing a more delicate brandy. The vineyards of Ténarèze make up the second district, and those in Haut-Armagnac form the third. All produce wines of the slope, the vines planted in tall *Y's*, their tendrils strung on wires.

The growers set their prices, and meet buyers, at the Café de France in Eauze, a tiny and charming village in the center of the vineyard districts. There, over glasses of the hard, local wine, they discuss their Armagnacs, arguing about vintages, exchanging tricks of the trade, discussing markets. Now and then, to prove a point, a grower will pull from his pocket a small sample bottle of his brandy, biting out the cork with his teeth.

Brandy is rarely drunk when being bought and sold, and much of it is rarely tasted. A few drops are poured into the palm and perhaps touched with the tongue, but usually the hands are rubbed together, then cupped in front of the nose. The brandy character can be detected best by the sense of smell. One grower claims that his father spent his entire life buying Armagnac and never tasted a drop.

After a few sniffs of the warmed and evaporating Armagnac on his palms, an old grower will have enough clues to be able to make good guesses as to the age of the brandy and the vineyards from which the original wine came, and perhaps even the particular lot from which the brandy was distilled. Buyers traveling around to growers in various districts are apt to depend more on their taste, however, for they must be able to detect in young Armagnacs those qualities that will make it distinctive after a quarter century of aging.

Because it is the land of the most famous of the Three Musketeers, most firms have their Réserve d'Artagnan, much the way Cognac firms resort to sticking Napoleon's name on a bottle. Perhaps the only person who really has the right to use the famous name is a direct descendant of that roistering gallant. He is the Marquis de Montesquiou, a mustached man who bears a marked resemblance to his ancient ancestor.

The Marquis is the owner of Château de Marsan, a great turreted castle near Auch, parts of which date from the tenth century. The paneled rooms and great halls are filled with portraits of a thousand years of famous ancestors. The Marquis, who is also the fifth Duc de Fezensac, which is a nearby commune full of vineyards whose wine becomes Armagnac, operates the château and its estate as a model farm and experimental station. He is apt to tell you that local legend says Armagnac is an aphrodisiac and was d'Artagnan's favorite drink.

The Marquis is one of the men primarily responsible for re-establishing the greatness of the name of Armagnac, for in this ancient land of French tradition little of the tradition attaches to the creation of fine Armagnac. In the days of Queen Victoria, Armagnac was thought to be too lusty a brandy, too powerful in aroma, to be allowed in the drawing room. Until *Appellation d'Origine* laws were passed, in fact, Armagnac was shipped north to be blended with Cognac. Today tastes are sturdier, and fine Armagnacs can again be drunk outside the region of its birth and under its own name.

Yet all Armagnac is not fine, and perhaps the principal reason is the lack of tradition among Armagnac shippers. Most shippers carry their businesses in their hats, and their concern is selling gallons of the local brandy, with little interest in maintaining a worldwide reputation for great quality. There is a great difference between fine and cheap Cognacs, but there is a still greater difference between Armagnacs, and many of them are simply bad. In France, when anybody wants a cheap brandy, he buys Armagnac, and few people in France realize that there are great Armagnacs as well. The Marquis feels that it is part of his heritage to make the most of the soil on which his family has lived for so many generations and to see that fine Armagnac is available outside the walls of his château. Some of the honest firms, such as Samalens and Cavé, work in cooperation with the Marquis to establish a tradition as great as that of Cognac, whose finest brandies can be obtained anywhere in the world, whether in Saigon or Saskatchewan. Armagnacs sell at the same price levels as Cognacs, yet it may be a hundred years before Armagnac's brandies will have made their reputation and established a tradition of excellence.

Armagnac was little known in the United States until the government passed a ruling permitting statements of age on bottles. These were immediately abused, and Armagnacs were shipped in and sold as being seventy-five years old; one company even sent over a shipment of brandies claimed to be ninety-eight years old if a day. In the spring of 1951 the government rescinded its ruling, so that today Armagnacs can bear no statement of age and must be at least three years old.

Age is not the only criterion when it comes to Armagnac, for peasant growers are scattered through districts whose vineyard product varies from fair to excellent, and blending can result in good or bad brandies. Armagnac, especially, is distinguished by a *goût de terroir* that reflects the quality of the soil in the taste of the brandy. Oak barrels and the skill used in distillation can all be reflected in the final result. Care during aging can also make an enormous difference. Many shippers show little concern with these details, but are anxious merely to buy the brandies from the peasants at the lowest possible price and sell them to gullible markets at the highest.

The strenuous efforts of the Marquis de Montesquiou and other honest merchants are beginning to bear fruit, however, for the quality of some of the great Armagnacs is being maintained. At the Château de Marsan it is customary to be served a dinner that features the traditional Gascony dish, *poule au pot,* a young chicken simmered for hours with vegetables and dumplings, followed by a fine old Armagnac. And in every bedroom it is the custom, as old as the brandy itself, to place a small decanter of Armagnac. It is considered an insult if any is left in the morning. The Marquis sees to it that brandy of the same quality goes into all bottles bearing his name. That has always been the tradition. It merely became necessary for someone to believe in it. The Marquis de Montesquiou, Duc de Fezensac, descendant of d'Artagnan, does.

APPENDIX

No wine glass can be to[o]
large. These classic win[e]
glasses of Baccarat cryst[al]
are big enough to brin[g]
out the quintessence of an[y]
great wine if one-third fille[d].

Champagne can be served i[n]
the tulip-shaped glass t[o]
the left or in the glass a[t]
bottom left, which is [a]
perfect all-purpose glass an[d]
the typical claret glas[s].

The glass directly belo[w]
and the glass by the top o[f]
the decanter are inspire[d]
by traditional shapes fro[m]
Burgund[y].

Photo: Robert Brandau[]

andy can be served in any
these three glasses, as
y form the proper chimney
brandy fumes and allow
warming in the palms
d for swirling.

e glass on the bottom
ht can also be used for
erries and liqueurs.

SERVING AND DRINKING WINES

Drinking wine is one of life's great pleasures. Through the centuries certain ideas about wine-drinking have been formulated, as guides to help you get the most from a bottle. Personal preferences are more important than any rules. The rules themselves are little more than tested preferences. Certain wines taste better than others with specific dishes.

If rules inhibit your enjoyment of wines, there should be no rules. As you learn about wines by tasting them with your own palate, you will invent your own guides. No rules about wine fall into the realm of etiquette; they merely indicate the most pleasing combinations of food and drink and help you to avoid unpleasant ones. What tastes right to your palate is likely to please another's.

FRENCH WINE-DRINKING

Wine and food go together, one bringing out the virtues of the other. The two complement each other. This basic fact is at the bottom of the Frenchman's surprise at the way other people eat and drink. American soda pop, for instance, and American cocktails are both an insult to the stomach; both tend to spoil the taste of food, and few Americans would try to deny this. But a Frenchman will sip a sweet and syrupy concoction before eating and think nothing of it, drink cheap and acid wine with his food, and top it off with an equally sickening and powerful liqueur. How you insult your stomach seems to depend on where you were brought up.

A dinner consists of a number of courses so that there will be time to have two or three different wines. Soup is served, for it acts as an alkalizer; the vegetables are served separately, for few taste good with wines. A cheese course is added before the dessert because cheese brings out the taste of wine better than anything else. And the whole meal is planned so that each course is better than the one before. The wines are also served in an ascending order of excellence.

Two wines are served, and a variety of courses, so that you will have a basis of comparison. One wine, the wine you like best, can give much satisfaction. But if more than one wine is served, it is possible to play that delightful gastronomic game fondly called the music of the wine. When the first wine is drunk with the first course, you leave a little of it in your glass. When the second wine comes along, you drink it with the second course and taste the first wine against it, and so on.

COCKTAILS

Outside of France, cocktails and highballs are favorite before-dinner drinks. Many wine-lovers are heartily opposed to them. There's no doubt that a strong cocktail, with a pronounced flavor, paralyzes your taste buds, and usually everything else as well, which is the reason why a glass of chilled dry Sherry or a dry Champagne often replaces the cocktail before a dinner where wines are being served. Sweet drinks, such as Manhattans or old-fashioneds, tend to make it difficult to taste the wines. When drinking wines, most pleasure is derived if drinks made only from grapes are served.

FOOD AND WINE

The only rules are that dry white wines taste best before red wines, and that great wines taste best when they follow lesser ones of a similar type. There are many classic marriages of food and wine, the fruits of centuries of trial and error. A fine Montrachet or Haut-Brion Blanc might taste fine with a chicken sandwich, but would taste glorious with poached sole or a perfectly roasted chicken. A smaller wine would better complement the sandwich, such as a Chablis or Vouvray. A Châteauneuf-du-Pape would marvelously add to the deliciousness of a barbecued steak; a Chambertin would be wonderful with a prime roast beef. The great gamut of French wines offers a wealth of choice for any dish. The detailed sections of this book covering the districts will offer suggestions that you can adopt to make your own combinations for wining and dining.

SMOKING

The French are much less strict about the ritual and regimen of serving wine than wine-lovers of England and America. Many wine-growers smoke while drinking wines, but never during meals.

SWEETS AND SOURS WITH WINES

Sour foods and tart dishes can spoil the taste of wines, as do highly spiced foods. One thing that completely destroys the taste of a dry wine is dessert. Sweet dishes and fruits completely deaden the taste for dry wine. Sweet wines exist for accompanying sweet foods, and there is a wide gamut of them to accompany fruits and custards. Champagnes and Vouvrays taste particularly wonderful with fruits, and the golden Sauternes and Barsacs can be perfect companions for other desserts.

BUYING WINES

VALUE

Many good wines are low in price—some only a dollar or two a bottle—but the value of a wine is always measured on how much you get for your money. A fake bottle of Burgundy at four dollars is expensive, a genuine bottle of Richebourg at ten dollars is a good value. A reliable shipper's Monopole, or regional wine, may be priced the same as a classified Bordeaux growth, but the first is a bad buy. For a dollar less it might be a good one.

WINE MERCHANTS

In the United States, at least, the customer often knows much more about wine than the seller, and the same is true in many restaurants. When a man pays for a bottle, he usually has an idea of what he's looking for, but the clerk or waiter usually knows little more than the price and where to find it on the shelf. One of the secrets of enjoying wines is to have a good wine merchant.

Many Americans refrain from buying French wines because they feel that all imported bottles are likely to be questionable, and that the trip ruins the wines. It is a matter of fact that it is easier to buy great estate-bottled Burgundies in New York or Los Angeles than in London or Paris, or even in Burgundy itself. Nowhere else is such a wide selection available. The wines from Bordeaux are also in large supply, and stocks in New York shops compare more than favorably with those in London and Paris. And although most experts believe that the ocean voyage adds a year or two to the age of a wine, this is of slight importance in buying a wine that may not mature for another decade or so.

RESTAURANTS

Some people distrust restaurant wines, and properly so. Not only are prices marked up enormously, anywhere from three hundred to four hundred per cent, but the wines are bought cheaply from dubious shippers, bear fancy labels, and are frequently of poor vintage. The theory is that the customers will not know the difference. There are many fine restaurants, however, that are exceptions. This is not limited to American restaurants, for a fine wine card is also a rarity in France. Few restaurants and hotels make any effort to carry or sell good wines. Their wine cards are a jumble of Sherries and Champagnes, Bordeaux and California wines, with no attempt to classify them into groups.

VINTAGE CHARTS

In England and America much wine-drinking is done from vintage charts. Wines from a district such as Burgundy or Bordeaux vary enormously in a single year, and a good vintage from one commune can be a bad one in the next.

It is perhaps easiest to think of vintage charts as a table of generalities, full of exceptions. In Burgundy, for instance, 1947 was the vintage of the century, and yet many growers made poor wine because their grapes were too high in sugar, which could not be converted properly to alcohol during fermentation. 1961 was rightly called a great year for white Burgundies, and yet the Chablis vineyards were ruined by hail early in the year, and no great wine was produced. In Burgundy, if you buy other than estate-bottled wines, the year on the label may not be the same as that of the wine in the bottle, for many shippers stretch good vintages with bad ones, or sell poor vintages as fine ones. There is no such difficulty, of course, when buying château-bottled Bordeaux, or wines from lesser or more southern districts where vintages are less important.

It is no wonder that shippers are tempted to put false vintage labels on bottles. Many wine-lovers are slaves to their charts, and if a year is not lauded in the tables, they will not consider the wine. Perfect examples are the 1958, 1960 and 1965 vintages, which were good in many districts, but 1960 and 1965 wines are hard to sell because they are rated low on most charts and thus have a poor reputation. A vintage chart can be a great help when buying wines, but it is a mistake to assume that the entire glorious gamut of wines can be reduced to a series of pat formulas on a tiny card. Wine-making methods have recently improved to such a large extent that in the Médoc district of Bordeaux, for instance, where a light year, because of improper vinification, used to turn out a poor wine, the wines are now of good quality, the difference being that they mature more quickly. A chart is most helpful when its limitations are appreciated. (See Vintage Chart, pages 233–5.)

HALVES AND MAGNUMS

Half bottles are good for trying out a wine for ordinary wines, their youngness protecting them. Great wines suffer from being in small bottles. They are better in magnum than in bottle.

LAYING AWAY WINES

Most people feel it is better to buy wines young and lay them away for a few years. Old bottles are expensive when bought in wineshops, and the wine-drinker can make enormous savings by buying great vintages when young, before the costs of long storing must be added to the price. Even so, great wines are never cheap. There are rarely such things as bargains in wine; wine advertised for quick sale can be poor or badly stored ones, and value for your money may be slight. Reputable merchants who know their business, however, can offer, through judicious buying, good wines at reasonable prices. Poor wine merchants also follow the practice of pushing cheap wines at bargain prices, always a poor value. The man who sells you the wine can be as important as the men who make it, for it is his job to select the good wine from the bad, out of all that is offered him.

SERVING WINES AND OPENING BOTTLES

For red wines, which cast a deposit, care must be taken in bringing the bottle from the cellar to the table, so that the sediment is undisturbed. The wax or foil wrapping around the bottle's mouth should be removed cleanly, so that bits will not fall into the glass. The neck should be wiped clean, and the corkscrew so used that no bits of cork drop into the wine. The wine should be served at its proper temperature, white wines cooled slowly, red wines cold from the cellar and allowed to warm gradually to room temperature, so that their delicate balance will not be destroyed.

CORKY BOTTLES

A cork is not infallible, and once in a while one will rot, particularly in old bottles. Some of the corks for wartime vintages were of poor quality. Once they are pulled, a glance will tell you if one is rotted. The wine waiter should smell the cork to see if the bottle is sound before he serves it, and he should let you smell it too. If the cork smells of cork, it's bad; the cork should smell of the wine. A corky wine loses all of its properties, and a wine that tastes of cork is no good. Send it back and ask for another bottle, just as you would if you were served a bad egg.

BASKETS AND DECANTING

There's nothing wrong with sediment in an old red wine, and in some years it is to be expected; but some wines with heavy deposits need decanting before being served. You can tell whether a wine should be decanted by holding the bottle up to the light. If there is half an inch or so of sediment in the bottle, the wine might better be decanted. Decanting is the simple process of transferring the wine from the bottle to another container, pouring carefully with a light behind the bottle so that you can note when the sediment begins to come out. If poured slowly and steadily, little of the wine is lost. When such a wine is not decanted, one must be especially careful when serving it.

A red wine of age and quality should stand upright for several hours before decanting or serving, to give the sediment plenty of time to settle to the bottom. Even when baskets are used, the wine should stand upright before serving. In any case, baskets are an unnecessary pretension, for they can never be a substitute for decanting. When you stand a bottle upright, it should be uncorked at least half an hour before serving, to allow the wine to breathe. This is not necessary when you decant the wine, for decanting allows the air to bring out all the imprisoned bouquet. This is extremely important if you want to get the most out of a fine red wine.

Many a wine-drinker has noticed that it is only when the bottle is nearly finished that the wine seems to come into its own, simply because it takes time for a wine to react to contact with the air. The swirling of wine while in the glass hastens this action, and that is why wineglasses are only half-filled, and why they should be large. Even in small Burgundian restaurants, glasses like large brandy snifters are used for all wines.

SERVICE

White wines should be served cool, the sweeter the cooler, but they lose their flavor when iced too much. A couple of hours in the refrigerator usually serves, although a wine bucket is thought to be better. In lieu of a wine bucket, some people fill a large salad bowl with ice and allow the bottles to cool in it. Any big bowl will do. Pink wines are also served chilled, but red wines are best at room temperature. A couple of hours before serving, the red wine can be brought to the dining-table and carefully tilted upright. In order not to disturb any sediment, some people like to use wine baskets or cradles; others think them a pretension. In any case, a wine that contains sediment should be poured in one continuous motion, not tilted repeatedly, and pouring should be stopped at the first sign of sediment. The host always pours a little of the newly opened wine into his own glass first, in case there are any particles of cork, both tasting and smelling it to see that it is sound and not corky.

GLASSES

Most people prefer clear crystal glasses for wine, unadorned, so that the sparkle of light on the wine is easily seen. The larger the glass, the better when serving fine Bordeaux and Burgundies. A water glass is usually better than most small wineglasses, for two thirds of the space can be left so that the wine can be swirled in the glass.

Wine is shown off by its glass, just as a girl is shown off by a pretty dress. Great wines can be ruined in small glasses, for the air cannot get at the surface of the wine to release its aroma. Equally, a mediocre wine is shown up for what it is in a large glass, for the quality of the wine is often judged by what it looks like in a fine glass. Wineglasses, like fine wines, have always been a symbol of civilized living. The finest glasses are large and tulip-shaped, clear and thin, without markings, the bowl the size of a large orange or an apple. When less than half-filled, such a glass permits the full enjoyment of the color, bouquet, and taste of a fine wine. France has made an art of clear crystal glasses.

Although there are many different shapes of glasses for different wines, a single glass, large, thin, and clear, can serve for all, making service and replacement simpler.

STORING WINES

When serving wine at home, a cool place is desirable for storing bottles, for a wine should rest for a week or two before being served, to allow it to recompose itself. This is particularly true of old wines, and those that have a heavy sediment, which must be allowed to settle.

The worst evil that can happen to a bottle of wine is a sudden change of temperature. But wines can stand extremes of temperature if they reach such extremes gradually. For this reason summer is usually easier on wines than winter, when steam heating warms up a storage space each day, while the temperature drops quickly during the night. A month or two of such sudden changes of temperature can destroy some wines, and improper storage near heat or in strong light can ruin one. Storing wines near steam pipes is particularly injurious.

White wines should be kept in the coolest spot practicable, usually nearest the floor, for they can spoil in a matter of months. Red Bordeaux can be placed above them, Burgundies on top, while the fortified wines can stand upright on the shelf beside your spirits. All natural wines should be laid on their sides, so that the wine wets the cork, keeping it from drying and shrinking. For this reason, places for storing wine should not be too dry.

CELLARS

A cellar is needed for storing extra cases of wines you like, ones that may become scarce or hard to get. There is also an immense saving with a cellar, for wines are cheaper by the case and can be bought young when prices are lower. Increase in prices of fine wines through the years of their maturing is greater than the amount of interest on the money invested in your cellar. Also, there's a delight in owning a cellar, for you have within your own home a bottled treasure of taste sensations, as full of potential pleasure as a fine library or a collection of records.

The size of a wine cellar depends on how often you serve wines. Consumed bottles should be replaced each year by new stocks, both bottles for current serving and others for laying down. A cellar gives most pleasure when there is a well-balanced stock to choose from. A cellar book in which you keep a record of your wines, with notes of your preferences, is a help when restocking your inventory, as well as a running diary for the pleasures you get from wines. With prices of wines listed in a cellar book, it is easier to replace wines of the same price category without insisting on the identical wine, so that you may drink several wines in a certain range over a period of time, rather than one wine, which may rise in price or deteriorate. Small wine cellars are simply made in a cool corner of the house cellar, away from steam pipes and light. They should be properly ventilated, and any nearby pipes should be wrapped with insulation.

BINS AND SHELVES

Three compartmented shelves will hold several dozen bottles in an area only a yard long. The compartments or bins need not be large for a small cellar, and a bin not much more than a foot square will hold almost a case, although one twice that size is more practical if you have the room. The best bins are diamond-shaped, for bottles piled in a flat bin may have a tendency to roll when one is removed, unless the bottles are braced. Wines take up little room when stored in bins. A thermometer should be hung nearby so that you can check to see that temperature remains constant, constancy being more important than degree, although 5° is considered ideal. The simplest arrangement is to transfer wine to whisky cases, standing the cases on edge in a closet.

A MODEL CELLAR

SMALL CELLAR

A small cellar of five to fifteen cases, as in all things concerning wine, should be based mainly on your taste. But for an adequate assortment of French wines, you might have the following quantities, which would cost between $650 and $800, depending on quality and vintages, and including Champagne and brandy. The wines alone would cost between $550 and $650.

3 Cases of Red Burgundy:

1 case of inexpensive Beaujolais of a very young vintage;

1 case at moderate price, such as estate-bottled Pommard or Nuits-Saint-Georges, from 2 to 7 years old;

1 case of a fine estate-bottled wine such as a Richebourg, Musigny, Chambertin Clos de Bèze, or Bonnes-Mares, from 3 to 7 years old. The more expensive the Burgundies, the slower they will be to mature and the longer they will last.

2 Cases of White Burgundy:

1 case of an estate-bottled Chablis from a good vineyard, from 1 to 5 years old, or a Pouilly-Fuissé of the same age;

1 case of estate-bottled Meursault Perrières or Blagny, from 2 to

5 years old; or a case of Chassagne, or Puligny-Montrachet from a good vineyard, preferably estate-bottled, of the same age.

3 Cases of Red Bordeaux:

1 case of inexpensive regional wine of a good shipper, from Margaux, Saint-Julien, Pomerol, or Saint-Émilion, 3 to 5 years old; an inexpensive château-bottled wine would be preferable.

1 case of château-bottled claret from the 2nd, 3rd, 4th, or 5th classified growths, 3 to 15 years old;

1 case of a fine château-bottled claret, such as the Châteaux of Haut-Brion, Latour, Lafite, Margaux, Mouton-Rothschild, Lascombes, Cheval-Blanc, Ausone, or Pétrus, of a good vintage, from 3 to 20 years old, depending on how soon you will drink it and how long you want to keep it.

1 or 2 Cases of White Bordeaux:

1 case of dry Graves from a good shipper, or preferably a château-bottled white Graves such as Haut-Brion, Domaine de Chevalier, Couhins, or Carbonnieux, from a good vintage, 1 to 5 years old;

1 case of château-bottled Sauternes or Barsac (if your taste runs to sweet wines), such as Yquem, Climens, La Tour Blanche, Filhot, Coutet, Roumieu.

2 Cases of Miscellaneous Wines:

1 case of *rosé* from Provence, Bordeaux, or Tavel, the youngest possible, as these wines do not improve with age;

1 case of Alsace, a Gewürz-Traminer, Riesling, or Sylvaner, from 1 to 3 years old, preferably young; or

1 case of Vouvray, Sancerre, Muscadet, or Pouilly-Fumé, from 1 to 4 years old.

1 Case of Champagne
An Assortment of 6 Bottles of Cognac and Armagnac.

MEDIUM CELLAR

A medium cellar usually ranges in size from 15 to 40 cases, and a good case assortment of French wines might be broken up as follows:

8 Cases of Red Burgundy:

3 cases from southern Burgundy, such as Beaujolais, Juliénas,

Fleurie, Morgon, or Moulin-à-Vent, for frequent use, from 1 to 4 years old;

2 cases of an estate-bottling, or from a reliable shipper, of Pommard, Volnay, Chassagne-Montrachet, Beaune, Corton, Nuits-Saint-Georges, Chambolle-Musigny or Vosne-Romanée, from 2 to 7 years old;

2 cases of estate-bottled Musigny, Bonnes-Mares, Chambertin Clos de Bèze, Richebourg, or Clos de Vougeot, from 2 to 7 years old, of a good vintage, for laying down until fully developed, which may take from 3 to 7 additional years;

1 case of older wines from the previous category, from 5 to 10 years old, of a good vintage, for drinking on special occasions.

5 or 6 Cases of White Burgundy:

1 or 2 cases of estate-bottled Chablis from a good vineyard, from 2 to 5 years old;

1 case of Pouilly-Fuissé, from a good shipper or estate-bottled, from 1 to 3 years old;

1 case of Chassagne-, or Puligny-Montrachet, estate-bottled or from a good shipper, from 2 to 5 years old;

1 case of estate-bottled Meursault-Blagny or Perrières, preferably the Clos des Perrières, or Corton-Charlemagne, of a good vintage, from 2 to 6 years old;

1 case, estate-bottled or from a good shipper, of Bâtard-Montrachet or Montrachet, of a good vintage, from 2 to 7 years old.

6 Cases of Red Bordeaux:

3 cases of a regional shipper's claret, or a *cru artisan,* or a *cru bourgeois,* from 2 to 4 years old;

1 case of château-bottled Saint-Émilion or Pomerol, or a 2nd, 3rd, 4th, or 5th classified growth of a good vintage, from 3 to 10 years old;

1 case of fine claret, such as Haut-Brion, Lafite, Latour, Margaux, Mouton-Rothschild, Lascombes, Cheval-Blanc, Ausone, or Pétrus, of a good vintage, from 3 to 8 years old, for laying down for 2 years or so;

1 case of wines from the above category, of a good vintage, from 6 years of age upward or as old as possible, for present drinking.

2 or 3 Cases of White Bordeaux:

1 or 2 cases of dry Graves, preferably Château Haut-Brion, Couhins, or Domaine de Chevalier, from 1 to 4 years old;

1 case of Sauternes or Barsac, château-bottled, from 3 to 10 years old.

1 Case of Rhône Valley Wine:

Estate-bottled or from a good shipper, red wine from Châteauneuf-du-Pape, Hermitage, or Côte Rôtie, from 2 to 7 years for the Châteauneuf, from 6 to 15 years for the others; or a case of white Hermitage of a good vintage, from 2 to 6 years old.

2 Cases of Rosé:

1 case from Provence or Bordeaux, and 1 case from Tavel, from 1 to 4 years old.

1 or 2 Cases of Assorted Wines:

1 case of Alsatian Riesling or Gewürz-Traminer, from 1 to 5 years old; and/or

1 case of Muscadet, Pouilly-Fumé, Sancerre, Vouvray, or Saumur, from 2 to 6 years old.

2 Cases of Champagne:

1 medium-priced of a lesser-known brand; 1 of a well-known brand.

An Assortment of 9 Bottles of Brandy:

4 bottles of 3-star or VO Cognac, or inexpensive Armagnac, the balance consisting of old Cognacs and Armagnacs, including a bottle of old Calvados and a bottle or more of *"alcool blanc,"* depending on your taste.

LARGE CELLAR

Even for a large cellar the quantities of sweet wines and minor wines would remain much the same. Quantities and varieties of Burgundies, Bordeaux, and Champagnes would increase most.

When stocking a large cellar, it is advisable to call in an expert, who will know the best buys among those wines currently available.

A portion of larger cellars should be made up of "vins de garde," wines bought young to be kept 2 to 5 years for proper maturing.

BOTTLE SIZES

BORDEAUX WINES

		Bottles	Ounces
$\frac{1}{10}$ gallon or 1 pint		$\frac{1}{2}$	12.5
$\frac{1}{5}$ gallon		1	24 to 25.5
Magnum		2	48 or 50 (1 quart, 1 pint)
Marie-Jeanne		3	72 to 84 (2 quarts, 8 ounces)
Double magnum		4	96 or 101 (3 quarts)
Jeroboam	(*approx.*)	5	120 (3 quarts, 1 pint, 8 ounces)
Imperial		8	192 ($1\frac{1}{2}$ gallons)

CHAMPAGNE

	Bottles	Ounces
Split	half pint	$6\frac{1}{2}$
Pint	usual short pint, $\frac{1}{10}$ gallon, regular $\frac{1}{2}$ bottle	13
Quart	usual short quart, $\frac{1}{2}$ gallon, regular bottle	26 or 27
Magnum	two bottles	52 or 54 (1 quart, 1 pint, 4 ounces)

COOPERAGE IN VARIOUS
WINE DISTRICTS OF FRANCE

The wine-buyer throughout France is confronted with a maze of various sized barrels, each referred to by a different name. As the wines are different, so are the barrels in which they mature. The following are some of the most useful names to retain.

BORDEAUX

The production of all the châteaux is always indicated in *tonneaux* of tons. All prices are quoted in *tonneaux*. There is no barrel of this size, however, A *tonneau* consists of 4 *barriques*, containing 225 liters. A fluctuation of 2.5 per cent is permitted in content. Wines are also sold in *feuillettes* (half a *barrique*) containing 112 liters, or a *quartaut* (a quarter of a *barrique*) containing 56 liters. A *barrique* yields 24 cases of 12 bottles each. A *tonneau*, consisting of 4 *barriques*, yields 96 cases.

BURGUNDY

In the Côte d'Or the regular barrel, called *pièce*, contains 226 to 228 liters; a half barrel, called *feuillette*, contains 114 liters; and a quarter barrel, called *quartaut*, contains 57 liters. The old French measure called *queue* is still used in Burgundy. The bids at the auction sale of the Hospices de Beaune are made in terms of *queue*, which means 2 *pièces*. Just as with the *tonneau* in Bordeaux, there is no actual barrel of this size. A *pièce*, once bottled, yields approximately 288 bottles, or 24 to 25 cases of 12 bottles each.

CHABLIS

The standard barrel of lower Burgundy is a *feuillette* containing 136 liters, which is larger than the *feuillette* of the Côte d'Or.

In the Mâconnais the *pièce* contains 215 liters; in the Beaujolais, 216 liters.

RHÔNE VALLEY

In and around Châteauneuf-du-Pape the *pièce* contains 225 liters. This barrel is slightly smaller than the *pièce* used in the Côte d'Or.

WINES OF THE LOIRE

In the province of the Touraine the wines of Vouvray are kept in *pièces* containing 225 liters, but farther down the river the wines of Anjou, Saumur, and Layon come in slightly smaller *pièces* of 220 liters.

CHAMPAGNE

The usual barrel is called *queue* and contains 216 liters. The half barrel, called *demi-queue,* contains 108 liters.

ALSACE

Sales are often made, as in Germany, in huge barrels, called *foudres* in France, containing 1,000 liters. The wine is shipped, however, in barrels of various sizes, often in small barrels called *aumes* containing 114 liters, which is the same size as the *feuillette* of the Côte d'Or.

ALGERIA AND THE MIDI

Wine is quoted in hectoliters, or 100-liter units. Prices vary according to alcoholic content. Most of the time, the wines are stored in large glass-lined vats although sometimes huge barrels called *demi-muids,* containing 600 to 700 liters, are used.

USEFUL FRENCH-AMERICAN MEASURES
LINEAR MEASURES
Metric System

Unit	Comparison	U.S. Equivalent
Millimeter (mm.)	——	.0394 inch
Centimeter (cm.)	10 mm.	.3937 inch
Meter (m.)	100 cm.	39.37 inches, or 3.28 feet
Kilometer (km.)	1,000 m.	0.621 miles

U.S. System

Unit	Comparison	Metric Equivalent
Inch (in.)	——	25.4001 mm.
Foot (ft.)	12 in.	.3048 m.
Yard (yd.)	36 in. 3 ft.	.9144 m.
Mile (mi.)	5,280 ft. 1,760 yd.	1,609 m. 1 km. 609 m.

UNITS OF AREA, OR SQUARE MEASURES
Metric System

Unit	Comparison	U.S. Equivalent
Square millimeter (mm.²)	——	.0015 sq. in.
Square centimeter (cm.²)	.0001 m.²	155 sq. in.
Square meter (m.²)	centare	10.7639 sq. ft.
Are (a.)	100 m.²	3.9537 sq. rd.
Hectare (ha.)	10,000 m², or 23 Burgundy *ouvrées*	2.471 acres
Square kilometer (km.²)	1,000,000 m.²	.3861 sq. mi.
Burgundy *ouvrée*	428 m.²	

U.S. System (Square Measures)

Unit	Comparison	Metric Equivalent
Square inch (sq. in.)	——	6.4516 cm.²
Square foot (sq. ft.)	144 sq. in.	.0929 m.²
Square yard (sq. yd.)	1296 sq. in. 9 sq. ft.	.8361 m.²
Acre	43,560 sq. ft. 4,840 sq. yd.	.4047 ha.
Square mile (sq. mi.)	27,878,400 sq. ft. 3,097,600 sq. yd. 640 acres	2.5900 km.²

UNITS OF VOLUME—CUBIC MEASURES

Metric System

Unit	Comparison	U.S. Equivalent
Cubic meter (m.³)	——	35.31 cubic feet

U.S. System

Unit	Comparison	Metric Equivalent
Cubic inch (cu. in.)	——	16.3872 cm.³
Cubic foot (cu. ft.)	1728 cu. in.	.0283 m.³
Cubic yard (cu.yd.)	46,656 cu. in. 27 cu. ft.	.7646m.³

WEIGHTS

Unit	Comparison	Avoirdupois
Gram (g.)	——	.0353 ounce
Kilogram (kg.)	1,000 grams	2.2046 pounds
Metric ton (tn.)	1,000 kil.	1.1023 short tn. .9842 long tn.

U.S. System

Unit	Comparison	Metric Equivalent
Ounce avoirdupois (oz. avdp.)	——	28.3495 g.
Pound (lb. avdp.)	16 ounces	.4536 kg.
Ton (tn.), short ton	2,000 pounds	.9072 metric tn.

UNITS OF CAPACITY—LIQUID MEASURE

Metric System

Unit	Comparison	U.S. Equivalent
Milliliter (ml.)	——	.0338 fluid ounces
Centiliter (cl.)	.01 l.	.3381 fluid ounces
Liter (l.)	100 cl.	1.0567 quarts, or 33.81 fluid ounces
Hectoliter (hl.)	100 l.	26.4178 gallons

Liquid Measures—U.S.

Unit	Comparison	Metric Equivalent
Fluid ounce (fl. oz.)	——	29.5729 ml.
Pint (pt.)	16 fl. oz.	.4732 l.
Quart (qt.)	32 fl. oz. 2 pt.	.9463 l.
Gallon (gal.)	8 pt. 4 qt.	3.7853 l.

FAHRENHEIT AND CENTIGRADE CONVERSIONS

To convert Fahrenheit to Centigrade, subtract 32 degrees and multiply by $5/9$; to convert Centigrade to Fahrenheit, multiply by $9/5$ and add 32 degrees.

CONVERSION OF ALCOHOLIC CONTENT

In order to convert the Gay-Lussac French measurement of alcoholic content by volume into American proof spirits, multiply by 2, which gives a close approximation. For complete accurate conversions reference should be made to special tables.

VINTAGE CHART

No vintage chart is a sure guide to the wines rated, for great wines cannot be standardized. Wines are a product of inconstant nature and fallible man. There will be enough enjoyable bottles in any one district in any off year to make exceptions invalidating anything so dogmatic as a vintage chart. Often overlooked, nevertheless a major factor in the purchase of wines, is the proper selection of wines that are sufficiently mature for present-day consumption. Very great years are often slow in maturing, hence your consideration of whether the wines will be consumed immediately or laid away for future consumption should be a determining factor in your selections.

Explanation of Ratings

20, 19—exceptionally great	9, 8—fair
18, 17—very great	7, 6—low average
16, 15—great	5, 4—poor
14, 13, 12—very good	3, 2, 1—very poor
11, 10—good	

N.B.: Many dry white wines may be too old for present-day consumption. All such wines are indicated by *italic figures*. All white Bordeaux older than 1966 which are not Sauternes, Barsac, or Ste. Croix-du-Mont should be considered as possibly being maderized.

Vintage	Red Bordeaux	White Bordeaux	Red Burgundy (Côte d'Or)	White Burgundy	Red Burgundy (Beaujolais)	Rhône	Loire	Alsace	Champagne
1929	20	19	19	19	19	19	16	17	17
1933	10	6	17	16	17	14	14	12	15
1934	17	16	17	17	17	16	13	14	15
1936	8	8	8	6	9	14	9	10	10
1937	15	18	17	16	13	16	14	15	16
1938	9	8	14	13	10	13	9	10	12
1939	5	6	3	3	8	10	8	4	8
1940	8	9	9	9	8	9	8	11	8
1941	2	1	4	4	5	9	7	8	12
1942	12	15	12	15	14	15	11	13	15
1943	15	15	14	15	15	15	14	15	18
1944	11	9	4	5	7	9	7	5	9
1945	20	19	19	16	20	19	18	17	16
1946	8	7	12	9	10	15	10	10	11
1947	19	19	19	20	19	19	19	19	19
1948	13	13	14	15	9	9	10	12	11
1949	18	18	19	17	19	16	13	16	17
1950	14	15	12	18	12	15	10	8	9
1951	9	6	8	8	7	9	7	9	7
1952	17	16	16	16	16	18	14	14	18
1953	19	17	19	17	19	13	17	17	17

Vintage	Red Bordeaux	White Bordeaux	Red Burgundy (*Côte d'Or*)	White Burgundy	Red Burgundy (*Beaujolais*)	Rhône	Loire	Alsace	Champagne
1955	**18–19**	*17*	**17**	*18*	*17*	**18**	*18*	*15*	*19*
1957	17	*16*	17	*18*	*18*	18	*18*	*17*	11
1958	11	*13*	9	*17*	*13*	16	*15*	*16*	*12*
1959	18	*18*	19	*18*	*18*	17	*19*	*19*	19
1960	13	*13*	8	*15*	*10*	20	*14*	*13*	*15*
1961	20	*19*	19	19	*20*	18	17	*17*	18
1962	17	*13*	15	*16*	*17*	12	16	16	16
1963	8	*6*	9	11	*9*	11	*9*	*11*	7
1964	17	*	15	15	*17*	13	15	15	17
1965	11	*10*	6	11	*11*	15	*10*	*10*	6
1966	17–18	†	15	16	*16*	17	15	14	18
1967	16	14	13	15	*14*	15	14	14	16
1968	10	††	6	6	*11*	10	10	11	9
1969	16	14	18	16	15	13	15	14	17
1970	18	18	14	15	15	15	14	13	16
1971	16	17	15	16	16	16	16	17	17
1972	16	**	15	14	13	14	13	13	14

* 16 dry   10 sweet

† 16 dry   11 sweet

††10 dry   7 sweet

**15 dry   13–15 sweet

BORDEAUX WINES

THE OFFICIAL CLASSIFICATION OF THE GREAT GROWTHS OF
THE GIRONDE. CLASSIFICATION OF 1855

The official production is given in tons (tonneaux), the Bordeaux standard measure, consisting of 4 barrels. A tonneau averages around 96 cases when it is bottled.

The following case figures of production are approximate, varying from year to year, and an estimate has been attempted by deducting the ullage or evaporation, which usually consists of 15 per cent.

MÉDOC WINES

1st Growths or Premiers Crus

	Township	Tonneaux	Average Production in Cases (*12 bottles each*)
Château Lafite	*Pauillac*	250	20,000
Château Margaux	*Margaux*	165	14,000
Château Latour	*Pauillac*	200	16,200
Château Haut-Brion [1]	*Pessac. Graves*	120	10,000

[1] This wine, although a Graves, is universally recognized and classified as one of the four First Growths of the Médoc.

Second Growths or Deuxièmes Crus

	Township	Tonneaux	
Château Mouton-Rothschild	*Pauillac*	135	11,000
Château Rauzan-Ségla	*Margaux*	160	14,000
Château-Rauzan-Gassies	"	90	7,600

	Township	Tonneaux	Average Production in Cases (*12 bottles each*)
Château Léoville-Las-Cases	*St.-Julien*	225	18,500
Château Léoville-Poyferré	"	160	13,000
Château-Léoville-Barton	"	100	8,000
Château Durfort-Vivens	*Margaux*	5	4,200
Château Gruaud-Larose	*St.-Julien*	250	20,500
Château Lascombes	*Margaux*	275	23,000
Château Brane-Cantenac	*Cantenac-Margaux*	300	26,000
Château Pichon-Longueville	*Pauillac*	100	8,500
Château Pichon-Longueville (Comtesse de Lalande)	"	180	14,000
Château Ducru-Beaucaillou	*St.-Julien*	160	13,000
Château Cos-d'Estournel	*St.-Estèphe*	210	18,000
Château Montrose	"	135	11,000

		3rd Growths or Troisièmes Crus	
Château Giscours	*Labarde-Margaux*	245	20,000
Château Kirwan	*Cantenac-Margaux*	60	4,800
Château d'Issan	"	150	13,000
Château Lagrange	*St.-Julien*	80	7,000
Château Langoa	"	75	6,100
Château Malescot-Saint-Exupéry	*Margaux*	40	3,500
Château Cantenac-Brown	*Cantenac-Margaux*	60	5,000
Château Palmer	"	110	10,000

	Township	Tonneaux	Average Production in Cases (*12 bottles each*)
Château La Lagune	*Ludon*	230	19,000
Château Desmirail	*Margaux*	0	0
Château Calon-Ségur	*St.-Estèphe*	200	17,000
Château Ferrière	*Margaux*	10	850
Château Marquis-d'Alesme-Becker	"	35	3,000
Château Boyd-Cantenac	*Cantenac-Margaux*	50	4,200

4th Growths or Quatrièmes Crus

	Township	Tonneaux	Average Production in Cases
Château Prieuré-Lichine	*Cantenac-Margaux*	80	6,800
Château Saint-Pierre	*St.-Julien*	50	4,000
Château Branaire-Ducru	"	120	10,000
Château Talbot	"	300	25,000
Château Duhart-Milon	*Pauillac*	60	5,000
Château Pouget	*Cantenac-Margaux*	20	1,400
Château La Tour-Carnet	*St.-Laurent*	50	4,000
Château Lafon-Rochet	*St.-Estèphe*	100	8,500
Château Beychevelle	*St.-Julien*	200	17,000
Château Marquis-de-Terme	*Margaux*	130	11,000

5th Growths or Cinquièmes Crus

	Township	Tonneaux	Average Production in Cases
Château Pontet-Canet	*Pauillac*	350	30,000
Château Batailley	"	150	12,500
Château Grand-Puy-Lacoste	"	85	7,000

	Township	Tonneaux	Average Production in Cases (*12 bottles each*)
Château Grand-Puy-Ducasse	"	35	2,800
Château Haut-Batailley	"	60	5,000
Château Lynch-Bages	"	160	13,000
Château Lynch-Moussas	"	20	1,600
Château Dauzac	*Labarde-Margaux*	60	4,800
Château Mouton-Baron-Philippe (formerly known as Château Mouton d'Armailhacq)	*Pauillac*	250	22,000
Château de Tertre	*Arsac-Margaux*	70	5,800
Château Haut-Bages-Libéral	*Pauillac*	40	3,300
Château Pédesclaux	"	35	3,000
Château Belgrave	*St.-Laurent*	90	7,100
Château Camensac	"	35	3,000
Château Cos Labory	*St.-Estèphe*	45	3,600
Château Clerc-Milon-Mondon	*Pauillac*	30	2,100
Château Croizet-Bages	"	90	7,500
Château Cantemerle	*Macau*	70	5,800

The average total production of classified growths in the Haut-Mèdoc for the three vintages of 1965, 1966, and 1967 has increased approximately 35 per cent in comparison to the average production of 1959, 1960, and 1961. There are two main reasons for this. The 1959 and two following vintages were still suffering from a lack of production because of the 1956 winter freeze, which destroyed a considerable amount of vines. The other reason is that many châteaux have increased their vineyards either through new plantings or by acquiring adjoining vineyards that were not classified. The latest production figures show that there are over 7,000 *tonneaux* produced per year, or just under 600,000 cases of all of the wines classified in 1855.

SHALL THE OLD ORDER CHANGE?

All wine-lovers know something about the classification of 1855. Most of them could successfully identify the first four growths, and would know a few other châteaux that appear on the list. This classification of 1855 was a most ambitious work. Not only did the men who made the list divide the sixty-two châteaux they retained for final consideration into five distinct classes, or growths, but they also entered every château in its "correct" position: Châteaux Ducru-Beaucaillou, Cos-d'Estournel, and Montrose—all second growths—were, for example, listed in exactly that order of merit.

Such a rigid insistence, not only on classifying sixty-two wines in a general order of merit but also on placing each growth in definitive position of order, has lost a great deal of its justification after 108 years. We are aware of so many possible reasons for differing quality that a classification made in the 1960's, even if it divided the wine into five growths, would not go to such limits of exactitude.

I owe much of the content of this classification I put forward to the discussion and comment of my friends in Bordeaux—brokers, proprietors, and shippers. Needless to say, however, I take full responsibility for the judgment I have made.

There was most general agreement, perhaps, on the need to change the original numerical divisions—"first growth," "second growth," etc. Airlines and steamship lines do not now offer second- and third-class accommodations; rather they divide their classes into "tourist," "economy," and "cabin." A great many people, if told that a wine was a fourth or fifth growth, not realizing that this was, in fact, a very, very honorable position, would regard it as a quite minor wine, and might well consider that a *Cru Exceptionnel* was a much finer wine.

Another accepted change was that a Bordeaux classification should include more than just the wines of the Médoc. In 1855 no account had been taken of the wines of Graves (with the exception of Haut-Brion), Pomerol, or Saint-Émilion, despite the fact that this classification was entitled "The Official Classification of the Great Growths of the Gironde." Although many wines of Saint-Émilion may lack the finesse of the great Médoc wines, there can be no doubt that the quality of some of them now deserves official recognition.

The principal basis for the suggested classification remains the selling price of the wines listed, but most of the experts consulted agreed that some properties should not be downgraded because of a few years of disappointing wines due to careless management, where a new owner would be able to take full advantage of the soil and the property to produce a far greater wine.

Recently, a group of owners belonging to the Committee of the 1855 Classified Growths requested that the official classification be changed to allow some important growths of the Médoc to obtain a better, more deserved position. In 1960 the Institut National des Appellations d'Origine was called in to be the final arbiter, but was declared legally incompetent by the committee in 1962 on the grounds that its jurisdiction was too limited to deal with this highly controversial subject. Now the entire matter of classification rests in the hands of the members of the *Comité des Grands Crus Classés de 1855*, most of whom are for a *status quo*. It is doubtful that the 1855 classification will ever be changed, but it is probable that a *new* classification will be established by the mid-seventies.

With the exception of the first wines in this classification, the wines have been listed in alphabetical order. I would like to stress that this is only a suggested listing, an attempt to reflect present quality and values in the hope that the increasing number of those who are just discovering the delights of good wine will find this a helpful, up-to-date guide.

THE SUGGESTED NEW CLASSIFICATION

Based on the standing of the Bordeaux vineyards as of 1962. Wines are listed alphabetically, with the exception of the Hors Classes, *or Outstanding Growths, category. The growths are in order of quality.*

Crus Hors Classes (*Outstanding Growths*)

MÉDOC	MÉDOC
Château Lafite-Rothschild	Château Mouton-Rothschild
Pauillac	*Pauillac*
Château Margaux	
Margaux	SAINT-ÉMILION
Château Latour	Château Cheval Blanc
	Château Ausone
Pauillac	
Château Haut-Brion	POMEROL
Pessac (Graves)	Château Pétrus

Crus Exceptionnels (*Exceptional Growths*)

MÉDOC	MÉDOC
Château Beychevelle	Château Durfort-Vivens
St.-Julien	*Margaux*
Château Brane-Cantenac	Château Gruaud-Larose
Cantenac-Margaux	*St.-Julien*
Château Calon-Ségur	Château Lascombes
St.-Estèphe	*Margaux*
Château Cantemerle	Château Léoville-Barton
Macau	*St.-Julien*
Château Cos-d'Estournel	Château Léoville-Las-Cases
St.-Estèphe	*St.-Julien*
Château Ducru-Beaucaillou	Château Léoville-Poyferré
St.-Julien	*St.-Julien*

Note: All Saint-Émilion and Pomerol châteaux classified in this list bear the strict commune designations of Saint-Émilion and Pomerol, respectively.

Bordeaux Wines,
New Classification (RED)

Crus Exceptionnels (*Exceptional Growths*)

MÉDOC

Château Lynch-Bages
    Pauillac

Château Montrose
    St.-Estèphe

Château Palmer
    Cantenac-Margaux

Château Pichon-Longueville
    Pauillac

Château Pichon-Longueville
 Comtesse de Lalande *Pauillac*

Château Rausan-Ségla
    Margaux

SAINT-ÉMILION

Château Belair

Château Canon

Château Figeac

Château La Gaffelière

POMEROL

Château La Conseillante

Château l'Évangile

Château Vieux-Château-Certan

GRAVES

Domaine de Chevalier
    Léognan

Château La Mission-Haut-Brion
    Pessac

Grands Crus (*Great Growths*)

MÉDOC

Château Branaire-Ducru
    St.-Julien

Château Cantenac-Brown
    Cantenac-Margaux

Château Duhart-Milon
    Pauillac

Château Durfort
    Margaux

Château Giscours
    Margaux

Château Grand-Puy-Lacoste
    Pauillac

Château d'Issan
    Cantenac-Margaux

Château La Lagune
    Ludon

Château Malescot-Saint-Exupéry
    Margaux

Château Mouton-Baron-Philippe
    Pauillac

Château Pontet-Canet
    Pauillac

MÉDOC

Château Prieuré-Lichine
    Cantenac-Margaux

Château Rauzan-Gassies
    Margaux

Château Talbot
    St.-Julien

SAINT-ÉMILION

Clos Fourtet

Château Magdelaine

Château Pavie

POMEROL

Château Certan-de-May

Château Gazin

Château Lafleur

Château Lafleur-Pétrus

Château Petit-Village

Château Trotanoy

GRAVES

Château Haut-Bailly
    Léognan

Château Pape-Clément
    Pessac

Crus Supérieurs (*Superior Growths*)

MÉDOC

Château Batailley

                Pauillac

Château Chasse-Spleen

                Moulis

Château Ferrière

                Margaux

Château Gloria

                St.-Julien

Château Grand-Puy-Ducasse

                Pauillac

Château Haut-Batailley

                Pauillac

Château Kirwan

                Cantenac-Margaux

Château Langoa-Barton

                St.-Julien

Château La Tour-de-Mons

                Soussans-Margaux

Château Marquis-d'Alesme-
Becker   *Margaux*

Château Marquis-de-Terme

                Margaux

SAINT-ÉMILION

Château l'Angélus

Château Beauséjour-
Duffau-Lagarosse

Château Beauséjour-Fagouet

Château Canon-la Gaffelière

SAINT-ÉMILION

Château Croque-Michotte

Château Curé-Bon-la-Madeleine

Château Larcis-Ducasse

Château Ripeau

Château Trottevieille

Château Villemaurine

POMEROL

Château Beauregard

Château Certan-Giraud

Clos de l'Église-Cinet

Clos l'Église

Château Lagrange

Château Latour-Pomerol

Château Nenin

Château La Pointe

GRAVES

Château Carbonnieux

                Léognan

Château Malartic-Lagravière

                Léognan

Château Smith-Haut-Lafitte

                Martillac

Château La Tour-Haut-Brion

                Talence

Château La Tour-Martillac
or La Tour-Kressmann

                Martillac

Bons Crus (*Good Growths*)

MÉDOC

Château Angludet

                Margaux

Château Bel-Air-
Marquis-d'Aligre

                Soussans-Margaux

Château Belgrave

                St.-Laurent

MÉDOC

Château Boyd-Cantenac

                Cantenac-Margaux

Château Capbern

                St.-Estèphe

Chateau Clerc-Milon-Mondon

                Pauillac

Bons Crus (*Good Growths*)

MÉDOC	SAINT-ÉMILION
Château Cos Labory	Château Baleau
St.-Estèphe	Château Balestard-la Tonnelle
Château Croizet-Bages	Château Cap-de-Mourlin
Pauillac	Château Le Chatelet
Château Dutruch-Lambert	Château La Clotte
Moulis	Château Corbin-Giraud
Château Fourcas-Dupré	Château Corbin-Michotte
Listrac	Château Coutet
Château Fourcas-Holstein	Château La Dominique
Listrac	Château Fonroque
Crus Gressier-Grand-Poujeaux	Château Grand-Barrail-Lamarzelle-
Moulis	Figeac
Château Haut-Bages-Libéral	Château Grand-Corbin
Pauillac	Château Grand-Corbin-Despagne
Château Lagrange	Château Grand-Murailles
St.-Julien	Clos des Jacobins
Château Lanessan	Château Saint-Georges-Côte Pavie
Cussac	Château Soutard
Château Lynch-Moussas	Château La Tour-du-Pin-Figeac
Pauillac	Château Troplong-Mondot
Château Les Ormes-de-Pez	
St.-Estèphe	POMEROL
Château Paveil	Château La Croix
Soussans-Margaux	Château La Croix-de-Gay
Château de Pez	Château Feytit-Clinet
St.-Estèphe	Château Gombaude-Guillot
Château Phélan-Ségur	Château la Fleur-Pourret
St.-Estèphe	Château Mazeyres
Château Poujeaux-Theil	Château Rouget
Moulis	Château de Sales
Château St. Pierre	
St.-Julien	GRAVES
Château Siran	Château Bouscaut
Labarde-Margaux	*Cadaujac*
Château La Tour-Carnet	Château Fieuzal
St.-Laurent	*Léognan*

Note: All Saint-Émilion and Pomerol châteaux classified in this list bear the strict commune designations of Saint-Émilion and Pomerol, respectively.

THE *CRUS BOURGEOIS* AND *CRUS ARTISANS* OF THE MÉDOC

The following figures of production are approximate, and indicate average annual output, as given by the townships and taken from their Déclarations de Récoltes *records.*

MINOR CHÂTEAUX OF THE HAUT-MÉDOC

	Township	*Hectares*	*Acres*	*Tonneaux*
Château Andron-Blanquet, Château St.-Roch	*St.-Estèphe*	13	32.5	52
Château Aney	*Cussac*	2	5	5
Château Angludet	*Cantenac-Margaux*	18	45	45
Château Antonic	*Moulis*	5	12.5	13
Château d'Arches	*Ludon*	2	5	5
Château d'Arcins	*Arcins*	19	47.5	20
Château Arnauld	*Arcins*	3	7.5	8
Cru Arnaud, Château du Brassat	*St.-Julien*	2	5	7
Château Balogues-Haut-Bages	*Pauillac*	6	15	7
Château Barateau	*St.-Laurent*	4	10	5
Cru Barraillot	*Margaux*	3	7.5	9
Château Barreyres	*Arcins*	11	27.5	26
Château Beaumont	*Cussac*	22	55	14
Château Beauregard	*St.-Julien*	2	5	6
Château Beauséjour	*Listrac*	2	5	6
Château Beauséjour, Château Picard	*St.-Estèphe*	17	42.5	41
Château Beau-Site-St.-Estèphe	*St.-Estèphe*	20	50	58
Château Beau-Site-Haut-Vignoble	*St.-Estèphe*	12	30	52

	Township	Hectares	Acres	Tonneaux
Château Bel-Air	St.-Estèphe	4	10	14
Château Bel-Air Lagrave	Moulis	4	10	11
Château Bel-Air-Marquis- d'Aligre	Soussans-Margaux	28	70	70
Château Belgrave	St.-Laurent	29	72.5	70
Château Bellegrave	Listrac	4	10	7
Château Bellevue	Cussac	3	7.5	7
Château Bellevue-les- Hautes-Graves	Soussans-Margaux	2	5	5
Château Bel-Orme	St.-Seurin-de- Cadourne	22	55	100
Cru Bibian Darriet	Listrac	2	5	9
Château Biston Brillette	Moulis	4	10	11
Château Bonneau	St.-Seurin-de- Cadourne	3	7.5	9
Château Bontemps- Dubarry	St.-Julien	2	5	5
Cru Bontemps	St.-Estèphe	2	5	6
Château Bouqueyran	Moulis	2	5	8
Château Bourgade de La Chapelle (*see* Château Rosemont)				
Château Bournac	St.-Estèphe	3	7.5	8
Château Branas	Moulis	3	7.5	4
Château du Brassat (*see* Cru Arnaud)				
Château du Breuil	Cissac	15	37.5	70
Château Brillette	Cussac	15	37.5	40
Château Bryette	St.-Seurin-de- Cadourne	2	5	8
Cru des Cachères	St.-Estèphe	2	5	6
Château Cadillon	Lamarque	4	10	7
Château Caillevet	Lamarque	3	7.5	14
Château Cambon	Blanquefort	2	5	5
Château Cambon La Pelouse	Macau	8	20	19
Domaine de Campion	Margaux	2	5	8
Château Canteloup	St.-Estèphe	15	37.5	50
Château Capbern, Château Capbern-Gasqueton,				

	Township	Hectares	Acres	Tonneaux
Château La Rose-Capbern, Château Grand Village Capbern, Château Moulin-de-Calon	St.-Estèphe	32	80	95
Château Capdeville	Listrac	3	7.5	4
Château Cap du Haut	Moulis	4	10	10
Château Capléon-Veyrin	Listrac	5	12.5	12
Château Caronne	St.-Laurent	20	50	45
Carruades du Château Lafite-Rothschild	Pauillac			64
Château du Cartillon	Lamarque	5	12.5	7
Clos Castets, Château St.-Seurin	St.-Estèphe	1	2.5	4
Château Chambert (Marbuzet)	St.-Estèphe	2	5	6
Cru Charmant	Margaux	6	15	20
Château Chasse-Spleen, Château Franquet	Moulis	42	105	120
Château Châteaufort de Vauban	Cussac	2	5	6
Château Chaux	Moulis	3	7.5	8
Château Chevalier d'Ars (Coopérative)	Arcins	50	125	122
Château Cissac	Cissac	2	5	12
Château Citran-Clauzel	Avensan	30	75	63
Château Clarke	Listrac	7	17.5	10
Château Clauzet	St.-Estèphe	4	10	21
Château de Côme	St.-Estèphe	2	5	5
Coopérative	St.-Sauveur		varies	
Coopérative (Grand Listrac)	Listrac	130	321	380
Coopérative "Grands Vins de St.-Estèphe"	St.-Estèphe	186	460	536
Coopérative "Cru La Paroisse St.-Seurin-de-Cadourne"	St.-Seurin-de-Cadourne	130	325	400
Coopérative La Rose Pauillac	Pauillac	210	525	700

	Township	Hectares	Acres	Tonneaux
Cru Cougot	*Arsac-Margaux*	2	5	5
Château Coutelin-Merville	*St.-Estèphe*	11	27.5	41
Château Curé-Bourse	*Margaux*	2	5	7
Château Deux Moulins	*Lamarque*	2	5	5
Château Deyrem-Valentin	*Soussans-Margaux*	4	10	9
Château Dillon	*Blanquefort*	9	22.5	29
Château Domeyne	*St.-Estèphe*	2	5	9
Château Donissan-Veyrin	*Listrac*	12	30	33
Château Duplessis Hauchecorne	*Moulis*	14	35	34
Château Dutruch Grand Poujeaux	*Moulis*	10	25	37
Domaine d'Esteau (*see* Château Fontesteau)				
Château Eyquem	*St.-Estèphe*	4	10	10
Château Fatin (*see* Château Le Crock)				
Château Felletin	*Lamarque*	5	12.5	9
Château Fellonneau	*Macau*	3	7.5	5
Clos de Ferrand	*St.-Estèphe*	1	2.5	10
Château Ferrey Gros Caillou, Cru Le Bécasse du Ferrey	*St.-Julien*	6	15	24
Cru des Fines Graves	*St.-Estèphe*	2	5	7
Château Fonbadet	*Pauillac*	30	75	100
Château Fonpetite (*see* Château Phélan-Ségur)				
Château Fonréaud	*Listrac*	25	62.5	60
Château Fontanet	*Le Taillan*	1	2.5	5
Château Fontesteau, Domaine d'Esteau	*Cissac*	11	27.5	15
Château Fourcas-Dupré	*Listrac*	12	30	38
Château Fourcas Hostein	*Listrac*	23	57.5	66
Château Foureau	*Listrac*	27	67.5	88
Château Gaciot	*Avensan*	4	10	10
Château Glana	*St.-Julien*	40	100	200
Château Gloria, Château Haut Beychevelle Gloria	*St.-Julien*	32	80	120
Château Gobineau-Graves-de-Lafon	*Listrac*	8	20	12

	Township	Hectares	Acres	Tonneaux
Domaine du Gona	*Cussac*	3	7.5	6
Cru Grammond	*Listrac*	2	5	5
Château du Grand-Clapeau	*Blanquefort*	5	12.5	9
Château Grandis	*St.-Seurin-de-Cadourne*	3	7.5	8
Château Grand-Jaugueyron	*Cantenac-Margaux*	3	7.5	7
Château Grand-Poujeaux-Theil	*Moulis*	32	80	100
Cru du Grand Rullong	*St.-Estèphe*	3	7.5	11
Château du Grand St.-Julien	*St.-Julien*	4	10	8
Château Grand-Soussans	*Soussans-Margaux*	3	7.5	4
Château Grand Village Capbern (*see* Château Capbern)				
"Grands Vins de St.-Estèphe" (*see* Coopérative)				
Château Granins	*Moulis*	3	7.5	10
Cru Granins	*Moulis*	1	2.5	5
Château Graves	*Moulis*	5	12.5	5
Cru des Graves	*Moulis*	1	2.5	5
Cru des Graves	*Listrac*	3	7.5	6
Château Cru du Gravier	*Arsac-Margaux*	2	5	6
Cru des Gravières	*Cussac*	2	5	6
Château Gressier Grand Poujeaux	*Moulis*	24	60	70
Château Guitignan	*Moulis*	3	7.5	9
Château Hanteillan	*St.-Estèphe*	20	50	65
Château Haut Bellevue	*Lamarque*	2	5	6
Château Haut-Carmail	*St.-Seurin-de-Cadourne*	4	10	13
Cru Haut Coutelin	*St.-Estèphe*	4	10	12
Château Haut Daubos, Château Mongrand Milon	*Pauillac*	3	7.5	4
Château Haut Hagna	*St.-Estèphe*	4	10	12
Cru Haut La Tour de Coutelin	*St.-Estèphe*	2	5	5
Château Haut Marbuzet	*St.-Estèphe*	12	30	24

	Township	Hectares	Acres	Tonneaux
Château Haut Plantey	*Listrac*	2	5	6
Château Haut Sieujean	*St.-Laurent*	3	7.5	8
Château Haut Verdon	*St.-Estèphe*	3	7.5	15
Château Héby	*Moulis*	2	5	5
Cru Hennebelle, Cru Landarey	*Lamarque*	3	7.5	7
Château Hortevie	*St.-Julien*	3	7.5	8
Château Hostein	*St.-Estèphe*	3	7.5	9
Château Houissant	*St.-Estèphe*	14	35	70
Château l'Abbégorsse-de-Gorsse	*Margaux*	4	10	11
Château La Bécade	*Listrac*	3	7.5	7
Cru La-Bécasse-du-Ferrey	*St.-Julien*	6	15	24
Château Labégorce	*Margaux*	4	10	11
Château Labégorce-Zédé	*Soussans-Margaux*	15	37.5	50
Cru La Chapelle	*St.-Estèphe*	3	7.5	7
Cru La Clidère	*Listrac*	2	5	6
Château La Closerie	*Moulis*	7	17.5	23
Château La Colonilla	*Margaux*	6	15	16
Château Laconfourque	*St.-Julien*	1	2.5	4
Château La Couronne	*Pauillac*	3	7.5	7
Château La Croix (*see* Château Phélan-Ségur)				
La Dame Blanche	*Le Taillan*	5	12.5	10
(*The white wine of Château du Taillan, which has only the Appellation Bordeaux Blanc Supérieur*)				
Château Ladouys	*St.-Estèphe*	4	10	10
Château Laffitte-Carcasset	*St.-Estèphe*	20	50	48
Château La Fleur	*St.-Laurent*	3	7.5	8
Château La Fleur Milon	*Pauillac*	7	17.5	16
Château Lafon	*Listrac*	6	15	10
Château La Galiane	*Soussans-Margaux*	4	10	9
Château La Gombaude	*Margaux*	5	12.5	15
Château Lagorce	*Moulis*	3	7.5	7
Château Lagravette-Peyredon	*Listrac*	5	12.5	10
Château La Gravière-Haut-Bages	*Pauillac*	1	2.5	4

	Township	Hectares	Acres	Tonneaux
Château La Gurgue	*Margaux*	8	20	30
Château La Haye	*St.-Estèphe*	5	12.5	12
Château Lalande (*see* Château Tronquoy)				
Château Lamothe-de-Bergeron	*Cussac*	10	25	21
Château La Mouline	*Moulis*	4	10	18
Château de Lamourous	*Le Pian*	4	10	16
Château de Lamouroux	*Margaux*	4	10	16
Cru Landarey (*see* Cru Hennebelle)				
Château Lanessan	*Cussac*	18	45	48
Cru Langa	*Cussac*	3	7.5	4
"Cru La Paroisse St.-Seurin-de-Cadourne" (*see* Coopérative)				
Château La Rose	*St.-Seurin-de-Cadourne*	2	5	6
Château La Rose (Co-opérative de Pauillac)	*Pauillac*	210	525	700
Château La Rose-Capbern (*see* Château Capbern)				
Château La Rose de France	*St.-Julien*	2	5	8
Château de Laroze	*Margaux*	2	5	7
Cru Larragay	*Listrac*	2	5	6
Château Larrieu-Terrefort-Graves	*Macau*	3	7.5	5
Château Larrivaux	*Cissac*	5	12.5	19
Château Lartigue	*St.-Estèphe*	2	5	13
Château La Tour d'Anseillan	*Pauillac*	9	22.5	20
Château La Tour l'Aspic	*Pauillac*	4	10	7
Château La Tour-de-Bessan (*see* Château La Tour-de-Mons)				
Château La Tour Brana	*St.-Estèphe*	2	5	5
Château La Tour Coutelin	*St.-Estèphe*	3	7.3	11
Château Latour-Dumirail	*Cissac*	10	25	16
Château La Tour du Haut Moulin	*Cussac*	7	17.5	15
Château La Tour Haut Vignoble (*see* Château Les Ormes-de-Pez)				
Château La Tour du Haut Vignoble	*St.-Estèphe*	12	30	52

	Township	Hectares	Acres	Tonneaux
Château La Tour de Leyssac	*St.-Estèphe*	3	7.5	12
Château La Tour Lichine (*see* Château Capbern)				
Château La Tour de Malescasse	*Lamarque*	5	12.5	9
Château La Tour de Marbuzet	*St.-Estèphe*	13	32.5	32
Château La Tour Marcillannet	*St.-Laurent*	6	15	9
Château La Tour-de-Mons, Château Riche-terre, Château La Tour-de-Bessan	*Soussans-Margaux*	24	60	65
Château La Tour Pibran	*Pauillac*	5	12.5	18
Château La Tour du Roc-Grand Poujeaux	*Arcins*	12	30	31
Château La Tour du Roch Milon	*Pauillac*	18	45	20
Château La Tour des Ternes	*St.-Estèphe*	12	30	13
Château Le Boscq	*St.-Estèphe*	13	32.5	39
Château Le Crock, Château Fatin, Château St.-Estèphe "La Croix"	*St.-Estèphe*	27	67.5	97
Château Lemoyne-Lafon-Rochet	*Le Pian*	3	7.5	10
Château Le Raux	*Cussac*	4	10	7
Château Le Roc	*St.-Estèphe*	1	2.5	5
Château Lescarjeau	*St.-Sauveur*	5	12.5	13
Cru Lescourt	*Listrac*	2	5	5
Château Les Graves de Germignan	*Le Taillan*	3	7.5	8
Château Les Ormes-de-Pez, Château Moulin Joli, Château La Tour Haut Vignoble	*St.-Estèphe*	21	52.5	80
Château Lestage	*Listrac*	29	72.5	43

	Township	Hectares	Acres	Tonneaux
Château Lestage	*St.-Seurin-de-Cadourne*	1	2.5	5
Château Lestage Darquier	*Moulis*	4	10	8
Château Lestage Darquier Grand Poujeaux	*Moulis*	4	10	13
Château L'Hôpital	*St.-Estèphe*	5	12.5	17
Château Liversan	*St.-Sauveur*	32	80	130
Domaine du Lucrabey	*Cissac*	5	12.5	7
Château Mac-Carthy	*St.-Estèphe*	4	10	12
Château MacCarthy Moula	*St.-Estèphe*	6	15	12
Château Malécot	*Pauillac*	7	17.5	21
Château Malescasse	*Lamarque*	4	10	11
Château Malmaison	*Moulis*	4	10	5
Château Marbuzet	*St.-Estèphe*	11	27.5	31
Château Marque	*St.-Seurin-de-Cadourne*	1	2.5	6
Clos du Marquis	*St.-Julien*	8	20	11
Château Marsac-Seguineau	*Soussans-Margaux*	3	7.5	9
Château Martinens	*Cantenac-Margaux*	19	47.5	14
Clos du Mas	*Listrac*	5	12.5	9
Château Maucaillou	*Moulis*	11	27.5	33
Château Maucamps	*Macau*	5	12.5	13
Château Médrac	*Moulis*	5	12.5	3
Château Meyney	*St.-Estèphe*	44	109	182
Château Milon-Mousset, Cru Milon	*Pauillac*	2	5	6
Château Mongrand Milon (*see* Château Haut Daubos)				
Château Monpelou	*Pauillac*	8	20	5
Château Montbrun	*Cantenac-Margaux*	5	12.5	25
Château Morin	*St.-Estèphe*	8	20	18
Clos du Moulin	*St.-Estèphe*	5	12.5	7
Cru du Moulin	*Cussac*	1	2.5	5
Château Moulin-à-Vent	*Moulis*	6	15	9
Cru du Moulin de Laborde	*Listrac*	4	10	10

	Township	Hectares	Acres	Tonneaux
Château du Moulin du Bourg	Listrac	6	15	31
Château Moulin de la Bridane	Pauillac	4	10	13
Château Moulin-de-Calon (see Château Capbern)				
Château Moulin de la Rose	St.-Julien	4	10	11
Château Moulin Joli (see Château Les Ormes-de-Pez)				
Château Moulin-Riche	St.-Julien	11	27.5	19
Château Moulin Rose	Lamarque	3	7.5	9
Château du Moulin Rouge	Cussac	4	10	6
Château Moulis	Moulis	6	15	16
Clos Muratel	Blanquefort	1	2.5	4
Cru Muscadet	St.-Estèphe	1	2.5	5
Château Nexon-Lemoyne	Ludon	2	5	10
Cru du Paléna	Listrac	2	5	5
Château Palmier	St.-Estèphe	5	12.5	18
Château Parempuyre-Cruse	Parempuyre	4	10	4
Château Parempuyre-Durand-Dassier	Parempuyre	3	7.5	10
Château Paveil	Soussans-Margaux	11	27.5	33
Château Pelon	St.-Laurent	3	7.5	8
Château Peyrabon	St.-Sauveur	9	22.5	16
Château Peyredon	Moulis	3	7.5	9
Château de Pez	St.-Estèphe	22	55	93
Château Phélan-Ségur, Château La Croix, Château Fonpetite, Château Roche	St.-Estèphe	44	109	175
Château Pibran	Pauillac	7	17.5	22
Château Picard (see Château Beauséjour)				
Château Pierre Bibian	Listrac	11	27.5	45
Château Piton Richebon	Moulis	5	12.5	14
Château Plaisance	Pauillac	7	17.5	13

	Township	Hectares	Acres	Tonneaux
Château Plantier-Rose	*St.-Estèphe*	7	17.5	23
Château Pomeys	*Moulis*	5	12.5	16
Château Pomiès-Agassac	*Ludon*	9	22.5	20
Château Pomys	*St.-Estèphe*	7	17.5	18
Cru Pontet-chappez	*Arsac-Margaux*	1	2.5	4

Château Pontoise-
    Cabarrus-Brochon
	*St.-Seurin-de-
	    Cadourne*
		7	17.5	20

Château Poujeaux-Theil	*Moulis*	16	40	47
Cru Poumarin	*St.-Estèphe*	3	7.5	5
Cru des Pradines	*St.-Estèphe*	2	5	5
Domaine des Pradines	*St.-Estèphe*	1	2.5	6
Château Renouil Franquet	*Moulis*	4	10	8
Château Reverdi	*Listrac*	3	7.5	7
Cru Ribeau	*St.-Estèphe*	2	5	6
Château Richeterre (*see* Château La Tour-de-Mons)				
Cru Richet-Marian	*Margaux*	2	5	8
Château Robert Franquet	*Moulis*	4	10	9
Château Robert Renouil-Grand Poujeaux	*Arcins*	2	5	8
Château Roche (*see* Château Phélan-Ségur)				
Château Roland	*Pauillac*	5	12.5	19

Château Rosemont,
    Château de Bourgade de
    La Chapelle
	Labarde	1	2.5	9

Château Rose Ste.- Croix	*Listrac*	5	12.5	13
Château Ruat	*Moulis*	4	10	5
Château St.-Estèphe	*St.-Estèphe*	3	7.5	9
Château St.-Estèphe "La Croix" (*see* Château Le Crock)				
Château St.-Louis- Dubosq	*St.-Julien*	1	2.5	4
Château St.-Martin	*Listrac*	2	5	8
Clos St.-Martin	*Pauillac*	3	7.5	6
Château St.-Paul	*St.-Seurin-de- Cadourne*	5	12.5	16

	Township	Hectares	Acres	Tonneaux
Cru St.-Pierre	*Margaux*	2	5	4
Château St.-Seurin (*see* Clos Castets)				
Château Saransot-Dupré	*Listrac*	4	10	18
Château Ségur-Bacqué	*Parempuyre*	5	12.5	10
Château Ségur-Fillon	*Parempuyre*	5	12.5	4
Château Sémeillan	*Listrac*	13	32.5	53
Château Sénéjac	*Le Pian*	10	25	22
Château Sénhilac	*St.-Seurin-de-Cadourne*	4	10	11
Château Siran	*Labarde-Margaux*	21	52.5	70
Château Sociando-Mallet	*St.-Seurin-de-Cadourne*	5	12.5	20
Château du Taillan	*Le Taillan*	5	12.5	10
(*The white wine is called Château La Dame Blanche*)				
Cru Taste	*St.-Estèphe*	3	7.5	6
Château Tayac-Plaisance	*Soussans-Margaux*	2	5	6
Château du Terrey	*St.-Sauveur*	12	30	10
Château Terrey-Gros-Caillou	*St.-Julien*	12	30	50
Château de Testeron	*Moulis*	2	5	5
Château Teynac	*St.-Julien*	4	10	10
Château Teynac, Clos St.-Julien	*St.-Julien*	4	10	12
Château Tourelle	*Listrac*	2	5	5
Château Tronquoy-Lalande	*St.-Estèphe*	16	40	60
Cru du Troupian	*St.-Estèphe*	2	5	5
Cru Vallière	*Margaux*	2	5	6
Château Verdignan	*St.-Seurin-de-Cadourne*	15	37.5	67
Château Villegeorge	*Avensan*	5	12.5	12
Château Vincent	*Cantenac-Margaux*	2	5	4

MINOR CHÂTEAUX OF THE MÉDOC (OR BAS-MÉDOC)

	Township	Hectares	Acres	Tonneaux
Domaine des Anguilleys (*see* Château Vieux Robin)				
Clos Beau Rivage	*Bégadan*	2	5	8
Château Bégadanet	*Bégadan*	4	10	12

	Township	Hectares	Acres	Tonneaux
Cru Bel Air Mareil	*Ordonnac-et-Potensac*	3	7.5	6
Château Belfort	*St.-Germain-d'Esteuil*	4	10	8
Château des Bellegraves	*Ordonnac-et-Potensac*	5	12.5	17
Château Bellerive	*Valeyrac*	9	22.5	35
Château Bellevue	*Valeyrac*	3	7.5	17
Château Bensse (*see* Coopérative de Prignac)				
Cru de Bert	*Couquéques*	3	7.5	8
Château Blaignan	*Blaignan*	4	10	11
Château Buscateau	*St.-Germain-d'Esteuil*	2	5	6
Château de By	*Bégadan*	7	17.5	28
Domaine de By	*Bégadan*	10	25	28
Cru Canteloup	*Blaignan*	2	5	6
Château Carcanieux-les-Graves	*Queyrac*	4	10	13
Château Castéra	*St.-Germain-d'Esteuil*	18	45	39
Cave Coopérative "St.-Jean"	*Bégadan*	560	1,384	1,200
Cave Coopérative "Belle Vue"	*Ordonnac-et-Potensac*	87	215	224
Cru Chantegric	*Prignac*	3	7.5	6
Château Chantelys	*Prignac*	4	10	11
Château des Combes	*Bégadan*	4	10	11
Coopérative	*Vertheuil*	—	—	300
Coopérative de Gaillan (Grand Vin du Vieux-Clocher)	*Gaillan*	15	37.5	26
Coopérative de Prignac, Château Bensse	*Prignac*	97	240	220
Coopérative de Queyrac, Château St.-Roch	*Queyrac*	15	37.5	50
Coopérative de St.-Yzans, Cave St.-Brice	*St.-Yzans*	96	238	220

	Township	Hectares	Acres	Tonneaux
Château Côtes de Blaignan, Cru Hontane	*Blaignan*	5	12.5	14
Cru Cruscaut-Graves-du-Pin	*Blaignan*	4	10	8
Cru des Deux-Moulins	*St.-Christoly*	13	32.5	48
Château Gaillais-Bellevue (*see* Château Potensac)				
Grand Vin du Vieux-Clocher (*see* Coopérative de Gaillan)				
Domaine et Clos des Graves	*Ordonnac-et-Potensac*	2	5	6
Château Haut-Blaignan	*Blaignan*	5	12.5	16
Cru de Haut Château Malendrin	*Couquéques*	2	5	6
Cru Haut-Garin	*Prignac*	3	7.5	8
Château Haut-Giras	*St.-Germain-d'Esteuil*	6	15	7
Château Haut-Graville	*Civrac*	8	20	16
Château Haut-Miqueu	*St.-Germain-d'Esteuil*	4	10	11
Clos Haut-Pouyzac	*St.-Christoly*	2	5	6
Cru Hontane (*see* Château Côtes de Blaignan)				
Château La Cardonne	*Blaignan*	34	85	98
Cru La Colonne	*St.-Yzans*	3	7.5	10
Château Lafitte	*Bégadan*	3	7.5	11
Domaine de Lafon	*Prignac*	3	7.5	7
Clos Laforest	*St.-Christoly*	4	10	11
Château La France	*St.-Yzans*	3	7.5	9
Château l'Aiglon	*St.-Germain-d'Esteuil*	2	5	4
Château La Gore	*Bégadan*	5	12.5	17
Château La Lagune	*St.-Germain-d'Esteuil*	1	2.5	6
Domaine de la Lagune	*Bégadan*	2	5	6
Château La Privera	*St.-Christoly*	2	5	8
Château La Roque de By	*Bégadan*	5	12.5	8
Château La Rose Garamay (*see* Château Livran)				
Château Lassalle	*Ordonnac-et-Potensac*	4	10	10
Château La Tour-Blanche	*St.-Christoly*	7	17.5	28

	Township	*Hectares*	*Acres*	*Tonneaux*
Château La Tour de By	*Bégadan*	31	77.5	62
Château La Tour Cordouan	*Bégadan*	2	5	6
Château La Tour du Haut-Caussan	*Blaignan*	3	7.5	10
Château La Tour-St.-Bonnet	*St.-Christoly*	15	37.5	52
Château Laujac	*Bégadan*	4	10	19
Château Le Bourdieu	*Vertheuil*	40	100	150
Château Le Clou	*Blaignan*	4	10	16
Château Le Grand-Trepeau	*St.-Christoly*	2	5	4
Château Les Lesques	*Lesparre*	11	27.5	11
Clos Les Moines	*Couquéques*	4	10	13
Château Les Ormes-Sorbet	*Couquéques*	8	20	27
Château Le Tertre-de-Caussan	*Blaignan*	5	12.5	18
Cru Les Tourelles	*Blaignan*	3	7.5	11
Château Le Tréhon	*Bégadan*	7	17.5	22
Château L'Hermitage	*Couquéques*	4	10	10
Château Livran, Château La Rose Garamay	*St.-Germain-d'Esteuil*	10	25	27
Château Loudenne	*St.-Yzans*	9	22.5	26
Château Lugagnac	*Vertheuil*	3	7.5	10
Clos Mandillot	*St.-Christoly*	3	7.5	5
Château Monthil	*Bégadan*	4	10	8
Clos Morteil	*Bégadan*	4	10	11
Clos du Moulin	*St.-Christoly*	4	10	15
Château Panigon	*Civrac*	8	20	16
Domaine de Patache	*Bégadan*	25	62.5	110
Château Pay-de-Lalo	*St.-Germain-d'Esteuil*	2	5	7
Château Plagnac	*Bégadan*	2	5	7
Château Potensac, Château Gallais-Bellevue	*Ordonnac-et-Pontensac*	9	22.5	35

	Township	Hectares	Acres	Tonneaux
Château Reysson	*Vertheuil*	34	85	65
Cru du Roc	*Couquéques*	2	5	6
Cru du Roc	*St.-Christoly*	6	15	15
Château Roquegrave	*Valeyrac*	5	12.5	19
Château de Roquetaillade	*Ordonnac-et-*			
	Potensac	3	7.5	12
Château St.-Anne	*St.-Christoly*	4	10	7
Château St.-Bonnet	*St.-Christoly*	13	32.5	37
Cave St.-Brice (*see* Coopérative de St.-Yzans)				
Château St.-Christoly	*St.-Christoly*	4	10	28
Château St.-Germain	*St.-Germain-*			
	d'Esteuil	2	5	8
Cru St.-Louis	*Couquéques*	3	7.5	11
Château St.-Roch (*see* Coopérative de Queyrac)				
Château St.-Saturnin	*Bégadan*	6	15	14
Cru Verdon	*Valeyrac*	3	7.5	12
Cru du Vieux-Château				
Landon	*Bégadan*	10	25	35
Château Vieux Robin,				
Domaine des Anguilleys	*Bégadan*	4	10	14

SAINT-ÉMILION

1955 OFFICIAL CLASSIFICATION

In mid-1955 the best Saint-Émilion wines were officially classified by the French Institut National des Appellations d'Origine as 1st Great Growths and Great Growths.

The following figures of production are approximate, and indicate average annual output, as given by the townships and taken from their Déclarations de Récoltes records.

1st Great Growths

	Tonneaux	Cases
Château Ausone	35	2,800
Château Beauséjour-Duffau-Lagarosse	25	2,000
Château Beauséjour-Fagouet	30	2,900
Château Belair	90	7,500
Château Canon	90	7,200
Château Cheval Blanc	150	12,000
Château Figeac	120	9,500
Clos Fourtet	80	6,700
Château La Gaffelière-Naudes	110	9,400
Château Magdelaine	40	3,200
Château Pavie	200	16,200
Château Trottevieille	40	3,250

Great Growths

(Acreage and production figures are given in the next section.)

Château l'Arrosée   Château Bergat
Château Balestard-la-Tonnelle   Château Cadet-Bon
Château Bellevue   Château Cadet-Piolat

Great Growths

Château Canon-la-Gaffelière	Château La Marzelle
Château Cap de Mourlin	Château l'Angélus
Château Chapelle Madeleine	Château Larcis-Ducasse
Château Chatelet	Château Larmande
Château Chauvin	Château Laroze
Château Corbin	Château Lasserre
Château Corbin-Michotte	Château La Tour-Figeac
Château Coutet	Château La Tour-du-Pin-Figeac
Château Croque-Michotte	Château Le Couvent
Château Curé-Bon	Château Le Prieuré
Château Fonplégade	Château Mauvezin
Château Fonroque	Château Moulin-du-Cadet
Château Franc-Mayne	Château Pavie-Decesse
Château Grand-Barrail- Lamarzelle-Figeac	Château Pavie-Macquin
	Château Pavillon-Cadet
Château Grand Corbin	Château Petit-Faurie-de-Souchard
Château Grand-Corbin-Despagne	Château Petit-Faurie-de-Soutard
Château Grand-Mayne	Château Ripeau
Clos des Grandes Murailles	Château St.-Georges-Côte-Pavie
Château Grand-Pontet	Clos St.-Martin
Château Guadet-St.-Julien	Château Sansonnet
Clos des Jacobins	Château Soutard
Château Jean Faure	Château Tertre-Daugay
Château La Carte	Château Trimoulet
Château La Clotte	Château Trois-Moulins
Château La Cluzière	Château Troplong-Mondot
Château La Couspaude	Château Villemaurine
Château La Dominique	Château Yon-Figeac
Clos La Madeleine	

Other Principal Growths

	Township	Hectares	Acres	Tonneaux
Domaine Allée-de- Lescours	*St.-Sulpice-de-Faleyrans*	4	10	11
Château Ambois	*St.-Georges-St.-Émilion*	1	2.5	4
Clos d'Armens	*St.-Pey-d'Armens*	2	5	7
Domaine d'Arriailh	*Montagne-St.-Émilion*	4	10	6

	Township	Hec-tares	Acres	Ton-neaux
Château d'Arthus	*Vignonet*	5	12.5	13
Clos d'Arthus	*Vignonet*	12	30	23
Château Austerlitz	*Sables-St.-Émilion*	5	12.5	18
Château Badette	*St.-Christophe-des-Bardes*	8	20	23
Château Badon (*see* Château Vieux-Ceps)				
Domaine de Badon-Patarabet	*St.-Émilion*	2	5	12
Château Baleau	*St.-Émilion*	12	30	41
Château Balestard-la-Tonnelle	*St.-Émilion*	7	17.5	31
Château Barbe-Blanche	*Lussac-St.-Émilion*	8	20	22
Château Barbey	*St.-Étienne-de-Lisse*	2	5	9
Château Barbeyron	*St.-Laurent-des-Combes*	4	10	13
Château Barde-Haut	*St.-Christophe-des-Bardes*	12	30	43
Château Bardoulet	*St.-Étienne-de-Lisse*	2	5	7
Domaine de Bardoulet	*St.-Étienne-de-Lisse*	3	7.5	15
Château Barraud	*Montagne-St.-Émilion*	4	10	21
Domaine de Barraud	*Montagne-St.-Émilion*	4	10	11
Château du Basque	*St.-Pey-d'Armens*	8	20	35
Château Bayard	*Montagne-St.-Émilion*	7	17.5	39
Clos Bayard	*Montagne-St.-Émilion*	5	12.5	22
Domaine de Bayard	*Montagne-St.-Émilion*	8	20	19
Château Béard	*St.-Laurent-des-Combes*	5	12.5	22
Clos Beaufort-Mazerat	*St.-Émilion*	2	5	9
Château Beau-Mazerat (*see* Château Grand-Mayne)				
Château Beauséjour	*Montagne-St.-Émilion*	6	15	30
Château Beauséjour	*Puisseguin-St.-Émilion*	14	35	58
Château Beausite	*Vignonet*	4	10	15
Château Beausite	*Lussac-St.-Émilion*	3	7.5	10
Château Bel-Air	*Lussac-St.-Émilion*	12	30	46
Château Bel-Air	*Montagne-St.-Émilion*	8	20	29
Château Bel-Air	*Puisseguin-St.-Émilion*	11	27.5	55
Château Belair-Sarthou	*St.-Étienne-de-Lisse*	5	12.5	19
Château Bel-Horizon	*Vignonet*	2	5	5
Château Belle-Assise	*St.-Sulpice-de-Faleyrans*	5	12.5	22
Château Bellefond-Belcier	*St.-Laurent-des-Combes*	11	27.7	42

	Township	Hec-tares	Acres	Ton-neaux
Château Bellegrave	*Vignonet*	8	20	40
Château Belles-Plantes	*Vignonet*	3	7.5	9
Château Bellevue	*St.-Émilion*	6	15	28
Château Bellevue	*Lussac-St.-Émilion*	11	27.5	32
Château Bellevue	*Montagne-St.-Émilion*	4	10	19
Clos Bellevue-Figeac	*St.-Émilion*	3	7.5	12
Cru Bellevue-Mondotte	*St.-Laurent-des-Combes*	2	5	7
Clos Bellevue-Peyblanquet	*St.-Étienne-de-Lisse*	3	7.5	7
Château Bellile-Mondotte	*St.-Laurent-des-Combes*	4	10	11
Cru Béouran	*St.-Émilion*	1	2.5	7
Château Bergat	*St.-Émilion*	3	7.5	8
Cru Berlière	*Parsac-St.-Émilion*	4	10	15
Domaine de Berlière	*Parsac-St.-Émilion*	3	7.5	5
Château Berliquet	*St.-Émilion*	7	17.5	19
Clos Bernachot	*St.-Sulpice-de-Faleyrans*	2	5	8
Clos Berthoneau (*see* Château du Roy)				
Château Bertineau-Goby	*Montagne-St.-Émilion*	9	22.5	28
Château Bézineau	*St.-Émilion*	13	32.5	53
Cru Bibey	*St.-Émilion*	6	15	18
Château Bicasse-Lartigue	*St.-Sulpice-de-Faleyrans*	3	7.5	11
Château Bigaroux	*St.-Sulpice-de-Faleyrans*	5	12.5	11
Château Billeron	*St.-Hippolyte*	8	20	27
Château Binet	*Parsac-St.-Émilion*	9	22.5	19
Cru Biquet	*St.-Hippolyte*	4	10	19
Château Bois-Grouley	*St.-Sulpice-de-Faleyrans*	3	7.5	14
Château Bois-Rond-Grand-Corbin	*St.-Émilion*	4	10	16
Château Bonneau, Château des Rochers	*Montagne-St.-Émilion*	9	22.5	43
Domaine de Bonneau	*Montagne-St.-Émilion*	4	10	12
Château Bord-Fonrazade	*St.-Émilion*	4	10	14
Château Bord-Lartigue	*St.-Émilion*	2	5	11
Château Boulerne	*St.-Sulpice-de-Faleyrans*	9	22.5	32
Château Bouquey	*St.-Hippolyte*	4	10	19
Domaine du Bourg	*St.-Christophe-des-Bardes*	2	5	13
Château Boutisse	*St.-Christophe-des-Bardes*	16	40	77

	Township	Hec-tares	Acres	Ton-neaux
Château Branne	*Montagne-St.-Émilion*	6	15	35
Château Brisson	*Vignonet*	4	10	13
Château Brisson, Château Destieux	*St.-Sulpice-de-Faleyrans*	9	22.5	30
Château Brun	*St.-Christophe-des-Bardes*	6	15	20
Clos Brun	*St.-Sulpice-de-Faleyrans*	3	7.5	13
Château Cadet-Bon	*St.-Émilion*	3	7.5	19
Château Cadet-Piolat	*St.-Émilion*	18	45	75
Château Calon	*Montagne-St.-Émilion*	20	50	71
Château Calon-Montagne	*St.-Georges-St.-Émilion*	3	7.5	11
Château Calon-St.-Georges	*St.-Georges-St.-Émilion*	3	7.5	12
Château du Calvaire	*St.-Étienne-de-Lisse*	6	15	23
Clos du Calvaire	*St.-Étienne-de-Lisse*	2	5	7
Château Canon-la-Gaffelière	*St.-Émilion*	18	45	61
Château Cante-Merle (*see* Château Ripeau)				
Château Cantenac	*St.-Émilion*	7	17.5	42
Clos Cantenac	*St.-Émilion*	5	12.5	27
Château Canteranne	*St.-Étienne-de-Lisse*	6	15	26
Château Cap de Mourlin	*St.-Émilion*	13	32.5	66
Château Cap-d'Or	*St.-Georges-St.-Émilion*	5	12.5	26
Château Caperot (*see* Château Monbousquet)				
Clos Caperot	*St.-Sulpice-de-Faleyrans*	3	7.5	10
Château Capet-Guillier	*St.-Hippolyte*	12	30	50
Château Cardinal-Villemaurine	*St.-Émilion*	7	17.5	35
Château Carteau-Bas-Daugay	*St.-Sulpice-de-Faleyrans*	4	10	18
Château Carteau-Côte-Daugay	*St.-Émilion*	3	7.5	12
Château Carteau-Pin-de-Fleurs	*St.-Émilion*	3	7.5	16
Domaine de Cassah	*Puisseguin-St.-Émilion*	6	15	12
Château Cassevert (*see* Château Grand-Mayne)				
Clos Castelot	*St.-Émilion*	10	25	43
Domaine de la Cateau	*St.-Émilion*	3	7.5	11

	Township	Hec-tares	Acres	Ton-neaux
Château Cauzin	*St.-Christophe-des-Bardes*	4	10	23
Clos de la Cavaille-Lescours	*St.-Sulpice-de-Faleyrans*	1	2.5	7
Cave Coopérative ⎫				1,760
Royal St.-Émilion ⎬	*St.-Émilion*	775	1,920	450
Côtes Rocheuses ⎭				270
Cave Coopérative des Côtes-de-Castillon	*St.-Étienne-de-Lisse*	3	7.5	14
Cave Vinicole de Puisseguin	*Puisseguin-St.-Émilion*	570	1,408	3,200
Château Champion	*St.-Christophe-des-Bardes*	5	12.5	16
Château Chante-Alouette	*St.-Émilion*	6	15	23
Château Chantecaille	*St.-Émilion*	3	7.5	17
Château Chantegrive, Château Destieux-Verac	*St.-Émilion*	5	12.5	20
Clos Chante-l'Alouette, Domaine Haut-Patarabet	*St.-Émilion*	4	10	24
Château Chapelle-de-la-Trinité (*see* Château Laniotte)				
Domaine du Chatain	*Montagne-St.-Émilion*	3	7.5	10
Château Chatelet	*St.-Émilion*	3	7.5	11
Château Chatelet (*see* Château Larques)				
Château Chauvin	*St.-Émilion*	12	30	59
Cru Chêne-Vert	*Parsac-St.-Émilion*	7	17.5	32
Château Chêne-Vieux	*Parsac-St.-Émilion*	8	20	34
Château Cheval-Brun	*St.-Émilion*	5	12.5	14
Château Cheval-Noir	*St.-Émilion*	4	10	11
Château du Clocher	*St.-Émilion*	3	7.5	13
Domaine de la Clotte	*St.-Hippolyte*	5	12.5	15
Domaine de la Clotte	*Montagne-St.-Émilion*	5	12.5	14
Château du Comte	*St.-Hippolyte*	3	7.5	5
Coopérative de Montagne	*Montagne-St.-Émilion*	145	358	706
Clos des Corbières	*Montagne-St.-Émilion*	2	5	8
Château Corbin	*St.-Émilion*	10	25	58
Château Corbin	*Montagne-St.-Émilion*	13	32.5	65
Château Corbin-Michotte	*St.-Émilion*	8	20	29

	Township	Hec-tares	Acres	Ton-neaux
Clos Cormey	*St.-Émilion*	7	17.5	29
Château Cormey-Figeac	*St.-Émilion*	10	25	43
Domaine de Corniaud	*Montagne-St.-Émilion*	5	12.5	15
Domaine de Corniaud-Lussac	*Lussac-St.-Émilion*	3	7.5	10
Château Côte de Bonde	*Montagne-St.-Émilion*	7	17.5	14
Château Côte de Rol-Valentin	*St.-Émilion*	3	7.3	9
Cru Côte-Migon-la-Gaffelière	*St.-Émilion*	1	2.5	6
Château Côtes-Bernateau	*St.-Étienne-de-Lisse*	8	20	50
Cru Côtes-du-Fayan	*Puisseguin-St.-Émilion*	8	20	23
Cru Côtes-Pressac	*St.-Étienne-de-Lisse*	2	5	8
Cru Côtes-Roland	*St.-Étienne-de-Lisse*	2	5	9
Clos Côtes-Roland-de-Pressac	*St.-Étienne-de-Lisse*	2	5	9
Cru Côtes-Veyrac	*St.-Étienne-de-Lisse*	3	7.5	19
Château Couchy	*Montagne-St.-Émilion*	11	27.5	45
Château Coudert	*St.-Christophe-des-Bardes*	3	7.5	12
Château Coudert-Pelletan	*St.-Christophe-des-Bardes*	9	22.5	36
Château Couperie-Dassault	*St.-Émilion*	16	40	52
Château du Courlat	*Lussac-St.-Émilion*	9	22.5	40
Château Coutet	*St.-Émilion*	12	30	30
Château Couvent-des-Jacobins	*St.-Émilion*	9	22.5	33
Domaine Croix-de-Grézard	*Lussac-St.-Émilion*	2	5	9
Château Croix-de-Justice	*Puisseguin-St.-Émilion*	5	12.5	14
Domaine de la Croix-Mazerat	*St.-Émilion*	2	5	5
Château Croix-du-Merle	*St.-Hippolyte*	3	7.5	8
Château Croix-Figeac	*St.-Émilion*	3	7.5	12

	Township	Hec-tares	Acres	Ton-neaux
Château Croix-Peyblanquet	*St.-Étienne-de-Lisse*	4	10	9
Château de la Croix-Simard	*St.-Émilion*	1	2.5	7
Château Croix-Villemaurine	*St.-Émilion*	1	2.5	5
Château Croque-Michotte	*St.-Émilion*	8	20	58
Château Cruzeau	*Sables-St.-Émilion*	3	7.5	14
Château Curé-Bon	*St.-Émilion*	5	12.5	15
Château Dassault	*St.-Émilion*	16	40	52
Clos Daupin	*St.-Émilion*	2	5	10
Clos Daviaud	*Parsac-St.-Émilion*	5	12.5	13
Château des Demoiselles	*St.-Christophe-des-Bardes*	1	2.5	5
Domaine des Dépend-ances Cru Jaugueblanc	*St.-Émilion*	3	7.5	13
Domaine Despagne	*St.-Sulpice-de-Faleyrans*	7	17.5	15
Château Despagnet	*St.-Sulpice-de-Faleyrans*	3	7.5	13
Château Destieu	*Vignonet*	4	10	15
Château Destieux	*St.-Émilion*	9	22.5	30
Château Destieux	*St.-Sulpice-de-Faleyrans*	7	17.5	25
Château Destieux (*see* Château Brisson, *St.-Sulpice-de-Faleyrans*)				
Château Destieux-Verac	*St.-Christophe-des-Bardes*	11	27.5	37
Château Divon	*St.-Georges-St.-Émilion*	4	10	19
Domaine des Escardos	*Vignonet*	7	17.5	12
Château Fagouet-Jean-Voisin	*St.-Émilion*	6	15	35
Château Faizeau	*Montagne-St.-Émilion*	7	17.5	32
Château Faleyrans	*St.-Sulpice-de-Faleyrans*	5	12.5	12
Château de Ferrand	*St.-Hippolyte*	30	75	148
Château Ferrandat	*St.-Laurent-des-Combes*	4	10	16
Cru Ferrandat	*St.-Laurent-des-Combes*	1	2.5	9
Château Figeac, Château Pont-de-Figeac, Château Grangeneuve	*St.-Émilion*	25	62.5	79
Clos Fleurus	*St.-Émilion*	1	2.5	8
Clos Fleurus	*St.-Sulpice-de-Faleyrans*	1	2.5	5

	Township	Hec-tares	Acres	Ton-neaux
Château Fombrauge	St.-Christophe-des-Bardes	38	94	150
Château Fond-de-Rol	St.-Émilion	1	2.5	5
Château Fond-Razade	St.-Sulpice-de-Faleyrans	4	10	8
Château Fongaban (*see* Château Mouchet)				
Château Fonplégade	St.-Émilion	10	25	33
Château Fonrazade	St.-Émilion	4	10	14
Clos Fonrazade	St.-Émilion	4	10	25
Château Fonroque	St.-Émilion	16	40	100
Clos Fontelle	St.-Étienne-de-Lisse	1	2.5	5
Château Fontmurée	Montagne-St.-Émilion	5	12.5	18
Domaine de Fontmurée	Montagne-St.-Émilion	10	25	39
Château Fougères	St.-Étienne-de-Lisse	9	22.5	45
Domaine de Fouquet	St.-Sulpice-de-Faleyrans	6	15	5
Château Fougueyrat, Cru La Tour-Laroze, Cru Le Châtelet	St.-Émilion	19	47.5	87
Clos Fourney	St.-Étienne-de-Lisse	4	10	14
Clos Fourney	St.-Pey-d'Armens	5	12.5	10
Château Franc (*see* Château Franc-Patarbet)				
Cru Franc-Baudron	Montagne-St.-Émilion	5	12.5	23
Domaine Franc-Baudron	Montagne-St.-Émilion	6	15	20
Château Franc-Beau-Mazerat	St.-Émilion	3	7.5	11
Château Franc-Cantenac	St.-Émilion	1	2.5	5
Château Franc-Cormey	St.-Émilion	2	5	4
Château Franc-Cros	St.-Émilion	4	10	14
Château Franc-Laporte	St.-Christophe-des-Bardes	9	22.5	50
Clos Franc-Larmande	St.-Émilion	3	7.5	9
Château Franc-la-Rose	St.-Émilion	4	10	20
Château Franc-Mayne	St.-Émilion	6	15	32
Cru Franc-Mazerat	St.-Émilion	2	5	8
Château Franc-Patarabet, Château Franc	St.-Émilion	4	10	20
Château Franc Peilhan	Vignonet	3	7.5	9
Château Franc-Petit-Figeac	St.-Émilion	3	7.5	22
Château Franc Pipeau	St.-Hippolyte	3	7.5	17
Château Franc Pourret	St.-Émilion	11	27.5	49

	Township	Hec-tares	Acres	Ton-neaux
Cru Franc-Rozier	*St.-Laurent-des-Combes*	3	7.5	15
Château Froquard	*St.-Georges-St.-Émilion*	3	7.5	15
Château Gadet-Plaisance	*Montagne-St.-Émilion*	4	10	12
Château Gaillard	*St.-Hippolyte*	8	20	11
Château Gaillard	*Sables-St.-Émilion*	4	10	16
Château Gaillard-de-Gorse	*St.-Étienne-de-Lisse*	3	7.5	10
Château Garderose	*Sables-St.-Émilion*	5	12.5	20
Château Gastebourse (*see* Château Pontet Clauzure)				
Château Gaubert, Clos des Moines	*St.-Christophe-des-Bardes*	16	40	55
Château Gay-Moulins	*Montagne-St.-Émilion*	7	17.5	27
Clos Gerbaud	*St.-Pey-d'Armens*	1	2.5	7
Clos Gilet	*Montagne-St.-Émilion*	3	7.5	13
Château Gironde	*Puisseguin-St.-Émilion*	4	10	5
Château Godeau	*St.-Laurent-des-Combes*	3	7.5	8
Clos Gontey	*St.-Émilion*	2	5	13
Château Goujon	*Montagne-St.-Émilion*	3	7.5	5
Domaine du Gourdins	*Sables-St.-Émilion*	1	2.5	6
Château Grand-Barrail-Lamarzelle-Figeac	*St.-Émilion*	23	57.5	123
Château Grand-Berc	*St.-Sulpice-de-Faleyrans*	4	10	13
Domaine du Grand-Bigaroux	*St.-Sulpice-de-Faleyrans*	2	5	9
Château Grand-Caillou-Noir	*Vignonet*	3	7.5	16
Domaine des Grands-Champs	*Montagne-St.-Émilion*	4	10	10
Château Grand-Corbin	*St.-Émilion*	13	32.5	71
Château Grand Corbin-Despagne	*St.-Émilion*	25	62.5	180
Grand Domaine Jean-Voisin	*St.-Émilion*	2	5	7
Clos Grand-Faurie	*Puisseguin-St.-Émilion*	4	10	24
Domaine du Grand-Faurie	*St.-Émilion*	4	10	17
Château Grand-Gontey	*St.-Émilion*	4	10	16

	Township	Hectares	Acres	Tonneaux
Clos Grand-Gontey	*St.-Émilion*	4	10	17
Domaine du Grand-Gontey	*St.-Émilion*	2	5	9
Château Grand Jacques	*St.-Christophe-des-Bardes*	11	27.5	46
Château Grand-Mayne, Château Cassevert, Château Beau-Mazerat, Château Grand-Mazerat	*St.-Émilion*	17	42.5	75
Château Grand-Mazerat (*see* Château Grand-Mayne)				
Château Grand-Mirande	*St.-Émilion*	6	15	32
Clos des Grandes-Murailles	*St.-Émilion*	2	5	10
Domaine des Grands-Pairs	*Lussac-St.-Émilion*	2	5	8
Château Grand-Peilhan-Blanc	*Vignonet*	7	17.5	34
Château Grand Pey-de-Lescours	*St.-Sulpice-de-Faleyrans*	24	60	112
Château Grand-Pontet	*St.-Émilion*	13	32.5	67
Château Grand-Rivallon	*St.-Émilion*	3	7.5	9
Château Grangeneuve (*see* Château Figeac)				
Château Grangey	*St.-Christophe-des-Bardes*	5	12.5	22
Château Grave-d'Armens	*St.-Pey-d'Armens*	3	7.5	5
Château des Graves	*St.-Pey-d'Armens*	4	10	24
Cru des Graves	*Vignonet*	2	5	6
Château Graves d'Arthus	*Vignonet*	5	12.5	21
Château des Graves-de-Mondou	*St.-Sulpice-de-Faleyrans*	4	10	14
Château Gravet	*St.-Sulpice-de-Faleyrans*	9	22.5	48
Clos Gravet	*St.-Sulpice-de-Faleyrans*	11	27.5	51
Domaine de Grimon	*St.-Georges-St.-Émilion*	5	12.5	20
Clos du Gros	*St.-Pey-d'Armens*	1	2.5	6
Château Gros-Caillou	*St.-Sulpice-de-Faleyrans*	8	20	32
Clos Gros-Caillou	*St.-Sulpice-de-Faleyrans*	3	7.5	8
Clos des Gros-Chênes	*Vignonet*	5	12.5	27

	Township	Hec-tares	Acres	Ton-neaux
Cru Grotte-d'Arcis	*St.-Laurent-des-Combes*	3	7.5	14
Château Guadet-le-Franc-Grâce-Dieu	*St.-Émilion*	5	12.5	19
Château Guadet-St.-Julien	*St.-Émilion*	5	12.5	20
Château Gueyrosse	*Sables-St.-Émilion*	4	10	15
Château Gueyrot	*St.-Émilion*	6	15	27
Château Guibeau	*Puisseguin-St.-Émilion*	11	27.5	76
Château Guibot-Lafourvieille	*Puisseguin-St.-Émilion*	13	32.5	59
Château Guillemot	*St.-Christophe-des-Bardes*	7	17.5	17
Château Guillou	*St.-Georges-St.-Émilion*	13	32.5	59
Château Guinot	*St.-Étienne-de-Lisse*	4	10	16
Clos Guinot	*St.-Étienne-de-Lisse*	6	15	40
Domaine du Haut-Badon	*St.-Émilion*	3	7.5	8
Domaine de Haut-Barbey	*St.-Étienne-de-Lisse*	2	5	7
Château Haut-Barbeyron	*St.-Laurent-des-Combes*	4	10	5
Château Haut-Bastienne	*Montagne-St.-Émilion*	4	10	20
Château Haut-Benitey	*St.-Laurent-des-Combes*	5	12.5	13
Château Haut-Berthonneau	*St.-Émilion*	1	2.5	7
Clos Haut-Bibey	*St.-Émilion*	2	5	11
Clos Haut-Cabanne	*St.-Émilion*	1	2.5	6
Château Haut-Cadet	*St.-Émilion*	13	32.5	36
Domaine Haut-Caillate	*St.-Georges-St.-Émilion*	2	5	10
Château Haut-Chéreau	*Lussac-St.-Émilion*	2	5	5
Domaine Haut-Corbière	*Sables-St.-Émilion*	2	5	11
Château Haut-Corbin	*St.-Émilion*	4	10	21
Domaine de la Haute-Faucherie	*Montagne-St.-Émilion*	3	7.5	12
Château Hautes-Graves-d'Arthus	*Vignonet*	9	22.5	47
Château Haut-Fonrazade, Cru La Tour-Fonrazade	*St.-Émilion*	11	27.5	43
Château Haut-Grâce-Dieu (*see* Château Peyrelongue)				
Château Haut-Grand-Faurie	*St.-Émilion*	4	10	21
Cru Haut-Grand-Faurie	*St.-Émilion*	1	2.5	5

	Township	Hec-tares	Acres	Ton-neaux
Château Haut-Gueyrot	*St.-Émilion*	2	5	6
Domaine Haut-Guillennay	*Sables-St.-Émilion*	2	5	10
Château Haut-Guitard	*Montagne-St.-Émilion*	4	10	20
Clos Haut-Jaugueblanc	*St.-Émilion*	1	2.5	5
Château Haut-Jean-Faure, Clos La Fleur-Figeac, Clos La Bourrue, Château Tauzinat-l'Hermitage	*St.-Émilion*	7	17.5	49
Château Haut-Jeanguillot	*St.-Christophe-des-Bardes*	4	10	17
Château Haut-Langlade	*Parsac-St.-Émilion*	4	10	14
Château Haut-Larose	*Lussac-St.-Émilion*	5	12.5	19
Château Haut-Lartigue	*St.-Émilion*	3	7.5	15
Château Haut-Lavallade	*St.-Christophe-des-Bardes*	4	10	23
Domaine Haut-Lavallade	*St.-Christophe-des-Bardes*	3	7.5	12
Clos Haut-Listrac	*Puisseguin-St.-Émilion*	4	10	14
Domaine de Haut-Marchand	*Montagne-St.-Émilion*	4	10	6
Château Haut-Mauvinon	*St.-Sulpice-de-Faleyrans*	8	20	28
Clos Haut-Mazerat, Vieux Château Mazerat	*St.-Émilion*	8	20	35
Clos Haut-Montaiguillon	*St.-Georges-St.-Émilion*	5	12.5	24
Château Haut-Musset	*Parsac-St.-Émilion*	5	12.5	17
Château Haute-Nauve	*St.-Laurent-des-Combes*	3	7.5	8
Château Haut-Panet-Pineuilh	*St.-Christophe-des-Bardes*	2	5	9
Domaine Haut-Patarabet (*see* Clos Chante-l'Alouette)				
Château Haut-Peyroutas	*Vignonet*	2	5	6
Château Haut-Piquat	*Lussac-St.-Émilion*	9	22.5	34
Château Haut-Plaisance	*Montagne-St.-Émilion*	7	17.5	29
Château Haut-Poitou	*Lussac-St.-Émilion*	2	5	9
Château Haut-Pontet	*St.-Émilion*	5	12.5	25
Château Haut-Pourret	*St.-Émilion*	5	12.5	30
Château Haut-Pourteau	*Lussac-St.-Émilion*	2	5	8
Château Haut-Rabion	*Vignonet*	5	12.5	17
Château Haut-Renais-sance	*St.-Sulpice-de-Faleyrans*	3	7.5	19

	Township	Hec-tares	Acres	Ton-neaux
Domaine Haut-Rimoulet	*St.-Émilion*	5	12.5	20
Clos Haut-Robin	*St.-Christophe-des-Bardes*	4	10	14
Château Haut-Rocher	*St.-Étienne-de-Lisse*	5	12.5	15
Domaine Haute-Rouchonne	*Vignonet*	4	10	16
Château Haut-St.-Georges	*St.-Georges-St.-Émilion*	2	5	9
Château Haut-Sarpe	*St.-Christophe-des-Bardes*	18	45	56
Château Haut-Segotte	*St.-Émilion*	7	17.5	42
Château Haut-Simard	*St.-Émilion*	5	12.5	29
Château Haut-Touran	*St.-Étienne-de-Lisse*	3	7.5	8
Château Haut-Troquard	*St.-Georges-St.-Émilion*	3	7.5	16
Clos Haut-Troquard	*St.-Georges-St.-Émilion*	1	2.5	6
Château Haut-Troquart	*St.-Émilion*	4	10	19
Domaine Haut-Vachon	*St.-Émilion*	4	10	18
Château Haut-Veyrac	*St.-Étienne-de-Lisse*	7	17.5	30
Clos des Jacobins	*St.-Émilion*	42	20	42
Château Jacqueblanc	*St.-Étienne-de-Lisse*	20	50	100
Clos Jacquemeau	*St.-Émilion*	1	2.5	5
Château Jacqueminot	*St.-Christophe-des-Bardes*	4	10	15
Château Jacquenoir	*St.-Étienne-de-Lisse*	4	10	20
Château Jaubert-Peyblanquet	*St.-Étienne-de-Lisse*	5	12.5	11
Château Jaugueblanc	*St.-Émilion*	5	12.5	21
Clos Jaumard	*Vignonet*	2	5	8
Château Jean-Blanc	*St.-Pey-d'Armens*	6	15	33
Château Jean Faure (*see* Château Ripeau)				
Clos Jean Guillot	*St.-Christophe-des-Bardes*	1	2.5	5
Cru Jeanguillot	*St.-Christophe-des-Bardes*	2	5	8
Domaine de Jean-Marie	*St.-Émilion*	2	5	6
Château Jean-Marie-Cheval-Brun	*St.-Émilion*	2	5	8
Château Jean-Voisin	*St.-Émilion*	5	12.5	14
Clos Jean-Voisin	*St.-Émilion*	3	7.5	9
Château Joly	*Vignonet*	6	15	27
Cru Jubilé	*St.-Christophe-des-Bardes*	2	5	9
Château Jupille	*St.-Sulpice-de-Faleyrans*	2	5	5
Château Jura-Plaisance	*Montagne-St.-Émilion*	8	20	34

	Township	Hec- tares	Acres	Ton- neaux
Château Justice	*St.-Étienne-de-Lisse*	3	7.5	15
Château La Barde	*St.-Laurent-des-Combes*	3	7.5	6
Clos La Barde	*St.-Laurent-des-Combes*	4	10	13
Château La Barthe	*St.-Pey-d'Armens*	4	10	17
Clos-Domaine-Château- La-Bastienne	*Montagne-St.-Émilion*	12	30	54
Domaine La Beillonne	*St.-Émilion*	2	5	14
Château La Blanque- Pinson	*St.-Sulpice-de-Faleyrans*	3	7.5	8
Clos La Bourrue (*see* Château Haut-Jean-Faure)				
Château La Bouygue	*St.-Émilion*	3	7.5	17
Clos Labrit	*St.-Sulpice-de-Faleyrans*	3	7.5	19
Clos La Cabanne	*Puisseguin-St.-Émilion*	4	10	22
Château La Carte	*St.-Émilion*	5	12.5	18
Château La Chapelle	*St.-Étienne-de-Lisse*	4	10	20
Château La Chapelle	*St.-Sulpice-de-Faleyrans*	2	5	9
Cru La Chapelle	*Parsac-St.-Émilion*	7	17.5	13
Domaine de la Chapelle	*St.-Étienne-de-Lisse*	3	7.5	15
Château La Chapelle- Lescours	*St.-Sulpice-de-Faleyrans*	3	7.5	18
Château La Clotte (*great growth*)	*St.-Émilion*	4	10	14
Château La Clotte	*Puisseguin-St.-Émilion*	2	5	4
Château La Clotte- Grande-Côte	*St.-Émilion*	4	10	11
Château La Cluzière	*St.-Émilion*	2	5	5
Château La Côte-Daugay	*St.-Sulpice-de-Faleyrans*	1	2.5	6
Château La Couronne	*Montagne-St.-Émilion*	4	10	21
Château La Couspaude	*St.-Émilion*	5	12.5	16
Clos La Croix	*St.-Pey-d'Armens*	9	22.5	49
Château La Crois-de-la- Bastienne	*Montagne-St.-Émilion*	2	5	12
Cru La Croix-Blanche	*Montagne-St.-Émilion*	2	5	7
Château La Croix-de- Blanchon	*Lussac-St.-Émilion*	5	12.5	16
Château La Croix- Chantecaille	*St.-Émilion*	6	15	32

	Township	Hec-tares	Acres	Ton-neaux
Clos La Croix-Figeac	*St.-Émilion*	3	7.5	18
Château La Croizille	*St.-Laurent-des-Combes*	4	10	9
Château La Dominique	*St.-Émilion*	17	42.5	63
Château La Fagnouse	*St.-Étienne-de-Lisse*	5	12.5	37
Château La Faucherie	*Montagne-St.-Émilion*	3	7.5	6
Château La Fleur	*St.-Émilion*	5	12.5	28
Château La Fleur-Cadet	*St.-Émilion*	4	10	14
Clos La Fleur-Figeac (*see* Château Haut-Jean-Faure)				
Château La Fleur-Perruchon	*Lussac-St.-Émilion*	5	12.5	17
Château La Fleur-Pourret	*St.-Émilion*	3	7.5	6
Château La Fleur-St.-Georges (*see* Château St.-Georges)				
Château La Fortine	*St.-Émilion*	2	5	6
Domaine de la Gaffelière	*St.-Émilion*	2	5	9
Château Lagaborite	*St.-Émilion*	2	5	8
Château La Garelle	*St.-Émilion*	12	30	48
Cru La Garelle	*St.-Émilion*	1	2.5	8
Clos La Glaye	*St.-Pey-d'Armens*	4	10	17
Château La Gomerie	*St.-Émilion*	2	5	12
Château La Grâce-Dieu, Château l'Étoile-Pourret	*St.-Émilion*	13	32.5	35
Château La Grâce-Dieu-les-Menuts	*St.-Émilion*	10	25	51
Château La Grande-Clotte	*Lussac-St.-Émilion*	5	12.5	19
Château Lagrave-Figeac	*St.-Émilion*	3	7.5	17
Château La Grenière	*Lussac-St.-Émilion*	5	12.5	16
Domaine de Lamaçonne	*Montagne-St.-Émilion*	3	7.5	12
Clos La Madeleine	*St.-Émilion*	2	5	8
Château La Marzelle	*St.-Émilion*	6	15	19
Château La Mauleone (*see* Château Pontet Clauzure)				
Château La Mayne	*Sables-St.-Émilion*	3	7.5	8
Château La Mélissière	*St.-Hippolyte*	10	25	11
Château La Méllisière	*St.-Sulpice-de-Faleyrans*	9	22.5	9
Domaine La Mélissière	*St.-Hippolyte*	1	2.5	6
Château La Mouleyre	*St.-Étienne-de-Lisse*	7	17.5	19
Domaine de la Mouleyre	*St.-Étienne-de-Lisse*	5	12.5	19

	Township	Hectares	Acres	Tonneaux
Château La Nauve	*St.-Laurent-des-Combes*	9	22.5	31
Clos La Nauve	*St.-Hippolyte*	2	5	5
Château l'Angélus	*St.-Émilion*	23	57.5	130
Château Langlade	*Parsac-St.-Émilion*	6	15	12
Château Laniotte, Château Chapelle-de-la-Trinité	*St.-Émilion*	5	12.5	26
Château La Paillette	*Sables-St.-Émilion*	3	7.5	10
Château Lapelletrie	*St.-Christophe-des-Bardes*	9	22.5	54
Château La Papeterie	*Montagne-St.-Émilion*	9	22.5	55
Château La Perrière	*Lussac-St.-Émilion*	5	12.5	20
Château Lapeyre	*St.-Étienne-de-Lisse*	8	20	35
Château La Picherie	*Montagne-St.-Émilion*	6	15	13
Domaine de Laplaigne	*Puisseguin-St.-Émilion*	7	17.5	31
Château La Plante	*Sables-St.-Émilion*	1	2.5	5
Château Larcis-Bergey	*St.-Émilion*	1	2.5	8
Château Larcis-Ducasse	*St.-Laurent-des-Combes*	10	25	57
Château Lardon-Jacqueminot	*St.-Christophe-des-Bardes*	15	37.5	74
Château Larmande	*St.-Émilion*	6	15	30
Clos Larmande	*St.-Étienne-de-Lisse*	4	10	15
Domaine Laroque, Château Nardon	*St.-Christophe-des-Bardes*	3	7.5	19
Clos Larose	*St.-Christophe-des-Bardes*	2	5	10
Cru La Rose	*Puisseguin-St.-Émilion*	5	12.5	17
Domaine de la Rose	*St.-Émilion*	2	5	12
Château La Rose-Côte-Rol	*St.-Émilion*	4	10	19
Château La Rose-Pourret	*St.-Émilion*	14	35	79
Château La Roseraie-du-Mont	*Puisseguin-St.-Émilion*	4	10	9
Château La Rose-Rol	*St.-Émilion*	4	10	19
Château Laroze	*St.-Émilion*	25	62.5	134
Château La Rouchonne	*Vignonet*	4	10	8
Chateau Larques, Château Châtelet	*St.-Christophe-des-Bardes*	19	47.5	36
Château Lartigue	*St.-Émilion*	3	7.5	9

	Township	Hec-tares	Acres	Ton-neaux
Clos Lartigue	St.-Émilion	1	2.5	5
Cru Lartigue	St.-Émilion	3	7.5	11
Clos Lartigues	St.-Pey-d'Armens	2	5	8
Château Larue	Parsac-St.-Émilion	4	10	13
Château La Sablière	St.-Émilion	6	15	28
Château La Sablonnerie	St.-Sulpice-de-Faleyrans	10	25	35
Château Lassègue	St.-Hippolyte	13	32.5	54
Château Lasserre	St.-Émilion	6	15	17
Cru Le Terte-de-Perruchon	Lussac-St.-Émilion	3	7.5	7
Château La Tête-du-Cerf	Montagne-St.-Émilion	6	15	15
Château Latour	Montagne-St.-Émilion	5	12.5	21
Château La Tour	St.-Christophe-des-Bardes	7	17.5	27
Château La Tour-Baladoz	St.-Laurent-des-Combes	3	7.5	12
Château La Tour-Ballet	Montagne-St.-Émilion	1	2.5	5
Château La Tour-Berthoneau	St.-Émilion	2	5	8
Château La Tour-Blanche	Parsac-St.-Émilion	3	7.5	19
Château Latour Blanche	St.-Hippolyte	1	2.5	4
Château La Tour-des-Combes	St.-Laurent-des-Combes	5	12.5	25
Château La Tour-Cravignac	St.-Émilion	3	7.5	16
Château La Tour-Figeac	St.-Émilion	5	12.5	27
Château La Tour-Fonrazade	St.-Émilion	4	10	17
Cru La Tour-Fonrazade (*see* Château Haut-Fonrazade)				
Château La Tour-Gilet	Montagne-St.-Émilion	6	15	34
Château La Tour-de-Grenet	Lussac-St.-Émilion	16	40	90
Château La Tour-Guillotin	Puisseguin-St.-Émilion	6	15	24
Château La Tour-Laroze (*see* Château Fougueyrat)				
Château Latour-Musset	Parsac-St.-Émilion	10	25	35
Château La Tour-Paquillon	Montagne-St.-Émilion	8	20	35

	Township	Hec-tares	Acres	Ton-neaux
Château La Tour-Peyblanquet	*St.-Étienne-de-Lisse*	6	14	21
Château La Tour-du-Pin-Figeac	*St.-Émilion*	17	42.5	111
Château Latour-Pourret	*St.-Émilion*	6	15	16
Château La Tour-St.-Émilion	*St.-Émilion*	4	10	18
Château La Tour-St.-Georges (*see* Ch. St.-Georges)		15	37.5	62
Château La Tour-St.-Pierre	*St.-Émilion*	6	15	30
Château La Tour-de-Ségur	*Lussac-St.-Émilion*	5	12.5	15
Château Latour-de-Ségur	*Lussac-St.-Émilion*	8	20	9
Château La Tour-Vachon	*St.-Émilion*	4	10	21
Château Lavallade	*St.-Christophe-des-Bardes*	11	27.5	56
Clos La Vallée-du-Roi	*Montagne-St.-Émilion*	3	7.5	8
Château Lavergne	*Vignonet*	2	5	15
Clos Lavergne	*St.-Pey-d'Armens*	9	22.5	46
Château Le Basque	*Puisseguin-St.-Émilion*	18	45	47
Château Le Bon-Pasteur	*St.-Émilion*	3	7.5	9
Clos Le Bregnet	*St.-Sulpice-de-Faleyrans*	5	12.5	22
Château Le Castelot	*St.-Sulpice-de-Faleyrans*	5	12.5	21
Château Le Cauze	*St.-Christophe-des-Bardes*	20	50	130
Château Le Chapelot	*Montagne-St.-Émilion*	4	10	8
Cru Le Châtelet (*see* Château Fougueyrat)				
Château Le Chay	*Puisseguin-St.-Émilion*	13	32.5	58
Château Le Couvent	*St.-Sulpice-de-Faleyrans*	3	7.5	12
Cru Le Franc-Rival	*Lussac-St.-Émilion*	2	5	9
Château Le Freyche	*St.-Pey-d'Armens*	4	10	13
Clos Le Freyche	*St.-Pey-d'Armens*	4	10	9
Clos de l'Église (*see* Château St.-Georges)				
Clos l'Église	*Montagne-St.-Émilion*	4	10	17
Clos de l'Église	*Parsac-St.-Émilion*	13	32.5	46
Château Le Grand-Barrail	*St.-Sulpice-de-Faleyrans*	3	7.5	11
Château Le Grand-Corbin	*St.-Émilion*	5	12.5	22

	Township	Hec-tares	Acres	Ton-neaux
Château Le Grand-Faurie	*St.-Émilion*	4	10	17
Château Le Gravier-Gueyrosse	*St.-Émilion*	3	7.5	12
Château Le Gueyrot	*St.-Émilion*	4	10	15
Château Le Jurat	*St.-Émilion*	9	22	39
Clos Le Loup	*St.-Christophe-des-Bardes*	6	15	5
Château Le Mayne	*Puisseguin-St.-Émilion*	3	7.5	9
Château Le Merle	*St.-Hippolyte*	6	15	12
Château Lenoir	*Sables-St.-Émilion*	4	10	13
Domaine du Léonard	*Puisseguin-St.-Émilion*	9	22.5	40
Clos Le Pas-St.-Georges	*St.-Georges-St.-Émilion*	6	15	31
Château Le Peillan	*St.-Laurent-des-Combes*	13	32.5	20
Château Lépine	*Sables-St.-Émilion*	2	5	7
Château Le Pont-de-Pierre	*Lussac-St.-Émilion*	3	7.5	15
Château Le Poteau	*St.-Christophe-des-Bardes*	4	10	17
Château Le Prieuré	*St.-Émilion*	5	12.5	15
Château Le Puy-St.-Georges (*see* Château St.-Georges)				
Château Le Roc-de-Troquard	*St.-Georges-St.-Émilion*	3	7.5	10
Château Le Rocher	*St.-Laurent-des-Combes*	3	7.5	10
Château Le Sable-Villebout	*St.-Laurent-des-Combes*	4	10	11
Château Les Bardes	*Montagne-St.-Émilion*	3	7.5	13
Château Les Bazilliques	*St.-Christophe-des-Bardes*	6	15	30
Château Les Carrières	*Montagne-St.-Émilion*	2	5	5
Château Les Côtes-de-Gardat	*Montagne-St.-Émilion*	5	12.5	24
Château Lescours	*St.-Sulpice-de-Faleyrans*	27	67.5	125
Château Les Eyguires, Château Haut-Sarpe, Clos du Vieux	*St.-Christophe-des-Bardes*	10	25	35
Domaine Les Genêts	*Montagne-St.-Émilion*	3	7.5	9
Château Les Grandes-Plantes-Haut-Béard	*St.-Laurent-des-Combes*	3	7.5	6
Château Les Grandes-Vignes	*Montagne-St.-Émilion*	2	5	10

	Township	Hec-tares	Acres	Ton-neaux
Clos Les Graves	*Vignonet*	4	10	12
Château Les Jacquets	*St.-Georges-St.-Émilion*	5	12.5	22
Domaine Les Jouans	*St.-Sulpice-de-Faleyrans*	3	7.5	15
Château Les Laurets	*Puisseguin-St.-Émilion*	43	106	165
Château Les Moulins	*St.-Sulpice-de-Faleyrans*	4	10	19
Château Les Moureaux	*St.-Étienne-de-Lisse*	4	10	23
Château Lespinasse	*St.-Pey-d'Armens*	4	10	19
Château Les Renardières	*St.-Georges-St.-Émilion*	4	10	14
Château Les Roquettes-Mondottes	*St.-Laurent-des-Combes*	3	7.5	10
Château Lestage	*Parsac-St.-Émilion*	8	20	47
Château Les Templiers	*St.-Émilion*	3	7.5	14
Château Les Tuileries	*St.-Étienne-de-Lisse*	3	7.5	18
Château Les Tuileries-de-Bayard	*Montagne-St.-Émilion*	8	20	29
Château Les Vieilles-Nauves	*St.-Laurent-des-Combes*	2	5	7
Château Les-Vieilles-Souches-La Marzelle	*St.-Émilion*	4	10	18
Château Les Vieux-Rocs	*Lussac-St.-Émilion*	3	7.5	5
Château Le Tertre	*St.-Laurent-des-Combes*	4	10	13
Château Le Thibaut	*St.-Étienne-de-Lisse*	9	22.5	33
Château Le Thibaut-Bordas	*St.-Étienne-de-Lisse*	3	7.5	13
Château l'Étoile-Pourret (*see* Château La Grâce-Dieu)				
Cru Le Vignot	*St.-Hippolyte*	1	2.5	7
Château l'Hermitage	*Montagne-St.-Émilion*	6	15	26
Château l'Hermitage-Mazerat	*St.-Émilion*	4	10	17
Domaine de Liamet	*St.-Étienne-de-Lisse*	2	5	8
Château de Lisse	*St.-Étienne-de-Lisse*	13	32.5	32
Domaine du Logis-de-Moureaux	*St.-Pey-d'Armens*	1	2.5	6
Domaine de Longat	*St.-Sulpice-de-Faleyrans*	3	7.5	6
Château de Long-Champ	*St.-Sulpice-de-Faleyrans*	4	10	26
Clos l'Oratoire (*see* Château Peyreau)				
Château L'Ormeau-Vieux	*Puisseguin-St.-Émilion*	7	17.5	23

	Township	Hec-tares	Acres	Ton-neaux
Château Lucas	*Lussac-St.-Émilion*	9	22.5	37
Château de Lussac	*Lussac-St.-Émilion*	20	50	88
Château Lyonnat	*Lussac-St.-Émilion*	49	121	218
Château Lyon-Perruchon	*Lussac-St.-Émilion*	4	10	11
Château Macureau	*Montagne-St.-Émilion*	6	15	26
Château Magnan-la-Gaffelière	*St.-Émilion*	8	20	40
Clos des Magrines	*Puisseguin-St.-Émilion*	3	7.5	6
Clos du Maine	*St.-Laurent-des-Combes*	2	5	10
Château Maison-Blanche	*Montagne-St.-Émilion*	25	62.5	134
Château Maisonneuve	*Parsac-St.-Émilion*	7	17.5	6
Clos Maisonneuve	*Parsac-St.-Émilion*	2	5	8
Domaine de Maison-neuve, Château St.-Georges-Macquin	*St.-Georges-St.-Émilion*	17	42.5	54
Château Malineau	*St.-Émilion*	4	10	14
Château Marrin	*St.-Christophe-des-Bardes*	6	15	33
Château Martinet	*Sables-St.-Émilion*	12	30	56
Château Matras	*St.-Émilion*	7	17.5	25
Château Maugot	*St.-Étienne-de-Lisse*	20	50	66
Clos Maurice	*St.-Sulpice-de-Faleyrans*	1	2.5	6
Château Maurillon	*St.-Christophe-des-Bardes*	1	2.5	7
Château Mauvezin	*St.-Émilion*	5	12.5	26
Château Mayne-Vieux	*St.-Étienne-de-Lisse*	5	12.5	17
Château Menichot	*St.-Hippolyte*	5	12.5	18
Clos des Menuts	*St.-Émilion*	2	5	8
Domaine des Menuts	*St.-Émilion*	1	2.5	5
Château du Merle	*St.-Hippolyte*	6	15	18
Clos Meylet-la-Gomerie	*St.-Émilion*	2	5	10
Château Meynard	*Sables-St.-Émilion*	6	15	11
Château Millery-Lapelletrie	*St.-Christophe-des-Bardes*	2	5	10
Château Milon-Feuillat	*St.-Christophe-des-Bardes*	3	7.5	10
Château Mitrotte	*St.-Laurent-des-Combes*	1	2.5	6
Château des Moines	*Montagne-St.-Émilion*	4	10	21
Château des Moines	*St.-Émilion*	4	10	23
Clos des Moines (*see* Château Gaubert)				

	Township	Hec- tares	Acres	Ton- neaux
Château Monbousquet, Château Caperot	*St.-Sulpice-de-Faleyrans*	31	77.5	144
Château Mondotte- Bellisle	*St.-Laurent-des-Combes*	6	15	16
Château Mondou	*St.-Sulpice-de-Faleyrans*	4	10	16
Clos Mondou	*St.-Sulpice-de-Faleyrans*	2	5	9
Château Monlot-Capet	*St.-Hippolyte*	8	20	37
Clos Monplaisir	*St.-Étienne-de-Lisse*	2	5	8
Château Montaiguillon	*Montagne-St.-Émilion*	23	57.5	128
Château Montaiguillon	*St.-Georges-St.-Émilion*	3	7.5	16
Château Montbelair	*St.-Étienne-de-Lisse*	2	5	8
Château Montesquieu	*Puisseguin-St.-Émilion*	14	35	63
Clos Montesquieu	*Montagne-St.-Émilion*	3	7.5	12
Château Montlabert	*St.-Émilion*	10	25	40
Domaine de Montlabert	*St.-Émilion*	2	5	10
Château Montremblant	*St.-Émilion*	5	12.5	25
Château Morillon	*St.-Christophe-des-Bardes*	2	5	8
Château Mouchet, Château Fongaban	*Puisseguin-St.-Émilion*	10	25	35
Château Mouchique	*Puisseguin-St.-Émilion*	4	10	17
Château du Moulin	*Puisseguin-St.-Émilion*	6	15	30
Château Moulin- Bellegrave	*Vignonet*	5	12.5	13
Château Moulin du Cadet	*St.-Émilion*	6	15	22
Château Moulin de Cantelaube	*St.-Émilion*	3	7.5	6
Château Moulin-du-Jura	*Montagne-St.-Émilion*	3	7.5	10
Château Moulin-de- Pierrefitte	*St.-Sulpice-de-Faleyrans*	3	7.5	14
Château Moulin-St.- Georges	*St.-Émilion*	11	27.5	48
Château Moulin-St.- Georges, Château Pin- du-Fleur	*St.-Émilion*	13	32.5	65
Cru Mourens	*St.-Hippolyte*	2	5	7
Château Musset	*Parsac-St.-Émilion*	7	17.5	28

	Township	Hec-tares	Acres	Ton-neaux
Château Myosotis	*St.-Émilion*	3	7.5	10
Château Naguet-La-Brande	*Parsac-St.-Émilion*	5	12.5	12
Cru Napoléon	*St.-Laurent-des-Combes*	2	5	7
Château Nardon (*see* Domaine Laroque)				
Clos de Naudin	*St.-Christophe-des-Bardes*	2	5	6
Château Négrit	*Montagne-St.-Émilion*	9	22.5	41
Château de Neuville	*St.-Christophe-des-Bardes*	1	2.5	7
Château Pailhas	*St.-Hippolyte*	12	30	51
Clos Pailhas	*St.-Hippolyte*	3	7.5	8
Clos du Palais-Cardinal	*St.-Sulpice-de-Faleyrans*	5	12.5	6
Château Panet	*St.-Christophe-des-Bardes*	22	55	80
Château Paradis	*Montagne-St.-Émilion*	5	12.5	28
Château Paradis, Château Patarabet	*Vignonet*	19	47.5	64
Château Parans	*St.-Étienne-de-Lisse*	7	17.5	35
Clos Pasquette	*St.-Sulpice-de-Faleyrans*	3	7.5	15
Domaine de Pasquette	*St.-Sulpice-de-Faleyrans*	5	12.5	26
Château Patarabet	*St.-Émilion*	3	7.5	11
Château Patarabet (*see* Château Paradis, *Vignonet*)				
Clos Patarabet	*St.-Émilion*	1	2.5	5
Cru Patarabet	*St.-Laurent-des-Combes*	1	2.5	4
Domaine Patarabet-la-Gaffelière	*St.-Émilion*	2	5	8
Clos Patarabet-Lartigue	*St.-Émilion*	2	5	9
Château Patris	*St.-Émilion*	5	12.5	29
Clos Patris	*St.-Émilion*	1	2.5	5
Château Pavie-Decesse	*St.-Émilion*	6	15	25
Château Pavie-Macquin	*St.-Émilion*	12	30	50
Château Pavillon-Cadet	*St.-Émilion*	6	15	11
Château Pavillon-Figeac	*St.-Émilion*	4	10	9
Château Pavillon-Fougailles	*St.-Émilion*	1	2.5	5
Château Peillan-St.-Clair	*Vignonet*	6	15	18
Château Pelletan	*St.-Christophe-des-Bardes*	5	12.5	16
Château Pérey	*St.-Sulpice-de-Faleyrans*	8	20	30
Domaine de Pérey	*St.-Sulpice-de-Faleyrans*	2	5	10

	Township	Hec-tares	Acres	Ton-neaux
Domaine Petit-Basque	*St.-Pey-d'Armens*	2	5	6
Château Petit-Bigaroux	*St.-Sulpice-de-Faleyrans*	5	12.5	15
Château Petit-Bois-la-Garelle	*St.-Émilion*	3	7.5	14
Château Petit Bord	*St.-Émilion*	1	2.5	4
Château Petit-Clos	*Montagne-St.-Émilion*	8	20	27
Domaine du Petit Clos	*St.-Hippolyte*	4	10	18
Petit Clos Figeac	*St.-Émilion*	3	7.5	15
Château Petit-Cormey	*St.-Émilion*	6	15	25
Château Petit-Faurie	*St.-Émilion*	1	2.5	5
Château Petit-Faurie-de-Souchard	*St.-Émilion*	10	25	52
Château Petit-Faurie-de-Soutard	*St.-Émilion*	8	20	43
Château Petit-Faurie-Trocard	*St.-Émilion*	4	10	21
Clos Petit-Figeac, Clos Pourret	*St.-Émilion*	3	7.5	16
Château Petit-Fombrauge	*St.-Christophe-des-Bardes*	2	5	6
Cru Petit-Gontey	*St.-Émilion*	2	5	9
Domaine du Petit-Gontey	*St.-Émilion*	3	7.5	9
Château Petit-Gravet	*St.-Émilion*	5	12.5	10
Domaine du Petit-Gueyrot	*St.-Laurent-des-Combes*	2	5	12
Château Petit-Mangot	*St.-Étienne-de-Lisse*	5	12.5	33
Château Petit-Refuge	*Lussac-St.-Émilion*	4	10	13
Château Petit-Val	*St.-Émilion*	5	12.5	27
Château Peygenestou	*St.-Émilion*	2	5	10
Château Peymouton	*St.-Christophe-des-Bardes*	3	7.5	10
Château Peyreau, Clos l'Oratoire	*St.-Émilion*	18	45	75
Château Peyrelongue, Château Haut-Grâce-Dieu	*St.-Émilion*	11	27.5	52
Château Peyrou	*St.-Étienne-de-Lisse*	5	12.5	24
Château Peyrouquet	*St.-Émilion*	1	2.5	7
Château Peyroutas	*Vignonet*	8	20	42

	Township	Hec-tares	Acres	Ton-neaux
Clos Pezat	*Vignonet*	1	2.5	6
Château Picon-Cravignac	*St.-Émilion*	4	10	12
Château Pidoux	*St.-Émilion*	2	5	10
Clos Piganeau	*St.-Émilion*	1	2.5	8
Château Pin-du-Fleur (*see* Château Moulin-St.-Georges)				
Château Piney	*St.-Hippolyte*	6	15	13
Cru Piney	*St.-Hippolyte*	1	2.5	4
Château Pipeau	*St.-Laurent-des-Combes*	19	47.5	112
Château Pipeau-Menichot	*St.-Hippolyte*	6	15	22
Château Piron	*Parsac-St.-Émilion*	6	15	17
Château Plaisance	*St.-Sulpice-de-Faleyrans*	6	15	29
Château Plaisance	*Montagne-St.-Émilion*	11	27.5	46
Clos Plaisance	*Parsac-St.-Émilion*	9	22.5	28
Cru Plaisance	*St.-Sulpice-de-Faleyrans*	4	10	20
Cru Plateau-Jappeloup	*St.-Étienne-de-Lisse*	3	7.5	6
Clos Plince	*Sables-St.-Émilion*	1	2.5	6
Château Pointe-Bouquey	*St.-Pey-d'Armens*	4	10	19
Château du Pont de Bouquey	*St.-Hippolyte*	3	7.5	11
Château Pont-de-Figeac (*see* Château Figeac)				
Château Pont-de-Mouquet	*St.-Pey-d'Armens*	12	30	40
Château Pontet	*St.-Émilion*	4	10	17
Château du Pontet	*St.-Étienne-de-Lisse*	3	7.5	12
Château Pontet Clauzure, Château La Mauléone, Château Gastebourse	*St.-Émilion*	8	20	43
Clos Pourret (*see* Clos Petit-Figeac)				
Château Pressac	*St.-Étienne-de-Lisse*	24	60	90
Clos Pressac	*St.-Étienne-de-Lisse*	7	17.5	32
Château du Puy	*Parsac-St.-Émilion*	6	15	24
Château Puy-Blanquet	*St.-Étienne-de-Lisse*	25	62.5	84
Château Puy-Bonnet	*Parsac-St.-Émilion*	5	12.5	10
Château du Puynormond	*Parsac-St.-Émilion*	7	17.5	24
Domaine du Puynormond	*Parsac-St.-Émilion*	5	12.5	21
Château Quentin	*St.-Christophe-des-Bardes*	35	87	93

	Township	Hec-tares	Acres	Ton-neaux
Château Quercy	*Vignonet*	4	10	22
Château Queyron	*St.-Émilion*	4	10	17
Château Queyron-Pin-de-Fleurs	*St.-Émilion*	4	10	27
Château Quinault	*Sables-St.-Émilion*	12	30	58
Château Rabat	*St.-Étienne-de-Lisse*	3	7.5	10
Château Rabion	*St.-Pey-d'Armens*	5	12.5	19
Domaine Rabion-Pailhas	*St.-Laurent-des-Combes*	4	10	14
Domaine de Rambaud	*Lussac-St.-Émilion*	3	7.5	6
Château Régent	*St.-Émilion*	4	10	20
Château Reine-Blanche	*St.-Émilion*	5	12.5	16
Château des Religieuses	*St.-Christophe-des-Bardes*	2	5	9
Clos des Religieuses	*Puisseguin-St.-Émilion*	3	7.5	8
Château Renaissance	*St.-Sulpice-de-Faleyrans*	5	12.5	24
Domaine de Rey	*St.-Émilion*	4	10	19
Château Reynard	*St.-Pey-d'Armens*	4	10	14
Château Rigaud	*Puisseguin-St.-Émilion*	3	7.5	10
Château Ripeau, Château Jean Faure, Château Cante Merle, Château Troquart	*St.-Émilion*	28	70	115
Château Rivallon	*St.-Émilion*	8	20	24
Domaine de Rivière	*St.-Pey-d'Armens*	5	12.5	21
Château Robin	*St.-Christophe-des-Bardes*	4	10	14
Château Robin-des-Moines	*St.-Christophe-des-Bardes*	5	12.5	7
Château Roc	*St.-Sulpice-de-Faleyrans*	4	10	20
Clos du Roc	*St.-Étienne-de-Lisse*	3	7.5	8
Château Roc-de-Puynormond	*Parsac-St.-Émilion*	6	15	10
Château Roc-St.-Michel	*St.-Étienne-de-Lisse*	4	10	18
Château Rochebelle	*St.-Laurent-des-Combes*	3	7.5	7
Château du Rocher	*St.-Étienne-de-Lisse*	9	22.5	39
Château Rocher-Bellevue-Figeac	*St.-Émilion*	8	20	14
Château Rocher-Corbin	*Montagne-St.-Émilion*	6	15	37
Château des Rochers (*see* Château Bonneau)				
Côtes Rocheuses (*see* Cave Coopérative)				

	Township	Hec-tares	Acres	Ton-neaux
Domaine des Rocs	*Lussac-St.-Émilion*	8	20	40
Château Rocs-Marchand	*Montagne-St.-Émilion*	9	22.5	9
Château de Rol	*St.-Émilion*	5	12.5	24
Côtes de Rol	*St.-Christophe-des-Bardes*	4	10	26
Domaine de Rol	*St.-Émilion*	3	7.5	13
Château Rol-de-Fombrauge	*St.-Christophe-des-Bardes*	4	10	20
Clos Rol-de-Fombrauge	*St.-Christophe-des-Bardes*	5	12.5	23
Cru Rol-de-Fombrauge	*St.-Christophe-des-Bardes*	4	10	15
Château aux Roquettes	*St.-Laurent-des-Combes*	2	5	7
Château Roucheyron	*St.-Christophe-des-Bardes*	6	15	28
Clos Roucheyron	*St.-Christophe-des-Bardes*	1	2.5	5
Château Roudier	*Montagne-St.-Émilion*	20	50	104
Château Roudier	*St.-Georges-St.-Émilion*	3	7.5	17
Domaine de Roudier	*Montagne-St.-Émilion*	7	17.5	9
Domaine du Rouy	*Vignonet*	2	5	9
Château du Roy, Clos Berthoneau	*St.-Émilion*	3	7.5	20
Royal St.-Émilion (*see* Cave Coopérative)				
Château Roylland-Matras	*St.-Émilion*	8	20	34
Château Rozier	*St.-Laurent-des-Combes*	10	25	43
Château Rozier	*St.-Sulpice-de-Faleyrans*	3	7.5	17
Château Rozier-Béard	*St.-Laurent-des-Combes*	6	15	22
Château des Roziers	*Montagne-St.-Émilion*	4	10	14
Clos du Sable	*St.-Christophe-des-Bardes*	2	5	5
Château Sablons	*Montagne-St.-Émilion*	5	12.5	20
Château St.-Christophe	*St.-Christophe-des-Bardes*	7	17.5	29
Château St.-Christophe	*St.-Sulpice-de-Faleyrans*	3	7.5	7
Clos St.-Émilion	*St.-Émilion*	8	20	44
Château St.-Georges, Château La Tour-St.-Georges, Château Le Puy-St.-Georges, Château La Fleur-St.-Georges, Clos de l'Église	*St.-Georges-St.-Émilion*	35	87	140
Château St.-Georges-Côte-Pavie	*St.-Émilion*	6	15	21
Château St.-Georges-Macquin (*see* Domaine de Maisonneuve)				

	Township	Hec-tares	Acres	Ton-neaux
Château St.-Jacques-Calon	*Montagne-St.-Émilion*	6	15	22
Domaine St.-Jean-de-Béard	*St.-Laurent-des-Combes*	4	10	11
Château St.-Julien	*St.-Émilion*	3	7.5	9
Château St.-Lô	*St.-Pey-d'Armens*	8	20	38
Château St.-Louis	*St.-Georges-St.-Émilion*	4	10	18
Château St.-Martial	*St.-Sulpice-de-Faleyrans*	2	5	9
Clos St.-Martin	*St.-Émilion*	1	2.5	7
Château St.-Michel	*Montagne-St.-Émilion*	2	5	9
Château St.-Paul	*Montagne-St.-Émilion*	5	12.5	23
Château St.-Pey	*St.-Pey-d'Armens*	9	22.5	59
Château St.-Pierre	*St.-Pey-d'Armens*	4	10	11
Château St.-Roch	*St.-Christophe-des-Bardes*	3	7.5	9
Clos St.-Valéry	*St. Émilion*	3	7.5	13
Domaine de la Salle (*see* Château Sansonnet)				
Château Samion	*St.-Georges-St.-Émilion*	9	22.5	35
Château Sansonnet, Château La Couspaude, Domaine de la Salle	*St.-Émilion*	9	22.5	27
Château de Sarenceau	*St.-Émilion*	5	12.5	26
Château de Sarpe, Château Vieux-Sarpe	*St.-Christophe-des-Bardes*	6	15	12
Clos de Sarpe	*St.-Christophe-des-Bardes*	3	7.5	10
Clos des Sarrazins	*St.-Hippolyte*	6	15	14
Château Saupiquet	*St.-Émilion*	1	2.5	9
Domaine Saupiquet	*St.-Émilion*	2	5	8
Domaine du Sème	*St.-Hippolyte*	4	10	20
Clos Sicard	*St.-Pey-d'Armens*	4	10	15
Château Simard	*St.-Émilion*	15	37.5	74
Clos Simard	*St.-Émilion*	3	7.5	13
Château Soleil	*Puisseguin-St.-Émilion*	5	12.5	21
Château Soutard	*St.-Émilion*	18	37.5	75
Château Soutard-Cadet	*St.-Émilion*	3	7.5	11
Château Tarreyre	*St.-Émilion*	2	5	11
Château Taureau	*Lussac-St.-Émilion*	3	7.5	11
Château Tauzinat	*St.-Christophe-des-Bardes*	3	7.5	5
Domaine Tauzinat	*St.-Christophe-des-Bardes*	3	7.5	10

	Township	Hec-tares	Acres	Ton-neaux
Château Tauzinat-l'Hermitage (*see* Château Haut-Jean-Faure)				
Château Teillac	*Puisseguin-St.-Émilion*	7	17.5	31
Château Terrien	*Lussac-St.-Émilion*	3	7.5	11
Château Tertre-Daugay	*St.-Sulpice-de-Faleyrans*	15	37.5	70
Château Tertre-de-la-Mouleyre	*Parsac-St.-Émilion*	2	5	8
Clos Teynac-Rival	*Lussac-St.-Émilion*	3	7.5	14
Château Teyssier	*Puisseguin-St.-Émilion*	98	70	120
Château Teyssier	*Vignonet*	4	10	16
Château Toinet-Fombrauge	*St.-Christophe-des-Bardes*	8	20	36
Château Tonneret	*St.-Christophe-des-Bardes*	2	5	10
Château du Touran	*St.-Étienne-de-Lisse*	4	10	25
Château des Tours	*Montagne-St.-Émilion*	59	147.5	275
Château Touzinat	*St.-Pey-d'Armens*	7	17.5	40
Château Trapaud	*St.-Étienne-de-Lisse*	11	27.5	94
Château Trapeau	*St.-Sulpice-de-Faleyrans*	8	20	47
Domaine de Trapeau	*St.-Sulpice-de-Faleyrans*	3	7.5	20
Château Trianon	*St.-Émilion*	5	12.5	21
Château Trimoulet	*St.-Émilion*	13	32.5	74
Clos Timoulet	*St.-Émilion*	4	10	21
Château Trois-Moulins	*St.-Émilion*	4	10	15
Château Troplong-Mondot	*St.-Émilion*	24	60	120
Château Troquart (*see* Château Ripeau)				
Château Truquet	*St.-Émilion*	4	10	18
Domaine Vachon	*St.-Émilion*	3	7.5	16
Château La Vaisinerie	*Puisseguin-St.-Émilion*	8	20	27
Château du Val-d'Or	*Vignonet*	3	7.5	19
Clos Valentin	*St.-Émilion*	4	10	21
Clos Verdot-Monbousquet	*St.-Sulpice-de-Faleyrans*	5	12.5	11
Clos Vert-Bois	*St.-Émilion*	4	10	10
Château Veyrac	*St.-Étienne-de-Lisse*	3	7.5	25
Domaine de la Vieille-Cloche	*St.-Émilion*	4	10	20
Château Vieille-Tour-La-Rose	*St.-Émilion*	3	7.5	16

	Township	Hec-tares	Acres	Ton-neaux
Clos du Vieux (*see* Château Les Eyguires)				
Château Vieux-Bonneau	*Montagne-St.-Émilion*	4	10	14
Vieux-Château-Calon	*Montagne-St.-Émilion*	5	12.5	24
Château Vieux-Castel-Robin	*St.-Christophe-des-Bardes*	4	10	17
Château Vieux-Ceps, Château Badon	*St.-Émilion*	6	15	28
Vieux-Château-Chauvin	*St.-Émilion*	4	10	18
Vieux-Château-Fortin	*St.-Émilion*	5	12.5	16
Château Vieux Garouilh	*St.-Sulpice-de-Faleyrans*	5	12.5	27
Vieux-Château-Goujon	*Montagne-St.-Émilion*	2	5	7
Château Vieux-Guillou	*St.-Georges-St.-Émilion*	4	10	17
Château Vieux-Guinot	*St.-Étienne-de-Lisse*	5	12.5	32
Vieux-Château-La-Beysse	*Puisseguin-St.-Émilion*	4	10	6
Château Vieux-Larmande	*St.-Émilion*	4	10	11
Château Vieux-Logis-de-Cazelon	*Montagne-St.-Émilion*	2	5	8
Vieux Château Mazerat (*see* Clos Haut-Mazerat)				
Vieux-Domaine-Menuts	*St.-Émilion*	3	7.5	7
Château Vieux Montaiguillon	*St.-Georges-St.-Émilion*	3	7.5	13
Château Vieux-Mouchet	*Montagne-St.-Émilion*	1	2.5	6
Château Vieux-Moulin-du-Cadet	*St.-Émilion*	3	7.5	16
Domaine du Vieux-Moulin-de-Calon	*Montagne-St.-Émilion*	1	2.5	6
Vieux-Château-Négrit	*Montagne-St.-Émilion*	10	25	54
Vieux-Château-Palon	*Montagne-St.-Émilion*	5	12.5	17
Vieux-Château-Peymouton	*St.-Christophe-des-Bardes*	9	22.5	37
Vieux-Château-Peyrou	*St.-Étienne-de-Lisse*	1	2.5	7
Clos Vieux-Pontet	*St.-Émilion*	2	5	6
Château Vieux-Pourret	*St.-Émilion*	4	10	19
Vieux Château St.-André	*St.-Georges-St.-Émilion*	3	7.5	7
Château Vieux-Clos-St.-Pierre	*Montagne-St.-Émilion*	4	10	19

Bordeaux Wines,
Saint-Émilion (RED)

	Township	Hec- tares	Acres	Ton- neaux
Château Vieux-Sarpe (*see* Château de Sarpe)				
Château Vieux-Taillefer	*Vignonet*	3	7.5	7
Clos Vieux Troquard	*St.-Georges-St.-Émilion*	1	2.5	5
Vieux-Château-Vachon	*St.-Émilion*	3	7.5	15
Domaine du Vieux- Vachon	*St.-Émilion*	3	7.5	8
Clos Vilet	*St.-Étienne-de-Lisse*	3	7.5	13
Château Villebout	*St.-Émilion*	2	5	10
Château Villemaurine	*St.-Émilion*	6	15	28
Clos Villemaurine	*St.-Émilion*	1	2.5	5
Château Viramont	*St.-Étienne-de-Lisse*	5	12.5	19
Château Yon	*St.-Christophe-des-Bardes*	7	17.5	27
Château Yon-Figeac	*St.-Émilion*	21	52.5	110
Château Yon-la-Tour	*St.-Émilion*	4	10	17
Clos Yon-St.-Martin	*St.-Émilion*	3	7.5	9
Clos Yveline	*Montagne-St.-Émilion*	2	5	5

POMEROL

The wines of Pomerol are not officially classified. Château Pétrus is recognized as being the outstanding Great Growth, followed by the eighteen other wines italicized below.

The following figures of production are approximate, and indicate average annual output, as given by the townships and taken from their Déclarations de Récoltes *records.*

Principal Growths

	Hectares	Acres	Tonneaux
Clos des Amandiers	2	5	11
Clos Barrail-du-Milieu, Clos du Pellerin	2	5	5
Château Beauchene (*see* Clos Mazeyres)			
Château Beaulieu	1	2.5	7
Château Beauregard	11	27.5	51
			(*3,800 cases*)
Clos Beauregard (*see* Château Taillefer)			
Château Beauséjour	2	5	6
Château Beau-Soleil	3	7.5	15
Château Bel-Air, Vieux-Château-Boënot	10	25	35
Clos Bel-Air (*see* Domaine La Pointe)			
Château Bellegraves	4	10	24
Château Bellevue	5	12.5	23
Château Boënot, Château Trintin	4	10	19
Clos Bonalgue	3	7.5	11
Château Le Bon-Pasteur	6	15	25
Domaine de Bourg-Neuf	1	2.5	6
Château Bourgneuf	9	22.5	36
Château Brun-Mazeyres	3	7.5	13
Domaine de Cantereau	1	2.5	6
Château du Casse	2	5	8

	Hectares	*Acres*	*Tonneaux*
Clos du Castel	2	5	9
Château Certan-Giraud	2	5	12
			(1,150 cases)
Château Certan-de-May	4	10	13
			(750 cases)
Château Certan-Marzelle	4	10	15
Château Clinet	6	15	39
Clos du Clocher, Château Monregard-			
Lacroix	5	12.5	28
Domaine des Clones	2	5	7
Clos du Commandeur	1	2.5	5
Cru Côte-Gazin	1	2.5	5
Clos du Fagnard	2	5	9
Château Ferrand	11	27.5	45
Château Feytit-Clinet	6	15	15
Château Franc-Maillet	4	10	22
Château Gazin	24	60	86
			(8,250 cases)
Château Gombaude-Guillot, Château			
Grandes-Vignes-Clinet	6	15	30
Château Gouprie	3	7.5	15
Château Grandes-Vignes-Clinet (*see* Château Gombaude-Guillot)			
Cru Grand-Mazeyres	2	5	7
Château Grand-Moulinet	1	2.5	5
Clos Les Grands-Champs, Château Guillot	5	12.5	23
Clos des Grands Sillons	3	7.5	20
Château Grange Neuve	4	10	16
Château Grate-Cap	4	10	19
Château Guillot (*see* Clos Les Grands-Champs)			
Château Haut-Cloquet	2	5	11
Domaine du Haut-Cloquet	1	2.5	5
Cru Haut-Groupey	2	5	6
Château Haut-Maillet	5	12.5	19
Clos Haut-Mazeyres	9	22.5	27
Domaine de Haut-Pignon	2	5	7
Domaine de Haut-Tropchaud	1	2.5	6
Château des Jacobins	1	2.5	5
Château La Cabane	9	22.5	35
Château La Chichonne	2	5	5

	Hectares	Acres	Tonneaux
Clos Lacombe	2	5	6
Château La Commanderie	5	12.5	20
Château La Conseillante	10	25	34
			(3,260 cases)
Château La Croix	8	20	23
			(2,000 cases)
Château La Croix-de-Gay	6	15	34
Château Lacroix-St.-Georges	4	10	21
Château La Croix-Taillefer	2	5	7
Château Lacroix-Toulifaut	1	2.5	11
Château Lafleur	4	10	12
			(1,150 cases)
Château Lafleur-Gazin	4	10	13
Château Lafleur-Pétrus	8	20	31
			(3,000 cases)
Château La Fleur-des-Rouzes	4	10	13
Château La Ganne	5	12.5	15
Château Lagrange	9	22.5	15
			(1,500 cases)
Château Lagrave	7	17.5	16
Château l'Angélus	1	2.5	5
Château La Patache	2	5	6
Château La Pointe	20	50	77
			(6,500 cases)
Domaine La Pointe, Clos Bel-Air	4	10	9
Château La Renaissance	1	2.5	5
Clos La Rose	3	7.5	13
Clos La Soulatte	2	5	8
Château Latour-Pomerol	8	20	27
			(2,400 cases)
Château La Violette	2	5	10
Château Le Caillou	5	12.5	30
Château Le Carillon	4	10	22
Château Le Gay	8	20	25
Clos l'Église	5	12.5	24
Domaine de l'Église	5	12.5	21
Clos de l'Église-Clinet	4	10	21
			(1,700 cases)
Château l'Enclos	7	17.5	34
Château Les Bordes	2	5	13

	Hectares	Acres	Tonneaux
Château Les Grandes-Vignes	1	2.5	5
Château Les Grands-Sillons	2	5	14
Château Les Hautes-Rouzes	2	5	9
Château l'Évangile	13	32.5	36
			(3,450 cases)
Château Margot	1	2.5	5
Château Mayne	3	7.5	11
Château du Mayne	2	5	11
Château Mazeyres	10	25	47
Clos Mazeyres, Château Beauchêne	6	15	26
Château Monregard-Lacroix (*see* Clos du Clocher)			
Château Moulinet	13	32.5	50
Château Nénin	20	50	76
			(7,300 cases)
Cru de la Nouvelle-Église	2	5	6
Clos du Pellerin (*see* Clos Barrail-du-Milieu)			
Château du Petit-Moulinet	3	7.5	12
Château Petit-Village	9	22.5	42
			(4,030 cases)
Château Pétrus	7	17.5	26
			(2,500 cases)
Château Pignon-de-Gay	2	5	10
Clos Pleville	1	2.5	5
Château Plince	7	17.5	34
Château Plincette	1	2.5	5
Château La Providence	3	7.5	7
Clos René	10	25	55
Domaine de René	3	7.5	8
Château Rève-d'Or	5	12.5	19
Domaine de Robert	4	10	13
Château Rocher-Beauregard	2	5	8
Château Rouget	10	25	35
			(3,400 cases)
Clos du Roy	3	7.5	12
Clos St.-André	2	5	12
Clos St.-Anne			
Château de Sales	31	77.5	110
Château Tailhas	9	22.5	54
Château Taillefer, Clos Beauregard, Clos			

	Hectares	*Acres*	*Tonneaux*
Toulifaut, Clos St.-Anne	21	52.5	102
Château des Templiers	3	7.5	17
Clos des Templiers	1	2.5	10
Château Thibéaud-Maillet	2	5	16
Château Toulifaut (*see* Château Taillefer)	1	2.5	5
Clos Toulifaut (*see* Château Taillefer)			
Château Tristan	1	2.5	5
Château Trintin (*see* Château Boënot)			
Château Trotanoy	7	17.5	23
			(2,200 cases)
Château de Valois	6	15	28
Domaine de la Vieille-École	1	2.5	5
Vieux-Château-Boënot (*see* Château Bel-Air)			
Vieux-Château-Bourgueneuf	3	7.5	18
Vieux-Château-Certan	14	35	56
			(5,370 cases)
Vieux-Château-Cloquet	2	5	7
Vieux-Château-l'Angélus	1	2.5	10
Vieux-Château-Tropchaud	2	5	6
Château Vieux-Maillet	1	2.5	5
Clos Vieux-Maillet	2	5	7
Château Vraye-Croix-de-Gay	4	10	13

CÔTES DE FRONSAC

The following figures of production are approximate, and indicate
average annual output, as given by the townships and taken from
their Déclarations de Récoltes _records._

		Principal Growths		
	Township	_Hectares_	_Acres_	_Tonneaux_
Clos du Alem	_Saillans_	10	25	24
Château Arnauton	_Fronsac_	11	27.5	20
Château Bardon-Ferrand	_St.-Aignan_	2	5	7
Château Bicot (Lambert)	_St.-Aignan_	1	2.5	3
Château Bicot (Rodier)	_Fronsac_	3	7.5	6
Château Bicot Latour	_St.-Aignan_	3	7.5	16
Château Cantelouve	_Fronsac_	10	25	25
Cru Cardeneau (Durand)	_Saillans_	4	10	12
Cru Cardneau (Godicheau)	_Saillans_	6	15	15
Domaine du Cardneau (Barraud)	_Saillans_	4	10	8
Domaine du Cardneau (Boussaye)	_Saillans_	2	5	7
Château du Carles	_Saillans_	13	32.5	28
Château Chadène	_St.-Aignan_	6	15	36
Domaine du Couprat	_Saillans_	5	12.5	9
Château du Fronsac	_Fronsac_	4	10	8
Château Gagnard	_Fronsac_	11	27.5	20
Château Gros Jean	_St.-Aignan_	4	10	22
Château Hauchat	_St.-Aignan_	1	2.5	5
Château Haut Rey	_Fronsac_	8	20	17
Château Jendeman	_St.-Aignan_	9	22.5	52
Domaine La Borie	_Saillans_	6	15	10
Domaine du Labrande	_Saillans_	5	12.5	12
Château La Croix	_Fronsac_	11	27.5	33
Château La Croix Gandineau	_Fronsac_	5	12.5	12

	Township	Hectares	Acres	Tonneaux
Château La Dauphine	*Fronsac*	6	15	14
Château La Faure	*Saillans*	13	32.5	27
Château La Fontaine	*Fronsac*	9	22.5	24
Château La Graves	*Fronsac*	3	7.5	7
Château Lague Bourdieu	*Fronsac*	4	10	14
Château Lambert	*St.-Aignan*	3	7.5	15
Château La Valade (Rupied)	*Fronsac*	11	27.5	20
Château La Valade (Roux)	*Fronsac*	4	10	13
Château La Venelle	*Fronsac*	4	10	13
Château La Vieille Curé	*Saillans*	14	35	32
Domaine Les Bernard	*Saillans*	4	10	12
Château Les Troix Croix	*Fronsac*	12	30	36
Château Magondeau	*Saillans*	9	22.5	38
Château de Malgarni	*Saillans*	3	7.5	6
Château Mayne-Vieil	*Galgon*	16	40	40
Château Moulins	*Saillans*	16	40	35
Château Musseau de Haut	*St.-Aignan*	2	5	12
Domaine Normand	*Saillans*	13	32.5	26
Château Pay de Pie	*Fronsac*	4	10	10
Château Peguilhem	*Saillans*	7	17.5	21
Château Peychez	*Fronsac*	4	10	8
Domaine Pillebourse	*Saillans*	3	7.5	6
Château Placette du Rey	*Fronsac*	4	10	7
Château Plainpoint	*St.-Aignan*	12	30	45
Château Richautey le Haut	*St.-Aignan*	2	5	6
Château Richodey	*St.-Aignan*	3	7.5	26
Château St.-Vincent	*St.-Aignan*	4	10	27
Château du Tasta	*St.-Aignan*	12	30	45
Château des Tonnelles	*St.-Aignan*	6	15	46
Clos des Tonnelles	*St.-Aignan*	4	10	18
Cru des Tonnelles	*St.-Aignan*	3	7.5	12
Clos Vieux Capot	*Fronsac*	2	5	5
Château Vieux Moulin	*Fronsac*	5	12.5	19
Château Vignes	*Fronsac*	2	5	5
Château Villars	*Saillans*	12	30	43
Château Vincent (Rigaud)	*St.-Aignan*	3	7.5	9
Château Vincent (Sudra)	*St.-Aignan*	5	12.5	32
Domaine de Vincent	*St.-Aignan*	4	10	17
Château Vincent La Mouleyre	*St.-Aignan*	2	5	14

CÔTES CANON-FRONSAC

The following figures of production are approximate, and indicate average annual output, as given by the townships and taken from their Déclarations de Récoltes *records.*

	Township	Hectares	Acres	Tonneaux
			Principal Growths	
Château Barrabaque	*Fronsac*	7	17.5	14
Château Belloy	*Fronsac*	5	12.5	10
Château Bodet	*Fronsac*	10	25	38
Château Canon	*Fronsac*	5	12.5	10
Château Capet-Bégaud	*Fronsac*	3	7.5	7
Château Cassange	*St.-Michel*	4	10	15
Château des Combes-Canon	*St.-Michel*	2	5	7
Château Coustolle	*Fronsac*	12	30	37
Château Gaby	*Fronsac*	6	15	12
Château du Gazin	*St.-Michel*	25	62.5	58
Château Gombeau	*Fronsac*	4	10	13
Château Grand Renouilh	*St.-Michel*	6	15	11
Château Haut-Caillou	*Fronsac*	3	7.5	9
Clos Haut-Caillou	*Fronsac*	3	7.5	8
Château Haut-Mazeris	*St.-Michel*	6	15	16
Château Junayme	*Fronsac*	13	32.5	34
Château La Chapelle-Lariveau	*St.-Michel*	5	12.5	16
Château La Marche	*Fronsac*	27	67.5	58
Clos La Marche	*Fronsac*	2	5	4
Château La Mausse	*St.-Michel*	7	17.5	17
Château Lariveau	*St.-Michel*	7	17.5	18
Château Larchevêque	*Fronsac*	5	12.5	10
Château Les Vignes	*Fronsac*	2	5	5
Château Mazeris	*St.-Michel*	7	17.5	15

	Township	*Hectares*	*Acres*	*Tonneaux*
Château Mazeris Bellevue	*St.-Michel*	6	15	12
Domaine du Mouchez	*Fronsac*	7	17.5	14
Château Moulin-à-Vent	*St.-Michel*	6	15	18
Château Moulin-Pey-Labrie	*Fronsac*	4	10	13
Clos Nardin	*St. Michel*	1	2.5	4
Château Panet	*Fronsac*	4	10	8
Château Perron	*Fronsac*	3	7.5	4
Château Pichelebre	*Fronsac*	5	12.5	15
Château Roulet	*Fronsac*	3	7.5	5
Château Roullet	*Fronsac*	3	7.5	7
Château du Tasta	*St.-Aignan*	2	5	11
Clos de Toumalin	*Fronsac*	2	5	5
Domaine de Toumalin	*Fronsac*	6	15	12
Domaine de Trepesson	*St.-Michel*	2	5	6
Château Vincent	*St.-Aignan*	7	17.5	12
Château Vrai Canon Bouché	*Fronsac*	5	12.5	13
Château Vrai Canon Bourret	*Fronsac*	2	5	6
Château Vrai Canon Boyer	*St.-Michel*	7	17.5	22

GRAVES

1959 OFFICIAL CLASSIFICATION

The following figures of production are approximate, and indi-cate average annual output, as given by the townships and taken from their Déclarations de Récoltes *records.*

CLASSIFIED RED WINES OF GRAVES

	Township	Tonneaux	Cases
Château Bouscaut	*Cadaujac*	180	16,000
Château Carbonnieux	*Léognan*	45	3,700
Domaine de Chevalier	*Léognan*	15	1,400
Château Fieuzal	*Léognan*	55	4,600
Château Haut-Bailly	*Léognan*	30	2,400
Château Haut-Brion	*Pessac*	125	10,000
Château La Mission-Haut-Brion	*Pessac*	125	10,000
Château La Tour-Haut-Brion	*Talence*	12	1,000
Château La Tour-Martillac	*Martillac*	45	3,750
Château Malartic-Lagravière	*Léognan*	30	2,400
Château Olivier	*Léognan*	14	1,200
Château Pape Clément	*Pessac*	125	10,000
Château Smith-Haut-Lafitte	*Martillac*	15	1,300

CLASSIFIED WHITE WINES OF GRAVES

	Township	Tonneaux	Cases
Château Bouscaut	*Cadaujac*	20	1,700
Château Carbonnieux	*Léognan*	90	7,000
Domaine de Chevalier	*Léognan*	9	700
Château Couhins	*Villenave-d'Ornon*	30	2,700

	Township	Tonneaux	Cases
Château Haut-Brion	*Pessac*	10	800
Château La Tour-Martillac (Kressman-Lafour)	*Martillac*	9	700
Château Laville-Haut-Brion	*Talence*	17	1,625
Château Malartic-Lagravière	*Léognan*	3	280
Château Olivier	*Léognan*	47	3,900

Other Principal Growths
(wh = white; r = red)

	Township		Hectares	Acres	Tonneaux
Château André-Lamothe	*Portets*	wh	2	5	11
		r	4	10	15
Domaine Andron	*St.-Selve*	wh	3	7.5	5
Château d'Arbanats	*Arbanats*	wh	6	15	10
Clos d'Armajan	*Budos*	r	2	5	4
Château d'Arricaud	*Landiras*	wh	12	30	49
Château des Arrocs	*Langon*	wh	3	7.5	10
Domaine Arzac	*St.-Selve*	wh	2	5	5
Clos L'Avocat	*Cérons*	wh	3	7.5	10
Château Bahans (minor growth of Château Haut-Brion)	*Pessac*	r	–	–	22
Château Bardins	*Cadaujac*	wh	2	5	2
		r			5
Château Baret	*Villenave-d'Ornon*	wh	12	30	17
		r			9
Domaine du Barque	*St.-Selve*	wh	6	15	3
		r			2
Clos Barreyre	*Virelade*	wh	3	7.5	8
Cru Barrouet	*Pujols*	wh	3	7.5	7
Domaine du Basque	*Pujols*	wh	3	7.5	12
Château Batsères	*Landiras*	wh	4	10	15
Château Beauchêne	*Beautiran*	wh	3	7.5	7
		r	2	5	5
Domaine du Beau-Site	*Portets*	wh	0.3	0.8	2
		r	3	7.5	9

	Township		Hec-tares	Acres	Ton-neaux
Château Bel-Air	*Portets*	wh	2	5	6
Château Bel-Air	*Le Haillan*	r	2	5	5
Château Bel-Air	*St.-Morillon*	wh	4	10	7
Château Bellefontaine	*St.-Pierre-de-Mons*	wh	3	7.5	7
Domaine Bellevue	*Toulenne*	wh	1	2.5	7
Domaine de Bellevue	*St.-Selve*	wh	4	10	13
Château Belon	*St.-Morillon*	wh	3	7.5	6
Domaine de Bequin	*Portets*	wh	5	12.5	11
		r	3	7.5	7
Château Bernard-Raymond	*Portets*	wh	3	7.5	13
		r	2	5	11
Cru du Bérot	*Arbanats*	wh	2	5	6
Cru Bichons	*La Brède*	wh⎱	5	12.5	11
		r ⎰			2
Domaine de Biot	*Arbanats*	wh	2	5	5
		r	2	5	4
Domaine de la Blancherie	*La Brède*	wh⎱	4	10	6
		r ⎰			2
Château Boiresse	*Ayguemortes*	wh	4	10	6
Domaine du Bonat	*St.-Selve*	wh	5	12.5	14
Clos de la Bonneterie	*Portets*	wh	2	5	6
		r	2	5	4
Cru de Borderie	*Portets*	wh	3	7.5	9
		r	2	5	8
Cru Boritz	*St.-Pierre-de-Mons*	wh	4	10	12
Domaine du Boscq	*St.-Morillon*	wh	2	5	5
Cru Bouyon	*Pujols*	wh	2	5	5
Château Boyrin	*Roaillan*	wh	6	15	16
Domaine de Brochon	*Arbanats*	wh	3	7.5	7
		r	2	5	3
Domaine de Brondelle	*Langon*	wh	2	5	4
Domaine de Brouillaud	*St.-Médard-d'Eyrans*	wh	7	17.5	19
Château Bruhaut	*St.-Pierre-de-Mons*	wh	2	5	4
Château de Budos	*Budos*	r	9	22.5	31
Clos Cabanes	*St.-Pierre-de-Mons*	wh	4	10	11
Clos Cabannes	*St.-Pierre-de-Mons*	wh	1	2.5	5

	Township		Hec-tares	Acres	Ton-neaux
Château Cabannieux	*Portets*	wh	3	7.5	7
		r	3	7.5	6
Cru de Cadenne	*Pujols*	wh	5	12.5	12
Cru du Caladis (*2 pro-prietors*)	*Portets*	r	3	7.5	9
		wh	4	10	7
		r			5
Cru Calens	*Beautiran*	r	7	17.5	17
Cru Camegaye	*Landiras*	wh	2	5	9
Château Cantalot	*St.-Pierre-de-Mons*	wh	7	17.5	22
Cru de Cap-de-Hé	*Pujols*	wh	2	5	6
Cru Capet-à-Corne	*Beautiran*	wh	3	7.5	5
Château Carmes-Haut-Brion	*Pessac*	r	2	5	8
Domaine Carros	*St.-Selve*	wh	2	5	9
Domaine de Casseuil	*Langon*	wh	4	10	6
Cru Castagnet	*Virelade*	wh	3	7.5	9
Domaine Castelnaud	*St.-Pierre-de-Mons*	wh	2	5	5
Château Catalas	*Pujols*	wh	6	15	17
Cru de la Cave	*Preignac*	wh	2	5	5
Château Cazebonne	*St.-Pierre-de-Mons*	wh	7	17.5	12
Cru Chanteloiseau	*Langron*	wh	5	12.5	12
Clos Charamel	*Castres*	wh	4	10	2
		r			4
Château Chaviran	*Martillac*	r	4	10	6
Clos Cherchy	*Pujols*	wh	4	10	11
Cru Cherchy	*Pujols*	wh	2	5	9
Château Chicane	*Toulenne*	wh	3	7.5	12
Domaine du Ciron	*Pujols*	wh	5	12.5	19
Domaine de Clare	*Landiras*	wh	3	7.5	8
Cru Coudillet	*Virelade*	wh	1	2.5	5
Cru du Couet	*St.-Pierre-de-Mons*	wh	2	5	5
Domaine de Courbon	*Toulenne*	wh	4	10	11
Domaine du Courreau	*St.-Médard-d'Eyrans*	wh	3	7.5	5
		r			3
Domaine du Courreau	*St.-Morillon*	wh	3	7.5	11

Bordeaux Wines,
Graves
(RED AND WHITE)

	Township		Hec-tares	Acres	Ton-neaux
Château Crabitey	*Portets*	wh	7	17.5	7
		r	8	20	13
Domaine de la Croix	*Langon*	wh	4	10	10
Château Cruzeau	*St.-Médard-*				
	d'Eyrans	wh	12	30	19
Clos Darches	*St.-Pierre-de-Mons*	wh	4	10	9
Clos Darrouban	*Portets*	wh	2	5	3
		r			3
Domaine de Darrouban	*Portets*	wh	3	7.5	15
		r	2	5	3
Château Despagne	*St.-Pierre-de-Mons*	wh	4	10	14
Clos Despagne	*St.-Pierre-de-Mons*	wh	4	10	16
Château Doms	*Portets*	wh	15	37.5	29
et Clos du		r			12
Monastère					
Domaine du Druc	*Landiras*	wh	2	5	6
Domaine de Durce,					
Domaine de Papoula	*Portets*	wh	2	5	7
		r	1	2.5	7
Domaine Étienne	*St.-Morillon*	wh	2	5	6
Cru Eyquem	*La Brède*	wh	5	12.5	12
Domaine de Faye	*Portets*	wh	1	2.5	6
		r	2	5	7
Château Fernon	*Langon*	wh	4	10	8
Château Ferran	*Martillac*	wh	3	7.5	11
		r	0.5	1.2	1
Château Ferrande	*Castres*	wh	10	25	33
Château Fieuzal	*Léognan*	wh	11	27.5	2
		r			20
Château Foncla	*Castres*	wh	13	32.5	21
		r			3
Château Foncroise	*St.-Selve*	wh	7	17.5	10
		r			4
Château des Fougères	*La Brède*	wh	2	5	5
Clos des Fougères	*Virelade*	wh	4	10	11
Château de France	*Léognan*	wh	8	20	6
		r			9

	Township		Hec-tares	Acres	Ton-neaux
Domaine des Gaillardins	*St.-Selve*	wh	4	10	8
Cru Galand	*Cérons*	wh	1	2.5	4
Clos du Gars	*La Brède*	wh	2	5	5
Château Gazin	*Léognan*	wh⎫			1
		⎬	7	17.5	
		r ⎭			10
Clos de Gensac	*Pujols*	wh	4	10	16
Domaine de la Girafe	*Portets*	wh	5	12.5	22
		r	2	5	11
Domaine de la Gleyre	*Pujols*	wh	2	5	9
Cru de Gonthier	*Portets*	wh	1	2.5	5
		r	2	5	7
Château Gorre	*Martillac*	wh	1	2.5	1
		r	2	5	3
Domaine du Grand-Abord	*Portets*	wh	5	12.5	18
		r	2	5	6
Château Grand Bourdieu	*Beautiran*	wh	6	15	10
Château Grand Chemin	*Cérons*	wh	2	5	8
Domaine de la Grande-Ferrade	*Villenave-d'Ornon*	r	4	10	8
Château Grandmaison	*Léognan*	wh⎫			5
		⎬	5	12.5	
		r ⎭			5
Domaine de la Grave	*St.-Selve*	wh	3	7.5	6
Cru des Graves	*Portets*	wh	3	7.5	6
		r	1	2.5	4
Domaine de Gravette	*St.-Morillon*	wh	15	37.5	33
Château Graveyron	*Portets*	wh	6	15	18
		r	4	10	13
Château de la Gravière	*Toulenne*	wh	7	17.5	25
Château des Gravières	*Portets*	wh	3	7.5	12
		r	2	5	10
Clos des Gravières	*Portets*	wh	2	5	5
		r	1	2.5	5
Domaine des Gravières	*Portets*	r	2	5	6
Domaine de Guérin	*Castres*	r	4	10	6
Château Guillaumot	*La Brède*	wh	13	32.5	41
Château des Guillemins	*Langon*	wh	8	20	28
Domaine de Guirauton	*St.-Morillon*	wh	4	10	9

	Township		Hec-tares	Acres	Ton-neaux
Cru des Guizats	*Pujols*	wh	2	5	8
Clos Harquey	*Langon*	wh	4	10	7
Château Haut-Bergey	*Léognan*	wh			2
			4	10	
		r			6
Cru du Haut-Blanc	*Pujols*	wh	1	2.5	4
Domaine du Haut-Blanc	*Pujols*	wh	4	10	12
Domaine Haut-Callens	*Beautiran*	wh	5	12.5	9
Cru du Haut-Claron	*St.-Morillon*	wh	3	7.5	7
Domaine du Haut-Courneau	*Portets*	wh	5	12.5	13
		r	5	12.5	13
Cru Haut-Gravette	*St.-Morillon*	wh	3	7.5	6
Château Haut-Madère	*Villenave-d'Ornon*	r	2	5	3
Château Haut-Nouchet	*Martillac*	wh			9
			9	22.5	
		r			6
Cru Hautes Plantes	*Landiras*	wh	3	7.5	8
Cru Haut-Reys	*La Brède*	wh	3	7.5	7
Château Jamnets	*St.-Pierre-de-Mons*	wh			5
			2	5	
		r			4
Clos Jamnet	*La Brède*	wh	8	20	18
Cru Janot-Bayle	*Budos*	r	8	20	16
Domaine du Jau	*St.-Morillon*	wh	3	7.5	5
Château des Jaubertes	*St.-Pierre-de-Mons*	wh	6	15	15
Clos Jean Dubos	*Pujols*	wh	2	5	4
Château Jean-Gervais, Clos Puyjalon	*Portets*	wh			38
			10	25	
		r			3
Clos Jean-de-Maye	*Portets*	wh			6
			5	12.5	
		r			11
Clos de l'Abbaye-de-la-Rame	*Mazères*	wh	6	15	12
Domaine de Labeillon	*St.-Pierre-de-Mons*	wh	2	5	5
Cru La Cabane	*Pujols*	wh	4	10	11
Cru La Camuse	*St.-Morillon*	wh	3	7.5	7
Château Côtes de Lacapère	*Landiras*	wh	2	5	6
Cru Lacapère	*Landiras*	wh	4	10	15

	Township		Hec-tares	Acres	Ton-neaux
Domaine de Lacapère	_Landiras_	wh	2	5	7
Cru Lafon	_St.-Pierre-de-Mons_	wh	2	5	9
Château La Garde	_Martillac_	r	13	32.5	40
Château Lagénie	_St.-Morillon_	wh	3	7.5	6
Château Lagueloup	_Portets_	wh	2	5	3
Cru La Hounade	_Pujols_	wh	2	5	9
Château La Louvière	_Léognan_	wh	28	70	45
		r			19
Clos Lamagine	_St.-Pierre-de-Mons_	wh	6	15	14
Cru La Mainionce	_Pujols_	wh	3	7.5	13
Cru La Médecine	_St.-Pierre-de-Mons_	wh	2	5	5
Cru de Lamoigon	_Pujols_	wh	3	7.5	5
Château Lamothe	_Cadaujac_	r	4	10	10
Château Lamothe	_St.-Mèdard-d'Eyrans_	wh	1	2.5	4
Clos Lamothe	_Portets_	wh	3	7.5	9
		r	2	5	11
Château Lamouroux	_Cérons_	wh	8	20	37
Château Laouilley	_Roaillan_	wh	3	7.5	3
Domaine La Peyrère	_St.-Selve_	wh	5	12.5	8
		r			2
Château La Prade	_St.-Médard-d'Eyrans_	wh	4	10	9
Cru Lardite	_Arbanats_	wh	2	5	13
		r	2	5	5
Domaine de Larnavey	_St.-Selve_	wh	4	10	9
Château Larrivet-Haut-Brion	_Léognan_	r	10	25	14
Cru Larroucat	_Pujols_	wh	2	5	8
Château La Salle	_Martillac_	wh	3	7.5	8
Domaine de Lassalle	_La Brède_	wh	6	15	26
Domaine La Solitude	_Martillac_	wh	2	5	4
		r	4	10	7
Cru La Terce	_Budos_	r	2	5	3
Château La Tour	_Léognan_	wh	5	12.5	9
		r			2
Château La Tour Bicheau	_Portets_	wh	3	7.5	9
		r	5	12.5	17
Château La Tour-de-Boyrin	_Langon_	wh	13	32.5	20

	Township		Hec-tares	Acres	Ton-neaux
Clos La-Tour-Cluchon	*Portets*	wh	2	5	3
		r	2	5	5
Château La Tourte	*Toulenne*	wh	6	15	16
Cru Le Bourut	*Pujols*	wh	2	5	9
Château Le Brouillaud	*St.-Médard-*				
	d'Eyrans	wh	5	12.5	16
Cru de l'Église	*Virelade*	wh	2	5	5
Cru Les Guizats	*Pujols*	wh	2	5	4
Cru Le Hiladey	*Portets*	wh	2	5	4
		r	4	10	4
Clos Léhoul	*Langon*	wh	4	10	8
Château Le Mayne	*Preignac*	wh			9
Château Le Méjean	*Ayguemortes*	wh	6	15	13
Château Le More	*St.-Selve*	wh	2	5	8
Château Le Pape	*Léognan*	wh⎫			3
		⎬	4	10	
		r ⎭			2
Château Les Charmettes	*Budos*	wh	2	5	4
Domaine Les Cluchets	*Langon*	wh	4	10	12
Cru Les Graves	*Toulenne*	wh	4	10	12
Cru Les Mengets	*Pujols*	wh	2	5	4
Château Lespault	*Martillac*	wh	4	10	3
		r	0.5	1.2	2
Château de l'Espérance	*La Brède*	wh	4	10	10
		r	—	—	1
Cru Les Pinsas	*Pujols*	wh	2	5	5
Cru Les Rocs	*Pujols*	wh	2	5	5
Cru Lestage	*Landiras*	wh	4	10	9
Domaine Lestang	*St.-Selve*	wh	5	12.5	8
Château Le Thil	*Léognan*	r	3	7.5	4
Cru de l'Hermitage	*Budos*	r	8	20	12
Château de l'Hospital	*Portets*	wh⎫			2
		⎬	5	12.5	
		r ⎭			9
Domaine de l'Hôpital	*Castres*	r	6	15	5
Clos Liché	*St.-Pardon-de-*				
	Conques	wh	3	7.5	7
Château Limbourg	*Villenave-d'Ornon*	wh⎫			5
		⎬	10	25	
		r ⎭			6

	Township		Hec-tares	Acres	Ton-neaux
Château Liot-Moros	*Pujols*	wh	5	12.5	17
Cru Lioy	*Budos*	r	3	7.5	4
Château Lognac	*Castres*	wh⎫			9
		⎬	14	35	
		r ⎭			2
Domaine de Louisot	*Virelade*	wh	4	10	13
Clos Louloumet	*Toulenne*	wh	3	7.5	8
Cru de Lubat	*St.-Pierre-de-Mons*	wh	8	20	14
Château des Lucques	*Portets*	wh⎫			12
		⎬	5	12.5	
		r ⎭			6
Domaine des Lucques	*Portets*	wh⎫			7
		⎬	7	17.5	
		r ⎭			6
Château Ludeman-Lacôte	*Langon*	wh	7	17.5	20
Cru des Luques	*Portets*	wh	2	5	6
		r	2	5	8
Château Lusseau	*Ayguemortes*	wh⎫			5
		⎬	8	20	
		r ⎭			6
Château Madélis	*Portets*	wh	2	5	6
		r	2	5	12
Château Madran	*Pessac*	r	3	7.5	4
Château Magence	*St.-Pierre-de-Mons*	wh	11	27.5	27
Cru Magnaud	*La Brède*	wh	5	12.5	11
Château Maillard	*Mazères*	wh	5	12.5	13
Clos de la Maison Blanche	*Budos*	wh	2	5	5
Château Malleprat	*Martillac*	wh	3	7.5	5
Domaine de Maron	*Landiras*	r	2	5	9
Domaine Martin	*Roaillan*	wh	2	5	6
Cru Massiot	*Martillac*	wh	2	5	6
Château de Mauves	*Podensac*	r	1	2.5	4
Domaine du May	*Portets*	wh	3	7.5	6
		r	2	5	5
Domaine du Mayne	*Langon*	wh	3	7.5	8
Cru Mayne d'Eyquen	*La Brède*	wh	5	12.5	14
Domaine de Metivier	*Ayguemortes*	wh	3	7.5	6
Château Millet	*Portets*	wh⎫			17
		⎬	10	25	
		r ⎭			20

	Township		Hec-tares	Acres	Ton-neaux
Château Mirabel	*Pujols*	wh	3	7.5	14
Château du Mirail	*Portets*	wh	5	12.5	16
		r	3	7.5	14
Château Moderis	*Virelade*	wh	5	12.5	10
Domaine de Mongenan	*Portets*	wh	5	12.5	13
		r			2
Clos de Mons	*La Brède*	wh	3	7.5	8
Cru Morange	*Virelade*	wh	2	5	7
Cru du Moulin-à-Vent	*Cérons*	wh	3	7.5	12
Cru du Moulin-à-Vent	*Landiras*	wh	3	7.5	9
Clos du Moulin-à-Vent	*St.-Pierre-de-Mons*	wh	5	12.5	18
Domaine le Mouniche	*Ayguemortes*	wh	5	12.5	7
		r			5
Château Mouteou	*Portets*	wh	2	5	6
		r	1	2.5	4
Château Moutin	*Portets*	r	1	2.5	5
Château Mouyet	*Budos*	r	2	5	11
Château Neuf	*Léognan*	wh	6	15	4
		r			4
Cru Nodoy	*Virelade*	wh	3	7.5	7
Clos Nouchet	*Castres*	wh	7	17.5	1
		r			6
Château de Nouguey	*Langon*	wh	2	5	6
Clos du Pape	*La Brède*	wh	6	15	19
Domaine de Papoula (*see* Domaine de Durce)					
Cru Patiras	*Toulenne*	wh	2	5	4
Château de Pavillon	*Roaillan*	wh	6	15	8
Château Pédebayle	*St.-Pierre-de-Mons*	wh	8	20	20
Château Péran	*Langon*	wh	8	20	17
Cru Perran	*Landiras*	wh	3	7.5	12
Domaine Perrin de Naudine	*Castres*	wh	5	12.5	1
		r			6
Château Perron	*Roaillan*	wh	14	35	37
Château Pesilla	*Landiras*	wh	4	10	16
Château Pessan	*Portets*	wh	6	15	14
		r	6	15	12

	Township		Hec-tares	Acres	Ton-neaux
Château Péyran	*Landiras*	wh	4	10	11
Château des Peyrères	*Landiras*	r	4	10	14
Cru Pezeau	*Beautiran*	wh	5	12.5	5
		r			1
Cru Pierret	*Castres*	wh	6	15	8
		r			3
Cru Pinaud	*Cérons*	wh	2	5	5
Château Pingoy	*Portets*	wh	5	12.5	21
		r	3	7.5	12
Château Pique-Cailloux	*Mérignac*	wh	7	17.5	13
Château Piron	*St.-Morillon*	wh	7	17.5	27
Clos des Places	*Arbanats*	wh	1	2.5	4
Domaine des Places	*Arbanats*	wh	2	5	9
		r	1	2.5	6
Domaine de Plantat	*St.-Morillon*	wh	9	22.5	16
Cru des Plantes	*Landiras*	wh	14	35	56
Domaine des Plantes	*Landiras*	wh	4	10	11
Domaine du Plantey	*Castres*	wh	2	5	2
		r			7
Château Pommarède	*Castres*	wh	4	10	5
		r			5
Château Pommarède-de-Bas	*Castres*	wh	5	12.5	11
		r			4
Château Pontac	*Villenave-d'Ornon*	wh	14	35	20
		r			15
Cru du Portail	*Landiras*	wh	2	5	7
Château de Portets	*Portets*	wh	7	17.5	18
		r	8	20	38
Cru de la Poste	*Virelade*	wh	4	10	6
Château Poumey	*Gradignan*	wh	4	10	4
		r			12
Clos Puyjalon (*see* Château Jean-Gervais)					
Château Queyrats, Clos d'Uza	*St.-Pierre-de-Mons*	wh	34	85	77

	Township		Hec-tares	Acres	Ton-neaux
Château Rahoul	*Portets*	wh	2	5	5
		r	5	12.5	26
Château Respide	*Langon*	wh⎫			55
		⎬	34	85	
		r ⎭			15
Château Respide	*St.-Pierre-de-Mons*	wh	4	10	5
Château Respide	*Toulenne*	wh	5	12.5	13
Château La Rocaille	*Virelade*	wh	9	22.5	13
Domaine Roland	*Langon*	wh	3	7.5	6
Château Roquetaillade	*Mazères*	wh	3	7.5	9
Château Rosario	*Eyzines*	wh	1	2.5	4
Château Rostang-Haut-Carré	*Talence*	wh	1	2	2
		r	3	7.5	6
Château Roubinet	*Pujols*	wh	8	20	32
Cru Roudet	*Pujols*	wh	5	12.5	17
Cru Sadout	*Virelade*	wh	6	15	19
Château Saige-Fort-Manoir	*Pessac*	r	5	12.5	11
Château St.-Gérôme	*Ayguemortes*	wh	4	10	7
Clos St.-Hilaire	*Portets*	wh	3	7.5	12
		r	3	7.5	8
Clos St.-Jean	*Pujols*	wh	8	20	23
Clos St.-Robert	*Pujols*	wh	26	. 65	54
		r	4	10	8
Domaine du Sapeur	*Portets*	wh⎫			9
		⎬	4	10	
		r ⎭			10
Cru Sarraguey	*Virelade*	wh	2	5	7
Domaine des Sarrots	*St.-Pierre-de-Mons*	wh	2	5	5
Clos Sentouary	*St.-Pierre-de-Mons*	wh	2	5	5
Cru Terrefort	*Pujols*	wh	3	7.5	10
Domaine de Teycheney	*Virelade*	wh	2	5	4
Domaine de Teychon	*Arbanats*	wh	4	10	16
Château Toumilon	*St.-Pierre-de-Mons*	wh	5	12.5	9
Cru Toumilon	*St.-Pierre-de-Mons*	wh	2	5	4
Château Tourteau-Cholet	*Arbanats*	wh	13	32.5	30

	Township		Hec-tares	Acres	Ton-neaux
Clos de la Tuilerie	*Portets*	wh	3	7.5	10
		r	2	5	10
Cru La Tuilerie	*Landiras*	wh	2	5	7
Château de Tuileries	*Virelade*	wh	3	7.5	14
		r	7	17.5	19
Château Tuquet	*Beautiran*	wh⎫			76
		⎬ 26	65		
		r ⎭			6
Château Tustoc	*Toulenne*	wh	8	20	26
Clos d'Uza (*see* Château Queyrats)					
Domaine des Vergnes	*Portets*	wh	2	5	4
		r	1	2.5	4
Clos Viaut	*St.-Pardon-de-*				
	Conques	wh	2	5	4
Clos Viaut	*St.-Pierre-de-Mons*	wh	9	22.5	25
Cru Videau	*Pujols*	wh	6	15	25
Château La Vieille-France	*Portets*	wh⎫			16
		⎬ 8	20		
		r ⎭			7
Château de Virelade	*Arbanats*	wh	3	7.5	9
		r	20	50	65

SAUTERNES AND BARSAC

As in the Médoc, the Sauternes vineyards were officially classified in 1855. This classification is known as the Official Classification of the Great Growths of the Gironde.

The total production from these vineyards represents approximately 25 per cent of the total Sauternes production, amounting roughly to 350,000 cases per year.

The following figures of production are approximate, and indicate average annual output, as given by the townships and taken from their Déclarations de Récoltes *records.*

	1st Great Growth	
	Tonneaux	*Cases*
Château d'Yquem	110	9,000
	1st Growths	
Château Guiraud	125	8,250
Château La Tour-Blanche	50	4,000
Château Lafaurie-Peyraguey	35	3,000
Château de Rayne-Vigneau	95	7,700
Château Rabaud-Sigalas	30	2,500
Château Rabaud-Promis	105	8,700
Clos Haut-Peyraguey	20	1,900
Château Coutet	75	6,000
Château Climens	55	4,500
Château de Suduiraut	115	9,600
Château Rieussec	85	7,000
	2nd Growths	
Château d'Arche	10	950
Château Filhot	50	4,000
Château Lamothe	10	750

	Tonneaux	*Cases*
Château Myrat	40	3,100
Château Doisy—Daëne	30	2,400
Château Doisy-Védrines	40	3,100
Château Filhot	50	4,000
Château de Malle	40	3,200
Château Nairac	30	2,300
Château Romer	15	1,200
Château Suau	15	1,200
Château Broustet	30	2,400
Château Caillou	40	3,200

Minor Growths

	Township	*Hectares*	*Acres*	*Tonneaux*
Château d'Arche-Lafaurie	*Sauternes*	19	47.5	48
Cru d'Arche-Pugnau, Château Peyraguey-le-Rousset	*Preignac*	15	37.5	32
Château d'Arches, Château Lamothe	*Sauternes*	15	37.5	40
Château d'Arche-Vimeney	*Sauternes*	5	12.5	11
Château d'Armajan-des-Ormes	*Preignac*	7	17.5	18
Cru d'Arrançon	*Preignac*	5	12.5	10
Cru Arrançon-Boutoc	*Preignac*	3	7.5	9
Château Augey	*Bommes*	10	25	26
Cru Baboye	*Fargues*	2	5	5
Château Barbier	*Fargues*	6	15	16
Cru de Barboye	*Bommes*	2	5	4
Cru Barjumeau	*Sauternes*	3	7.5	6
Château Barjumeau-Chauvin	*Sauternes*	3	7.5	9
Clos Barreau	*Fargues*	1	2.5	4
Château Barrette	*Sauternes*	5	12.5	14
Cru Barrette	*Fargues*	1	2.5	2
Cru Bas-Peyraguey	*Preignac*	2	5	4
Château Bastor-Lamontagne	*Preignac*	38	95	90
Château Batsalle	*Fargues*	4	10	9
Cru Batsalle	*Fargues*	1	2.5	3
Château Baulac-Dodigeos	*Barsac*	5	12.5	12
Cru Baylieu	*Fargues*	7	17.5	13
Château Béchereau	*Bommes*	12	30	22

	Township	Hec-tares	Acres	Ton-neaux
Cru Bel-Air	*Preignac*	2	5	4
Château Bergeron	*Bommes*	5	12.5	15
Cru Bergeron	*Preignac*	4	10	11
Château Bernisse	*Barsac*	3	7.5	8
Cru Bernisse	*Barsac*	1	2.5	4
Cru Bignon	*Bommes*	1	2.5	3
Cru Bordesoulles	*Preignac*	3	7.5	7
Château Bousclas	*Barsac*	3	7.5	8
Cru Bousclas	*Barsac*	4	10	12
Cru Boutoc	*Preignac*	5	12.5	10
Cru Boutoc	*Sauternes*	2	5	5
Château Bouyot	*Barsac*	6	15	15
Cru Bouyreou	*Preignac*	1	2.5	2
Château Brassens-Guitteronde	*Barsac*	5	12.5	14
Cru Camelong	*Bommes*	1	2.5	2
Château Cameron et Raymond-Louis	*Bommes*	9	22.5	35
Château Camperos, Château Monta-livet, Château Mayne-Bert	*Barsac*	12	30	27
Château Cantegril	*Barsac*	14	35	38
Cru Caplane	*Bommes*	2	5	5
Cru Caplane	*Sauternes*	5	12.5	16
Domaine de Caplane	*Sauternes*	5	12.5	25
Cru Carbonnieu	*Bommes*	6	15	23
Château de Carles	*Barsac*	6	15	16
Cru du Carrefour	*Sauternes*	1	2.5	2
Cru de la Cave	*Preignac*	2	5	5
Cru du Chalet	*Barsac*	2	5	5
Cru du Chalet	*Preignac*	1	2.5	3
Domaine de la Chapelle	*Preignac*	2	5	4
Château de la Chartreuse	*Preignac*	5	12.5	10
Cru Chauvin	*Sauternes*	2	5	4
Cru Claverie	*Fargues*	2	5	6
Château Closiot	*Barsac*	5	12.5	11
Clos Cloziot	*Barsac*	1	2.5	2
Cru Cluziot	*Barsac*	1	2.5	2
Cru Commarque	*Bommes*	1	2.5	3
Château Commarque	*Sauternes*	4	10	10
Cru Commarque	*Sauternes*	6	15	11

	Township	Hec- tares	Acres	Ton- neaux
Cru Commet-Magey	*Preignac*	4	10	8
Cru Commet-Magey-Briatte	*Preignac*	4	10	11
Domaine Cosse	*Fargues*	6	15	12
Domaine de Couite	*Preignac*	3	7.5	8
Cru Coussères	*Fargues*	1	2.5	2
Château Coustet	*Barsac*	6	15	21
Cru Coustet	*Barsac*	1	2.5	2
Domaine du Coy	*Sauternes*	3	7.5	8
Château de Coye	*Sauternes*	1	2.5	3
Cru Druerin	*Bommes*	2	5	4
Château Ducasse	*Barsac*	5	12.5	12
Cru Ducasse	*Fargues*	2	5	5
Château Dudon	*Barsac*	8	20	20
Domaine Duperneau	*Bommes*	3	7.5	9
Cru Duzan	*Barsac*	1	2.5	3
Clos d'Espagnet (*see* Château Esterlin)				
Château Esterlin, Clos d'Espagnet	*Sauternes*	3	7.5	7
Château de Fargues	*Fargues*	7	17.5	16
Château Farluret	*Barsac*	4	10	11
Cru Fillau	*Fargues*	4	10	10
Château Fleury, Château Terre-Noble	*Barsac*	2	5	4
Clos Fontaine	*Fargues*	2	5	6
Château Fontebride	*Preignac*	2	5	7
Domaine de la Forêt	*Preignac*	21	52.5	61
Cru Gavach	*Fargues*	3	7.5	7
Château Gilette, Domaine des Justices, Château Les Rochers, Château Les Remparts, Château Lamothe	*Preignac*	14	35	30
Clos Girautin	*Barsac*	1	2.5	3
Château Grand-Carretey	*Barsac*	1	2.5	2
Cru Grand-Carretey	*Barsac*	6	15	16
Cru Grand-Jauga	*Barsac*	2	5	6
Château Grand-Mayne-Qui-Né-Marc	*Barsac*	1	2.5	3
Cru Gravailles	*Preignac*	2	5	4
Château Gravas	*Barsac*	8	20	20
Château Grillon	*Barsac*	6	15	18
Cru Guillem-du-Rey	*Preignac*	7	17.5	22
Château Guimbalet	*Preignac*	1	2.5	4

	Township	Hec- tares	Acres	Ton- neaux
Cru Guitteronde	Barsac	1	2.5	3
Château Guitteronde-Bert	Barsac	9	22.5	22
Château Guitteronde-Sarraute	Barsac	4	10	10
Château du Haire	Preignac	4	10	9
Cru du Haire	Preignac	6	15	18
Château Hallet	Barsac	10	25	24
Château Haut-Bergeron	Preignac	4	10	13
Château Haut-Bommes	Bommes	7	17.5	14
Château Haut-Claverie	Fargues	4	10	8
Cru Haut-Lagueritte	Bommes	2	5	4
Château Haut-Mayne	Fargues	2	5	5
Cru Haut-Piquan	Sauternes	1	2.5	3
Cru du Hère	Preignac	2	5	2
Château Hourmalas (see Château St.-Marc)				
Cru Hourmalas	Barsac	2	5	6
Château Jany	Barsac	2	5	6
Clos Jauguet	Barsac	1	2.5	3
Cru Jauguet	Barsac	5	12.5	14
Château Jean-Galant	Bommes	2	5	7
Château Jean-Laive	Barsac	4	10	11
Clos de Jeanlaive	Barsac	5	12.5	11
Cru Jeannonier	Bommes	3	7.5	4
Domaine Jean-Robert	Preignac	1	2.5	3
Château du Juge	Preignac	4	10	10
Cru Junka	Preignac	3	7.5	4
Château Les Justices	Preignac	3	7.5	6
Domaine des Justices (see Château Gilette)				
Cru La Bernisse	Barsac	3	7.5	7
Château La Bouade	Barsac	12	30	31
Clos La Bouade	Barsac	3	7.5	8
Domaine de Labouade-Rambaud	Barsac	1	2.5	3
Cru La Bouchette	Bommes	1	2.5	2
Cru Labouchette	Preignac	2	5	5
Château La Brouillère	Bommes	4	10	9
Cru Labrousse	Barsac	2	5	5
Château La Chapelle-St.-Aubin	Bommes	3	7.5	6
Château La Clotte	Barsac	5	12.5	12
Cru Lacoste	Barsac	2	5	4

	Township	Hec- tares	Acres	Ton- neaux
Cru La Côte	*Fargues*	5	12.5	9
Château Lafon, Château Le Mayne	*Sauternes*	6	15	19
Château Lafon-Laroze	*Sauternes*	3	7.5	5
Cru Lagardan	*Bommes*	3	7.5	10
Cru l'Agnet	*Bommes*	2	5	3
Château Lagravette	*Bommes*	2	5	5
Cru La Gravière	*Preignac*	2	5	5
Cru Lahonade-Peyraguey	*Bommes*	2	5	6
Château Lahouilley	*Barsac*	3	7.5	9
Château La Hourcade	*Preignac*	4	10	13
Cru Lalot	*Preignac*	6	15	16
Cru La Maringue	*Bommes*	4	10	8
Château Lamothe (*see* Château d'Arches)				
Château Lamothe (*see* Château Gilette)				
Cru Lamothe	*Sauternes*	6	15	14
Château La Mourette	*Bommes*	3	7.5	8
Cru Lanère	*Sauternes*	11	27.5	21
Château Lange	*Bommes*	5	12.5	12
Cru Lanusquet	*Fargues*	2	5	5
Clos Lapachère	*Barsac*	4	10	10
Château Lapelou	*Barsac*	6	15	16
Château Lapinesse	*Barsac*	16	40	44
Cru Lapinesse	*Barsac*	7	17.5	19
Cru La Pinesse	*Barsac*	2	5	5
Domaine de Laraude	*Sauternes*	2	5	5
Château Laribotte	*Preignac*	5	12.5	9
Domaine de l'Arieste	*Preignac*	8	20	21
Clos l'Arieste	*Preignac*	3	7.5	8
Cru Larode	*Sauternes*	1	2.5	2
Château La Tour	*Barsac*	2	5	4
Château Latrezotte	*Barsac*	7	17.5	20
Cru l'Aubépin	*Bommes*	10	25	26
Cru l'Aubépine	*Bommes*	2	5	4
Cru l'Aubépins	*Sauternes*	3	7.5	6
Château Lauvignac	*Preignac*	3	7.5	6
Château Laville	*Preignac*	11	27.5	22
Château Le Coustet	*Barsac*	5	12.5	10

	Township	Hec-tares	Acres	Ton-neaux
Cru Le Haut Bommes	Bommes	0.5	1.2	2
Château Le Hère	Bommes	6	15	10
Château Le Mayne (*see* Château Lafon)				
Château Le Mayne	Preignac	13	32.5	34
Château Le Mouret	Fargues	6	15	6
Cru Le Pageot	Bommes	2	5	4
Château l'Ermitage	Preignac	7	17.5	13
Cru Le Roc	Preignac	1	2.5	3
Château Le Rose-et-Monteil	Preignac	5	12.5	14
Cru Le Rousseau	Bommes	2	5	3
Château Les Arrieux	Preignac	5	12.5	15
Château Le Sauhuc	Preignac	3	7.5	9
Cru Les Cailloux	Bommes	2	5	4
Cru Les Gravilles	Barsac	1	2.5	2
Château Les Plantes	Barsac	5	12.5	14
Cru Les Quints	Barsac	1	2.5	2
Château Les Remparts (*see* Château Gilette)				
Château Les Rochers	Preignac	7	17.5	18
Château Les Rochers (*see* Château Gilette)				
Cru Les Rochers	Preignac	2	5	4
Cru Les Tuileries	Fargues	1	2.5	3
Château Liot	Barsac	11	27.5	29
Château de Luzies	Barsac	3	7.5	9
Cru Mahon	Bommes	1	2.5	4
Cru Mahon	Preignac	2	5	6
Cru de Mahon	Preignac	2	5	3
Clos des Maraings	Preignac	3	7.5	6
Château Masereau	Barsac	7	17.5	15
Château Mathalin	Barsac	11	27.5	35
Domaine de Mathalin	Barsac	1	2.5	3
Château Mauras	Bommes	10	25	24
Cru Mauras	Bommes	3	7.5	5
Cru Mauvin	Preignac	6	15	16
Château du Mayne	Barsac	7	17.5	17
Château du Mayne	Preignac	2	5	5
Château Mayne-Bert (*see* Château Camperos)				
Clos Mayne-Lamouroux	Barsac	2	5	5

	Township	Hec- tares	Acres	Ton- neaux
Cru Menate	Barsac	1	2.5	2
Château Menota, Château Menota-Labat	Barsac	17	42.5	54
Château Menota-Labat (see Château Menota)				
Château Mercier	Barsac	2	5	4
Clos Mercier	Barsac	3	7.5	8
Cru Mercier	Barsac	1	2.5	4
Clos de Miaille	Barsac	1	2.5	2
Cru Miaille	Barsac	1	2.5	3
Cru Miselle	Preignac	3	7.5	7
Château du Mont	Preignac	4	10	11
Château Montalivet (see Château Camperos)				
Château Monteau	Preignac	9	22.5	21
Cru Monteil	Bommes	3	7.5	7
Cru Monteils	Preignac	1	2.5	2
Domaine de Monteils	Preignac	7	17.5	19
Cru Montjoie	Preignac	2	5	4
Château Montjou (see Château Terre Noble)				
Cru Mothes	Fargues	8	20	13
Cru du Moulin Neuf	Preignac	1	2.5	2
Château Mounic	Fargues	1	2.5	2
Domaine de Mounic	Fargues	1	2.5	2
Château Moura	Barsac	1	2.5	4
Cru Mouret	Fargues	3	7.5	7
Cru Mussotte	Fargues	1	2.5	3
Clos de Nauton	Fargues	4	10	7
Château Padouen-Terre-Noble	Barsac	7	17.5	10
Château Pageot	Sauternes	5	12.5	12
Cru du Pajeot	Bommes	4	10	7
Château Paloumat	Fargues	2	5	2
Château du Pape	Preignac	3	7.5	12
Clos du Pape	Fargues	5	12.5	11
Château Partarrieu	Fargues	8	20	9
Cru Passérieux	Barsac	3	7.5	7
Château Pébayle	Barsac	5	12.5	15
Château Peillon-Claverie	Fargues	9	22.5	26
Château Pechon-Terre-Noble	Barsac	3	7.5	9
Château Pernaud	Barsac	17	42.5	35

	Township	Hec-tares	Acres	Ton-neaux
Cru du Perret	*Bommes*	2	5	6
Château Perroy-Jean-Blanc	*Bommes*	7	17.5	17
Cru Petit-Grillon	*Barsac*	2	5	5
Cru Peyraguey	*Preignac*	8	20	22
Château Peyraguey-le-Rousset (*see* Cru d'Arche-Pugnau)				
Château de Peyre	*Fargues*	1	2.5	3
Cru de Peyre	*Fargues*	1	2.5	3
Clos Peyret	*Preignac*	1	2.5	3
Château Peyron	*Fargues*	4	10	17
Château Piada, Clos du Roy	*Barsac*	11	27.5	29
Cru Pian	*Barsac*	2	5	7
Château Piaut	*Barsac*	9	22.5	22
Château du Pick	*Preignac*	23	57.5	59
Clos de Pierrefeu	*Preignac*	4	10	10
Cru Pilote	*Fargues*	3	7.5	8
Cru Piquey	*Bommes*	1	2.5	2
Cru de Pistoulet-Peyraguey	*Bommes*	2	5	4
Cru du Placey	*Barsac*	1	2.5	3
Cru Planton	*Barsac*	1	2.5	3
Château Pleytegeat	*Preignac*	12	30	51
Cru Pouteau	*Fargues*	2	5	4
Cru Pouton	*Preignac*	2	5	6
Clos des Princes	*Barsac*	2	5	6
Château Prost	*Barsac*	8	20	21
Château Pugnau	*Preignac*	3	7.5	8
Cru Puydomine	*Bommes*	2	5	4
Château Raspide	*Barsac*	5	12.5	16
Château Raymond-Lafon	*Sauternes*	3	7.5	4
Château des Remparts	*Preignac*	1	2.5	4
Cru Richard Barbe	*Bommes*	2	5	5
Cru Ripaille	*Preignac*	1	2.5	2
Château du Roc	*Barsac*	2	5	5
Château des Rocs	*Preignac*	1	2.5	3
Château de Rolland	*Barsac*	14	35	39
Domaine de la Roudette	*Sauternes*	2	5	6
Château Roumieu	*Barsac*	18	45	46
Château Roumieu-Lacoste	*Barsac*	5	12.5	14
Clos Rouquette	*Preignac*	6	15	17

	Township	Hec-tares	Acres	Ton-neaux
Clos du Roy (*see* Château Piada)				
Château Sahuc	*Preignac*	2	5	5
Château Sahuc-Latour	*Preignac*	4	10	8
Château St.-Amand	*Preignac*	7	17.5	20
Château St.-Marc, Château Hourmalas	*Barsac*	6	15	14
Château St.-Michel	*Barsac*	1	2.5	3
Cru St.-Michel	*Barsac*	1	2.5	3
Clos St.-Robert	*Barsac*	1	2.5	3
Cru St.-Sardeau	*Fargues*	2	5	6
Cru Saubade-Terrefort	*Sauternes*	2	5	3
Château Simon	*Barsac*	4	10	12
Château Simon-Carretey	*Barsac*	4	10	7
Château Solon	*Preignac*	4	10	13
Cru Soula	*Fargues*	4	10	9
Château Suau	*Barsac*	5	12.5	14
Domaine Tchit	*Fargues*	1	2.5	3
Cru Terrefort	*Bommes*	4	10	11
Domaine de Terrefort	*Sauternes*	3	7.5	6
Château Terre Noble, Château Montjou	*Barsac*	9	22.5	24
Château Terre-Noble (*see* Château Fleury)				
Cru des Terres Rouges	*Barsac*	2	5	4
Château Thibaut	*Fargues*	2	5	4
Cru Thibaut	*Fargues*	7	17.5	15
Château de Touilla	*Fargues*	3	7.5	4
Château Trillon	*Sauternes*	8	20	20
Cru Tucan	*Barsac*	2	5	3
Château Tucau	*Barsac*	3	7.5	9
Cru Tucou	*Preignac*	1	2.5	2
Château Valmont-Mayne	*Barsac*	2	5	4
Château Veyres	*Preignac*	10	25	30
Cru Vigne-Vieille	*Barsac*	3	7.5	8
Château Villefranche	*Barsac*	6	15	13
Château du Violet	*Preignac*	7	17.5	24
Cru du Violet	*Preignac*	1	2.5	5
Cru du Violet-et-Lamothe	*Preignac*	5	12.5	12
Château Voigny	*Preignac*	6	15	18

CÉRONS

The following figures of production are approximate, and indicate average annual output, as given by the townships and taken from their Déclarations de Récoltes *records.*

	Township	Principal Growths		
		Hec-tares	Acres	Ton-neaux
Château Archambeau	*Illats*	4	10	34
Clos Avocat	*Cérons*	4	10	8
Clos de la Avocat	*Cérons*	3	7.5	9
Château Balestey	*Cérons*	10	25	20
Clos de Barial	*Illats*	9	22.5	22
Clos du Barrail	*Cérons*	8	20	19
Château Beaulac	*Illats*	3	7.5	7
Cru Bel-Air	*Illats*	3	7.5	12
Clos du Bos-Lancon	*Illats*	4	10	12
Cru de Bouley	*Illats*	4	10	8
Domaine de Bourdac	*Illats*	7	17.5	40
Clos Bourgelet	*Cérons*	7	17.5	15
Cru de Boutec	*Illats*	5	12.5	20
Cru de Braze	*Illats*	7	17.5	18
Cru Brouillaou	*Podensac*	11	27.5	28
Cru de Cabiro	*Illats*	3	7.5	11
Château Cages	*Illats*	5	12.5	17
Domaine du Caillou	*Cérons*	5	12.5	10
Domaine Caillou Rouley	*Podensac*	8	20	15
Château Cantau	*Illats*	4	10	9
Clos Cantemerle	*Cérons*	3	7.5	7
Château de Cérons	*Cérons*	15	37.5	28
Domaine de la Citadelle	*Illats*	4	10	14
Cru Cleyrac	*Cérons*	5	12.5	15

	Township	Hec- tares	Acres	Ton- neaux
Cru des Deux Moulins	*Illats*	4	10	8
Cru Ducas	*Illats*	2	5	6
Domaine du Freyron	*Cérons*	3	7.5	5
Domaine de Gardennes	*Illats*	3	7.5	6
Château Grand Chemin	*Cérons*	4	10	8
Cru du Grand-Chênes	*Cérons*	3	7.5	6
Grand Enclos du Château de Cérons	*Cérons*	11	27.5	30
Château Hauret	*Illats*	4	10	9
Cru Haut-Buhan	*Illats*	7	17.5	18
Château du Haut-Gravier	*Illats*	11	27.5	22
Cru Haut La Hountasse (P. Banos)	*Illats*	3	7.5	6
Cru Haut La Hountasse (R. Banos, J. Banos)	*Illats*	5	12.5	15
Château Haut-Mayne	*Cérons*	5	12.5	10
Cru Haut-Mayne	*Cérons*	2	5	5
Cru de Haut-Mayne	*Cérons*	3	7.5	6
Château Haut-Rat	*Illats*	16	40	40
Château Huradin, Domaine du Salut	*Cérons*	8	20	30
Clos du Jaugua	*Illats*	4	10	8
Domaine de Jaussans	*Illats*	8	20	20
Château LaLanette Ferbos	*Cérons*	5	12.5	12
Château Lamouroux	*Cérons*	10	25	22
Château Lanette	*Cérons*	5	12.5	12
Cru Larrouquey	*Cérons*	7	17.5	18
Domaine Larrouquey	*Cérons*	5	12.5	12
Château La Salette	*Cérons*	5	12.5	12
Domaine Le Cossu	*Podensac*	5	12.5	11
Château de L'Émigré	*Cérons*	2	5	5
Château Le Huzet	*Illats*	7	17.5	18
Cru Le Tinan	*Illats*	3	7.5	6
Cru de Lionne	*Illats*	7	17.5	18
Château Madère	*Podensac*	12	30	28
Cru Madérot (Édouard Sterlin)	*Podensac*	9	22.5	18
Cru Madérot (Étienne Sterlin)	*Podensac*	2	5	6
Cru Majans	*Cérons*	3	7.5	6
Cru Marc	*Illats*	5	12.5	16
Château des Mauves	*Podensac*	7	17.5	16
Château Mayne d'Anice	*Podensac*	4	10	9
Cru Maynine	*Illats*	3	7.5	10

	Township	Hec-tares	Acres	Ton-neaux
Domaine de Menaut Larrouquey	*Cérons*	12	30	32
Cru de Menjon	*Illats*	3	7.5	9
Château Moulin-à-Vent	*Cérons*	4	10	12
Clos des Moulins-à-Vent	*Cérons*	5	12.5	**14**
Cru des Moulins-à-Vent (Lafond)	*Cérons*	3	7.5	6
Cru des Moulins-à-Vent (Lapujade, Despujols)	*Cérons*	9	22.5	14
Cru du Moulin-à-Vent (Baron)	*Illats*	2	5	6
Cru Moulin-à-Vent (Biarnes)	*Illats*	16	40	51
Cru Moulin de La Glorie	*Illats*	2	5	7
Domaine des Moulins-à-Vent	*Illats*	9	22.5	21
Cru du Noulin	*Cérons*	3	7.5	6
Cru des Parrajots	*Illats*	3	7.5	8
Cru du Perliques	*Illats*	3	7.5	8
Château du Peyrat	*Cérons*	8	20	21
Cru Peyroutene	*Cérons*	4	10	9
Cru Pinaud	*Cérons*	4	10	10
Domaine de Prouzet	*Illats*	7	17.5	13
Château du Roc	*Cérons*	5	12.5	8
Clos des Roches	*Illats*	2	5	6
Cru St.-Roch	*Illats*	2	5	5
Domaine du Salut (*see* Château Huradin)				
Château du Seuil	*Cérons*	3	7.5	13
Château Sylvain	*Cérons*	11	27.5	28
Château Thomé-Brousterot	*Illats*	8	20	18
Château Uferic	*Cérons*	6	15	14
Cru Voltaire	*Cérons*	4	10	7

LOUPIAC

The following figures of production are approximate, and indicate average annual output, as given by the townships and taken from their Déclarations de Récoltes *records.*

Principal Growths

	Hectares	Acres	Tonneaux
Château Barbe Morin	5	12.5	16
Cru Barberousse	4	10	15
Château Bel-Air	5	12.5	16
Château Bertranon	2	5	5
Château Bouchoc	2	5	4
Château Caudiet	10	25	36
Domaine du Chay	12	30	29
Château Chichoye	2	5	7
Clos de Ciron	4	10	9
Château Clos Jean	12	30	40
Château Couloumet	5	12.5	12
Château du Cros	21	52.5	56
Château Dauphine Rondillon	15	37.5	55
Château de l'Ermitage	2	5	7
Château La Nève	9	22.5	40
Château La Tarey	5	12.5	13
Château Le Pavillon	4	10	14
Château Loupiac-Gaudiet	10	25	45
Château de Malendure	3	7.5	6
Cru Marges Dusseau	4	10	17
Château Mazarin	16	40	42
Côtes de Mossac	2	5	7
Château Moulin Neuf	10	25	40
Cru de Moulin Vieux	5	12.5	18
Château du Noble	7	17.5	15

	Hectares	Acres	Tonneaux
Château Peyruchet	12	30	34
Cru du Plainier	5	12.5	14
Château Pontac	10	25	36
Château Ricaud	36	90	78
Domaine de Roby	5	12.5	20
Château Rondillon	12	30	40
Cru de Rouquette	8	20	18
Cru de la Sablière	4	10	13
Cru St.-Romain	4	10	11
Château Terrefort	8	20	34
Clos de Terrefort	3	7.5	6
Cru de Terrefort	4	10	16
Cru de Terrefort Pierre Noire	3	7.5	11
Château Turon Lanère (Dalas)	3	7.5	10
Château Turon Lanère (David)	5	12.5	18
Château du Vieux-Moulin	9	22.5	40

SAINTE-CROIX-DU-MONT

The following figures of production are approximate, and indicate average annual output, as given by the townships and taken from their Déclarations de Récoltes *records.*

Principal Growths

	Hectares	Acres	Tonneaux
Cru Abraham	4	10	15
Cru Baret-les-Arrivaux	3	7.5	12
Château Bel-Air	12	30	46
Clos Belle-Vue	4	10	17
Château de Bertranon	2	5	9
Château Bouchoc	3	7.5	13
Domaine du Bougan	3	7.5	6
Domaine du Bugat	3	7.5	14
Cru du Canet	3	7.5	6
Château des Coulinats	3	7.5	13
Château Coullac	5	12.5	26
Domaine de Coullander	1	2.5	5
Clos du Crabitan	5	12.5	21
Domaine Damanieu	3	7.5	12
Domaine de d'Escaley	2	5	9
Domaine du Gaël	2	5	10
Cru de Gaillardet	1	2.5	4
Château Gensonne	2	5	5
Cru de Guerisson	3	7.5	7
Château Haut de Baritault	5	12.5	15
Cru Haut-Larrivat	3	7.5	12
Cru Haut-Medouc	3	7.5	15
Domaine de l'If	3	7.5	15
Château Jean-Lamat	4	10	16
Château Laborie	6	15	24

	Hectares	Acres	Tonneaux
Château La Caussade	5	12.5	20
Domaine de Lacoste	2	5	9
Cru de La Côte Doré	2	5	8
Château Lafuë	10	25	35
Cru La Grave	2	5	6
Château La Grave	6	15	17
Château La Gravière	11	27.5	51
Château La Graville	4	10	19
Château Lamarque	15	37.5	60
Château La Mouleyre	4	10	8
Clos La Mouleyre	4	10	16
Cru La Mouleyre	3	7.5	12
Cru Lapeyrère	5	12.5	26
Clos L'Arabey	2	5	7
Château La Rame	5	12.5	20
Cru La Rame	6	15	27
Clos Larrivat	3	7.5	13
Château Laurette	15	37.5	66
Château Le Grand Peyrot	5	12.5	11
Clos Le Haut-Crabitan	2	5	8
Château Le Pin	3	7.5	13
Château L'Escaley	5	12.5	23
Clos Les Arrivaux	3	7.5	11
Cru Les Arroucats	2	5	7
Domaine Les Marcottes	4	10	20
Cru Le Tarrey	5	12.5	23
Château Loubens	10	25	34
Domaine de Louqsor	1	2.5	5
Château Lousteau Vieil	7	17.5	33
Château des Mailles	6	15	24
Cru Medouc	4	10	8
Clos du Medouc	2	5	7
Cru Medouc La Grave	2	5	8
Château Megnien	3	7.5	13
Château du Mont	7	17.5	30
Cru de Montagne	5	12.5	19
Domaine des Noyers	7	17.5	25
Clos du Palmiers	3	7.5	12
Domaine de Pampelune	3	7.5	15

	Hectares	Acres	Tonneaux
Domaine de Parenteau	4	10	19
Château de la Princesse	2	5	9
Château du Pavillon	4	10	17
Cru Peillot	2	5	9
Cru du Pin	2	5	6
Château Roustit	9	22.5	40
Château de Tastes	6	15	18
Château Terfort	3	7.5	11
Cru du Terrefort	2	5	9
Château Vertheuil	10	25	25
Domaine du Vignots	2	5	7

NOTE: In addition to all the châteaux listed in this Appendix there are approximately 1,500 others in the communes of Bordeaux that do not have separate listings.

ACKNOWLEDGMENTS

I could not have written this book without the friendly assistance of a great many people—growers, cellar-masters, shippers, and others connected with the great wine industry of France. It is a pleasure to list some of their names here and to offer to each of them again my grateful thanks.

Sam Aaron, of New York.

Dr. Maynard A. Amerine, Professor of Oenology, University of California, Davis, California.

Mignot-Aubert, former President of the Growers Association of Indre-et-Loire.

André Balaresque, Wine Broker, of Bordeaux.

J. Bavard, of Puligny-Montrachet.

James A. Beard, of New York, author of *The Fireside Cookbook* and *Fish Cookery*.

The late E. Besserat de Bellefon, of Ay.

Henri Binaud, former President, Syndicat des Négociants en Vins, Bordeaux.

R. E. Boillot, of Volnay.

Baron Le Roy de Boiseaumarié, the late President of the Association of the Wine Growers of France.

The late J. Bouteiller, of Château Pichon-Longueville (Baron), Pauillac.

Marc Bredif, of Vouvray.

Inspector Canal, of the Institut National des Appellations d'Origine des Vins et Eaux-de-Vie, Armagnac.

Mademoiselle Chabert, President of the Cave Coopérative, Fleurie.

Georges S. Chappaz, Vice-President of the Institut National des Appellations d'Origine des Vins et Eaux-de-Vie, Paris.

Henri Coquillaud, Director, Bureau National Interprofessionel du Cognac.

Paul Damiens, Technical Adviser of the I.N.A.O.

The late Pierre Damoy, of Gevrey-Chambertin.

J. Dargent, of the Comité Interprofessionnel du Vin de Champagne, Épernay.

Jean Delamain, of Jarnac.

A. Devlétian, Institut National des Appellations d'Origine des Vins et Eaux-de-Vie, Paris.

M. Droin-Mary, of Chablis, former President of the Chablis Growers Association.

Joseph Drouhin, of Beaune.

Mme. Drouhin-Laroze, of Gevrey-Chambertin.

The Abbe Dubaquié, late Directeur Honoraire de la Station Oenologique de Bordeaux.

Georges Duboeuf, of Romanèche-Thorins.

The late Pierre J. Dubos, of Château Cantemerle, Macau-Médoc.

Dr. Philippe Dufays, of Chateauneuf-du-Pape.

René Engel, of Vosne-Romanée.

The late Louis Eschenauer, of Bordeaux.

Henri de Fonroque-Mercié, of Bordeaux.

The late Armand Achille Fould, owner of Château Beychevelle, Saint-Julien.

Georges Fouquier, of Bordeaux.

J. Fourcaud-Laussac, Château Cheval-Blanc, of Saint-Émilion.

Madame Fournier, owner of Château Canon, Saint-Émilion.

The late Edouard Gasqueton, proprietor, Château Calon-Ségur, Saint-Estèphe.

Pierre Gauthier, wine buyer, Alexis Lichine & Co.

Bernard Ginestet, of Château Margaux.

Pierre Ginestet, owner of Château Margaux, former President of the Syndicate of Bordeaux Wine Shippers.

Jean Godet, of La Rochelle.

The late Henri Gouges, President of the Burgundy Growers Association, Nuits-Saint-Georges.

The late Louis Gros, of Vosne-Romanée.

M. Guillaume, of Mesnil-sur-Oger.

Patrick Hennessy, of Cognac.

François Hine, of Jarnac.

Jean Hugel, of Riquewihr.

Michel Jaboulet-Vercherre, of Pommard.

Pierre Janneau, of Condom.

Alfred A. Knopf, of New York.

Eduard Kressmann, of Bordeaux.

René Kuehn, of Ammerschwihr.

Count and Countess Durieu de Lacarelle, Château Filhot, Sauternes (Gironde).

Georges Lawton, of Bordeaux.

Daniel Lawton, of Bordeaux.

The late Marquis de Lur-Saluces, of Château d'Yquem, Sauternes.

G. Lung, of Bordeaux.

Henri Martin, President, Comité Interprofessionnel des Vins de Bordeaux, and Mayor of Saint-Julien.

René Masson, of Reims.

Jean Michel, of Chablis.

Duc Pierre de Montesquiou-Fezensac, Château de Marsan, Auch.

C. Moreau, of Vosne-Romanée.

Guy Moreau, of Chablis.

Jean-Pierre Moueix, of Libourne.

Mme. Mugnier, of Chambolle-Musigny.

Dr. E. Peynaud, of the Station Oenologique de Bordeaux.

Prince de Polignac, of Reims.

Charles Quittanson, Inspector of Fraud, Institut National des Appellations d'Origine des Vins et Eaux-de-Vie, Dijon.

Claude Ramonet, of Chassagne-Montrachet.

Comte E. de Rohan-Chabot, Château de Saint-Martin, Taradeau, President of the Syndicat de Defense de Côtes de Provence.

Ed. Rolland, of the Académie des Vins de Bordeaux, and Château Coutet, Barsac.

Baron Philippe de Rothschild.

Joseph Salzmann, of Kaysersberg.

Étienne Sauzet, of Puligny-Montrachet.

Noël Sauzet, of Jarnac.

Guy Schyler, of Chateau Lafite, Pauillac.

Marcel Servin, of Chablis.

Pierre Sevez, President, Société du Vermouth Dolin, Chambéry.

Claude Taittinger, of Reims.

Colonel Teed, of Cassis.

Baron Thénard, of Givry.

H. Gregory Thomas, Grand Master, Commanderie de Bordeaux, of New York.

Nicolas Trambitsky, of Paris.

Louis Trapet, of Gevrey-Chambertin.
J. Vidal-Fleury, of Ampuis.
H. Seymour Weller, Château Haut-Brion, Pessac.
Anthony Wood, of Los Angeles.
Georges Yard, of Beaune.

INDEX

quenelles: de brochet, 53, 142;
   Nantua, 149
Quenot, M., 83
Quetsch, defined, 198
queue, defined, 124
quiche Lorraine, 174
Quincy: *maps*, 2, 164; 163, 166

rabbit (*lapin*), *terrine* of, 69, 133,
   166
Rabelais, 170, 173; quoted, 78, 169,
   170
racking, defined, 192
Rameau, A., 88
Rameau-Saguin, A., 107
Ramonet, Claude, 87, 119–20, 137–8,
   139
Ramonet, Pierre, 119
rancio, defined, 59
Rapet, C., 86, 88
Rasteau: *map*, 148
Réas, Aux, 111
Rebourseau, Domaine, 80, 83, 107
Recoules, Les (Hermitage vd.),
   152
régisseur, defined, 26; in Burgundy,
   102
Reims: *map*, 2; 188, 189, 191
Remy, 80
Remy, H., 85
Remy, J. H., 82, 85, 97
Renardes (Aloxe-Corton vd.), 83,
   122
Renow, A., 86
Restaurants: 218; Auberge Paul
   Bocuse (Lyon), 149; Bonne
   Auberge (Antibes), 158; Beausite
   (Orbey), 174; Café de France
   (Eauze), 207–8; Campo (Mar-
   seille), 157; Chapon Fin
   (Bordeaux), 12; Château de
   Madrid (near Monte Carlo), 158;
   Château Trompette' (Bordeaux),
   12; du Chevreuil (Meursault),
   133; de Choiseul (Amboise), 166;
   de la Côte d'Or (Saulieu), 51;
   Dubern (Bordeaux), 12; de
   l'Étoile (Chablis), 85–6; de

France et d'Angleterre (Mâcon),
   142; Mère Brazier (Lyon), 149;
   Mère Germaine (Châteauneuf-du-
   Pape), 153; Mère Guy (Lyon),
   149; Mule du Pape (Châteauneuf-
   du-Pape), 153; Nandron (Lyon),
   149; Oliver (Langon), 46; Pic
   (Valence), 153; Pont de Cisse
   (Vouvray), 166; Pyramide
   (Vienne), 149; Relais de
   l'Empereur (Montélimar), 153;
   La Réserve (Beaulieu), 158;
   Splendide (Bordeaux), 12;
   Strasbourg (Marseille), 157; *see
   also* hotels
Reugny (Vouvray vd.), 166
Reuilly; *maps*, 2, 164; 163, 166
Revolution, French, effect on vds.,
   55, 56
Rheingau, 42, 178
Rhine River, 54, 174, 175
Rhône: *maps*, 2, 52, 148; 43, 149–
   56; barrels, 229; shippers, 154–5;
   vds., 150, 152, 153, 154–5;
   vintages, 155–6, 233–5; wines
   for blending, 55
Rhône River, 53, 146, 183
Ribeauvillé, 174
Ribereau-Gayon, M., 16
Richebourg (Vosne vd.): *map*, 92;
   81, 110, 111, 113; price, 217;
   w. characteristics, 112
Richelieu, 170
Richelieu, Duc de, 5
Richemone, La (Vosne vd.), 114
Riesling (grape), 177
rillettes, 166, 188
rince cochon ("pig rinse"), 79
Rinces, Les (Pouilly-Fuissé vd.),
   143
Riquewihr, 174, 175
Rivesaltes, 183
Riviera, 157–8, 184
Roasted Slope: *see* Côte Rôtie
robe, defined, 96
Roblot, Raymond, 85, 107
Roche-aux-Moines, La (Savennières-
   Loire vd.), 172

ALEXIS LICHINE is a wine grower who owns Chateâu Prieuré-Lichine in the Médoc area of Bordeaux and until recently had been co-owner of Château Lascombes for twenty years. In 1960 he organized an exhibit of contemporary art entitled La Vigne et le Vin *(The Vine and Wine), which was held annually until 1971 at Château Lascombes. In 1964 he sold the wine-shipping company bearing his name in Bordeaux. In 1967 his* Encyclopedia of Wines and Spirits, *considered by many to be the most authoritative book on the subject, was published by Alfred A. Knopf. He produced a unique record album,* The Joy of Wine, *designed to introduce beginners to the subject of wine. In addition, he is a director of several European companies, including the Marbella Beach Hotel, S. A., in Spain.*

Born in Moscow, Alexis Lichine was taken to France after the Revolution and came to the United States in 1934. During the Second World War, he served in Europe and North Africa with the United States Army Military Intelligence. After his discharge as a major, he started his wine business in France. He belongs to the Académie des Vins de Bordeaux, the only American among the organization's forty members. He is an Officer of the Legion of Honor.

Although his base of operations is now New York, for years he has probably spent more time in the vineyards of France than any other man writing in English.

A NOTE ON THE TYPE

This book was set on the Linotype in DeVinne, a modern type face. The modern faces are sharply drawn with an almost mathematical exactness and are designed for use on hard, smooth-surfaced papers, in contrast with the old style faces, which are more freely drawn and were originally designed for use on the softer handmade sheets. DeVinne, alone among the moderns, has a most interesting character when used on antique papers, as it frequently is. The modern types were first made about 1790. Becoming immensely popular, they were soon grossly distorted, each type founder trying to outdo his competitors by exaggerating the modern characteristics. It was not until late in the nineteenth century that the modern type was brought back to a useful sanity of design, largely through the influence of the great American printer Theodore Low DeVinne, in whose honor this type face was named.

This book was composed, printed, and bound by Kingsport Press, Inc., Kingsport, Tennessee.

Typography and binding design by Elton Robinson.